The Unitarian Universalist Pocket Guide

Edited by
HARRY B. SCHOLEFIELD

Skinner House Books
Boston

Our Unitarian Universalist congregations are as unique as fingerprints, and as similar.

— Joan Goodwin

The Unitarian Universalist pocket guide / edited by Harry B. Scholefield.
— Rev. ed.
p.   cm.
Bibliography: p.
ISBN 0-933840-45-4
1. Unitarian Universalist Association. 2. Unitarianism. 3. Universalism. I. Scholefield, Harry Barron. II. Unitarian Universalist Association.
BX9841.2.U55 1988
288' .32--dc19   88-23906
                                             CIP

Library of Congress Catalog Card No. 88-050971

ISBN 0-933840-45-4

The Unitarian Universalist Association wishes to thank the following for permission to reprint: Excerpt from "The Dry Salvages" in Four Quartets, copyright 1943 by T.S. Eliot, renewed 1971 by Esme Valerie Eliot, reprinted by permission of Harcourt Brace Jovanovich, Inc. "Geography of This Time" by Archibald Macleish from *Actfive and Other Poems* (Boston: Houghton Mifflin, Inc., © 1948).

Cover design by Suzanne Morgan.

Contents

Unitarian Universalist Principles

We, the member congregations of the Unitarian Universalist Association, covenant to affirm and promote:

> The inherent worth and dignity of every person;
> Justice, equity, and compassion in human relations;
> Acceptance of one another and encouragement to spiritual growth in our congregations;
> A free and responsible search for truth and meaning;
> The right of conscience and the use of the democratic process within our congregations and in society at large;
> The goal of world community with peace, liberty, and justice for all;
> Respect for the interdependent web of all existence of which we are a part.

> — from the By-Laws of the Unitarian Universalist Association

Foreword

This *Pocket Guide* provides a general statement of Unitarian Universalist beliefs, practices, history and organization. It offers no body of official doctrine, for there is none. It does present the affirmative beliefs and values, and the covenant on which the Unitarian Universalist Association is founded. And it describes the long, loving traditions of openness and truth-seeking which characterize our liberal religious movement. Those who have contributed chapters are:

David O. Rankin, Minister of the Fountain Street
    Church, Grand Rapids, Michigan
Joan Goodwin, Religious Education Director, Church
    of the Larger Fellowship
Harry Scholefield, Minister Emeritus of the First
    Unitarian Church of San Francisco, California
Christopher Gist Raible, former minister in Toronto,
    Ontario and Worcester, Massachusetts
William F. Schulz, President, Unitarian Universalist
    Association
Jean Starr Williams, former Director of Education,
    Unitarian Universalist Association.

I thank those who have contributed chapters to the Guide, and I especially thank the Rev. Mark W. Harris, Director of Information for the Unitarian Universalist Association, for his considerable help in publishing this edition.

The bibliography will be of interest to those who wish to pursue further reading on Unitarian Universalist beliefs and history. Those who wish information on the wide variety of books and pamphlets currently available are invited to write to the UUA Bookstore, 25 Beacon Street, Boston, MA 02108-2800 for the UUA Bookstore Catalog. The chapter, "About the Church of the Larger Fellowship," will be of special interest to readers who live in areas where there are no local Unitarian Universalist congregations.

It was in 1954, nearly thirty-five years ago, that I edited the first edition of the *Pocket Guide*. Over the years it has gone through many printings and some seven different editions. Thousands have used it as an introduction to our liberal religion. It is always in the process of being revised and rewritten. If you have suggestions for improving future editions, you are cordially invited to write to me. If you wish to make further inquiries, please write to the Information Office, Unitarian Universalist Association, 25 Beacon Street, Boston, MA 02108-2800. If there is a congregation of Unitarian Universalists in your neighborhood, pay them a visit. You will be warmly welcomed.

Harry Scholefield
344 Mt. Shasta Drive
San Rafael, CA 94903

Our Beliefs

David O. Rankin

I believe in God the Father
And in Christ Jesus, His only Son, our Lord.
Who was born of the Holy Spirit and the Virgin Mary
Who was crucified under Pontius Pilate and was buried
And the third day rose from the dead.
Who ascended into heaven
And sitteth on the right hand of the Father
Whence He cometh to judge the living and the dead.
And in the Holy Ghost - the Holy Catholic Church
The remission of sins - the resurrection of the flesh
And life everlasting.
Amen.

This is the Apostles' Creed, written in the year 340 C.E. It is a creed millions of Protestants and Roman Catholics still recite on Sunday morning, and that I, myself, recited for fifteen years in a small Methodist church in Pennsylvania.

But, there came a time in my life when I could no longer believe in the creed. The words stuck in my throat, my tongue tied with doubt. Questions welled up in me about the Holy

Spirit, the Holy Ghost, and the Holy Catholic Church. I was filled with doubt about the resurrection, the final judgment, and promises of life everlasting.

My silent rebellion rose as I felt my acceptance of the church creeds ebbing. Within myself, I was beginning to refuse to conform.

It became impossible for me to obediently repeat words I no longer believed; to pray; to sing hymns. In the end I was unable to attend church at all.

I turned against the religion of my youth with a vengeance. The church was an aged relic, mired in its own hypocrisy. The religion itself was weak, remote, and irrelevant. The minister droned on in ignorance of the world around him. To me, it seemed there was a clear choice to be bound or to be free. I chose to be free.

I abandoned the church for nine years. My friends and I joked with amused condescension over drinks; we had been that route. We were young, well educated, and independent. What use was church or religion? I could think for myself.

There was an odyssey of return. Slowly, with difficulty, I did come back. The journey, born out of strange longing, was often jagged and random.

> Out of the emptiness and despair of the secular world;
> Out of the hunger and the thirst for the meaning of life;
> Out of the weariness and the boredom of daily routine;
> Out of the desire and the need to relate to community;
> Out of the wonder and the mystery of my own
>   existence;

I did return to find a religious community. Eventually, I became a minister myself.

As a Unitarian Universalist minister, I speak to many people who are former Methodists, Catholics, and Presbyterians; former Jews, Mormons, and Congregationalists; former Anglicans, Baptists, and Lutherans. I ask that they remember the words of T.S. Eliot from "The Dry Salvages":

> There is no end, but addition: the trailing
> Consequence of further days and hours,
> While emotion takes to itself the emotionless
> Years of living among the breakage
> Of what was believed in as the most reliable —
> And therefore the fittest for renunciation.

I want them not to let negative feelings from the past dominate their newly found religious lives. It is only by cherishing and respecting our earliest experiences of community religion that we can integrate them with Unitarian Universalism.

It is commonly charged that the Unitarian Universalist churches have become a haven for people who cannot quite make up their minds.

One wit has written that a Unitarian Universalist is a person who walks the thin line between confusion and indecision.

Another has written that if you are a Unitarian Universalist, bigots burn a question mark on your lawn.

It is true that ours is a free, tolerant, and creedless church. There is acceptance of people from all traditions and backgrounds—with no theological dogmas, with no intellectual restraints, with no prohibition on religious expression. But, that's not where it ends. It is important that a person accepts his or her own past and accepts any negative feelings that go with it; this is the first step. But beyond finding peaceful closure with what has been, people joining the Unitarian Universalists need to build a new and positive commitment to religion.

There are ways in which we are similar to other religions. Like the Roman Catholics, we have a long tradition extending over many parts of the world from India to Hungary to the

Americas. Like the Jews, we have our heroes and heroines: Servetus, David, and Fuller; Murray, Channing, and Emerson; Barton, Anthony, Steinmetz, and many others. We have a system of democratic polity, like the Baptists, with the congregation acting as the ultimate authority. There is an elected Board of Trustees, and a pulpit characterized by freedom of expression.

As with the Confucianists, we have emphasized reason, wisdom, and knowledge. We have an eclectic system of theology, like the Hindus, which encourages each individual to develop a personal faith that is not dependent on the demands of an institution. Like humanists, we have our roots in the experience of the world as it is known through touch, sight, sound, taste, and smell. Like Buddhists, we accent the beauty, mystery, and holiness of every man, woman, and child, seeing each as a sacred vessel.

The similarities of belief are not an accident of history. Rather, they spring from the receptivity of Unitarian Universalism to the surrounding culture. While our roots are deep in the Christian tradition, they also extend to the Greek philosophers, the Hebrew prophets, the Renaissance thinkers, the mystics of the East, and the secular thinkers of the modern world.

Although there are many similarities between Unitarian Universalism and other religions, there are also differences. Robert L'H. Miller, Professor of Religion at Tufts University, sought to discover whether there is a value system in Unitarian Universalism that differs distinctly from that of Catholicism, Protestantism, Judaism, and secularism. He conducted a scientific survey and described his results in "The Religious Value System of Unitarian Universalists." He concluded that there was, in fact, a distinctive composition of values. Unitarian Universalists placed self-respect, wisdom, inner harmony, mature love, a world of beauty, and an exciting life much higher than did people in other religious groups. The values of social recognition, pleasure, a comfortable life, family security, and salvation were ranked lower. Indeed, salvation came close to being a disvalue, ranking consistently as the lowest of eighteen selections. (It was first among orthodox Christians.)

It was found that of instrumental values, Unitarian Universalists place lovingness, independence, intellectualism, imagination, and logic much higher than did people of other religious groups. The values of obedience, cleanliness, politeness, self-control, and forgiveness were ranked lower. (Indeed, the disdain for obedience and politeness goes far toward explaining the occasional chaos of our meetings together.) It is good that we are loving.

It can be said, then, that people who choose to be part of a Unitarian Universalist church do have a special pattern of values. These people can best be described as self-actualizing, intellectual, independent, ethically committed, and this-worldly. In the language of Miller's article:

> ... the data support the conclusion that being a Unitarian Universalist is characterized by holding a constellation of values which differentiates such persons from other kinds of religious communities and, at the same time, develops an internal sense of commonality and a homogeneous community. (*Review of Religious Research*, 17:3, Spring, 1976, 207-08).

In other words, there are ways to seek religious fulfillment, handle joy and sorrow, search for profound and satisfying relationships, wonder at the place of human destiny in the wider scheme of things, and find mature self-awareness that are particular to Unitarian Universalism.

One of the themes of the 400 years of Unitarian Universalist history has been to preserve and extend a pattern of values which is genuinely our own—not merely the remains and borrowings of other religions. Unlike the orthodox, with their emphasis on obedience and authority, we believe in freedom and independence. And unlike the Fundamentalists, with their emphasis on self-denial and surrender, we believe in self-fulfillment and affirmation. We are not like the Witnesses, who emphasize death and salvation. We believe in life and beauty. And we are not like the Mormons, who emphasize security and prosperity. We believe in risk and excitement. Finally, we differ from the New Age religions, with their emphasis on serenity and adjustment. We believe in an inner harmony that will lead to ethical action.

Usually it is very difficult for the newcomer to understand our approach to the religious life. I have seen many people outwardly reject the tenets of an orthodox religion, but still cling to them unconsciously. It takes time and patience to educate people in the ways of Unitarian Universalism, and encourage them gradually to adopt a new system of beliefs.

It is important to understand the traditional religious themes in order to approach an entire understanding of the Unitarian Universalist faith. We cherish diversity of belief as an institution; we call for commitment as individuals.

On God: There is acceptance of agnosticism, humanism, even atheism; there is also an understanding that belief in God can be manifested in many ways—from an idea of a "personal God" to an idea of God as an "Ultimate Reality."

On Jesus: There is a belief in the Galilean as the highest model of the religious life: At the same time, there is an interpretation of Jesus that equates his ministry with that of Moses, Buddha, Socrates, and Mohammed.

On Scripture: There is belief in the Bible as especially unique and inspired: There is also a belief that every revelation of truth in every era of human history should be highly revered and esteemed.

On Human Nature: There is a belief in the devastating power of evil; and a belief that all people can do good if their innate capacity for goodness is well nurtured and guided.

On Immortality: There is a belief that death brings the absolute cessation of mind and body: there is also a belief in other numerous possibilities—from the immortality of the soul to the Hindu concept of reincarnation.

Unitarian Universalism is a great disappointment for those who desire a creedal statement on the traditional themes of religion, or feel that everyone in a church should hold the same theological views. For those who feel the need to build their own personal theology, without the constraints of an institutional formula or the authority of an ecclesiastical hierarchy, Unitarian Universalism is an exciting adventure.

There is a peculiar genius to the eclecticism of the Unitarian Universalist faith, which lies, I think, in its recognition that religion is not an isolated incident or event, but is the expression of a single human spirit's relationship to the world in the search for meaning and the joy of discovery.

Religion is singing, dancing, praying;
Religion is reason, emotion, longing;
Religion is dreaming, playing, creating;
Religion is biology, morality, politics.

Faith is a well from which insight and courage can be drawn to confront the problems of life. A religion that dealt only with intellectual abstraction would not answer this human need. In the end, the only relevant and essential test of a religion is how it teaches us to act in response to the hardest challenges before us; to face grief, despair, tragedy. Unitarian Universalism is connected, at its core, to actual experience; its essence does not lie in a distant and separate realm.

George Marshall writes in *Challenge of a Liberal Faith*:

> One is free to believe what one's conscience, mind, experience, and emotions lead one to affirm. Our fellowship is founded upon the free-mind principle, and ours is an association that seeks to help a person develop the religion that is within each, rather than merely to give an external religion that can be put on like a suit of clothing. What can be put on can be taken off, and we feel too many people find they have no religion when the chips are down. What makes sense when we have background organ music or the filtered light of colored windows often escapes us when we are involved in the hustle and bustle of everyday life. Accordingly, if we can develop our own religion in terms of our beliefs, they can assist us in meeting the issues of life.

The following "Ten Points" provide a summary of the essential beliefs of Unitarian Universalists:

1. We believe in the freedom of religious expression. All individuals should be encouraged to develop a personal theology, and to openly present their religious opinions without fear of censure or reprisal.

2. We believe in tolerance of religious ideas. The religions of every age and culture have something to teach those who listen.

3. We believe in the authority of reason and conscience. The ultimate arbiter in religion is not a church, a document, or an official, but the personal choice and decision of the individual.

4. We believe in the search for truth. With an open mind and heart, there is no end to the fruitful and exciting revelations that the human spirit can find.

5. We believe in the unity of experience. There is no fundamental conflict between faith and knowledge; religion and the world; the sacred and the secular.

6. We believe in the worth and dignity of each human being. All people on earth have an equal claim to life, liberty, and justice; no idea, ideal, or philosophy is superior to a single human life.

7. We believe in the ethical application of religion.   Inner grace and faith finds completion in social and community involvement.

8. We believe in the force of love, that the governing principle in human relationships is the principle of love, which seeks to help and heal; never to hurt or destroy.

9. We believe in the necessity of the democratic process. Records are open to scrutiny, elections are open to members, and ideas are open to criticism, so that people might govern themselves.

10. We believe in the importance of a religious community. Peers confirm and validate experience, and provide a critical platform, as well as a network of mutual support.

I refer those who would like a short definition for the purpose of explaining to friends and relatives to a statement by Earl Morse Wilbur in *Our Unitarian Heritage:* "Unitarian Universalism is a progressive movement toward perfect freedom of thought and speech in religion, within the context of a democratic religious community."

I would like to close with a personal word. The return to organized religion has been one of the most significant events of my life. I have found in the Unitarian Universalist faith a religion that suits my needs and temperament; that offers joy and hope in daily living; that provides an impetus for ethical commitment; that encourages a community of love and trust. It is good to be home.

I know now that I am also able to look back on the small Methodist church of my youth with a sense of gratitude. The people were tender and kind. The ministers were earnest and dedicated. The church was warm and friendly. Even the Apostles' Creed, seen from a new perspective, has elements that are interesting and penetrating. It's good to remember with affection my former home.

Our Caring Communities

Joan Goodwin

Our Unitarian Universalist congregations are as unique as fingerprints, and as similar. Scattered across the United States and Canada are approximately one thousand groups ranging in size from maybe a dozen to over a thousand people. They meet in private homes, large Victorian houses, geodesic domes, A–frames, rented rooms at the "Y," classic white-steepled meeting houses, modern architects' dreams, and Gothic-revival churches.

Our Sunday morning programs are as varied as the meeting places themselves. They can include formal communion, served from pre-Revolutionary silver, lectures on the widest possible range of subjects, free-for-all discussions, family canoe trips, and innovative experimental worship services, as well as more traditional services. Our children's programs include creative worship, arts, discovery learning, and family-oriented activities.

Although individual religious and political philosophies differ widely, our congregations have one thing in common:

they exist because we need one another. As religious liberals, we sometimes feel ourselves to be a misunderstood minority, and our church home—whatever shape it takes—gives us the courage to be more fully ourselves than we might be without it. A sense of community is part of the vital support system we all need in order to live whole, productive, satisfying lives.

Many thoughtful social critics believe that our age is marked by an unprecedented speed-up in social change and that transience and alienation have never been more pronounced. We are well aware of these trends in our churches. In one small Unitarian Universalist congregation in central Illinois the average length of stay is less than five years. Among its membership are many people with previous associations in two or three other Unitarian Universalist societies. It is significant that a religious community means so much to some of us that the presence or absence of a Unitarian Universalist group in a given area is an important factor in the choice of job relocation. People on the move, spatially as well as spiritually, find themselves at home in our midst.

The breakdown in family stability has placed more importance on the church community. Increasingly, our congregations are composed of divorced men and women, some of them parents; single people, many of them widowed. There are many single women with children, and high school and college students living away from home. Even intact families struggle to meet their members' emotional needs. In modern history the family has been the primary institution to include and look out for people throughout their lives. With the family unable in many instances to provide stability, it is often to the church that people turn in their hunger for community.

Alvin Toffler, author of *Future Shock,* spoke to the General Assembly of our churches, addressing himself to ways in which our churches can work to offset the current trends toward dehumanization and alienation. As immense institutions become more and more impersonal, men and women are viewed more and more as disposable, consumable products rather than as persons to be respected and loved for their uniqueness. One thing our churches can do, said Toffler, is "to expand the love network." Unitarian Universalism's traditional valuing of individuality, joy in diversity, and willingness to include give us the potential to make a reality of Toffler's vision.

In seeking to develop a guideline philosophy, a group of Unitarian Universalists asked the question, "Why do people come to our church?" Their carefully considered answer was that people come out of hope—hope to become part of an "ideal family" that each person helps to mold, and within which all can find sanctuary, love, and growth. Their next question was a challenging one, "How can the hope be transformed into reality?"

One Unitarian Universalist who is without personal family ties put it this way: "I felt I'd become a member of a family as well as a church. If multiplying fishes and loaves to feed a crowd was regarded as miraculous, having a ready–made family spring up around me after my own was gone seemed no less impressive. I knew it was a family and not just a pretty illusion because its members called on me for help and support, which not only made me feel valued and included but also assured me I was free to call on them, too. It was nothing grand or flowery that gave me the feeling of family, but the everyday details, the commonplace stuff... I learned the church was really family because we worked hard and close enough with one another to get mad and argue as well as sing hymns together." (Dan Wakefield, *Returning: A Spiritual Journey*).

While trying not to violate the privacy of any person who wishes to avoid "togetherness," our congregations also work to avoid the seemingly cool, intellectual aloofness of which they are often accused. From hospitality committees to governing boards; from Women's Federation programs to conferences for young people; in small fellowships, large churches, in cities, and at the level of countries, astonishing amounts of time, energy, and imagination are devoted to building a caring community.

The many adult religious education programs are key elements in community building. *Cakes for the Queen of Heaven* is a ten-session curriculum by Shirley Ranck designed to help women explore feminist theology through history, mythology, and their own life experience. In more than one congregation, the "Cakes" groups have gone on to develop their own continuing programs to maintain the friendship and shared interest they discovered.

Building Your Own Theology, a course created by Richard S. Gilbert, was so successful in developing a feeling of closeness among participants that a second "BYOT" course was created in response to their demand. Adult groups have also formed around Robert and Christopher Nelson's *Parents as Resident Theologians*, and other UUA programs. Meditation and journal-writing have attracted people and added to the sense of family within our congregations.

More and more frequently, UU churches and fellowships are building into their calendars regular overnight or weekend retreats that bring families, leadership, or special interest groups together, away from the regular meeting place. They worship together, share outdoor activities, talk, play games, cook and clean, and get to know each other in greater depth than they might be able to under the usual circumstances.

In our churches it is traditionally the role of the minister to provide personal counseling and help to families in crisis, and to celebrate the rites of passage by dedicating children, accepting newcomers and young people into membership, and performing marriage and memorial ceremonies. Unitarian Universalist ministers and religious educators have been among the first to accept and create new forms for such observances—forms which speak directly and personally to the life experiences of the people involved. Such services are at the very core of the church's community outreach.

However, many Unitarian Universalist congregations have no minister or director of religious education. In all of our congregations, lay leadership is of the highest importance, but where there is no professional staff person, lay members have a much larger responsibility. When questions arise as to how this kind of religious community can minister to the needs of its members, the answers are varied and interesting. A small ministerless congregation in the Twin Cities area of Minnesota has no trouble reaching a minister in one of several metropolitan Unitarian Universalist churches when the need arises. But they want to be able to provide as fully as possible for people with their own resources. In one instance they designed a memorial service to be conducted by the church family and friends. When it was presented to the congregation at a Sunday morning service, people were moved and discussion was spurred about individual feelings regarding death and the importance of the church community when a death occurs.

In some instances, legal provision is made for marriages to be performed by persons other than ordained ministers. A Texas Unitarian Universalist group had just moved into its new building when the lay president was asked to perform the marriage ceremony for a young woman who had regularly cared for the babies and toddlers during Sunday services. This first wedding in the new church was a significant event for the entire congregation. They were happy to be able to meet this need for a beloved member of their community.

A word should be said here about youth organizations and activities. There is nothing like a youth conference for community. Our young people from twelve to twenty-two find in their YRUU groups an opportunity for mutual support that can provide warmth and belonging through difficult adolescent years. There are often problems in youth organizations, some having to do with negotiating with the adult congregation. But despite these challenges, the youth groups do provide a valuable opportunity for the young people of our community to work and grow together.

A relatively new organization is the Unitarian Universalist Young Adult Network, formed to meet the special needs of college-age people, whether or not they are enrolled in academic programs. With career preparation lengthened and marriage postponed, people in their twenties and thirties often find themselves somewhat adrift, away from the families in which they grew up and not yet having established families of their own. They may not be within reach of a UU congregation, or they may feel that congregational programs do not meet their needs. The Network provides a variety of programs and conferences for young adults that help them stay in touch with their liberal faith, or find a new spiritual path if they have, like most of us, come from other faith traditions.

Lay leaders, even in societies that have professional leadership, are doing more and more ministering—with effectiveness and enjoyment. In one Ohio Valley church, the minister's impending sabbatical led to training in hospital and home visitation for members who were interested. They carried on this part of the pastoral work while the minister was away, and reported it as one of the most successful aspects of the sabbatical period. One of our ministers in a center city church conducted a Lay Ministry Workshop on developing caring skills, reminding participants that a congregation becomes a deeply caring community only to the degree that the members give of themselves.

Special leadership training offered at various levels of denominational organization provides experience in designing and presenting worship services, increasing knowledge of liberal religious history and theology, and improving management skills. In some of our districts the training takes place at week-long leadership schools. Other districts have programs in which a lay leader chosen by a local society works with a minister who teaches that leader ministerial skills in a course of individualized study. Both the lay people and the ministers who participate in these programs more richly experience themselves as Unitarian Universalists. They strengthen the quality of the caring and celebrating that they share with their congregations.

It is impossible to think of the Unitarian Universalist community without giving some attention to the annual summer conferences held in many parts of the continent. From Ferry Beach on the New England coast to de Benneville Pines in the California Sierra, religious liberals gather for a week or two of diverse programs. Some weeks are family oriented, others are for young people, or for those interested in religious education, or science, or international affairs, or personal growth. A common element—and perhaps the principal one— is the formation and renewal of friendships. Children who grow up in small congregations constantly explaining themselves to neighbors and classmates are astonished and relieved to find that there are many other Unitarian Universalists in the world with the same problem. Families who move frequently are sustained by knowing that they can spend summer vacations with old friends at Lake Geneva, Wisconsin, or Star Island, New Hampshire. They may also be delighted to find in their new congregations people they have already met at Unitarian Universalist conferences. These are the ways the community of religious liberals extends itself.

Mention should also be made of our Church of the Larger Fellowship, described at the back of this Guide. Conceived and designed in 1944 to meet the needs of religious liberals isolated from participation in a church or fellowship, it has its own unique, caring dimension, serving its members by mail from publications, a library of sermons on tape, and lifespan religious education materials for home use. Some congregations extend their caring communities by providing CLF services to their homebound members and to students away from home.

Unitarian Universalists are known for reaching out into the larger community, in addition to caring for the needs of their own. Many congregations have been involved in providing sanctuary for Central American refugees. In metropolitan areas, UU societies have joined interfaith efforts to provide for the homeless and hungry, often by establishing overnight shelters in their own buildings, and by setting up regular meal programs for street people. Our caring extends as well to the natural environment the "interdependent web of all existence of which we are a part," in the words of the UUA Principles and Purposes.

Unitarian Universalism is made up of many rich and caring communities. There is the endless potential for growth within the community, individually and collectively, into the larger community. At every turn we seek better ways of caring for one another and sharing what we have and know. Whether this occurs in programs and ventures already in progress or in those yet to be conceived; whether it occurs in our largest or our smallest congregations, care is at the center of our communities—the medium by which we "expand the love network."

Our Roots

Harry Scholefield

The Unitarian Universalist Association is of recent origin. It came into being in Boston, Massachusetts in 1961, with the merging of the American Unitarian Association and the Universalist Church of America. But the Unitarians and the Universalists each have their own separate histories. So it is that the Association and the approximately 1,000 churches and fellowships which form its constituency have roots that run to the distant past.

The term Universalism has taken on different meanings at different times. There is an important element of truth in the comment by Universalist minister L.B. Fisher: "Universalists are often asked to tell where they stand. The only true answer to give to this question is that we do not stand at all, we move." In 1791, the Universalist Benjamin Rush, a physician and a signer of the Declaration of Independence, described Universalism as "A belief in God's universal love to all his creatures." He went on to say that God "will finally restore all of them who are miserable to happiness." Taken by itself this was a remarkable statement in an age when belief in eternal hellfire and damnation was common. But Rush went further and declared that the belief in God's universal love "leads to truths upon all subjects, more especially upon the subject of government. It establishes the *equality* of mankind - it abolishes the punishment of death for any crime and converts jails into houses of repentance and reformation." The fact that the early American Universalists saw social action growing inevitably out of theological belief should not be lost upon us. Scholars trace Universalism all the way back to the Alexandrian Christian School and the early church fathers, Clement of Alexandria and Origen. The Universalist belief that the whole human race will be "saved," was condemned as a heresy by a Church Council in 544.

Unitarianism is similarly ancient and heretical. The first official use of the term occurred in 1638 in Transylvania, a province of Hungary which became part of Romania after World War I. It referred to those who believed in the unity of God, but not in the dogma of the Trinity. Again, some meanings of the word go back to theological controversies in the church that were settled—more or less—by the decisions of the famous Council of Nicaea in 325. Other chapters in this *Pocket Guide* deal with contemporary meanings of Unitarianism and Universalism. But we note that the meanings have never stood still for long. It has been central to our tradition to understand truth as an evolving, growing reality, and to understand that no one person, church, science, or generation can grasp the whole of truth, or define it once and for all.

Our churches have existed and our beliefs have been foreshadowed in different places at different times. Michael Servetus was perhaps the earliest of the Reformation anti-Trinitarians. He bore the unique distinction of being burned in effigy by the Roman Catholics and in actuality by the Protestants. He was burned at the stake in Geneva in 1553. In his book, *Hunted Heretic*, Roland Bainton writes that Servetus "brought together in a single person the Renaissance and the left wing of the Reformation. He was at once a disciple of the Neoplatonic Academy at Florence and of the Anabaptists. The scope of his interests and accomplishments exhibits the type of the 'universal man' of the Renaissance, for Servetus was proficient in medicine, geography, Biblical scholarship, and theology. In him the most diverse tendencies of the Renaissance and the Reformation were blended."

Our connections with the Renaissance have been underscored, also, by the Unitarian Universalist historian Arnold Crompton, who, in an earlier edition of this *Pocket Guide*, wrote, "Under the still powerful influence of the Renaissance, scholar preachers in the university towns of Florence, Bologna and Padua practiced complete freedom of inquiry. They appealed to conscience and reason as they searched the scriptures. Some of these scholar preachers, such as Bernadino Ochino, reached a Unitarian Universalist position not unlike that of the American Universalist Hosea Ballou in the early 19th century."

In 1565, Giorgio Biandrata, a refugee from Italy, founded the first anti–Trinitarian church in Poland. Faustus Socinus, an Italian, like Biandrata, became the leader of the Polish anti–Trinitarians, who were then known as Socinians. Francis David, who moved from Catholicism through Lutheranism and Calvinism to Unitarianism, became the great leader of the Transylvanian Unitarians. He was martyred in 1579. But the Unitarian churches he founded have remained vital and strong to this day.

In England, the beginnings of Unitarianism are associated with John Biddle, who was often persecuted and imprisoned for his Unitarian beliefs. He died in prison in 1662. Joseph Priestley, the discoverer of oxygen, was a major figure in eighteenth-century English Unitarianism. He was both a Unitarian minister and a scientist. He was a radical in both his theology and in his politics, sympathizing with the aims of both the American and French revolutions. In 1791 his meeting house and his laboratory were destroyed by a mob outraged by his radical views. A few years later, he emigrated to America and gave a series of lectures in Philadelphia when it was still the capital of the United States. A number of leaders in the new nation attended these lectures, including Priestley's friend, Thomas Jefferson. The lectures led to the founding of the First Unitarian Church of Philadelphia, the first permanently established church in the country to take the Unitarian name.

Priestley emigrated to Pennsylvania in 1794. Forty-three years earlier, in 1751, George de Benneville, an important figure in early American Universalism, had come to the same state. De Benneville was a lay preacher and a physician. In his boyhood he had become convinced of the truth of Universalism. As a result of this conviction, he was ostracized by the French Protestant Church in England when he was fourteen. Prior to coming to America, he preached Universal Salvation in Germany, England, Holland, and France. He was imprisoned in France and was saved from being beheaded by the intervention of King Louis XV. When he came to America, he was warmly welcomed by and very much at home with the Pennsylvania pietist groups such as the Dunkers, the Universal Baptists, and the Quakers. In the opinion of the Unitarian Universalist minister and historian, Clinton Lee Scott, George de Benneville is as entitled as any one person to be called the founder of American Universalism. In *The Universalist Church of America: A Short History*, Scott reminds us that "When Universalists today emphasize individual freedom of belief, the unrestricted use of reason, religion as a way of living, human beings and their welfare as central in organized life, truth as the only authority, the nurture of the inner spirit, and the Bible as one of the many forms of revelation, they are stressing principles which were central to the faith of the

Spiritual Reformers. To leave this heritage out of consideration is to render difficult the understanding of the Universalism of the present day." Of course, these words apply to Unitarian Universalism as a whole. The past and the present have an organic, dynamic, living relationship to each other.

In 1759, *Union*, an important statement on Universalism by James Relly, was published in England. It became a target of the ministers of the period, who were out looking for heretics. A young man, John Murray, heard Methodist ministers attacking Relly, and resolved to approach him in person and bring the light to this heretic. But when he got to Relly, the tables were turned. James Relly proved to be a man of good conscience and strong persuasive powers. He convinced Murray of the soundness of the Universalist position. Murray became a Universalist.

Debts, time spent in debtors' prison, and the death of his wife and baby motivated Murray to come to America. It was his intention not to preach Universalism in his new country, but circumstances, as well as the depth of his beliefs decreed otherwise. In 1770, under dramatic circumstances, he landed at Good Luck on Barnegat Bay, New Jersey, and was given hospitality by a Universalist, Thomas Potter. At Potter's urging, Murray began to preach again. Nine years later, he organized the First Universalist Church in America at Gloucester, Massachusetts. And in Gloucester, he and his followers won several important battles for religious freedom. Universalism had been present in America before Murray's arrival. Indeed, he was invited to Gloucester by a group that was studying James Relly's *Union*. But Murray was its catalyst and organizer. His energy and his courage were limitless. He brought the Universalists together and laid the foundation of the denomination. He made its doctrines known to the general public and was a most important part of its original dynamic.

A significant portion of our American roots can be traced to events that took place in Pennsylvania in the second part of

24   Unitarian Universalist Pocket Guide

the eighteenth century. This is especially true of Universalism.
However, the major events leading to the establishment of the
American Unitarian and Universalist denominations themselves took place in New England. Early in the eighteenth century, there were ministers in the Congregational churches who
sowed the seeds of a more rational and liberal interpretation of
the Christian faith. These men were characterized by great
breadth of mind and spirit. Among them were Ebenezer Gay,
who took a liberal stand on the doctrine of the Trinity as early
as 1740, Charles Chauncy, and Jonathan Mayhew. Clinton Lee
Scott characterizes Chauncy as "a pronounced Universalist with
Unitarian convictions" and Mayhew as "a pronounced Unitarian with Universalist convictions." These men remained tied to
the Congregational church, but over the years the Congregationalists proved unwilling to tolerate the liberals.

William Ellery Channing, minister of the Federal Street
Church in Boston, Massachusetts, and one of the greatest figures in American Unitarian history, emerged as the leader of
the liberal Congregationalists. A sermon that he delivered in
1819 in Baltimore, Maryland became the rallying point for a
new liberal religious movement and led to the organization of
the American Unitarian Association in Boston in May, 1825.
The controversy affected many of the oldest churches in New
England; out of the twenty-five oldest churches in New England, twenty soon took the Unitarian position. In all, approximately one hundred twenty-five churches became Unitarian
and either withdrew or were forced from the Congregational
denomination. These churches were led by men and women
very much at home in the scientific and literary currents of the
day. Their ministers were for the most part Harvard-educated.

With the Universalists it was not a question of large numbers of strong, established churches banding together to form
a new denomination. Ministers like John Murray, Elhanan
Winchester, Hosea Ballou, and others drew into new congrega-

tions men and women who, like the Unitarians within Congregationalism, sought a more liberal interpretation of Christianity. They came from different denominations. A very large number came from the Baptists. They were for the most part self-educated, less affluent, and more representative of the people at large than the Unitarians of the period. The Unitarians stressed free will. The Universalists put more emphasis on God as love. This led to the humorous but pertinent remark of Thomas Starr King (1824-1864), son of a Universalist minister, who, during his brief but brilliant ministry, had served both Universalist and Unitarian churches: "The one thinks God is too good to damn them forever, and the other thinks they are too good to be damned forever." The Universalists came together to create a denomination in Oxford, Massachusetts in 1785, and again in Philadelphia, Pennsylvania in 1790. In 1894 they made the Universalist General Convention their national governing body, and in 1942 they adopted the name The Universalist Church of America. As noted earlier, the American Unitarian Association was organized in 1825.

It is important to remember that we were born during a revolutionary period, and that the humanistic values of the period saturated the lives of our late-eighteenth-and early-nineteenth century-forebears. The links we had with the American Revolution are many. Suffice it to say that most of the signers of the Declaration of Independence were what we would today call "religious liberals."

One of our most precious inheritances is our congregational polity, which came to us from the congregational churches and other churches of the free spirit. From the beginning, it was accepted that ultimate decision–making power rests in the hands of the individual, autonomous churches. Local congregations select and ordain their ministers, determine their forms of worship or celebration, set their own requirements—or lack of requirements—for membership, and are responsible for all aspects of church government.

We have already seen that our beliefs change over the generations, and that the beliefs of individuals differ within the same generation and the same congregation. One way to catch a glimpse of the ways in which our beliefs have changed, and of the spirit and attitudes that unite us, is to go directly to the words of those who set us on our way. Fortunately, what might be called the founding declarations have been brought together in two highly readable, well edited books. On the Universalist side, there is *Universalism in America, A Documentary History*, edited by Ernest Cassara, published by Skinner House Books. It opens with a historical sketch and then presents selections from Universalist writings, beginning with the writings of George de Benneville (1703-1793) and concluding with those of a contemporary Unitarian Universalist minister and poet, Kenneth L. Patton.

On the Unitarian side, there is *The Epic of Unitarianism, Original Writings from the History of Liberal Religion* by David B. Parke, also published by Skinner House Books. It begins with selections from the writings of Michael Servetus (1511-1553) and concludes with selections from the contemporary Unitarian Universalist scholar, theologian and social reformer, James Luther Adams. To read these documents is to actually spend time in the company of Michael Servetus, Faustus Socinus, George de Benneville, Joseph Priestley, Benjamin Rush, Thomas Jefferson, Hosea Ballou, William Ellery Channing, Ralph Waldo Emerson, Abner Kneeland, Adin Ballou, Augusta J. Chapin, Horace Greeley, Henry W. Bellows, Olympia Brown and others.

Olympia Brown, suffragist pioneer in municipal reform, was ordained by the Northern (New York) Universalist Association in 1863. She was thus the first denominationally ordained woman minister in the United States. In his bicentennial historical essay on American Universalism, George Huntston Williams, retired Professor of Ecclesiastical History at Harvard University, writes: "Perhaps the most conspicuous feature of the Centennial Convention (the Universalist Centennial Convention held in Gloucester, Massachusetts in 1870) was the prominence of women in the Universalist cause." Other prominent figures are Universalist, Judith Sargent Murray and the Unitarian, Margaret Fuller. To be a member of this company is to know that Unitarian Universalism is always reaching out and striving for greater understanding.

Unitarians in Canada, by Phillip Hewett, minister of the Unitarian Church of Vancouver, British Columbia, was published in 1978. With scholarship, wit, and insight, Hewett describes the role Unitarians have played in Canadian life for more than 150 years. He brings to life our recent, as well as more distant history within and outside of Canada. His is one of a number of books published in the last decade that remind us of the depth and strength of our roots.

The Unitarian Church in Montreal (Church of the Messiah) was organized in 1842, but the presence of Unitarians in the city was known to the public as early as 1821. The Universalist Unitarian Church of Halifax was organized as a Universalist Church in 1843. The 1827 census listed fifty-five Universalists living in Nova Scotia. The First Unitarian Congregation of Toronto was organized in 1845. The Canadian Unitarian Council—Counseil Unitaire Canadien—was organized in 1961. It is located at 175 St. Clair Ave. W., Toronto, Ontario M4V 1P7, and is affiliated with the Unitarian Universalist Association.

In the years preceding the Civil War, much of the energy of the Unitarians and Universalists in the United States was taken up with issues such as the preservation of the Union and the abolition of slavery. The years of war made their own extraordinary demands. After the war it gradually became clear to each denomination that their survival and vibrancy depended on each one's capacity to bring its members together and find a stronger, renewed sense of conviction within each church as a whole. Twelve thousand Universalists gathered in a General Convention in Gloucester, Massachusetts in 1870 to celebrate the centennial of John Murray's arrival in America. In a fascinating bicentennial essay published by the Universalist Historical Society in 1971, George Huntston Williams observed that in that 1870 General Convention, "Universalism completed the overhaul of its ecclesiastical structure, as did many another denomination after the Civil War, adopting a comprehensive new constitution for 'a uniform organization of the Universalist Church.'"

It has been a chronic problem for both Unitarians and Universalists to reconcile their love of individual freedom and autonomy with necessary church structures. There has been a strong bias against any kind of organizational—particularly *denominational*—structure, or consensus on belief. In 1884, at a meeting of the National Conference of Unitarians, an event of great importance took place. The Unitarians transformed the American Unitarian Association from an association of individuals who paid annual dues of one dollar for voting privileges into an association of autonomous churches. This was done through the leadership of Henry W. Bellows, minister of the First Unitarian Church of New York City (now All Souls). Bellows was an organizing genius. During the Civil War he had organized the United States Sanitary Commission to serve the war-wounded. A comment on Bellows made by one of his ministerial colleagues exaggerates a bit, but will bear repetition: "Dr. Bellows is the only leader the Unitarian body ever had."

Our history teaches us the importance of institutions, ideas, and beliefs; measured by the lives they help us live. By our traditions, that kind of life should be the one that is both for ourselves and for others. The Unitarian Universalist record of living to do good by others was good in the mid-nineteenth century. Some of our activists include: Susan B. Anthony, pioneer in the struggle for women's rights, anti-slavery leader; Adin Ballou, radical pacifist, severe critic of the injustices of capitalism, founder of Hopedale; Henry Bergh, one of the founders of the American Society for the Prevention of Cruelty to Children; Clara Barton, organizer of the American Red Cross; Dorothea Dix, crusader for the reform of institutions for the mentally ill; Samuel Gridley Howe, pioneer in work with the blind; Horace Greeley, crusading newspaper editor, champion of labor unions and cooperatives; Abner Kneeland, advocate of land reform, public education, birth control, pioneer in the commune movement, founder of Salubria; Judith Sargent Murray and Margaret Fuller, intellectuals, essayists, pioneer feminists; and Joseph Tuckerman, pioneer social worker.

There was probably no denomination in nineteenth-century America that had more humanitarian leverage on society than the Unitarians and Universalists. This is not to say that the road was easy, or that there was unanimity—this has never been our strong point. But the reformers represented the cutting edge. They demonstrated to their contemporaries and to us that liberal religion is a powerful motivating force for both personal growth and involvement in social change.

To help those who wish to further study our early history, I have underscored the importance of David Parke's *The Epic of Unitarianism*, Ernest Cassara's *Universalism in America*, and Phillip Hewett's *Unitarians in Canada*. There are many other fine books available in book shops, and in church and public libraries. Some of these books and periodicals are listed at the back of this Guide.

It has not been our custom to reflect often on our history. We tend to be in a hurry to get things done, and look forward rather than backward. This, too, is one of our traditions. But stopping to look at our past is reassuring and exciting. Our story is adventurous and full of hope; discovering the depth and strength of our roots is a nourishing experience that feeds us the inspiration and stamina we need in order to meet today's challenges. The following lines from "Geography of This Time," by Archibald MacLeish are part of the liturgy of our churches, and come swiftly to the point:

> What is required of us, Companions, is the recognition
>   of the frontiers across this history, and to take heart
>   and cross over.
> To persist and cross over and survive.
> But to survive
> To cross over.

Our Ways of Worship

Christopher Gist Raible

The Celebration of Life

For all our diversity, worship is the most common activity among Unitarian Universalists. Week after week, year after year, whatever else a congregation does, it gathers for worship.

The "celebration of life" is an oft-quoted definition of worship. Coined earlier in this century by Von Ogden Vogt (a Unitarian whose theories made a major contribution to Protestant liturgical thought), the phrase suggests that an act of worship expresses feeling more than it adores a deity (though, for many it may do both).

"Celebration" is a common phenomenon for us. We celebrate through services that mark anniversaries, special events, and our own versions of Christian or Jewish holidays. Some even prefer to describe our regular weekly gatherings as "celebrations," rather than as gatherings of "worship." The word "celebrate" has its root in the Latin word for "speed" (as in "accelerate") and by extension "to frequent." Thus a celebration should occur frequently or regularly, even though it's a special occasion. The demands of life make it necessary that we make time to come together to affirm its worth and consider its meaning.

Common Worship

Although worship can, of course, refer to times of individual contemplation, meditation, or reflection, it is common worship that is central to the life of a UU church or fellowship. The regular gatherings of the people express the values of the religious community.

At least one Unitarian Universalist commentator, Alice Blair Wesley, has suggested that our worship ought be seen more as an intransitive than a transitive verb. That is, we gather as a people more to worship than to worship something. It is the subject (the people) rather than the object (God), which is essential. For many congregations, worship is an experience (or a recalling of an experience) of the Divine Mystery, Presence, Reality; thought of in subject-object terms. Even so, the bond of Unitarian Universalist worshippers is revealed in what we do together. When we worship, we gather, we pause, we reflect, we share, we serve.

The Place and Time of Worship

It is we the people who create the church, the fellowship. Where we meet becomes sacred by what we create together. As Ethical Culture founder, Felix Adler wrote years ago, when selecting a meeting place, "to seek the highest is holy ground." The space may be a simple hall or a formal sanctuary, but it is holy space because people are there, not because things are there. No altar, sacrament, nor symbol makes the place the church-the people worshipping and serving make it a church.

A place of Unitarian Universalist worship is not, however, likely to be barren. Flowers, plants or clear windows offer reminders of the natural world. Art and symbolism express connection with religious tradition. Light and human scale help the worshipper to be inspired without being overwhelmed. Natural materials and setting create an environment which is warm and nurturing.

Not all of our buildings are this way, but many are—from the oldest New England colonial meeting houses to the most modern structures. In the early-nineteenth century Charles Bulfinch and in the twentieth century Frank Lloyd Wright (both Unitarians) created Unitarian or Universalist churches that continue to be among their finest works of influence. In the last three decades, many of the best known of North American architects have designed new UU church buildings.

We the people gather for worship in a particular place at a particular time. The time is usually Sunday morning, though there may be services at other times. (A recent survey to determine the hymns we sing most often revealed that three of the top four had "morning" themes—the most popular, "Morning Has Broken.") The regularity of time and place is an important aspect of worship. This is a time of ordering and of giving shape.

At regular intervals members congregate for a service. Forms and substance may vary widely from one group to another—or even for the same group from one week to another—but there are common elements to our worship.

The Order of Worship

When we gather for worship, there is a general pattern or order for what we do. For some congregations the style is informal, with no intent to establish strict guidelines. A few congregations insist that within the regularity of time and place, the services themselves should always be different.

Many others are more formal. They have an "order of service" which all can follow. These orders may vary somewhat from week to week, or be changed on special occasions. Or, they may be a reasonably steady procedure that has evolved over a period of years.

Nevertheless, the formal and informal worship services still share common elements. Music, readings, hymns or songs, meditation or prayers are all found in most services, as is an announcement period and probably the taking of a collection. How these and other worship elements—spoken affirmations, periods of silence, responses—all fit together is probably determined by the minister or worship leader.

Some take a thematic approach. Various elements of nature have been selected to express a particular theme for the morning service. The themes include: seasons, values, images, historic events, personalities, social concerns, personal concerns. The possibilities are many. In such a thematic service, whether formal or informal, the worshippers' focus is guided to a single idea or ideal.

Others are more liturgical ("liturgy" means "the people's work.") Services are deliberately designed to lead the worshippers through various moods or feelings, lending a universalness to the service, regardless of the speaker's particular subject. Liturgical services are more likely to be structured, with different sections of the service focusing on designated emotional concepts such as centering, emptying, sharing, affirming, or dedicating.

The theories of Von Ogden Vogt, Unitarian minister, educator and author, developed largely in the 1920s and 1930s, still inform much of this liturgical approach. Patterning his ideas on the call of the prophet Isaiah (Isaiah 6:1-8), Vogt moved in a service from "Vision" through "Humility," "Exaltation" and "Illumination" and ultimately to "Dedication." Vogt's later writings modified the theory somewhat, but the basic pattern still held.

Although the services Vogt developed have largely fallen into disuse, his ideas have profoundly influenced contemporary Unitarian Universalist liturgical worship. In particular, an organization called "Abraxas" has in recent years developed liturgical programs. Its attitude toward worship, which is serious yet light, has aroused both skepticism and respect within our denomination.

The Tradition of the Word

Regardless of the form or theme, central to almost every UU service is the spoken word. Whatever else congregants may like or dislike in worship, all look forward to the sermon or address. We are a people of the word.

This centrality of preaching reflects our Puritan rather than sacramental tradition. In modern dress, we still practice some essentially Puritan principles.

In the Catholic or sacramental tradition, the climax of the mass is the communion. It is the giving of divine power— the grace of God—by the priest to the communicant. The sacraments (which also include baptism, marriage, etc.) are by the authority of the church, the channels for God's grace. A member attends mass—worships—to receive that grace.

The Puritan tradition rebelled against such authority. God's will was to be found not in church dogma but in scripture. To understand and to practice biblical teaching, free men and women came together for worship. To the Puritan, the Bible was the Word of God. Worship was preparation to receive that word through preaching, in order that it could be incorporated into one's life.

Our Unitarian and Universalist forebears accepted the authority of biblical truth, but affirmed that it must be reasonably interpreted. The advancement of human knowledge and experience over the years has led Unitarians and Universalists to find truth in many written works as well as to accept scholarly criticism of the Bible. Nevertheless, this speaking of the truth, as the minister or other speaker best understands it, is still basic to us. Each individual congregant must, of course, determine for him or herself what rings true. It is not required that people agree with all that is said.

Words of Worship

This tradition of the word may contribute to our uneasiness over particular words. Our rejection of creeds is not a rejection of beliefs; it reflects, rather, our doubt that truth can ever be said in a way that is absolutely and eternally right. The ultimate mystery can never be fully described.

Many, perhaps most of our churches, have revised the words used in worship in hymns, affirmations, and responsive readings, to move them beyond gender references. They seek to express their faith in more inclusive language than words like "men" for all human beings or "he" for any individual. References to deity such as "Father," "Lord" or "King" are felt to reflect a cultural masculine bias that is inappropriate to contemporary understanding. Such changes are not easy to make because historical, aesthetic, and even nostalgic influences are not easily dismissed, to say nothing of the integrity of the original authorship. But still, the Unitarian Universalist tradition of hymnody and other words of worship has been a tradition of constant change and alteration to fit the liturgical needs of the time. Throughout our history, words and music have been revised for both emotional and theological reasons.

For example, the Unitarians deleted references to the Trinity and the Universalists removed "hell" from many hymns.

Arguments over the words of worship reflect a central problem for any congregation, but especially for Unitarian Universalist congregations. Words spoken or sung by the people need to be words that they can all affirm and that are in some sense already familiar. Congregational vocalizing is a community expression of faith. If any significant number of persons feels they are excluded and that the words are not right for them for any reason, then the words have failed. Of course, poetic metaphors ought not to be taken too literally, new materials ought not to be rejected without trial, and personal differences to some extent have to be overlooked.

Perhaps the biggest wonder is that with all our individuality we ever manage to find common words at all. Yet most of us do sing hymns and repeat words. One Unitarian Universalist hymnal, *Hymns of the Spirit*, published in 1937, had liturgical orders of service based on Vogt's work that are little used, but the book's hymns and responsive readings are still voiced in a number of our churches. *Hymns for the Celebration of Life*, published in 1964 (its title perpetuates Vogt's phrase), is widely used. Much of the new material in this later volume is the work of Kenneth Patton, whose naturalistic humanistic poetry has found a wide audience among us. Many of the other poets in the hymnal were included largely a result of Patton's research and influence.

Moods and needs change; every decade or two there is need for a new work. A number of our congregations are compiling their own supplementary hymn or songbooks, many in looseleaf form. The First Unitarian Church of Los Angeles, California published *Songs of Faith in Man* (later revised to *How Can I Keep From Singing?*) which is used in a number of churches and fellowships. A hymnbook commission, appointed in 1986, is currently at work on a new work, projected to be completed by 1992. Meanwhile, revised and new materials for worship continue to be published by the Unitarian Universalist Association and related organizations.

Singing hymns was especially important in nineteenth century Unitarian and Universalist churches when music had become almost as important to worship as preaching. Although few Universalist hymns from the period have survived, many Unitarian hymns—by Longfellow, Adams, Hedge, Holmes, Howe and others—have found their way into the hymnals of most denominations. Some of these, like "Nearer My God to Thee" and "In the Cross of Christ I Glory," are now rarely sung in UU circles, but the dated form of their poetry ought not obscure the personal and human qualities of it that are still important to us today.

The inclusion in *Hymns for the Celebration of Life* of material drawn from non-Judeo-Christian sources reflects our openness to inspiration from many sources. Hindu scripture, Chinese philosophy, and contemporary poetry are all represented along with familiar psalms and traditional hymns. The tension between the affirmation of our Western heritage and our desire to cultivate a universal world view is unlikely to be resolved. Such tensions of opposites—particularity and universality, individuality and community, familiarity and novelty, reflection and action, confirmation and confrontation, nurture and challenge, immediacy and patience—are part of the creative dynamic of our Unitarian Universalist religious life.

Seasons of Worship

The worship of a UU congregation extends far beyond any one Sunday service. The cycle of the year, the rhythms of life, the changing ethical issues of society, and the important events of a church's ongoing history all find their expression in our worship. Individual members may attend events regularly or sporadically, but there is a communal continuity through the months and years.

Our worship is seasonal in several ways. Recognizing the changing seasons and the religious holidays of Thanksgiving, Christmas, and Easter (some congregations also include Jewish high holy days or other cultural festivals) gives the year shape. Modern urban living is not completely divorced from an elemental awareness of nature's changes.

The "seasons of the soul" are also essential aspects of worship. Some human emotions, such as joy, praise, gratitude, love, and courage are often voiced in worship. Others, such as sorrow, fear, infirmity, and confusion are more difficult to express, but through worship a voice and place may be found for them.

The seasons of life, from birth through death, are also part of worship. Marriage and funeral services in our practice combine traditional and personal elements. Many ministers would testify that the planning and performing of a wedding or of a memorial service are among the most important tasks of ministry. Services for new children, variously called "christening," "dedication," "welcoming" or "naming," are usually incorporated into a regular Sunday service. Some congregations have also developed a rite of passage for adolescents who are becoming members.

Our worship is not limited to adults. Indeed, the religious education program for children has had an effect on adult worship. "Intergenerational" services, or sections of the regular service that include the presence of children, are important to the life of many congregations. Moreover, the pioneering religious education philosophy of Sophia Lyon Fahs, developed in the 1940s and 1950s, opened many adults, as well as children, to an understanding that religion is part of normal everyday experience. Worship may involve smell, touch or even taste, along with sight and sound. Time taken to consider a flower or hold a crystal may be an act of worship. The "experience of beauty" along with the "celebration of life" was, in fact, one of Vogt's definitions of worship.

Worship as Shaping

The word "worship" comes from the Anglo-Saxon "weorth-scipe," which means to affirm what is of worth. It also means more. The "scipe" means to shape, as in "scoop" and "shovel." Hence, worshipping is shaping that which is already known to be of worth—shaping values, shaping ideals, shaping beliefs. In addition, it may mean not only shaping, but being shaped by them.

When Unitarian Univeralists worship, we are shaping, formulating, organizing, and ordering our faith. We are actively, individually and together, also allowing our lives to be shaped by our faith. In this sense we are engaged in a celebration of life.

Our Concern for Social Justice

William F. Schulz

"Somebody, after all, had to make a start."

These were the words of Sophie Scholl before the People's Court in Munich, Germany, on February 22, 1943. Along with her brother Hans, Sophie was about to be convicted for her participation in the revolt against Hitler of the small group of students known collectively as the White Rose. Armed only with leaflets and a conscience, but convinced that Nazism was responsible for incomparable horrors, these children of German Protestants sought to reassert the values of human dignity and civility in the midst of the most terrible oppression. Their words alone, they knew, could not destroy the Third Reich, but to remain silent was unthinkable and, so, Sophie said, "Somebody, after all, had to make a start."

We North American Unitarian Universalists have never had to face the kind of Nazi terror that confronted the White Rose. Yet many of our churches and fellowships celebrate each year at lovely Flower Communion Services the heroism of Norbert Capek, a Czechoslovakian Unitarian minister that the

Nazis put to death at Dachau in October of 1942. And throughout our two hundred year history, our leaders, members, and institutions have stood witness, sometimes with little company, for values of social justice.

We proudly remember Benjamin Rush and his timely defense of social equality in the late eighteenth century, and Theodore Parker's passionate advocacy of abolition in the mid-nineteenth century. We remember Adin Ballou, with his critique of industrial society, and William Ellery Channing, with his abhorrence of poverty. Olympia Brown was ordained to the ministry in 1863, the first denominationally ordained woman minister in the United States, and we remember her along with Clara Barton, founder of the Red Cross, Dorothea Dix, Susan B. Anthony, and many others.

In more recent times, John Haynes Holmes, pacifist and human rights advocate, co-founder of the War Resisters League and the American Civil Liberties Union, stands as an exemplar of our concern for social justice. There is Donald Thompson's outspoken commitment to civil rights as a Unitarian Universalist minister in Jackson, Mississippi in the early 1960s, and the multiple gunshot wounds he sustained because of that commitment; I think of Thompson's Unitarian Universalist colleague, James Reeb, beaten to death on the streets of Selma, Alabama in March, 1965 because of the same commitment. One of our most historic churches, the Arlington Street Church in Boston, Massachusetts, offered warm hospitality to Dr. Benjamin Spock, Michael Ferber, and other partisans of draft resistance during the Vietnam War. And I remember also the Unitarian Universalist Association's decision to publish the controversial Pentagon Papers, despite government harassment, and of the Association's commitment to gay and lesbian rights long before other denominations had recognized the call. Many of our local churches and fellowships have responded in one way or another to injustice.

Like the White Rose, we have always been few in numbers. But our energies, when wisely spent and keenly tailored, have often made a difference. Elaine Noble, a former member of the Massachusetts Legislature, suggested that the Unitarian Universalist signature in support of a piece of legislation puts lawmakers on notice that the issue will eventually be taken seriously by the larger liberal constituency.

All this is well and good, and yet sometimes we Unitarian Universalists are asked how we can take institutional political action and at the same time maintain our fealty to individual freedom of belief. Consider, for example, the resolutions on a wide variety of social issues that are debated and then either approved or rejected by representatives of our churches and fellowships at our General Assemblies. These do not attempt by any means to bind all individual Unitarian Universalists or our local societies. But they are important attempts to state a general consensus in order to focus attention and guide the Association in its social responsibility efforts. Do they compromise our creedlessness? Ought a religious institution engage in social action at all? The search for an answer tells us much about Unitarian Universalism and our approach to religion and the world. It raises issues both theological and practical.

Being and Power

Plato believed that the definition of being is power, that by the simple fact of one's existence, one commands a share of personal power. I believe that. I think of how a disturbed child can dominate a family, or how a newborn baby commands its parents' world, or how a person in a coma radically alters loved ones' lives.

If the equation "Being = Power" holds for individuals, it is even more characteristic of institutions. By virtue of its very existence the church possesses power. By their property and their wealth, prestige and people, their ministries, mailing lists, and mimeos, their visibility and vision, our local societies and our Association are de *facto* possessors of power. We cannot avoid it.

Nor can we avoid exercising that power. It is still true that "not to decide is to decide," that neutrality in the face of injustice comes close to endorsing it. This is most obvious when an institution is forced to be an active agent of a tyrannous authority, as occurred during the Vietnam War when a ten percent federal tax was placed on all telephone charges to pay for the war effort. To carry on "business as usual" was obviously, in this case, to contribute to the military operations. The inseparable link between religion and politics is often more subtle, but still quite real.

Every decision, whether tacit or explicit, about the use of our institutional resources, or power, is a political decision and a reflection of what we value. Please understand this is not to suggest that the church's only business—or even its primary business—ought to be social action. But it is to say that every act, including the tacit choice to remain passive, is a statement about our relationship with the public realm. A congregation that closes its doors to the community six–and–a–half days a week makes as profound a political comment as one that regularly participates in social activism. The question, then, is not whether we possess power and the means to use it, but rather whether we are willing to use it in the interest of our ideals.

Our Heritage of Interference

No matter what our theological beliefs, I think Unitarian Universalists would be hard pressed not to agree in some sense with the Koran that "one hour of justice is worth seventy years of prayer." We believe religion must have an impact on the world. It cannot be all chanting and incense or even coffee and conversation, or it risks becoming too far removed from experience. Our entire tradition, from Francis David, the Transylvanian Unitarian, who was martyred in 1579, to the contemporary social ethicist, James Luther Adams, and from Origen to the late Clarence Skinner, educator, pacifist and social reformer, asserts that it is not enough merely to be in the world; it is necessary to judge the world in religious and ethical terms.

One of the measurements of that judgment is whether or not every individual receives a certain measure of respect; respect that may be tempered only by what William Ellery Channing called the "death of goodness in the breast." To withhold respect on any other grounds is to do damage to the spirit.

This is our faith and the only way to teach it to our children is by making it visible in the way we live. This may be done in a quiet way, in individual acts of kindness. But in addition to that our children must also learn about politics and power and our relation to both. We may not be able to provide our young people with the certainty and finality of other faiths, but we can offer them models of conviction and consistency and we can encourage in them the strength to live with integrity.

Surely religion speaks of mysterious things, such as transcendence and redemption, but it must also speak of the mundane. If, in view of eternity, people need the promise of glory, it is also the case that in the face of persecution they require the possibilities of power. For Unitarian Universalism to refuse, when necessary, to shatter tranquility, or refuse to interfere on behalf of those who are powerless, or to reject the prophet Nathan's role when confronted with King David, would be to betray our heritage. Judgment, witness, sympathy, and devotion are all synonymous with our tradition.

46 Unitarian Universalist Pocket Guide

The Liberation of Blessings

Clarence Darrow's family always told him that the long trek up the snowy hill was not worth the short sledding trip down, but Darrow never believed them. Snowy hills and the excitement of sledding are gifts of grace that come to us unsought. But Unitarian Universalism reminds us that you can't get up a snowy hill if your legs are broken and you can't get back down if you don't own a sled.

The world is full of blessings, and rich with opportunity. "Grace" is the theological term for all unsolicited favor. Grace is not something we can deliberately seek and find, or ask for and be granted, but it is within our power to create circumstances that block its appearance. Blessings cannot be sought, but they can be smothered; every instance of oppression lessens the possibilities of being found by grace.

Dietrich Bonhoeffer, the great German theologian who was martyred by the Nazis, distinguished between cheap and costly grace. "Those who believe in cheap grace," he said, "believe that it comes without preparation or price, the Church's inexhaustible treasury from which she showers blessings with generous hands, without asking questions or fixing limits." But those who know that true grace is costly know that it requires an open and committed heart and a discipleship to the powers of transformation.

Social involvement with the world is merely an extension of our broader religious sympathies. It is prompted by worship and liturgy; nurtured by the aesthetic; implied in our devotions. The second reason, then, that Unitarian Universalists work in the world is to help make the blessings of life available for as many as possible. Cheap grace and snowy hills are fine for the affluent, but before a poor person can revere the sun she requires decent housing to shelter her from it. It is exactly because we so cherish the gift of the sun that we attend first to the procurement of housing.

The Amending of History

People are often distinguished more for their memories than for their characters. Elie Wiesel tells of the young student who read one night for the first time about the Holocaust and who awoke the next morning to find his hair turned white. White hair and vivid memory are testimony to the unforgotten.

Those of orthodox Christian persuasion believe that the meaning of history is contained within it, whole and complete, signaled by the Cross and renewed by each conversion. But we Unitarian Universalists believe that the meaning of history is still in the making, undetermined.

A sign is displayed above the entrance to the concentration camp at Bergen Belsen: "O Earth," it reads, "conceal not the blood shed on thee." But long after the Allies knew the purpose of Auschwitz, they refused to bomb the ovens or the railroad lines because those were not critical to their military objectives. History threatens to convince us of life's unspeakable emptiness. But every time we find a voice and lend a hand, we bring blood into the open, bomb the ovens, and try to rectify the wrongs of history. Even though we may fail to reach our goals, there is a difference between failure and futility.

Unitarian Universalists take this tack not because we can do no wrong, but because we know we, ourselves, are capable of cruelty. "If only it were all so simple!" cried Solzhenitsyn in *Gulag Archipelago*. "If only there were evil people somewhere committing evil deeds and it were necessary only to separate them from the rest of us and destroy them. But the dividing line between good and evil cuts through the heart of every human being. And who is willing to destroy his [her] own heart?" Our hands already drip with history's blood and only dirt can cleanse them.

Power and Being

To be faithful to a heritage, to liberate blessings, and to amend history might be reason enough to act justly. But why, exactly, should our political acts take an institutional form? Aren't the manifold individual acts of conscience enough? Once again we are drawn back to a discussion of power.

Power manifests primarily through institutions. The individual conscience, noble as it may sometimes be, is feeble before the conglomerates of government, business, and, yes, even other religious faiths. If we are to act as a "countervailing force" to injustice, we need at least the power to demand a confrontation. To advocate individual witness alone is in effect to be smugly (or naively) satisfied with martyrdom. (There were many others in the White Rose besides Hans and Sophie.) "Attitudes do not become effective in public life," says James Luther Adams, a prominent Unitarian Universalist theologian, "until they find an institutional instrument." Changes are made through associations, and only rarely by a single hero. We turn now to discussion of our formal organizations for social change.

The Unitarian Universalist Association (UUA)

Each General Assembly of the UUA since 1961 has passed a series of resolutions on various social issues of the day. It is the task of the UUA and, in particular, its Department for Social Justice (UUA–SJ), to implement those resolutions, and thereby transform rhetoric into reality.

General Assembly resolutions are initiated at the local society or district level. The UUA Commission on General

Resolutions receives proposed resolutions, reviews and edits them, and then places up to ten of them on the "parish poll" that is distributed to all congregations each spring. The three that receive the highest number of positive votes from the congregations are placed on the agenda of the General Assembly.

In the first year a resolution appears on the agenda, the Assembly only decides whether or not to refer that resolution to congregations for a year's worth of study. UUA–SJ provides background material for such study and congregations are encouraged to give feedback to the Commission on every resolution. After a year's study, the proposed guidelines, now amended in accord with the responses from congregations, go before the Assembly again for final action.

UUA–SJ does not work alone to implement our resolutions. It belongs to a host of interreligious and secular advocacy coalitions, including the Interfaith Center for Corporate Responsibility, the Religious Network for Equality for Women, the Coalition for a New Foreign and Military Policy, Project Equality, the Leadership Conference on Civil Rights, the AIDS Action Council, and numerous others. The UUA Washington Office directly represents our concerns to elected and appointed officials in Washington, D.C.

Finally, the Department for Social Justice offers training in social change and advocacy to our local congregations in order that they might witness more effectively at the local level for our religious principles. In 1936 the Commission on Appraisal wrote, "Religion that does not express itself through action in society is not in any true sense religion at all." (Commission on Appraisal, *Unitarians Face a New Age.*)

Social Action Clearing House (SACH)

The UUA Department for Social Justice is not by any means the only Unitarian Universalist agency involved in the struggle for a more just and peaceful world. SACH is an umbrella network of Unitarian Universalist social action organizations that meet quarterly to coordinate efforts. Each April a training and lobbying session in Washington, D.C. is sponsored by SACH. Among those agencies included in the Clearing House are the following five:

Unitarian Universalist Service Committee (UUSC)

Independent of the UUA, the Service Committee brings its energy and expertise to bear upon a limited number of social change projects. Founded in 1939 as a rescue mission to reach Jews and liberals in Nazi-threatened Prague, the UUSC has sponsored war relief, medical assistance, and community development projects around the world. Through its staff and network of volunteers, UUSC works for basic social change in the United States, especially in the areas of criminal justice and aging, and for health, women's rights, economic development, and human rights in Central America, the Caribbean, India, and Africa.

Unitarian Universalist United Nations Office (UU-UNO)

The co-directors of UU-UNO are the officially accredited representatives of the UUA and the International Association for Religious Freedom to the UN and UNICEF. The UU-UNO staff monitor UN activities with special emphasis on disarmament, the status of women, aging, population, and religious freedom. UU-UNO sponsors an annual youth conference and an intergenerational seminar for UUs across the continent. A network of local contacts (called "UN Envoys") links UU-UNO with local congregations.

Unitarian Universalist Women's Federation (UUWF)

The mission of the UUWF is to enable Unitarian Universalist women to join together for mutual support, personal growth, and spiritual enrichment and, through their combined strength and vision, to work toward a future where all women will be empowered to live their lives with a sense of wholeness and integrity. The Federation is made up of local units in Unitarian Universalist Societies as well as individual members.

Unitarian Universalist Peace Fellowship (UUPF)

Organized in 1955 as the Liberal Religious Peace Fellowship, this group combined the Unitarian Pacifist Fellowship and the Adin Ballou Fellowship of the Universalist Church of America. It is affiliated with the Fellowship of Reconciliation. A membership organization linking UU pacifists and other peace activists, it supports conscientious objection, provides peace education, and publishes the newsletter *UNIPAX*.

Unitarian Universalist Peace Network (UUPN)

The UU Peace Network was established in 1984 as a result of growing denominational concern for nuclear disarmament. It is made up of the UUA, UUSC, UUUNO, UUWF, UUPF, and the International Association for Religious Freedom. The Network provides programs and initiates action on the economics of the nuclear arms race, the social and political impact of sustained high levels of military spending, and the positive aspects of a peaceful world.

Our Local Churches and Fellowships

These organizations are national or international in scope. They provide outstanding resources for our local congregations, but it is in the church or fellowship that the most important work gets done. Whether petitioning legislators, supporting boycotts, sponsoring refugees, encouraging the presentation of unpopular views, or engaging in a host of other kinds of social concerns, it is the local society that provides the community that puts our faith into practice.

If the instruments of our efforts are institutional, the rewards are distinctly personal. And this transformation of being may be one final and overriding reason why we Unitarian Universalists seek to manifest our faith in acts. Whether it is thought of as pity, mercy, compassion, or self-respect, it follows this story: a wise man once went to preach righteousness to Sodom and Gomorrah, but without success, and soon someone asked him why he continued when he knew he could not change the people of Sodom and Gomorrah. And the wise man replied, "Now I know I must continue so that the people of Sodom and Gomorrah do not change me."

Action may come out of outrage, guilt, passion, resentment, or even the search for truth. But as it was written on the walls of a Spanish harbor, "I am seeking God, but I do not find God. I am seeking myself, but I do not find me. But I do find my neighbor and the three of us go on our way together."

Our Ways of Education

Jean Starr Williams

In our liberal church, education of the people of all ages is, at its best, the responsibility of the people.

We do not have a creed or a body of doctrine which, when assimilated by a person, identifies that person as religious. Nor do we have a holy writ, which, when known and understood by a person makes that person religious.

We say that someone is religious who is striving with mind, spirit, and body to live by a set of values that empower and enhance that individual's thought and action. We believe that living by these values would empower and enrich the lives of the peoples of the earth.

The members of the Unitarian Universalist community plan study programs, field trips, celebrations, worship, dialogues, and artistic experiences for peer groups and intergenerational groups, as well, to help further each person's religious process. We think of our three-year olds as beings with spirit and awareness. The world of their religious community lies most effectively and enduringly in their homes and the arms of their parent(s). But the church environment is designed to stimulate, comfort, and sustain children, feeding their developmental needs as well as possible.

We think of each person and each constellation of persons in our community as being in need of intellectual enlightenment. It is not enough to know only the worlds we ourselves move in. Each of us must be invited, encouraged, even prodded to look beyond our immediate surroundings to the wider world around us. We need to strive toward an educated outlook, which has as its roots a longing for justice, compassion, and peace for all humankind.

We know it takes more than our intellects to encompass such a monumental personal goal. It takes the education of the conscience and spirit. The good Samaritan needed more than a quick mind to analyze the situation. He needed a heart that had been educated to act in a compassionate and caring way.

Such a process of personal development is a long journey. In our culture, as soon as we leave home to go to school and see more of the world, we encounter language, action, and religious points of view that run counter to those we were raised with. Within the family of our church fellowship, we can, at any age, identify confusing and contrary forces in our lives. Once we identify and understand these forces we can explore ways to respond to them—positively or negatively.

I am reminded of a young Unitarian Universalist who was told he could not be a Boy Scout because he would not take the Scout Oath. "But I do not believe in God," he insisted. Or the six–year–old girl who asked her mother, "Can I go to hell?" I think of the first openly gay person ordained into our ministry in 1979. I remember James Reeb, who was born in 1927 and ordained into our ministry in 1958, and in the spring of 1965, at the age of 38, was murdered in Selma, Alabama by men of his own color—white. In a paper Jim wrote prior to his ordination, he said:

Because the members of the Unitarian Church [the Unitarian and Universalists movements had not yet merged] are not bound to a creed or to certain conceptions held to be absolute truths, except that the pursuit of truth is always of ultimate importance, they can respond to new ideas and truths no matter what their source or how evidently they contradict previously held beliefs.

Since there is a recognition that there will always be people at different stages of opinion among sincere and dedicated people as to the nature of life and the good life, the responsibility and freedom of each individual to proceed along the pathways that are more productive for him [sic] are emphasized.

Finally, the development of people so that they may approach ever nearer to full fruition is accepted as the primary task of religion. (Duncan Howlett, *No Greater Love, The James Reeb Story.*)

All our ventures in education are designed so that, at any age, a person will receive support and encouragement to grow and live in a religious way. We are all engaged perpetually in formulating and living out values. We seek to know truth as well as joy, and have fun as well as understand the sobriety and sometimes trauma of living.

Our goals are worthy of our struggles to achieve them. It is safe to say that our strivings date as far back as 1790 when the Universalist, Benjamin Rush, founded an organization in Philadelphia for the religious education of youth, known as the "First Day" or "Sunday School Society."

In 1837, the Unitarian William Ellery Channing clearly stated the aims and methods of liberal religious education as they apply to the young at home or in church. This statement still stands as a goal to be achieved in our churches and fellowships. Any tendency to use secular education to achieve religious goals is a travesty in Channing's eyes. He wrote in "The Sunday School":

The great end in religious instruction, whether in the Sunday School or *family*, is, not to stamp our minds irresistably on the young, but to stir up their own; not to make them see with our eyes, but to look inquiringly and steadily with their own; not to give them a definite amount of knowledge, but to inspire a fervent love of truth; not to form an outward regularity, but to quicken and strengthen the power of thought; not to bind them by ineradicable prejudices to our particular sect or peculiar notions, but to prepare them for impartial, conscientious judging of whatever subjects may, in the course of Providence, be offered to their decision; not to impose religion upon them in the form of arbitrary rules which rest on no foundation but our own word and will, but to awaken the consciousness, the moral discernment, so that they may discern and approve for themselves what is everlastingly right and good.

Over many years the curricula of both the Unitarian and the Universalist movements have evolved and changed. We have moved from a graded and thoroughly biblical content to an approach that is more eclectic with regard to both the origins and the applications of religion. This expansion is identified by the Reverend A.W. Gould, President of the Western Unitarian Sunday School Society, in his annual address to the Society in 1899 (Western Unitarian Conference, 1899):

First, it (the Western Unitarian Sunday School Society) had helped our schools beyond the idea that all religion was confined to a chosen people and their scripture.

Second, it had taught that all life is religious, and

that our own social institutions have fully as great religious lessons for our children as had the tabernacle of Moses.

Third, it had shown that all nature is religious, that our own pond-lilies are just as religious as the lilies of the field of which Jesus spoke.

Fourth, it was showing that all true art is religious, so that we can use pictures not alone as incidental illustrations of passages studied in our Sunday-school, but as objects of study in themselves. A fine picture will speak to the mind of the child long before the words will do so, will cultivate his religious taste (which in itself is a religious work), and impress it with lessons that cannot be conveyed to it in any other way.

In 1901, the Universalists made available to all their churches a curriculum called "The Universalist Graded Lessons." This curriculum was centered on the Bible but not exclusively so. In 1909, the Unitarian Sunday School Society created a wholly graded curriculum, the Beacon Series.

The Unitarians and the Universalists were both moving from Bible-centered curricula to an educational approach which was child-centered and more related to experience.

In 1912, a Department of Religious Education was established by the American Unitarian Association and a new curriculum was developed called the Beacon Course. In the words of Unitarian Universalist minister David Parke: "The Beacon Course presupposed the interrelatedness of religion and life, the validity of both Biblical and Modern sources, and the centrality of the child within a Christian framework." This material proved increasingly unsatisfactory during the decades of the 1920s and 1930s.

In 1937, the New Beacon Series appeared under the author/editorship of Sophia Fahs. Fahs' conception of curriculum is precisely described in the following words by Hugh Hartshorne, in "A School of the Christian Life": "(Curriculum) does not depend for the progress of its work upon any printed texts. It uses printed material not as an end in itself to be mastered, but rather as an adjunct of teaching... The real curriculum is found in the children's own growing experience and in the helpful experiences of [hu]mankind." The New Beacon Series met a great need, not only among our churches and fellowships, but also among other liberal religious groups such as the Friends and the Ethical Culture Society. It should be noted that the philosophy of education embodied in the New Beacon Series was also set forth in the writings of the Universalist Educator, Angus MacLean, for many years Professor of Religious Education at the Theological School of St. Lawrence University.

As a matter of fact, Unitarians and Universalists embarked on joint ventures in religious education some years before they merged. The merger took place in 1961, but seven years earlier, in 1954, the denominational departments of religious education were joined.

In 1965, as a merged denomination, we entered into a new era of curriculum development identified as our Multi-Media Programs. Hugo Hollerorth was the author/editor. The multimedia programs came out of a perceived need to respond to the growing complexity of our world and its effect on all of us—children, young people, and adults. Throughout our lives, each of us needs to be able to question and sort through the barrage of events that move about us. Twenty programs were developed, for ages as young as kindergarten, to adults. The programs ranged in themes from *Decision Making, Freedom and Responsibility*, and *About Your Sexuality*, to a trilogy on UUism: *Disagreements Which Unite Us, Our Experiencing, Believing and Celebrating*; and *Our Ways of Relating*. Hollerorth continued to work within the basic framework of the *New Beacon Series*, but he broadened it philosophically, in addition to adding new tools for learning. Hollerorth's *Relating to Our World* is recommended reading.

In 1981, the Religious Education Futures Committee, which was appointed by the UUA Board of Trustees and administration to assess the needs of religious education throughout the Association, recommended that curriculum and programs be created that were based on the religious principles broadly affirmed by Unitarian Universalists. It further recommended that each local congregation undertake the process of exploring, formulating and articulating a philosophy of religious education, and then sharing it with the UUA, whose Department of Religious Education would prepare a composite statement of a Unitarian Universalist philosophy of religious education for the Association. To facilitate this task, a process guide was designed for use by UU societies: *Philosophy-Making for UU Religious Growth and Learning*. A comprehensive plan of curriculum development has been drawn up and new programs for education of all age groups are being put together for use over the next ten years (*Report of the Religious Education Futures Committee to the UUA Board of Trustees*, October, 1981). The subject areas come from six major sources: Unitarian Universalist history and traditions, Jewish and Christian heritages, other world religions and cultures, the arts, secular literature, and contemporary and historical events and forces.

What is the place of parents in all of this? We remember that Channing's words included *the home*. This is where the most earnest religious education takes place. Over time, our values tend to become our children's values, as do our enthusiasms and loyalties. It is not enough that our children be aware of what we have rejected from our early faiths; they must also be made aware of what it is in our Unitarian Universalist faith that sustains us and compels us to more intentionally live out and articulate our Unitarian Universalist values and convictions. No child escapes the imprint of the religious education he or she receives at home. The quality of that religious education is the responsibility of the parents. In turn, it is our responsibility to see that our church or fellowship provides us with the tools to give good home religious education. Go now and teach, for in the best of all possible religious communities, each of us is a model for learning for all the others in our church or fellowship.

Important Dates
in Unitarian Universalist History

Early Christian History

325　Nicene Creed adopted at Council of Niceaea
　　　establishes dogma of the Trinity.

544　Belief in universal salvation condemned as
　　　heresy by a church council.

The Reformation

1511　Birth of Michael Servetus (the most famous of the
　　　sixteenth-century anti-Trinitarians).

1527　Martin Cellarius publishes *On the Works of God*
　　　(the earliest anti-Trinitarian book).

1531　Michael Servetus publishes *On the Errors of the
　　　Trinity*.

1553　Michael Servetus is burned at the stake in Geneva.

Polish Socinianism

1539　Birth of Faustus Socinus (leader of the Polish
　　　Socinian or Unitarian movement).

1546   Anti-Trinitarianism appears in Poland.

1579   Faustus Socinus arrives in Poland.

1585   Founding of the Rakow press (the first official Unitarian press).

1591   The Socinian Church in Krakow is destroyed by a mob.

1658   The Polish Diet banishes Socinians.

Transylvania (Hungarian) Unitarianism

1510   Birth of Francis David (leader of Transylvanian Unitarians).

1566   Francis David preaches against the doctrine of the Trinity.

1568   King John Sigismund (the Unitarian King) proclaims the earliest edict of complete religious toleration.

1579   Francis David, condemned as a heretic, dies in prison.

1821   English and Transylvanian Unitarians discover one another.

English Unitarianism and Universalism

1550	The Church of the Strangers (Socinian in influence) is established in London.
1615	Birth of John Biddle (the founder of English Unitarianism).
1654	John Biddle is banished to the Scilly Isles.
1703	Thomas Emlyn is imprisoned at Dublin for anti-Trinitarian beliefs.
1703	Birth of George de Benneville (one of the leaders of American Universalism) in London.
1723	George de Benneville undertakes first preaching mission on the European continent.
1723	Birth of Theophilus Lindsey (one of the founders of the English Unitarian movement).
1733	Birth of Joseph Priestley (one of the greatest scientists of his age, a founder of both the English and American Unitarian movements).
1741	John Murray (the founder of American Universalism) born in Alton, England.
1741	George de Benneville emigrates to Pennsylvania.

1750   James Relly, an associate of the evangelist George
         Whitefield, withdraws from this connection and
         establishes himself as an independent preacher of
         Universalism.

1759   *Union* (a theological treatise on universal
         salvation by James Relly) published in London.

1774   Essex Street Chapel opened in London (marking
         the beginning of permanently organized
         Unitarianism in England).

1791   Riots against Joseph Priestley and other Unitarians
         in Birmingham.

1794   Joseph Priestley emigrates to America.

1825   The British and Foreign Unitarian Association
         founded.

Canadian Unitarianism and Universalism

1832   First recorded meeting of Unitarians in Montreal.

1842   First permanent Unitarian Church established in
         Montreal.

1843   A Universalist Church established in Halifax.

1845   First Unitarian Church of Toronto established.

1891   An Icelandic-speaking Unitarian Church organized
        in Winnipeg. (Between 1891 and 1931 other
        Icelandic-speaking Unitarian Churches organized.

1961   Canadian Unitarian Council organized.

1962   Cercle Unitaire de Langue Francaise, a French
        language fellowship, founded in Montreal.

1962   Canadian Unitarian Council/Conseil Unitaire
        Canadien relates itself officially to the UUA.

American Unitarianism and Universalism

1637   Samuel Gorton (a pioneer of Christian Universalism)
        driven out of Massachusetts for his political and
        religious radicalism.

1684   Joseph Gatchell has his tongue pierced with a red-
        hot iron for his statement "All men should be
        saved."

1740   High point of the Great Awakening (whose
        emotional excesses stimulated a desire for
        a more rational religion).

1743   Christopher Sower (a Universalist Quaker) with the
        assistance of George de Benneville, prints the first
        Bible in America translated into German. Passages
        supporting the universal character of religion
        produced in heavier type.

1770   John Murray arrives at Good Luck on Barnegat Bay, New Jersey.

1770   On September 30 Murray preaches his first sermon in America in the meeting house of Thomas Potter.

1771   Birth of Universalist Hosea Ballou, in Richmond, New Hampshire.

1774   John Murray preaches in Gloucester, Massachusetts.

1778   Caleb Rich organizes the General Society (Universalist) to ordain ministers and issue preaching licenses.

1779   Gloucester Universalists organize the first Universalist church in America and call John Murray as minister.

1785   Liturgy of King's Chapel Boston, is revised, omitting references to the Trinity.

1785   The first Universalist Convention (with delegates from churches) held in Oxford, Massachusetts.

1786   Gloucester Universalists successfully contest the right of the state to raise taxes for the established church.

1786   A Universalist church (called the Universal Baptist Church) organized in Philadelphia.

1787   Congregation of King's Chapel, disregarding
        Episcopal procedures, ordains lay reader James
        Freeman as its minister, thereby becoming the first
        independent church of Unitarian beliefs.

1788   Murray wins the right of Universalists and
        dissenting ministers to be recognized as ordained
        ministers with authority to perform marriages.

1790   The Philadelphia Convention of Universalists
        adopts a declaration of faith and a set of principles
        of social reform.

1796   Joseph Priestley advocates Universalism and
        Unitarianism in Philadelphia. Founding of the First
        Unitarian Church of Philadelphia with the
        encouragement of Priestley.

1802   The oldest Pilgrim church in America (founded
        at Plymouth in 1620) becomes Unitarian.

1803   Winchester Profession of Faith adopted by
        Universalists at Winchester, New Hampshire.

1805   Hosea Ballou writes *A Treatise on Atonement* (the
        first book published in America openly rejecting
        the doctrine of the Trinity).

1816   Harvard Divinity School established.

1819   William Ellery Channing delivers his Baltimore
        sermon (a landmark statement of Unitarian
        principles).

1819   *The Christian Leader* (Universalist) begins publication
        (originally named *The Universalist Magazine*).

1821   *The Christian Register* (Unitarian) begins publication.

1825   The American Unitarian Association is organized.

1833   Formation of The General Convention of
        Universalists in the United States (with advisory
        powers only).

1838   Ralph Waldo Emerson delivers "The Divinity School
        Address" (a major event in religious liberalism).

1841   Theodore Parker delivers his South Boston sermon
        "The Transient and Permanent in Christianity"
        (in defense of natural religion).

1844   Meadville Theological School established.

1847   The Universalist General Reform Association is
        organized.

1852   Tufts College founded by Universalists at Medford,
        Massachusetts.

1852   Western Unitarian Conference is organized in
        Cincinnati, Ohio.

1854   Publication of the first book under American
        Unitarian Association imprint — *Grains of Gold or
        Select Thoughts on Sacred Themes* by the Rev. Cyrus A.
        Bartol, Jr.

1856   St. Lawrence University and Theological School
        founded by Universalists at Canton, New York.

1856   Children's Sunday started, Universalist Church,
        Chelsea, Massachusetts.

1862   The Universalist Publishing House established.

1863   Ordination of Olympia Brown, first woman to be
        ordained by any denomination.

1865   The National Conference of Unitarian Churches
        organized.

1866   Organization of the Universalist General
        Convention (renamed in 1942 the Universalist
        Church of America).

1867   The Free Religious Association is organized.

1869   Women's Centenary Association formed (in 1939
        became the Association of Universalist Women).

1880   The General Alliance of Unitarian and Other
        Liberal Christian Women (originally called
        Women's Auxiliary Conference) is organized.

1884   The American Unitarian Association becomes an
        association representative of and directly
        responsible to its member churches.

1889   Young People's Christian Union formed (later
        called Universalist Youth Fellowship).

1890   Universalists establish churches in Japan.

1896   Unitarian Young People's Religious Union organized.

1899   "Essential Principles of Universalism" adopted at Boston, Massachusetts.

1899   First Merger Commission founded.

1900   The International Congress of Free Christians and Other Religious Liberals formed.

1902   Beacon Press launched (broadening the American Unitarian Association's book-publishing program). First title: *Some Ethical Phases of the Labor Question*, by Carroll Wright.

1904   Starr King School for the Ministry founded in Berkeley, California, as Pacific Unitarian School of the Ministry.

1908   The Unitarian Fellowship for Social Justice organized.

1913   The General Sunday School Association organized at Utica, New York.

1917   The first denomination-wide Unitarian Youth Sunday held.

1920   The Unitarian Laymen's League organized.

1921   Universalist women acquire Clara Barton
        homestead (developed into camp for diabetic girls).

1931   Second Merger Commission.

1933   Free Church of America formed.

1934   Commission on Appraisal appointed by American
        Unitarian Association.

1935   Washington Statement of Faith adopted by
        Universalists.

1936   AUA Commission on Appraisal publishes
        Unitarians Face a New Age.

1937   The Unitarian Sunday School Society merged
        with the Religious Education Department of
        the American Unitarian Association.

1937   Frederick May Eliot elected president of the AUA;
        Sophia Lyon Fahs appointed Children's Editor.

1938   The Beacon press pioneers a series of publications in
        religious education.

1939   Unitarian Service Committee organized.

1941   Young People's Christian Union reorganized into
        Universalist Youth Fellowship.

1942   The Young People's Religious Union reorganized
        into American Unitarian Youth.

1942   The Universalist General Convention renamed the Universalist Church of America.

1943   The Unitarian Service Committee makes plans for medical missions to war-devastated countries.

1944   The Church of the Larger Fellowship organized to serve Unitarians living in areas without Unitarian churches.

1945   The Universalist Service Committee formed.

1948   Continental program to establish Unitarian fellowships begun.

1950   American and English Unitarians jointly celebrate the 125th anniversary of their respective denominational organizations.

1953   Liberal Religious Youth, Inc., is formed by the merger of American Unitarian Youth and Universalist Youth Fellowship.

1953   The Council of Liberal Churches (Universalist-Unitarian) Inc., is organized for the federation of the departments of publications, education and public relations.

1953   *The Christian Leader* renamed *The Universalist Leader*.

1956   Unitarians and Universalists create Joint Commission on Merger to examine feasibility of merging the two denominations.

1958   *The Christian Register* renamed *The Unitarian Register*.

1961   The American Unitarian Association and the Universalist Church of America officially consolidate and organize the UnitarianUniversalist Association.

1961   *The Unitarian Register* and *The Universalist Leader* are merged as the Unitarian Universalist *Register-Leader*.

1962   The Unitarian Laymen's League and the National Association of Universalist Men join to form the Laymen's League (Unitarian-Universalist).

1963   The Alliance of Unitarian Women and the Association of Universalist Women join to form the Unitarian Universalist Women's Federation.

1963   The Unitarian Service Committee and the Department of World Service of the Unitarian Universalist Association unite to form the Unitarian Universalist Service Committee, Inc.

1965   James Reeb, Unitarian Universalist minister, murdered in Selma, Alabama in civil rights protest organized by Martin Luther King, Jr. As a result, protest intensifies across the nation.

1967   Black Unitarian Universalist Caucus organized.

1970   *Unitarian Universalist World* succeeds *Register-Leader*.

1972   Beacon Press publishes *Pentagon Papers* and the federal government investigates UUA bank records.

1973   UUA organizes National Conference on American Freedom.

1973   UUA initiates "Sharing in Growth" renewal program.

1974   Federal judge dismisses UUA Pentagon Papers Case without prejudice after U.S. Attorney's statement that the investigation would not be resumed.

1979   Death of President Paul Carnes; election of President O. Eugene Pickett.

1985   Election of President William F. Schulz.

1987   Tabloid *Unitarian Universalist World* becomes *The World*, publishing in magazine format.

About the
Unitarian Universalist Association

The Unitarian Universalist Association (UUA) represents the consolidation in 1961 of two religious denominations: the Universalists, organized in 1793 and incorporated in 1866, and the Unitarians, organized in 1825 and incorporated in 1847.

The Association is composed of member congregations serving more than 180,000 adults and church school children in more than 1,000 churches and fellowships in the United States and Canada. Its uniting purpose is set forth in its By-laws:

We, the member congregations of the Unitarian Universalist Association, covenant to affirm and promote:

- The inherent worth and dignity of every person;

- Justice, equity and compassion in human relations;

- Acceptance of one another and encouragement to spiritual growth in our congregations;

- A free and responsible search for truth and meaning;

- The right of conscience and the use of the democratic process within our congregations and in society at large;

- The goal of world community with peace, liberty and justice for all;

- Respect for the interdependent web of all existence of which we are a part.

The Association's policy–setting body is its General Assembly, which meets annually and is made up of delegates from the churches and fellowships. The General Assembly makes overall policy for carrying out the Association's purposes, reviews the program, and elects for stated terms a president, a moderator, a financial advisor and four other members of the Board of Trustees. Twenty members of the Board are elected regionally. The Board conducts the affairs of the Association and carries out policies and directives as provided by law.

At present, the Association has ten departments for carrying forward programs of service to the churches and fellowships: Development, Communications, Publications, Ministry, Social Justice, Extension, Religious Education, District Services, Finance, and Beacon Press. Beacon Press is a nonprofit publisher dedicated to the responsible exploration of the human condition. Over half a million Beacon Press books are sold each year.

The churches and fellowships that constitute the Association's member bodies are completely autonomous and self-governing. Ultimate authority and responsibility is vested in the membership of each congregation. Membership is open to all without regard to color, race, sex or national origin.

Continentally, the Association is organized into twenty-three geographic districts. Each district serves the congregations in its area with a variety of programs and promotes increased participation in the life of the denomination. Professional staff from the UUA and the districts offer counsel and assistance in many matters to districts, area councils or "clusters," and individual congregations.

Among the many functions and services of the Association are the following: aiding congregations, organizing new groups, encouraging area leadership, providing building loans, producing pamphlets and devotional materials, keeping more than 100,000 UU families informed with issues of *The World* magazine, creating a sense of continental unity and purpose, maintaining interfaith relationships, providing financial advice, managing an investment trust, furnishing worship art suggestions, creating religious education curricula, exchanging information on social action, supporting a UU voice in Washington, accrediting men and women for the ministry, assisting congregations to find new ministers, and raising funds to accomplish and sustain the many programs of the Association.

Many (but by no means all) Unitarian Universalist ministers receive their theological education at one of three schools: Meadville/Lombard Theological School, affiliated with the University of Chicago; Thomas Starr King School for Religious Leadership in Berkeley, California; and Harvard (University) Divinity School.

A number of organizations are related to the Association to express specific Unitarian Universalist needs. These include the UU Service Committee, the UU Women's Federation, the UU Ministers Association, Young Religious Unitarian Universalists, UU United Nations Office, and many others.

UU congregations in Canada have a national voice and conduct many programs through the Canadian Unitarian Council (Conseil Unitaire Canadien) with offices in Toronto. The Association maintains contact with liberal religious groups throughout the world through the International Association of Religious Freedom, which has its headquarters in Frankfurt, West Germany.

For further information on the Unitarian Universalist Association and related organizations, write to the Information Office, UUA, 25 Beacon St., Boston, MA 02108-2800. Phone (617) 742—2100.

About the
Church of the Larger Fellowship

The Church of the Larger Fellowship was organized in 1944 to meet the needs of religious liberals isolated for geographical, occupational, psychological or health reasons from participation in a local Unitarian Universalist church or fellowship. It thus meets a need which goes back to our nation's early history. In 1825 Thomas Jefferson wrote to Dr. Benjamin Waterhouse, "The population of my neighborhood is too slender and is too much divided into other sects to maintain any one preacher well. I must therefore be contented to be a Unitarian by myself." Later, in 1884, "The Post Office Mission" was organized. CLF is the legal and logical successor carrying on this extension-by-mail program.

Today, men and women who cherish religious convictions that are liberal in character can find warmth and stimulation and a variety of practical resources in this unusual "church," which has more than 2,500 member families and serves over 500 children and young people. Its members live in some 1,700 communities in the United States and Canada, and it has over 300 members living in sixty-three countries in other parts of the world.

Monthly mailings of sermons and other reading materials are sent to its members, each of whom is given a subscription to *The World* published by the Unitarian Universalist Association. A monthly bulletin, *Quest*, keeps members informed of the activities of other members and of a variety of church activities. The CLF adapts denominational materials for home use, with particular emphasis on religious education. In addition, it provides a Lending Library of books of particular interest to religious liberals, a Liberal Religious Braille Library for the blind, a Cassette Library of sermons, and an opportunity to participate in the many varied humanitarian and educational activities of the Unitarian Universalist Association. Correspondence study and personal discussions-by-mail are invited. The Church has its own full-time minister.

CLF was incorporated in 1970 as an independent or autonomous organization. The Church is managed by its own Board of Directors which is responsible to CLF members. An Every Member Canvass is held each fall to meet the current expense budget (approximately $125,000) and members have the opportunity to support the UUA Annual Program Fund and Unitarian Universalist Service Committee. An Endowment Fund honoring Frederick May Eliot and Clinton Lee Scott, founding ministers, creates a perpetual foundation. Further, CLF has a "Society of Sponsors," individuals, most of whom are members of existing churches and fellowships, who recognize the service that CLF provides the denomination. Not only does CLF introduce liberal religion to hundreds of new people each year, but a majority of fellowships have a nucleus of CLF members. Each member of the Society of Sponsors pledges a specific amount per annum to the Church of the Larger Fellowship.

CLF also has a category of "Associate Members" made up of small churches and fellowships that are experiencing programming difficulties, particularly with their religious education programs for children. CLF's home service to its regular members has been enlarged to meet the needs of its Associate Members.

For further information about the Church of the Larger Fellowship, write to The Minister, Church of the Larger Fellowship, Unitarian Universalist Association, 25 Beacon St., Boston, MA 02108-2800.

Bibliography

History

Ballou, Hosea, *A Treatise on Atonement*, with an introduction
by Ernest Cassara (Boston: Skinner House, 1986).
First published in 1805, the major work of the great
nineteenth-century Universalist theologian.
American Transcendentalism: An anthology of criticism.
Edited by Brian M. Barbour. (Notre Dame: University
of Notre Dame Press, 1973).
Cassara, Ernest, *Universalism in America* (Boston: Skinner
House, 1984).
A documentary history of Universalism's first two
hundred years.
Crompton, Arnold, *Unitarianism on the Pacific Coast: The First
Sixty Years* (Boston: Beacon Press, 1957).
Hewett, Philip, *Unitarianism in Canada* (Canadian Unitarian
Council/Conseil Unitaire Canadien, 1967).
The origin of individual Unitarian and Universalist
Churches in Canada as well as the history of the
Canadian Unitarian Council.
_____, *Unitarians in Canada* (Ontario: Fitzhenry and White
Side, 1978.)
How the Unitarians have exerted a powerful
inflence on Canadian life for over 150 years.

Howe, Daniel Walker, *The Unitarian Conscience*, 2nd ed.
(Middletown: Wesleyan University Press, 1987).
A study of moral philosophy taught at Harvard and
its influence on outstanding New England
Unitarians from 1805 to 1861.

Hutchison, William R., *The Transcendentalist Ministers* (New
Haven: Yale University Press, 1959).
A study of nineteenth-century transcendentalist
ministers and their ideas.

Lavan, Spencer, *Unitarians and India: A Study in Encounter
and Response* (Boston: Skinner House, 1977).

Lyttle, Charles H., *Freedom Moves West: A History of the
Western Unitarian Conference* (Boston: Beacon Press,
1952).

Marshall, George, *Challenge of a Liberal Faith* (Boston: Skinner
House, 1987).

The Transcendentalists, edited by Perry Miller (Cambridge:
Harvard University Press, 1950).

Miller, Russell E., *The Larger Hope: History of the Universalist
Church in America*, 2 Vols. (Boston: Unitarian Universalist Historical Society, 1979, 1985).

Morrison-Reed, Mark D., *Black Pioneers in a White Denomination* (Boston: Beacon Press, 1984).

The Epic of Unitarianism, edited by David Parke, (Boston:
Skinner House, 1980).
Original writings from the history of liberal religion
from the sixteenth century to the twentieth.

Parke, David, *The Historical and Religious Antecedents of the
New Beacon Series in Religious Education* (Ann Arbor:
University Microfilms International, 1978).

Persons, Stow, *Free Religion: An American Faith* (New Haven:
Yale University Press, 1947).
A study of the origin, development and implications
of the free religious movement which emerged from
Unitarianism following the Civil War.

Robinson, David, *The Unitarians and the Universalists* (Westport, CT: Greenwood Press, 1985).

Robinson, Elmo Arnold, *American Universalism: Its Origins, Organization and Heritage* (Jericho: Exposition Press, 1970).

Scott, Clinton Lee, *The Universalist Church of America: A Short History* (Boston: Universalist Historical Society, 1957).
   An introductory essay on the history of American Universalism.

Wilbur, Earl Morse, *A History of Unitarianism* in two volumes: Volume I. *Socinianism And Its Antecedents.* (Cambridge: Harvard University Press, 1945). Vol. II.

_____, *A History of Unitarianism in Transylvania, England and America.* (Cambridge, MA: Harvard University Press, 1952).
   A definitive work on the origins of Unitarianism.

_____, *Our Unitarian Heritage* (Boston: Beacon Press, 1956).
   An introductory history of Unitarianism from early Christianity through the first quarter of the twentieth century.

Williams, George Huntston, *American Universalism, A Bicentennial Historical Essay* (Boston: Skinner House, 1983).
   A study of the first one hundred years of Universalism with special attention to its impact on American Society.

Wright, Conrad, *The Beginnings of Unitarianism in America* (Boston: Beacon Press, 1955).
   Considers eighteenth-century religious liberals as a unified group in the social structure of New England from 1735 to 1805.

_____, *The Liberal Christians* (Boston: Skinner House, 1979).
   Six essays on American Unitarian history in its relationship to some of the dominant forces in American life.

Wright, Conrad, *Three Prophets of Religious Liberalism:*
>   *Channing, Emerson, Parker*, 2nd ed. (Boston: Skinner
>   House, 1986).
>> In addition to an introductory essay, includes
>> William Ellery Channing's *Unitarian Christianity*,
>> Ralph Waldo Emerson's *Divinity School Address*, and
>> Theodore Parker's *The Transient and Permanent in
>> Christianity*.

*A Stream of Light: A Sesquicentennial History of American
>   Unitarianism*, edited by Conrad Wright (Boston:
>   Skinner House, 1975).

Wintersteen, Prescott B., *Christology in American Unitarianism*
>   (Boston: Unitarian Universalist Christian Fellowship,
>   1977).

Biography

Bainton, Roland H., *Hunted Heretic* (Boston: Beacon Press,
>   1953).
>> A biographical study of the most famous of the six-
>> teenth century anti-Trinitarians, Michael Servetus,
>> who was burned at the stake in Geneva in 1553.

Cassara, Ernest, *Hosea Ballou: The Challenge to Orthodoxy*
>   (Lanham, MD: University Press of America, 1982).
>> A study of the life and works of the great nine-
>> teenth-century Universalist and their implications
>> for religious liberalism.

Commager, Henry Steele, *Theodore Parker: Yankee Crusader*
>   (Boston: Skinner House, 1982).
>> A biography of the Unitarian reformer, preacher,
>> scholar whom Ralph Waldo Emerson called one of
>> the three great men of the age.

Howlett, Duncan, *No Greater Love: The James Reeb Story* (New
>   York: Harper & Row, 1966).

Hunter, Edith F., *Sophia Lyon Fahs: A Biography* (Boston:
    Beacon Press, 1976).
Hitchings, Catherine, *Universalist and Unitarian Women
    Ministers* (Boston: Unitarian Universalist Historical
    Society, 1985).
        Includes the biographies of more than 150 deceased
        Universalist and Unitarian women ministers.
Mendelsohn, Jack, *Channing, The Reluctant Radical* (Boston:
    Skinner House, 1979).
        A contemporary biography of William Ellery Chan-
        ning, major nineteenth-century Unitarian leader.
Richardson, Robert D., Jr., *Henry Thoreau: A Life of the Mind*
    (Berkeley: University of California Press, 1987).
Rusk, Ralph L., *The Life of Ralph Waldo Emerson* (New York:
    Charles Scribner & Sons, 1949).
Skinner, Charles R., and Alfred S. Cole, *Hell's Ramparts Fell*
    (Boston: Universalist Publishing House, 1941).
        A biography of John Murray, the founder of Ameri-
        can Universalism.

Contemporary Statements

Marshall, George, *Challenge of A Liberal Faith* , 3rd Ed. (Bos-
    ton: Skinner House, 1987).
        An affirmation of Unitarian Universalist values with
        a brief account of beliefs and history.
Mendelsohn, Jack, *Being Liberal in an Illiberal Age — Why I am
    a Unitarian Universalist* (Boston: Beacon   Press,
    1985).

Social Justice

The Commission on Appraisal, *Empowerment* (Boston: Uni-
    tarian Universalist Association, 1984)

Gilbert, Richard, S. *The Prophetic Imperative* (Boston: Unitarian Universalist Association, 1980)

Resolutions and Resources, A Social Responsibility Handbook, (Boston: Unitarian Universalist Association, 1988, with annual updates)

Unitarian Universalist Association, *Task Force on Social Responsibility and Accompanying Paper #1* (Boston: Unitarian Universalist Association, 1985)

Pamphlets

"A Voice for Lesbian and Gay Human Rights" edited by Donna Scalcione-Conti, 1981

"Avoiding Sexist Language" by Robin Behn and Doris Pullen, 1987

"Facts on Military Service and Conscientious Objection" by Kathleen Skerrett, 1987

"Social Concern is Necessary But Not Sufficient" by Loretta Williams, 1969

Additional resource material is available from:

Unitarian Universalist Service Committee, 78 Beacon Street, Boston, MA 02108

Unitarian Universalist United Nations Office, 777 U.N. Plaza, New York, NY 10017

Unitarian Universalist Peace Network, 5808 Green Street, Philadelphia, PA 19144.

Unitarian Universalist Women's Federation, 25 Beacon Street, Boston, MA 02108

Religious Education

Anastos, M. Elizabeth, Editor, *Curriculum Mapping: A Guide to Curriculum Planning for Unitarian Universalist Societies* (Boston: Unitarian Universalist Association, 1985)

Anastos, M. Elizabeth and David Marshak, *Philosophy-Making for Unitarian Universalist Religious Growth and Learning: A Process Guide* (Boston: Unitarian Universalist Association, 1983)

Hollerorth, Hugo, *Relating to Our World* (Boston: Unitarian Universalist Association, 1974)

MacLean, Angus, *The Wind in Both Ears*, Second Ed. (Boston: Skinner House, 1987)

Navias, Eugene B., *Parish Ministry and Pedagogy: 1823-1983-A Past and Future Look at Religious Education*, essay given at the Berry Street Conference, 1983.

Stone House Conversations, edited by Hugo J. Hollerorth. (Boston: Unitarian Universalist Association, 1979). Created by people representing twelve groups within the UUA, verbatims of critique of twelve papers exploring the questions: 1) What is UUism? 2) What are the objectives of UU religious education? 3) What content and experiences should be included in our curriculum to fulfill these objectives?

Unitarian Universalism in the Home, edited by Ellen Johnson-Fay and others (Boston: Unitarian Universalist Association, 1982)

Pamphlets

"Can I Believe Anything I Want?," by Elizabeth Strong, 1987

"Cornerstones of Religious Education: Sophia Lyon Fahs Speaks," edited by Rosemarie Smurzynski, 1985

"It's A New Day for Religious Education," by Eugene B.
    Navias, 1986
"Unitarian Universalism for Young People," by Lois Eck-
    lund and Jan Rugh, 1985

PERIODICALS AND PAMPHLETS

For subscriptions to periodicals, write directly to addresses
    given below.

Periodicals:

The Humanist
    A magazine of religious, social and literary comment
    and criticism, published by the American Humanist
    Association. (7 Harwood Drive, P.O. Box 146,
    Amherst, NY 14226-9982.)
The Inquirer
    "The oldest dissenting weekly paper in Britain," con-
    taining Unitarian news of England and the Common-
    wealth, plus articles of general interest. (1-6 Essex St.,
    London, WC2R 3 HY.)
Proceedings of the Unitarian Universalist Historical Society
    Research articles and critical reviews of current
    literature in the history of Unitarian Universalism. (25
    Beacon St., Boston, MA 02108-2800.)
Religious Humanism
    The quarterly journal of the Fellowship of Religious
    Humanists. (P.O. Box 278, Yellow Springs, OH 45387.)
Synapse
    Newspaper of the Young Religious Unitarian Univer-
    salists. Published several times per year. (YRUU, 25
    Beacon Street, Boston, MA 02108).

Unitarian Universalist Christian
> News, articles and sermons of Unitarian Universalist Christianity in the modern world. (P.O. Box 66, Lancaster, MA 01523-0066.)

The Universalist Herald
> A bulletin of information, ideas and ideals. Started in 1847. (P.O. Box 185, Canon, GA 30520.)

The World
> The official journal of the Unitarian Universalist Association. (25 Beacon Street, Boston, MA 02108-2800).

Pamphlets:

"Introducing Unitarian Universalism" by John Nicholls Booth, 1986

"Meet the Unitarians and Universalists" by Jack Mendelsohn, 1987

"Unitarians and Universalists Believe" by George Marshall, 1986

"The Faithfulness of Unitarian Universalists" by Alice Blair Wesley, 1988

Unitarian Universalist Views Series:
> UU Views of the Bible
> UU Views of Christmas
> UU Views of Death and Immortality
> UU Views of Easter
> UU Views of God
> UU Views of Jesus
> UU Views of Science and Religion
> UU Views of World Religions
> UU Views of Worship

Write to the Information Office, UUA, 25 Beacon St., Boston, MA 02108-2800 for a current list of pamphlets.

Sources

A large and varied stock of books, pamphlets, and teacher resources relating to Unitarian Universalism are listed in the UUA Bookstore Catalog. It may be requested from the UUA Bookstore, 25 Beacon Street, Boston, MA 02108-2800.

In addition to *The World*, Journal of the Unitarian Universalist Association, a number of periodicals and journals are published by different groups and organizations within the UUA, or by groups which have a special interest in Unitarian Universalism. For information on these periodicals, contact the Information Office, UUA, 25 Beacon Street, Boston, MA 02108-2800.

About the Author

BORN IN Neuchâtel in Switzerland, in 1906, Denis de Rougemont was educated in Switzerland and in Vienna, but made his home in France, where, until the outbreak of the second world war, he was active as one of the leaders of the new "personnaliste" movement. He founded, together with E. Mounier and A. Dandieu, the two personalist reviews *Esprit* and *L'Ordre Nouveau,* and launched simultaneously a review of existential theology, *Hic et Nunc.* In 1941, Mr. de Rougemont was sent to the United States and put in charge of the French transmissions of the Voice of America; he also taught at the Ecole Libre des Hautes Etudes in New York.

After his return to Europe in 1946, he devoted himself to the cause of European Federalism, becoming one of the guiding spirits of the European Federalist Movement. Since 1950 he has directed the European Cultural Center in Geneva, of which he is the founder, and he also presides over the Congrès pour la Liberté de la Culture, which has its seat in Paris.

A brilliant writer, whose work has been translated into twelve languages, Mr. de Rougemont has published eighteen works in the fields of literary criticism, religion, philosophy and politics, three volumes of journals, and a tragedy which has been set to music by Arthur Honegger. His masterful analysis of modern society and its dislocations, *The Devil's Share,* has found an enthusiastic audience in the United States.

Love
in the
Western
World

DENIS DE ROUGEMONT

translated by
MONTGOMERY BELGION

—

REVISED AND
AUGMENTED EDITION

A FAWCETT PREMIER BOOK

Fawcett Publications, Inc., Greenwich, Conn.
Member of American Book Publishers Council, Inc.

Preface to the 1956 Edition

It was at the suggestion of my English publisher that I undertook to revise this book.

Three times five years have passed since it first appeared, and there has been a war, and much has been experienced to put my contentions to a stern test. I have forgotten nothing and have learned a little; for that matter, I have learned more from life than from reading my critics, as these have been far from mutual agreement. Some of them have nevertheless swayed me. In this new version I have replaced one or two wild flourishes of the pen by a little analysis, even though I feel that this worsens my case.

The historians deplored my insistence upon the disturbing relations which I noted between Cathars and troubadours. They, for want of evidence, do not find them disturbing. Several theologians, either Roman or Greek, complained with friendliness that I contrast Eros with Agape in too uncompromising a fashion,[1] one which does not allow for the intermediate kind of love without which we should be unable to live. To the historians I shall reply simply that I was in quest of an existential *meaning*. Hence I had no idea of poaching upon their preserves. The documents which I quote, the juxtapositions which I propose, are intended to serve less as evidence than as illustrations. However, as far back as 1940 fresh research began to strengthen my theory. I have taken advantage of this to rewrite nearly the whole of Book II, which deals with the twelfth century, with Catharism, the troubadours, and Tristan. That is what is mainly new.

To the critics who disputed the actual *meaning* which I thought I was justified in putting on the facts, I am tempted to give way on a number of points. My original task was to clear the ground and mark decisive contrasts; I could not always qualify or draw distinctions. A chapter now added to Book VI,

[1] Cf. in particular the excellent book by Father M. C. D'Arcy, S.J., *The Mind and Heart of Love* (London, 1945), which is largely devoted to a critical exposition of the standpoints represented by Anders Nygren in his *Eros and Agape* and by the present book.

and innumerable corrections of detail, will show, I hope, that I have gained in realism.

My central purpose was to describe the inescapable conflict in the West between passion and marriage; and in my view that remains the true subject, the real contention of the book as it has worked out.

The topicality of my inquiry seems to have suffered in no way from the second world war. Particularly at the end of Book V, I mentioned the possibility of a conflict which might put an end to the problems propounded in this study. My fear very nearly proved right, and I need now but transfer it to the foreseeable results of an inter-continental atomic war. Furthermore, seven years spent in the United States have afforded me the opportunity of seeing that the passion myth—now degraded to mere romance—is not in sight of exhausting its effects. The cinema[1] propagates those effects the entire world over, and the statistics of divorce show us how strong they are. If our civilization is to endure, it will have to carry through a great revolution. It will have to recognize that marriage, upon which its social structure stands, is more serious than the love which it cultivates, and that marriage cannot be founded on a fine ardour.

The ways of such a revolution are not yet to be forecast. On that I dwell in Book VI. My ambition is confined to making readers sensitively alive to the presence of the myth, and thereupon to enabling them to detect its radiation into real life as much as into works of art. It will perhaps not be altogether in vain for a few minds to be brought to grow conscious of what is being implied around them. For if it is true that the mutations of the heart are matured, and indeed happen, in the unconscious, they begin with their epiphany in expression, whether that is written, plastic, or pictorial, even as a love affair with its first avowal.

D. de R.

[1] It is curious to note that several films have taken their plots from my account of passionate love. Cf. B. Amengual, *Le Mythe de Tristan au Cinéma* (Algiers, 1951).

Contents

Love
in the
Western
World

Book I

THE TRISTAN MYTH

1

Behind the Vogue of the Novel

"My Lords, if you would hear a high tale of love and death . . ." [1]

We know we could listen to nothing more delightful; and this opening of Bédier's *Tristan* should serve accordingly as a model for the beginning of a novel. It must be an unerring art that can at once thrust us into the state of absorbed suspense thanks to which narrative imparts the illusion of veracity. Where does the spell come from? And why should our feelings go halfway to meet the emotional effect of such a profound rhetorical device? One thing the tremendous vogue of the romantic novel makes immediately clear: the chord that awakens in us the most sonorous echoes has for its tonic and dominant, so to speak, the words "love" and "death." There are other and more occult grounds for thinking that this is one clue to the European mind.

Love and death, a fatal love—in these phrases is summed up, if not the whole of poetry, at least whatever is popular, whatever is universally moving in European literature, alike as regards the oldest legends and the sweetest songs. Happy love has no history. Romance only comes into existence where love is fatal, frowned upon and doomed by life itself. What stirs lyrical poets to their finest flights is neither the delight of the senses nor the fruitful contentment of the settled couple; not the satisfaction of love, but its *passion*. And passion means suffering. There we have the fundamental fact.

Our eagerness for both novels and films with their identical type of plot; the idealized eroticism that per-

[1] Joseph Bédier, *The Romance of Tristan and Iseult,* translated by Hilaire Belloc (London, 1913).

15

vades our culture and upbringing and provides the pictures that fill the background of our lives; our desire for "escape," which a mechanical boredom exacerbates —everything within and about us glorifies passion. Hence the prospect of a passionate experience has come to seem the promise that we are about to live more fully and more intensely. We look upon passion as a transfiguring force, something beyond delight and pain, an ardent beatitude. In "passion" we are no longer aware of that "which suffers," only of what is "thrilling." And yet actually passionate love is a misfortune. In this respect manners have undergone no change for centuries, and the community still drives passionate love in nine cases out of ten to take the form of adultery. No doubt lovers can invoke numerous exceptions. But statistics are inexorable, and they confute our poetic self-deception.

Can we be in such a state of delusion, can we have been so thoroughly "mystified," as *really* to have forgotten the unhappy aspect of passion, or is it that in our heart of hearts we prefer to what must seemingly fulfil our ideal of a harmonious existence something that afflicts and yet elevates us? Let me examine the contradiction more closely, notwithstanding that to do so *must* seem disagreeable, since it threatens to uncover what we would rather not see. To assert that passionate love is actually tantamount to adultery is to insist upon a fact which our cult of love both conceals and distorts; it exposes what by the cult is dissimulated, repressed, and left unnamed, so as to leave us free to give ourselves up ardently to something we should never dare claim as our due. In the reader's very objection to recognizing that passion and adultery are commonly indistinguishable in contemporary society, we have a first indication of the paradox that we now desire passion and unhappiness only on condition we need never admit wishing for them as such.

To judge by literature, adultery would seem to be one of the most remarkable of occupations in both Europe and America. Few are the novels that fail to allude to it; and the vogue of the others, how we make allowances for these, the very passion with which we sometimes denounce them—all that shows well enough what couples dream about in the grip of a rule that has turned marriage into a duty and convenience. Without adultery, what would happen to imaginative writing? Novels and plays subsist on the so-called "breakdown of marriage." Probably, also, they help to prolong the breakdown, on the one hand by extolling what religion regards as a crime and law as an infringement, and, on the other hand, by making fun of this and drawing from it an inexhaustible fund of situations either comic or shameless. Whether the subject is idealized by speaking of the divine rights of passion, refined away by means of a smart, worldly psychology, or mocked by the popularity which the eternal triangle enjoys in the theatre, we are constantly *betraying* how widespread and disturbing is our obsession by the love that breaks the law. Is this not the sign that we wish to escape from a horrible reality? To turn the situation into either a farce or something mystical is equally to confess that it is unbearable. Ill-assorted couples, the disappointed, the rebellious, the intense, the shameless, the unfaithful or the deceived (whether in fact or in dreams, in remorse or in terror, in the delight of revolt or the disquiet of temptation)—few men and women will fail to see that they belong to at least one of these categories. The word "adultery" sums up one half of human unhappiness—renunciation, compromises, separations, neurasthenia, together with the irritating and petty confusion of dreams, obligations, and secret acquiescence. Although so many books are being produced, or perhaps on that very account, it sometimes seems as if nothing has yet been said about the reality of our unhappiness, and that some of the most ingenuous problems in this department have more often been solved than propounded.

For instance, once the existence of the ill has been recognized, must the institution of marriage bear the blame for it, or is there something fatal to marriage at the very heart of human longing? Has the so-called "Christian" notion of marriage, as many people suppose, really brought about all this turmoil, or is there a notion of love abroad in the world which, although we do not yet realize it, renders the marriage bond intolerable in its very essence? It is obvious that Western Man is drawn to what destroys "the happiness of the married couple" *at least as much* as to anything that ensures it. Where does the contradiction come from? If the breakdown of marriage has been simply due to the attractive-

ness of the forbidden, it still remains to be seen why we
hanker after unhappiness, and what notion of love—what
secret of our existence, of the human mind, perhaps of
our history—this hankering must hint at.

2

The Myth

There is one great European myth of adultery—the
Romance of *Tristan and Iseult*. In the midst of our
chaotic conduct, and piercing the jumble of moral systems and immorality which the chaos fosters, there are
purely dramatic moments when this mythical shape looms
out like a watermark. It is then a bold and simple
design, a kind of archetype of our most complex feelings
of unrest. And as poets, in order to get away from the
current linguistic confusion, are wont to seek the remote
origin of a word—the thing or action which this word
first denoted—so I wish to connect with this myth part
of the disorder in contemporary manners. I am undertaking an *etymology of the passions,* which promises to
be less inconclusive than actual etymology, because it is
our lives, and not some theoretical science, that will supply its instant verification.

It may at once be asked if the Romance of *Tristan* is
indeed a myth, and if in that case to try to analyse it is
not to destroy its *charm*. But we are no longer at the
stage of supposing that the mythical is tantamount to un-
reality or illusion. Too many myths now display their
indisputable power over us. And yet abuse of the term has
made a fresh definition needful. Speaking generally, a
myth is a story—a symbolical fable as simple as it is
striking—which sums up an infinite number of more or
less analogous situations. A myth makes it possible to
become aware at a glance of certain types of *constant
relations* and to disengage these from the welter of everyday appearances.

More narrowly, a myth expresses the *rules of conduct*

of a given social or religious group. It issues accordingly from whatever *sacred* principle has presided over the formation of this group. Symbolical accounts of the life and death of gods, legends accounting for either sacrifices or the origin of taboos, are examples of myths. It has frequently been noted that myths never have an author. The origin of a myth has to be *obscure*, and so to some extent has its meaning. A myth stands forth as the entirely anonymous expression of collective—or, more exactly, of common—facts. Therefore, a work of art—whether poem, tale, or novel—differs radically from a myth. The validity of a work of art depends on nothing but the talent of its author. What matters about it is exactly what does not matter as regards a myth—its "beauty" or its "verisimilitude," together with all its qualities of singular success, such as originality, skill, style, etc. *But the most profound characteristic of a myth is the power which it wins over us, usually without our knowing.* If a story, an event, or some leading human figure may turn into a myth, it is precisely by virtue of coming to hold sway over us as though against our will. A work of art, as such, never exerts, properly speaking, any *compulsion* upon its spectators or auditors. However splendid and powerful it may be, it is always open to criticism and can always be enjoyed on individual grounds. With a myth it is otherwise. The statement of a myth disarms all criticism, and reason, if not silenced, becomes at least ineffective.

I propose to consider *Tristan,* not as a piece of literature, but as typical of the relations between man and woman in a particular historical group—the dominant social caste, the courtly society, saturated with chivalry, of the twelfth and thirteenth centuries. The group in question was indeed long ago dissolved. Yet its laws remain our laws in an unsuspected and diluted form. Profaned and repudiated by our official legal codes, these laws have become the more compelling in that they wield no power over us except in our *dreams.*

The Tristan legend has many features indicative of a myth. First of all these is the fact that the author—supposing the legend to have had one, and one only—is entirely unknown. The five "original" versions that have come down to us are artistic rearrangements of an

archetype it is impossible to trace.[1] Another sign of the
mythical in the Tristan legend is its making use of a
sacred principle.[2] The advance of the action, and the
effects which this action was intended to have on an audi-
tor, depend (to an extent I hope to make clear) on a set
of rules and ceremonies which are no other than those
of the custom of medieval chivalry. And the "orders" of
chivalry were often called "religions." "A religion" is
what Chastellain, the fifteenth-century Burgundian chron-
icler, calls the Order of the Golden Fleece—the latest
of such orders in point of time—and he refers to it as a
sacred mystery, notwithstanding that he wrote at a period when chivalry was no more than a survival.[3] Fi-

[1] Critical comparison makes it easy to eliminate the individual
vagaries of the five authors. When I come below (Chap. 5)
to analyse the content of the legend, I shall neglect such variations,
because they are very easily accounted for by ephemeral circumstances or else by the personal tastes of each writer.

[2] In order to forestall misconception, I must insist that I am
concerned only with the Tristan legend as *written*. That alone is
what I refer to wherever I speak of the original myth. No doubt
much can be made out of the sacred attributes of the characters of
Tristan and Iseult (or Essylt) in Celtic mythology. And unquestionably many details of the bardic oral tradition were incorporated with the legend (cf. Book II, Chap. 12, below). But
it is equally certain that none of the five authors—neither
Béroul, Thomas, Eilhart, nor the author of the *Roman en prose*,
nor the author of *La Folie Tristan*—had been initiated to this
tradition. Not one of them is aware of the sacred and symbolical
significance originally inhering in the characters whose loves he
relates. Moreover, the myth of passionate love is all contained in
the legend as this was set down by twelfth-century poets after
they had endowed it with a new significance, and *that alone is
what is still active within us today*.

[3] J. Huizinga, the *The Waning of the Middle Ages,* translated
by F. Hopman (London, 1924), says (p. 56):
"Medieval thought in general was saturated in every part with the
conceptions of the Christian faith. In a similar way and in a more
limited sphere, the thought of all those who loved in the circles
of court or castle was impregnated with the idea of chivalry. . . .
This conception even tends to invade the transcendental domain.
The primordial feat of arms of the archangel Michael is glorified
by Jean Molinet as 'the first deed of knighthood and chivalrous
prowess that was ever achieved.' From the archangel 'terrestrial
knighthood and human chivalry' take their origin, and in so far

nally, the very *obscurity* which we find in the legend denotes its deep relation to a myth.

As a rule, the obscurity of a myth does not reside in its form of expression.[1] The obscurity belongs in part to the mystery of the origin of the myth, and in part to the vital import of what the myth symbolizes. If this were not obscure, or *if there were no reason to conceal its origin and its bearings so that it might escape challenge,* a myth would lack a *raison d'être.* A law, a moral treatise, or even some little tale able to serve as a mnemonic summary, would do instead. No myth arises so long as it is possible to keep to the obvious and to express this obvious openly and directly. On the contrary, a myth arises whenever it becomes dangerous or impossible to speak plainly about certain social or religious matters, or affective relations, and yet there is a desire to preserve these or else it is impossible to destroy them. There is, for example, no need of myths nowadays in order to set forth scientific truths, which we deal with from an entirely "lay" standpoint and which therefore have everything to gain from individual criticism. *But a myth is needed to express the dark and unmentionable fact that passion is linked with death,* and involves the

---

are but an imitation of the host of the angels around God's throne."

Again (p. 57):

"The conception of chivalry constituted for these authors [Froissart, Monstrelet, d'Escouchy, Chastellain, La Marche, etc.] a sort of magic key, by the aid of which they explained to themselves the motives of politics and history. . . . What they saw about them looked primarily mere violence and confusion. War . . . tended to be a chronic process of isolated raids and incursions; diplomacy was mostly a very solemn and very verbose procedure, in which a multitude of questions about juridical details clashed with some very general traditions and some points of honour. All notions which might have enabled them to discern in history a social development were lacking to them. Yet they required a form for their political conceptions, and here the idea of chivalry came in. By this traditional fiction they succeeded in explaining to themselves, as well as they could, the motives and the course of history, which thus was reduced to a spectacle of the honour of princes and the virtue of knights, to a noble game with edifying and heroic rules."

[1] Here the form of expression is the language of the poem; and we know that this is extremely simple.

destruction of any one yielding himself up to it with all
his strength. For we have wanted to preserve passion
and we cherish the unhappiness that it brings with it;
and yet at the same time both passion and unhappiness
have stood condemned in the sight of official morals
and in the sight of reason. Hence, thanks to the obscurity,
we have been able to receive and enjoy imaginatively
the disguised content of the myth, and yet have not grown
sufficiently aware of the nature of this content to be
confronted by the contradiction. In this way certain
human facts which are, we either realize or suspect,
fundamental, have escaped challenge. The myth *expresses*
those realities to the extent exacted by our instinct, but
it also veils them to the extent that broad daylight and
reason [1] might imperil them.

The origins of the mythical romance of *Tristan* are unknown or but half-known, its nature was once *sacred,*
and it veils what it is disclosing, so that it may be wondered if it fully possesses the *compelling* features of a true
myth. The question is not to be shirked. It carries us
into the heart of the problem and shows the problem
to be important for the present day. In the thirteenth
century the rules of chivalry did indeed operate with
absolute compulsion, but in the romance they are introduced only as a *mythical obstacle* and as *ritualistic figures*
of rhetoric. They provide the tale with pretexts for re-
newals of impetus, and, above all, the tale would not,
without them, have been accepted unquestioningly by its
audiences. It has to be recognized that these social "ceremonies" are means of obtaining allowance for an anti-
social *content,* and this content is passion. In this context,
indeed, the word "content" acquires its full force. The
rules of chivalry literally "contained" the passion of
Tristan and Iseult; and only on that condition was the
passion open to being expressed in the twilight of a myth.
Because, in being the passion that wants Darkness and
triumphs in a transfiguring Death, it must represent, for

---

[1] The kind of reason I have in mind here is the "profaning"
activity that operates at the cost of what is collectively sacred and
emancipates the individual from the compulsions which this exerts.
Although rationalism has been raised to the status of an official
doctrine, we ought not to forget its strictly *sacrilegious,* anti-social,
and "disruptive" power.

any society whatsoever, a threat overwhelmingly intolerable. The social groups then in existence had therefore to be capable of withstanding it by means of a strongly framed structure, so that while obtaining an outlet it nevertheless did not do too much damage.

Let the social bonds subsequently slacken, or the social group disintegrate, and the myth must cease to be such in the strict sense. But what it then loses in compelling force and ability to be communicated in a veiled and tolerable guise, it gains in occult influence and in lawless violence. *Pari passu* with the loss of the last virtues of chivalry, even in the profaned guise of good form—the conventions to be observed by gentlemen—the passion "contained" in the original myth spread out into everyday life, invaded the subconscious, and invoked or, if necessary, invented new compulsions. For, as will be shown presently, it was not only the nature of society, but also the very ardour of the dark passion, that required the avowal to be *masked*.

The myth itself, in the strict sense, was formed in the twelfth century, at the very time the leading caste was making a great effort to establish social and moral order. The intention was, indeed, "to contain" the surges of the destructive instinct; for religion, in attacking this instinct, had been exacerbating it. Contemporary chronicles, sermons, and satires show that in this century there occurred an early "breakdown of marriage," and the breakdown made a vigorous reaction imperative. The achievement of the Romance of *Tristan* was thus to set passion in a framework within which it could be expressed in symbolical satisfactions.[1] Let such a framework disappear, and passion will nevertheless subsist. It will still be as dangerous to the life of society, and will still drive society to attempt a corresponding restoration of order. Hence, not the myth in its original guise, but *that need of a myth* which the Romance met, remains historically permanent.

Enlarging my definition, I shall henceforth intend by the term "a myth" this permanence of a type of relations together with the corresponding reactions. The myth of

---

[1] Rather with the same aim and to the same effect, the Church took paganism into its ritual.

Tristan and Iseult I shall consider to be, not merely the Romance, but the peculiarity which the Romance illustrates—something the influence of which has gone on extending all the way down to our own day. The myth that has been agitating us for eight hundred years as spell, terror, or ideal, is at one and the same time a passion sprung from dark nature, an energy excited by the mind, and a pre-established potentiality in search of the coercion that shall intensify it. In having shed its original guise, it has merely become more dangerous. Fallen myths can distil venom even as the dead truths alluded to by Nietzsche.

3

Topicality of the Myth, or Reasons for Its Analysis

There is no need to have read Béroul's *Tristan* or M. Bédier's, and no need to have heard Wagner's opera, in order to undergo in the course of everyday life the nostalgic dominion of such a myth. It is manifested in the majority of novels and films, in the popularity these enjoy with the masses, the acceptance which they meet with in the hearts of middle-class people, from poets, from ill-assorted couples, and from the seamstresses who dream of having a miraculous love-affair. The myth operates wherever passion is dreamed of as an ideal instead of being feared like a malignant fever; wherever its fatal character is welcomed, invoked, or imagined as a magnificent and desirable disaster instead of as simply a disaster. It lives upon the lives of people who think that love is their fate (and as unavoidable as the effect of the love-potion is in the Romance); that it swoops upon powerless and ravished men and women in order to consume them in a pure flame; or that it is stronger and more real than happiness, society, or morality. It lives upon the very life of the romanticism within us; it is the great mystery of that religion of which the poets of the nineteenth century made themselves the priests and prophets.

Of this influence, and that it is the influence of a myth, there is immediate evidence, evidence provided in this very place by the reader's reluctance to face squarely what it is I am proposing to do. The Romance of Tristan is "sacred" for us precisely to the extent that it seems "sacrilegious" on my part to attempt to analyse it. No doubt the charge of sacrilege now has a very mild quality. In primitive societies it resulted, not in the reluctance which I anticipate, but in the execution of the guilty person. The sacred which is involved here amounts to no more than an obscure and weak survival. The only risk I run is that the reader may close the book at this point, and not open it again. True, the unconscious intent of such an act does not fall short of getting me put to death, but the intent is without effect. However, supposing you spare me, dear Reader, am I to conclude that the passion is not sacred for you? Possibly people are nowadays as feeble in passion as in acts of reproof. In the absence of open foes, perhaps it is against themselves that writers must show the daring which is being demanded of them, and perhaps it is only the enemy in our own breasts that we can really contend with.

I confess I was vexed to find one commentator describing the Tristan legend as "an epic of adultery." The phrase may be accurate enough in respect of the dry bones of the Romance. That does not make it any the less vexatious and "prosaically" narrow. I doubt if it can be maintained that the real subject of the legend is the moral fault. How assert that Wagner's *Tristan,* for example, is no more than an opera about adultery? For that matter, is adultery but a nasty word, or a breach of contract? Adultery is that too, and in all too many cases no more than that. But it often is a great deal more—a passionate and tragic atmosphere beyond good and evil, and a drama either lofty or dreadful; in short, a drama—a *romance.* And "romanticism" derives from "romance."

The problem expands splendidly—and my case worsens proportionately. I shall set out my reasons for going on, and it can then be decided if they are diabolical. First, social confusion has now reached a point at which the pursuit of immorality turns out to be more exhausting than compliance with the old moral codes. The cult of passionate love has been *democratized* so far as to have lost its aesthetic virtues together with its spiritual and tragic values; and we are left with a dull and diluted pain, something unclean and gloomy. In profaning the falsely sacred causes of this, I cannot believe that we have anything to lose. The literature dealing with passion, the advertising which passion gets, the business-like "vogue" of what used to be a religious secret—all that needs to be attacked and made war upon, if only to rescue the myth from being abused in its excessive popularization. And whatever sacrilege we may thereby commit will not matter; for poetry has other outlets.

My second reason is a desire to be quite clear about contemporary life. I fasten upon the Tristan myth because it enables me to offer a *simple explanation* of our present confusion and at the same time to set forth certain *permanent relations* which the scrupulous vulgarities of current psychologies submerge. Furthermore, I can lay bare a particular *dilemma*, the stern reality of which we are in process of overlooking as a result of our frenzied living, the state of our culture, and the purr of current moral doctrines.

To raise up the myth of passion in its primitive and sacred vigour and in its monumental integrity, as a salutary comment upon our tortuous connivances and inability to choose boldly between the Norm of Day and the Passion of Night—such is my first purpose. It means raising up that image of the Dying Lovers which is excited by the disturbing and vampire-like crescendo of Wagner's second act. And what I aim at is to bring the reader to the point of declaring frankly, either that "That is what I wanted!" or else "God forbid!"

I am not certain that complete self-awareness is useful either in a general way or *per se*. I do not hold that practical truths can be made plain in the market place. But whatever the "usefulness of my undertaking, we who dwell in the Western world are destined to become more and more aware of the illusions on which we subsist. And possibly it is the job of philosophers, moralists, and creators of ideal forms, simply to increase our self-awareness—the consciousness which is of course also a bad conscience.

With that I pass to the promised analysis. Remaining deaf and blind to the "charms" of the tale, I am going to try to summarize "objectively" the events it relates and the reasons which it either gives for these events or very oddly omits.

4

What the Tristan Romance[1] Seems to Be About

Amors par force vos demeine!—BÉROUL.

Tristan is born in misfortune. His father has just died, and Blanchefleur, his mother, does not survive his birth. Hence his name, the sombre hue of his life, and the lowering stormy sky that hangs over the legend. King Mark of Cornwall, Blanchefleur's brother, takes the orphan into his castle at Tintagel and brings him up there.

Tristan presently performs an early feat of prowess. He vanquishes the Morholt. This Irish giant has come like a Minotaur, to exact his tribute of Cornish maidens or youths. Tristan is of an age for knighthood—that is, he has just reached puberty—and he obtains leave to fight him. The Morholt is killed, but not before he has wounded Tristan with a poisoned barb. Having no hope of recovery, Tristan begs to be put on board a boat that is cast adrift with neither sail nor oar. He takes his sword and harp with him.

He lands in Ireland. There is only one remedy that can save him, and, as it happens, the Queen of Ireland is

[1] In summing up the chief episodes of the Romance, I shall make use (except here and there) of M. Bédier's *Concordance* (contained in his study of Thomas's poem) for the five twelfth-century versions—those by Béroul, Thomas and Eilhart together with *La Folie Tristan* and *Le Roman en prose*. The later versions by Gottfried of Strasbourg, or by German, Italian, Danish, Russian, Czech, and other imitators, are all derived from those five. I also take into account the more recent critical undertakings of Messrs. E. Muret and E. Vinaver.

alone in knowing its secret. But the giant Morholt was this queen's brother, and so Tristan is careful not to disclose his name or to explain how he has come by his wound. Iseult, the queen's daughter, nurses him and restores him to health. That is the Prologue.

A few years later a bird has brought to King Mark a golden hair. The king determines to marry the woman from whose head the hair has come. It is Tristan whom he selects to go in quest of her. A storm causes the hero to be cast ashore once again in Ireland. There he fights and kills a dragon that was threatening the capital. (This is the conventional motif of a virgin delivered by a young paladin.) Having been wounded by the dragon, Tristan is again nursed by Iseult. One day she learns that the wounded stranger is no other than the man who killed her uncle. She seizes Tristan's sword and threatens to transfix him in his bath. It is then that he tells her of the mission on which he has been sent by King Mark. And Iseult spares him, for she would like to be a queen. (According to some of the authors, she spares him also because she then finds him handsome.)

Tristan and the princess set sail for Cornwall. At sea the wind drops and the heat grows oppressive. They are thirsty. Brengain, Iseult's maid, gives them a drink. But by mistake she pours out the "wine of herbs" which the queen, Iseult's mother, has brewed for King Mark and his bride after they shall have wed. Tristan and Iseult drink it. The effect is to commit them to a fate from "which they can never escape during the remainder of their lives, *for they have drunk their destruction and death*." They confess that they are now in love, and fall into one another's arms.

Let it be noted here that according to the archetypal version, which Béroul alone has followed, the effect of the love-potion is limited to three years.[1] Thomas, a sensitive psychologist and highly suspicious of marvels,

---

[1] Verses 2137–2140:

> A conbien fu determinez
> Li lovendrins, li vin herbez:
> La mere Yseut, qui le bolli,
> A trois anz d'amistié le fist.

The quotation is from Béroul, as are those in Chapter 8, below. I follow A. Ewert's text (*The Romance of Tristan* (Oxford, Black-

which he considers crude, minimizes the importance of the love-potion as far as possible, and depicts the love of Tristan and Iseult as having occurred spontaneously. Its first signs he places as early as the episode of the bath. On the other hand, Eilhart, Gottfried, and most of the others attribute unlimited effect to the magic wine. Nothing could be more significant than these variations, as we shall see.)

Thus the fault is perpetrated. *Yet Tristan is still in duty bound to fulfil the mission with which King Mark has entrusted him.* So, notwithstanding his betrayal of the king, he delivers Iseult to him. On the wedding night Brengain, thanks to a ruse, takes Iseult's place in the royal bed, thus saving her mistress from dishonour and at the same time expiating the irretrievable mistake she made in pouring out the love-potion.

Presently, however, four "felon" barons of the king's go and tell their sovereign that Tristan and Iseult are lovers. Tristan is banished to Tintagel town. But thanks to another trick—the episode of the pine-tree in the orchard—Mark is convinced of his innocence and allows him to return to the castle. Then Frocin the Dwarf, who is in league with the barons, lays a trap in order to establish the lovers' guilt. In the spear-length between Tristan's bed and the queen's he scatters flour, and persuades Mark to order Tristan to ride to King Arthur at Carduel the next morning at dawn. Tristan is determined to embrace his mistress once more before he rides away. To avoid leaving his foot-marks in the flour he leaps across from his own bed to the queen's. But the effort reopens a wound in his leg inflicted the previous day by a boar. Led by Frocin, the king and the barons burst into the bedchamber. They find the flour blood-stained. Mark is satisfied with this evidence of adultery. Iseult is handed over to a party of a hundred lepers, and Tristan is sentenced to the stake. On the way to execution, however, he is allowed to go into a chantry on the cliff's edge. He forces a window and leaps over the cliff, thus effecting his escape. He rescues Iseult from the lepers, and together they go and hide in the depths of the Forest of Morrois.

well, 1939)), which is later than E. Muret, and I am also indebted to Ewert's glossary for my translations. "For how long was the love potion, the herb wine? Mother Yseut, who brewed it, made it to three years of love."—Translator's Note.

There for three years they lead a life "harsh and hard."
It happens one day that Mark comes upon them while
they are asleep. But on this occasion Tristan has put
between Iseult and himself his drawn sword. Moved by
this evidence of innocence, as he supposes it to be, the
king spares them. Without waking them, he takes up
Tristan's sword and sets his own in its place.

*At the end of three years the potency of the love-potion
wears off* (according to Béroul and the common ancestor of the five versions). It is only then that Tristan
repents, and that Iseult wishes she were a queen again.
Together they seek out the hermit Ogrin, through whom
Tristan offers peace to the king, saying he will surrender
Iseult. Mark promises forgiveness. As the royal procession approaches, the lovers part. But before this happens Iseult has besought Tristan to stay in the neighbourhood till he has made certain that Mark is treating her
well. Then, with a final display of feminine wiles, she
follows up her advantage in having persuaded Tristan to
agree to this, and declares she will join him at the
first sign he makes, for nothing shall stop her from doing
his will, "neither tower, nor wall, nor stronghold."

They have several secret meetings in the hut of Orri
the Woodman. But the felon barons are keeping watch
and ward over the queen's virtue. She asks and is granted
"a Judgement of God." Thanks to a subterfuge, the ordeal is a success. Before she grasps the red-hot iron
which will not harm one who has spoken the truth, she
swears that no man has ever held her in his arms except
the king and a poor pilgrim who has just carried her
ashore from a boat. And the poor pilgrim is Tristan in
disguise.

However, fresh adventures carry Tristan far away from
Iseult, and he then comes to suppose that she no longer
loves him. So he agrees to marry "for her beauty and
her name" [1] another Iseult, Iseult "of the White Hand."
And indeed this Iseult remains unstained, for after their
marriage Tristan still sighs for 'Iseult the Fair."

At last, wounded by a poisoned spear and about to die,
Tristan sends for the queen from Cornwall, she who alone
can save his life. She comes, and as her ship draws near
it hoists a white sail as a sign of hope. But Iseult of the

---

[1] "Pur belté e pur nun d'Isolt" (Thomas).

White Hand has been on the look-out, and, tormented
by jealousy, she runs to Tristan and tells him that the sail
is black. Tristan dies. As he does so, Iseult the Fair lands,
and on arriving at the castle, she lies down beside her
dead lover and clasps him close. Then she dies too.

5

Some Riddles

Thus summarized, and with all the "charm" destroyed, the most absorbing of poems appears, on
cool consideration, to be straightforward neither in its
matter nor in its progression. I have passed over numerous accessory episodes, but over none of the motives alleged for the central action. Indeed, these motives
I have rather stressed. They have been seen not to amount
to much. Tristan delivers up Iseult to the king, *because*
bound by the fealty of a knight. At the end of the three
years spent in the forest, the lovers part, *because* the
love-potion has lost its potency. Tristan marries Iseult
of the White Hand *"for her beauty and her name."* If
these "reasons" are discounted—although we shall return
to them—the Romance turns out to depend on a series
of puzzling contradictions.

I have been struck by the passing comment of one recent editor of the legend. All through the Romance Tristan is made to appear the physical superior of all his foes
and particularly of the king. It follows that no external
power prevents him from carrying off Iseult and thus
fulfilling his fate. The manners of the time sanctioned the
rights of the stronger; they made these rights divine without qualification; and this was especially the case with a
man's rights over a woman. *Why does Tristan not take
advantage of these rights?*

Put on the alert by this first question, our critical suspicions lead us to discover other riddles, no less curious
and obscure. *Why has the sword of chastity been placed
between the two sleepers in the forest?* The lovers have

already sinned, and they refuse to repent just then.
Furthermore, they do not expect that the king will discover
them. Yet in all five versions there is neither a line nor a
word to explain the sword.[1] Again, *why does Tristan restore the queen to Mark,* even in those versions where at
that time the love-potion is still active? If, as some say,
the lovers part because they now sincerely repent, why
do they promise one another to meet again in the moment they undertake to part? And why later does Tristan
go forth upon fresh adventures when he and Iseult have
made a tryst in the forest? Why does the guilty queen
ask for "a Judgement of God?" She must know that
the ordeal is bound to go against her. It is only successful thanks to a trick improvised at the last moment; and
this trick, it is implied, deceives God Himself, since the
miracle ensues.[2] Moreover, the judgement having gone
in the queen's favour, her innocence is thereupon taken
for granted. But if she is innocent, so is Tristan; and it becomes quite impossible to see what prevents his return
to the king's castle, and *hence to Iseult's side.*

At the same time it is surely very odd that thirteenth-
century poets—so punctilious in matters of honour and
suzerain fealty—should let pass without a word of comment so much thoroughly indefensible behaviour. How
can they hold up Tristan as a model of chivalry when he
betrays his king with the most shameless cunning, or the
queen as a virtuous lady when she is not only an adulteress, but does not shrink from committing an astute
blasphemy? On the other hand, why do they call "felons"

---

[1] It is true that in Bédier's edition of Thomas's poem (Vol.
I, p. 240), the king's huntsman is said to have gone to the
lovers' retreat, where he has seen "Tristan" lying asleep, and across
the cave was Iseult. The lovers were resting from the great heat,
and lay apart from one another because. . . ." At this point
the text breaks off! And Bédier notes: "An unintelligible passage."
What diabolical agency can have partly destroyed *the one text*
likely to have solved the riddle?

[2] Gottfried of Strasbourg brazenly insists:
　　　　　'Twas thus made manifest
　　　　　And averr'd before all
　　　　　That Christ most glorious
　　　　　Will mould like cloth for garments.
　　　　　. . . He complies with ev'ry one's wish,
　　　　　Whether honest or deceitful.
　　　　　He ever is as we would have Him be.

the four barons who defend Mark's honour and who, even
if actuated by jealousy, neither deceive nor betray
(which is more than can be said of Tristan)?

Even the validity of what few motives are mentioned
remains open to question. For if the rule of suzerain
fealty required that Tristan should deliver to Mark the
betrothed he had been to fetch,[1] his compliance with
this rule must seem both very belated and hardly sincere, inasmuch as once he has delivered up Iseult he
knows no rest till he has contrived to get back into the
castle and is with her again. And as the love-potion was
brewed for Mark and his queen, it must be wondered
why its potency is not permanent. Three years of married bliss are not much. And when Tristan marries another Iseult "for her beauty and her name," but does
not touch her, it is surely obvious that nothing has compelled him either to marry or to be guilty of his insulting
chastity, and that by marrying a woman whom he cannot make his wife he has put himself into a position
from which the only way out is death.

6

Chivalry v. Marriage

The Romance of *Tristan and Iseult* brings home to us
the antagonism which grew up in the second half of
the twelfth century between the rule of chivalry and feudal custom. Perhaps the extent to which the Arthurian romances reflect and foster this antagonism has not hitherto
attracted the notice it deserves. In all likelihood, courtly
chivalry was never more than an ideal. The earliest
writers to mention it commonly lament its decay, but in
doing so they overlook that in the form which they would
like it to assume it has only just come into existence in
their dreams. It is of the essence of an ideal that its
decay should be lamented in the very moment it is clumsily

---

[1] But to whom he had won a full title *himself* by delivering
her from the dragon, as Thomas does not omit to stress.

striving for fulfilment. Moreover, to contrast the *fiction* of some ideal of living with tyrannical reality is precisely something possible in a romance. A preliminary answer to several of the riddles propounded by the legend can be sought in this direction. Once it is granted that Tristan's experience was intended to illustrate a conflict between chivalry and feudal society—and hence a conflict between two kinds of *duty* and even between two "religions" [1]— a number of episodes are made intelligible. At any rate, even if not disposing of every difficulty, the hypothesis significantly delays a solution.

Arthurian romance, which supplanted the *chanson de geste* with astonishing swiftness in the middle of the twelfth century, differs from this *chanson* in that it allots to a woman the part formerly taken by a suzerain. An Arthurian knight, exactly like a troubadour of the South, regarded himself as the vassal of some chosen Lady, when, actually, he remained the vassal of a lord; and this gave rise to a number of conflicting claims of which the Romance supplies examples.

Let me go back to the four "felon" barons. According to feudal morals, it was the duty of a vassal to warn his lord of anything that might endanger the latter's rights or honour. He was a "felon" if he did not. Now, in *Tristan* the barons go and tell King Mark how Iseult is behaving. They should therefore be considered feal and true. If, then, the author refers to them as "felons," he must evidently do so in virtue of some other code, which can only be the code of southern chivalry. For instance, according to a well-known judgement delivered by the Gascon courts of love, whosoever discloses the secrets of courtly love is a felon. The single instance is enough to show that the authors of the different versions of the Romance were deliberately siding with "courtly" chivalry against feudal law. But there are further grounds for thinking so. Alone the view of fidelity and of marriage that was adopted in courtly love will explain some of the striking contradictions in the tale.

According to the theory officially received, courtly love arose as a reaction to the brutal lawlessness of feudal manners. It is well known that the nobles in the twelfth century made of marriage simply a means of enriching themselves, either through the annexation of

[1] As was hinted at on p. 20, above.

makes it possible for the tale to move forward again.[1]
In itself this explains nothing. It is all too easy to dispose of every one of our questions by saying: Events happen thus because *otherwise* there would be no story. Such a reply will appear convincing only owing to a lazy custom of literary criticism. Actually, it answers nothing. It simply raises the fundamental question: Why has there to be a story? And *this* story in particular? There is an unconscious wisdom in calling such a question ingenuous, for it is not asked without peril. In fact, it carried us into the heart of the problem; and undoubtedly it involves far more than the particular case of this myth.

If, by an effort of abstraction, we place ourselves outside the process common to both novelist and reader so that we can overhear the intimate dialogue that goes on between them, we see that a tacit convention, or, rather, a mutual *encouragement,* unites them. They both wish the novel to go on, or, as the saying is, to rebound. Suppress that *wish,* and there can be no verisimilitude whatsoever. This is exemplified in scientific history. The reader of a "serious" book is all the more exacting for being aware that neither his wishes nor the author's fancies can govern the sequence of events. Suppose, instead, these wishes to operate unchecked, and then nothing is too far-fetched. That is the situation for fiction. Between the two extremes there are as many levels of verisimilitude as there are plots. Or, if you like, what shall be verisimilitude in any given piece of literary fiction depends on the nature of the passions which this piece of fiction is intended to please. In short, a reader pays no heed to distortions or to twistings of the "logic" of current observation so long as the licence thus taken produces the *pretexts* necessary to the passion which he longs to feel. Hence it is in the kink of "tricks of the trade" employed by the author that the real plot of a given piece of fiction is disclosed, and

[1] I should make this quite clear. 1. The codes are respected each in turn as the result of a secret calculation; for if either was chosen to the entire exclusion of the other, the situation would be resolved too soon. 2. The codes are not always respected: for instance, when the lovers sin together as soon as they have drunk the love-potion they are committing a sin according to courtly love just as much as according to Christian and feudal morality. But were it not for that first fault there would be no romance at all.

a reader condones these tricks precisely to the extent that he shares the author's intentions.[1]

I have shown that the external barriers to the fulfilment of Tristan's love are in one sense arbitrary, and, after all, only fictional contrivances. And it follows from what has just been said about verisimilitude that it is precisely the arbitrary character of the obstructions introduced into a tale that may show what this tale is really about and what is the real nature of the passion it is concerned with. In this respect everything, it must be realized, is symbolical. Everything holds together and is connected after the manner of a *dream*, and not in accordance with our lives. This is equally true of the pretexts devised by the author, the conduct of his two leading characters, and the secret inclinations which he assumes to exist in his reader. The events narrated are but images or projections of a longing and of whatever runs counter to this longing, excites it, or merely protracts it. Everything the knight and princess do betrays that they act in virtue of a necessity they are unaware of—and that perhaps the author has been unaware of too—but *that is stronger than the need of their happiness*. Objectively, not one of the barriers to the fulfilment of their love is insuperable, and yet each time they give up. It is not too much to say that they never miss a chance of getting parted. When there is no obstruction, they invent one, as in the case of the drawn sword and of Tristan's marriage. They invent obstructions as if on purpose, notwithstanding that such barriers are their bane. Can it be in order to please author and reader? It is all one; for the demon of courtly love which prompts the lovers in their inmost selves to the devices that are the cause of their pain is the very demon of *the novel* as we in the West like it to be.

What, then, is the legend really about? The partings of the lovers? Yes, but in the name of passion, and for love of the very love that agitates them, in order that this love may be intensified and transfigured—at the cost of their happiness and even of their lives.

The secret and disturbing significance of the myth is beginning to loom out—the *peril* it at once expresses and

---

[1] The twentieth-century detective story is the best illustration of this. Verisimilitude there becomes a function of the amateur's "technical" pleasure and is nothing else.

veils, the passion to which to yield is like a swoon. But it is too late to turn away. We are affected, we are under the spell, we grow alive to the "exquisite anguish." It would be idle to condemn; swooning cannot be condemned. But is it not a philosopher's passion to meditate in the act of swooning? Perhaps knowledge is but the effort of a mind that resists the headlong fall and holds back in the midst of temptation.

8

The Love of Love

"De tous les maux, le mien diffère; il me plaît; je me réjouis de lui; mon mal est ce que je veux et ma douleur est ma santé. Je ne vois donc pas de quoi je me plains; car mon mal me vient de ma volonté; c'est mon vouloir qui devient mon mal; mais j'ai tant d'aise à vouloir ainsi que je souffre agréablement, et tant de joie dans me douleur que je suis malade avec délices." CHRESTIEN DE TROYES. [1]

It is only "silly" questions that can enlighten us; for behind whatever seems obvious lurks something that is not. Let us then boldly ask: Does Tristan care for Iseult, and she for him? The lovers do not seem to be brought together in any normal *human* way. On the contrary, at their first encounter they confine themselves to having ordinary polite relations; and later, when Tristan returns to Ireland to fetch Iseult, the politeness, it will be remembered, gives place to open hostility. Everything goes to show that they would never have chosen one another were they acting *freely*. But no sooner have they drunk the love-potion than passion flares between them.

---

[1] "From all other ills doth mine differ. It pleaseth me; I rejoice at it; my ill is what I want and my suffering is my health. So I do not see what I am complaining about; for my ill comes to me by my will; it is my willing that becomes my ill; but I am so pleased to want thus that I suffer agreeably, and have so much joy in my pain that I am sick with delight."

Yet that any fondness supervenes to unite them as a result of the magic spell I have found, among the thousands of lines of the Romance, only a single indication. When, following Tristan's escape, it has been told how they have gone to live in the Forest of Morrois, there occur these lines:

> Aspre vie meinent et dure:
> Tant s'entraiment de bone amor
> L'un por l'autre ne sent dolor.[1]

If it should be imagined that poets in the Middle Ages were less emotional than we have grown to be and felt no need to insist on what goes without saying, let the account of the three years in the forest be read attentively. Its two finest passages—which are no doubt also the most profound passages in the whole legend—describe the lovers' two visits to the hermit Ogrin. The first time they go to see him, it is in order to make confession. But instead of confessing their sin and asking for absolution, they do their best to convince him that they are not to blame for what has befallen, since after all *they do not care for one another!*

> Q'el m'aime, c'est par la poison
> Ge ne me pus de lié partir,
> N'ele de moi——[2]

So speaks Tristan, and Iseult says after him:

> Sire, por Deu omnipotent,
> Il ne m'aime pas, ne je lui,
> Fors par un herbé dont je bui
> Et il en but: ce fu pechiez.[3]

They are thus in a thrillingly contradictory position. They love, but not one another. They have sinned, but cannot repent; for they are not to blame. They make confession, but wish neither to reform nor even to beg forgiveness. Actually, then, like all other great lovers, they

[1] "Harsh life led they and hard, so entertaining good love for one another. One by the other was ne'er exposed to pain."

[2] "If she loves me, it is by the poison which holds me from leaving her and her from leaving me."

[3] "Lord, by almighty God, he loves me not, nor I him; except for a herb potion which I drank and which he drank; it was a sin."

imagine that they have been ravished "beyond good and evil" into a kind of transcendental state outside ordinary human experience, into an ineffable absolute irreconcilable with the world, but that they feel to be *more real than the world*. Their oppressive fate, even though they yield to it with wailings, obliterates the antithesis of good and evil, and carries them away beyond the source of moral values, beyond pleasure and pain, beyond the realm of distinctions—into a realm where opposites cancel out.

Their admission is explicit enough: "Il ne m'aime pas, ne je lui." Everything happens as if they could neither see nor recognize one another. They are the prisoners of "exquisite anguish" owing to something which neither controls—some alien power independent of their capacities, or at any rate of their conscious wishes, and of their being in so far as they are aware of being. Both characters, the man as much as the woman, are depicted physically and psychologically in an entirely conventional and rhetorical manner. He is "the strongest;" she, "the most beautiful;" he, the knight; she, the princess; and so on. It is impossible to believe that any human feeling can grow between two such rudimentary characters. The friendship mentioned in connexion with the length of time the effect of the love-potion lasts is the opposite of a true friendship; and, what is still more striking, if moral friendship does at last appear, it is at the moment their passion declines. And the immediate consequence of their nascent friendship, far from being to knit them more closely together, is to make them feel that they have everything to gain from a separation. This last point deserves to be considered more closely.

> L'endemain de la saint Jehan
> Aconpli furent li troi an.[1]

Tristan is out in the forest after game. Suddenly he is reminded of the world. He sees in his mind's eye King Mark's castle. He sighs for "the vair and grey" and for the pomp of chivalry. He thinks of the high rank he might hold among his uncle's barons. He thinks too of his beloved—apparently for the first time! But for him she

[1] "On the morrow of St John's Day, the three years were accomplished."

might be "in fine rooms . . . hung with cloth of silk."
Simultaneously Iseult is filled with similar regrets. In the
evening they are together, and they confess to one another what is newly agitating them—"en mal uson nostre
jovente." It does not take them long to agree to part.
Tristan talks of making off to Brittany. But first they will
seek out Ogrin the Hermit and beg his forgiveness—and
at the same time King Mark's forgiveness of Iseult.

It is at this point that there occurs a highly dramatic
short dialogue between the hermit and the two penitents:

> Amors par force vos demeine! [1]
> Conbien durra vostre folie?
> Trop avez mené ceste vie.

So Ogrin admonishes them.

> Tristan li dist: or escoutez [2]
> Si longuement l'avons menee
> Itel fu nostre destinee.

On top of this comes one more feature. When Tristan
hears that the king agrees to Iseult's return:

> Dex! dist Tristan, quel departie! [3]
> Molt est dolenz qui pert s'amie!

It is with his own pain that he commiserates; not a
thought for "s'amie!" And she too, we are made to feel,
finds it much more pleasant to be back with the king
than she ever did with her lover—happier in the unhappiness of love than she ever was in the life they led together in the Morrois.

---

[1] "Love by force dominates you. How long will your folly
last? Too long you have been leading this life." *Amors par force
vos demeine*—the most poignant description of passion ever penned
by a poet! We must pause to admire it. In a single line the whole
of passion is summed up with a vigour of expression making all
romanticism look pallid! Shall we ever recover this sturdy "dialect
of the heart"?

[2] "Tristan quoth to him: 'Now hearken, if for long we have
been leading this life, that is because it was our destiny.'"

[3] "God!" quoth Tristan, "What a fate! Wretched he who loseth
his mistress."

For that matter, later on—as we have seen—passion seizes the lovers again, notwithstanding that the effect of the love-potion has worn off, and this time they are so carried away that they die—"he by her, she by him." The seeming *selfishness* of their love is enough to account for the many "chance" happenings and tricks of fate that obstruct their attainment of happiness. But this selfishness, in its profound ambiguity, still wants explaining. Selfishness, it is said, always ends in death. But that is as a final defeat. Theirs, on the contrary, requires death for its perfect fulfilment and triumph. To the problem this raises there is only one answer worthy of the myth.

Tristan and Iseult do not love one another. They say they don't, and everything goes to prove it. *What they love is love and being in love.* They behave as if aware that whatever obstructs love must ensure and consolidate it in the heart of each and intensify it infinitely in the moment they reach the absolute obstacle, which is death. Tristan loves the awareness that he is loving far more than he loves Iseult the Fair. And Iseult does nothing to hold Tristan. All she needs is her passionate dream. Their need of one another is in order to be aflame, and they do not need one another as they are. What they need is not one another's presence, but one another's absence. *Thus the partings of the lovers are dictated by their passion itself,* and by the love they bestow on their passion rather than on its satisfaction or on its living object. That is why the Romance abounds in obstructions, why when mutually encouraging their joint dream in which each remains solitary they show such astounding indifference, and why events work up in a romantic climax to a fatal apotheosis.

The duality is at once irrevocable and deliberate. "Molt est dolenz qui pert s'amie," Tristan sighs: and yet he then already sees, glimmering in the depths of the approaching night, that hidden flame which absence rekindles.

9

The Love of Death

But we must push on further still. Augustine's *ama-bam amare* is a poignant phrase with which he himself was not content. I have repeatedly referred to *obstruction*, and there is the way in which the passion of the two lovers *creates obstruction*, its effects coinciding with those of narrative necessity and of the reader's suspense. Is this obstruction not simply a *pretext* needed in order to enable the passion to progress, or is it connected with the passion in some far more profound manner? If we delve into the recesses of the myth, we see that this obstruction is what passion really *wants*—its true object.

I have shown that the Romance is given its motive power by the repeated partings and reunions of the lovers. For convenience, here once more, briefly, is what happens. Tristan, having landed in Ireland, meets Iseult and then parts from her without being in love. He turns up in Ireland again, and this time Iseult wants to kill him. They take ship together and drink the love-potion, and then sin. Next, Iseult is delivered up to Mark, and Tristan is banished from the castle. He and Iseult meet under a pine-tree, their talk being overheard by Mark. Tristan comes back to the castle, and Frocin and the barons discover evidence of his crime. They are parted. They meet again, and for three years go to live in the forest. Then, once more, they part. They meet at the hut of Orri the Woodman. Tristan goes away. He comes back, disguised as a poor pilgrim. He goes away again. The separation this time is prolonged, and he marries Iseult of the White Hand. Iseult the Fair is about to rejoin him when he dies. She dies too. More briefly still: They have one long spell together ("L'aspre vie"—"The harsh life"), to which corresponds a lengthy separation

44

—and Tristan's marriage. First, the love-potion; lastly, the death of both. In between, furtive meetings.

They are led to part so often either by adverse external circumstances or by hindrances which Tristan devises; and it is to be noted that Tristan's behaviour varies according to which kind of cause is operating. When social circumstances—for example, Mark's presence, the barons' suspiciousness, the Judgement of God—threaten the lovers, Tristan leaps over the obstruction (this is symbolized by his leap from his own bed to the queen's). He then does not mind pain (his wound reopens) nor the danger to his life (he knows he is being spied upon). Passion is then so violent—so brutish, it might be said—that in the intoxication of his *déduit* (or delight) he is oblivious to pain and perils alike. Nevertheless, the blood flowing from his wound betrays him. This is the "red stain" that apprises the king of what is happening. And it also apprises the reader of the lovers' secret—that they are seeking peril for its own sake. But so long as the peril comes from without, Tristan's prowess in overcoming it is an affirmation of life. At this stage Tristan is simply complying with the feudal practice of knights. He has to prove his "valour" and show he is either the stronger or the more wily. We have seen that if he persevered in this direction he would carry off the queen, and that established law is only respected here because this gives the tale an excuse to rebound.

But the knight's demeanour becomes quite different when nothing external any longer separates the two lovers. Indeed, it becomes the opposite of what it has been. When Tristan puts his drawn sword between himself and Iseult although they are lying down fully clothed, this is again prowess, but on this occasion against himself, *to his own cost*. Since he himself has set up the obstruction, it is no longer one *he can overcome!* It must not be overlooked that the hierarchy of events corresponds closely to the hierarchy of both the story-teller's and the reader's *preferences*. The most serious obstruction is thus the one preferred above all. It is the one must suited to intensifying passion. At this extreme, furthermore, the wish to part assumes an emotional value *greater than that of passion itself*. Death, in being the goal of passion, kills it.

Yet the drawn sword is not the ultimate expression of

the dark desire and of the actual *end* of passion (in both senses of the word "end"). The admirable episode of the exchange of swords makes this clear. When the king comes upon the lovers lying asleep in the cave, he substitutes his own sword for that of his rival. The meaning of this is that in place of the obstruction which the lovers have wanted and have deliberately set up he puts the sign of his social prerogative, a legal and objective obstruction. Tristan accepts the challenge, and thereby enables the *action* of the tale to rebound. At this point the word "action" takes on a symbolical meaning. Action prevents "passion" from being complete, for passion is "what is suffered"—and its limit is death. In other words, the action here is a fresh postponement of passion, which means a delaying of Death.

There is the same shift as regards the two marriages in the Romance, that of Iseult the Fair to the king and that of Iseult of the White Hand to Tristan. The first is an obstruction in fact. The concrete existence of a *husband* symbolizes its character, husbands being despised in courtly love. Making the obstruction that leads to adultery a husband is unimaginative, the excuse most readily thought of, and most in keeping with everyday experience.[1] See how Tristan shoves the husband aside, and enjoys making sport of him! But for the existence of a husband, the love of Tristan and Iseult would not have lasted beyond three years! And old Béroul showed his good sense in limiting the effect of the love-potion to that length of time:

> La mere Yseut, qui le bolli,
> A trois anz d'amistié le fist.

But for the existence of a husband, the lovers would have had to get married; and it is unbelievable that Tristan should ever be in a position to marry Iseult. She typifies the woman a man does not marry; for once she became his wife she would no longer be what she is, and he would no longer love her. Just think of a Mme Tristan! It would be the negation of passion—at least of the passion we are concerned with here. The spontaneous ardour of a love crowned and not thwarted is essentially

[1] Romanticism was later on to devise more refined excuses.

of short duration. It is a flare-up doomed not to survive the effulgence of its fulfilment. But its *branding* remains, and this is what the lovers want to prolong and indefinitely to renew. That is why they go on summoning fresh perils. But these the knight's valour drives him to overcome, and so he has to go away, in quest of more profound and more intimate—and it even seems, more interior —experiences.

When Tristan is sighing quietly for his lost Iseult, the brother of Iseult of the White Hand thinks his friend must be in love with his sister. This confusion—produced by identity of name—is the sole "cause" of Tristan's marrying. It is obvious that he could easily have cleared up the misunderstanding. But here again honour supervenes —of course, as a mere pretext—to prevent him from drawing back. The reason is that he foresees, in this new ordeal which is *self-imposed,* the opportunity of a decisive advance. This merely formal marriage with a woman he finds beautiful is an obstruction which he can remove only by achieving a victory *over himself* (as well as over the institution of marriage, which he thus damages from within). This time his prowess goes against him. His chastity now he is married corresponds to the placing of the drawn sword between himself and the other Iseult. But a self-imposed chastity is a symbolical suicide (here is the hidden meaning of the sword)—a victory for the courtly ideal over the sturdy Celtic tradition which proclaimed its pride in life. It is a way of purifying desire of the spontaneous, brutish, and active elements still encumbering it. "Passion" triumphs over desire. Death triumphs over life.

Hence Tristan's inclination for a *deliberate obstruction* turns out to be a desire for death and an advance in the direction of Death! But this death is for love, a deliberate death coming at the end of a series of ordeals thanks to which he will have been purified; a death that means transfiguration, and is in no way the result of some violent chance. Hence the aim is still to unite an external with an internal fate, which the lovers deliberately embrace. *In dying for love they redeem their destiny and are avenged for the love-potion.* So that at the last the struggle between passion and obstruction is inverted. At this point the obstruction is no longer serving irresistible passion, but has itself become the goal and end wished

for for its own sake. Passion has thus only played the part
of a purifying ordeal, it might almost be said of a penance, in the service of this transfiguring death. Here we
are within sight of the ultimate secret.

The love of love itself has concealed a far more aw-
ful passion, a desire altogether unavowable, something
that could only be "betrayed" by means of symbols such
as that of the drawn sword and that of perilous chastity.
Unawares and in spite of themselves, the lovers have
never had but one desire—the desire for death! Unawares,
and passionately deceiving themselves, they have been
seeking all the time simply to be redeemed and avenged
for "what they have suffered"—the passion unloosed by
the love-potion. In the innermost recesses of their hearts
they have been obeying the fatal dictates of a wish for
death; they have been in the throes of *the active passion
of Darkness*.

•

10

The Love-Potion

And thereupon we perceive, now that it is half-dis-
closed, what caused the *myth* to take form and the
very necessity whereby it was brought forth. So
dreadful and unutterable is the real meaning of passion
that not only are those persons who undergo it unable
to grow aware of its end, but also writers wishing to
depict it in all its marvellous violence are driven to employ the *deceptive* language of symbols. I shall set aside
for the moment the question whether or not the authors
of the five original poems were aware of what they were
writing about. In all fairness, it is first imperative to
make plain what I wish to imply by the word "deceptive"
which I have just used.

Thanks to the popularization of psycho-analysis, we
now commonly take it for granted that the existence of
a repressed wish is invariably manifested, though in such
a way as to disguise the true nature of this wish. A for-

bidden passion or a shameful love finds expression in the symbols of a hieroglyphic language which consciousness leaves undeciphered. The language is essentially equivocal; in both senses of the verb, it "betrays" what it wishes to say without saying it. A single gesture or a single metaphor may thus express at one and the same time both the object of a wish and what condemns the wish. The prohibition is thus recognized, and the object is not, and yet the latter is being alluded to. In this way irreconcilable demands are to some extent simultaneously satisfied. Two needs—that of speaking of what delights, and that of avoiding to decide whether the delightful is good or bad—and two instincts—that of courting danger and that of taking care—are all four gratified. If anybody using this language is asked why the predilection for this or that apparently weird image, the answer will be that "it's perfectly natural," that "he hasn't the remotest idea," or that "he doesn't think it matters." If the person questioned is a poet, he will drag in inspiration or poetic licence. In no circumstances will he have any hesitation in showing that he is in no way *responsible*.

Now, consider the problem that must have confronted the author of the original Romance. The symbolical material available in the twelfth century for concealing what had also to be expressed was magic, on the one hand, and the rhetoric of chivalry on the other. How convenient are these forms of expression is something immediately obvious. Magic persuades without giving reasons, and is perhaps persuasive to precisely the extent that it withholds reasons. Like all rhetoric, the rhetoric of chivalry is a means of passing off the most obscure statements as "natural." It was an ideal mask; for it ensured secrecy all right, and also ensured that the approval of the reader would be *unconditional*. Chivalry was the rule which the leading caste was hoping to employ to check the wildest "follies" that were felt to be threatening the framework of its society. The customs of chivalry were thus bound to supply the Romance with its armature. And I have repeatedly indicated how the prohibitions of chivalry prove to be "perfect pretexts" for the progression of the narrative. Magic comes in because the passion which has to be depicted has a fascinating violence not to be accepted without qualms. Passion appears uncouth in its effects. The Church proscribes it as sinful, and common sense looks upon it as a morbid excess. It is thus not open to admiration till it has been freed from every kind of visible connexion with human responsibility. That is why it was indispensable to bring in the love-potion, which acts willy-nilly, and—better still—is drunk by mistake.[1]

The love-potion is thus an *alibi* for passion. It enables each of the two unhappy lovers to say: "You see, I am not in the least to blame; you see, it's more than I can help." Yet, thanks to this deceptive necessity, everything they do is directed towards the fatal fulfilment they are in love with, and they can approach this fulfilment with a kind of crafty determination and a cunning the more unerring for not being open to moral judgement. Our least calculated actions are sometimes the most effective. A stone which we throw "without aiming" hits the mark. Actually, we aimed at the mark all right, but consciousness was not given time to interfere and deflect our spontaneous movement. That is why the finest passages in the Romance are those where the authors did not see how to dilate upon events and wrote as if in perfect innocence. There would be no myth and no romance if Tristan and Iseult were able *to say* what is the end they are making ready for in the depths—indeed, in the abyss —of their wills. Who would dare admit that he seeks Death and detests offensive Day, that what he longs for with all his being is the annihilation of his being.

Much later on poets arose who did dare to make this crowning avowal. But the masses said of them: "They are mad!" And the passion which most novelists wish to please in the reader is seemingly something weaker. It is unlikely ever to be driven to proclaim itself by undeniable excess, by a death in which it would be manifested beyond any possible repentance! Some of the mystics have gone further than avowal. They have understood and explained. But if they were able to face "the Dark Night" with a most strict and lucid passion, it was because, through faith, they had won a pledge that an altogether

---

[1] Thomas, who seeks to minimize the part played by this magical influence, is driven to making passion less inhuman and hence more tolerable to a moralist. Inferior in this respect to Béroul, he is the first writer to degrade the myth.

personal and "luminous" Will would take the place of theirs. Their will power was not seized upon by the nameless god of the love-potion, a blind force or Nothingness, but by the God who promises His grace, and "the living flame of love" that burns in the "deserts" of the Night.

But Tristan can make no avowal. His longing is as if he had it not. He confines himself inside an unverifiable and unjustifiable "truth," from any understanding of which he recoils with horror. He has his excuse ready, and it is pervasively specious: it is the poison which "par force le demeine." And yet, that he has chosen his fate, and willed and welcomed it in a dark and complete assent, is betrayed by everything he does, down to his desperate flight, a sublime coxcombry! And at the same time it is essential to the exemplary grandeur of his life that he should be unaware of this fate. Night has its reasons which are not those of Day, and they cannot be made known to Day.[1] Day they despise. Tristan has delivered himself over to a madness that must rob him of wisdom, "truth," and life itself. He has travelled beyond our pleasure and pain. He is hastening forward to the supreme moment in which delight is all concentrated on *foundering*.

Night cannot be described in the language of Day. But this particular form of desire has not lacked, and has indeed produced, an "artful music." Arise, deep-sounding tempests of Tristan and Isolde's death! The hero sings:

> Old tune so full of sadness
> That sing'st thy sad complaint.

[1] In Wagner's drama, when the king surprises the lovers and asks "for the undiscovered deep and secret cause of all," Tristan replies (F. Jameson's translation of the poem):
> King Marke, that *I can never tell thee;*
> and what thou ask'st that canst thou ne'er discover.
Later, when dying, Tristan says too:
> Where I awoke I stayed not;
> yet where I tarried, that *I can never tell thee. . . .*
> It was where I had been for ever,
> Where I for aye shall go;
> the boundless realm of night's domain.
> There one thing alone is ours:
> deep, eternal, all forgetting! . . .
> This terrible yearning wasting my heart;
> *if I could name it, if thou couldst know it!*

Through evening breezes came that strain,
as once my father's death I learned in childhood;
through morning twilight, sadder sounding,
as to me my mother's fate was told.
He who begot me died, she dying gave me birth.
The olden ditty's mournful plaint,
E'en so to them its numbers came,
that strain that asked, that asks me still,
what fate for me was chosen,
when there my mother bore me,
what fate for me?
The olden ditty once more tells me:
'tis yearning and dying! . . .
				Yearning now calls.
for death's repose.

He may curse his stars and his birth, but the music is indeed artful, and its notes make known tremendously the lovely secret. It is he who has willed his own fate.

The terrible draught that this anguish has brought,
'tis I myself by whom it was wrought! . . .
				What I have drunken,
what day by day has gladdened my spirit.

11

Unhappy Mutual Love

Passion means suffering, something undergone, the mastery of fate over a free and responsible person. To love love more than the object of love, to love passion for its own sake, has been to love to suffer and to court suffering all the way from Augustine's *amabam amare* down to modern romanticism. Passionate love, the longing for what sears us and annihilates us in its triumph—there is the secret which Europe has never allowed to be given away; a secret it has always repressed—and preserved! Hardly anything could be more tragic; and the way passion has persisted through the centuries should cause us to look to the future with deep despondency.

Here let me note a feature which will presently call for consideration. Both passion and the longing for death which passion disguises are connected with, and fostered by, a particular notion of how to reach understanding which in itself is typical of the Western *psyche*. Why does Western Man wish to suffer this passion which lacerates him and which all his common sense rejects? Why does he yearn after this particular kind of love notwithstanding that its effulgence must coincide with his self-destruction? The answer is that he reaches self-awareness and tests himself only by risking his life—in suffering and on the verge of death. The third act of Wagner's drama represents far more than a romantic disaster; it represents the *essential disaster* of our sadistic genius—the repressed longing for death, for self-experience to the utmost, for the revealing shock, a longing which beyond question manifests the most tenacious root of the war instinct we nourish.

From this tragic extreme—illustrated, avowed, and evidenced by the myth in its pristine purity—let us step down to passionate experience as men undergo it today. The tremendous success of the Tristan Romance shows, whether we like it or not, that we have a secret preference for what is unhappy. According to the sturdiness of our spirit, this unhappiness may be the "delightful sadness" and spleen of nineteenth-century decadence, a transfiguring torment, or a challenge which the mind flings down to the world. But in any case, what we pursue is what promises to uplift and excite us, so that in spite of ourselves we shall be transported into the "real life" spoken of by poets. But this "real life" is an impossible one. What is heralded by the sky with high-riding clouds and by the empurpled heroic sunset is not Day; it is Night! "Real life is *elsewhere*," Rimbaud said. "Real life" indeed is but another name for Death, and the only name we have dared *to invoke* it by—even while we were pretending to fend it off. Why is it that we delight most of all in some tale of impossible love? Because we long for the *branding;* because we long to grow *aware* of what is on fire inside us. Suffering and understanding are deeply connected; death and self-awareness are in league;[1] and European romanticism may be compared to a man for whom sufferings, and especially the sufferings of love, are a privileged mode of understanding.

Of course, this is only true of the best romantics among us. Most people do not bother about understanding or about self-awareness; they merely go after the kind of love that promises the most *feeling*. But even this has to be a love delayed in its happy fulfilment by some obstruction. Hence, whether our desire is for the most self-conscious or simply for the most intense love, secretly we desire obstruction. And this obstruction we are ready if needs be to invent or imagine.

This seems to me to explain much of our psychological nature. Unless the course of love is being hindered there is no "romance"; and it is romance that we revel in—that is to say, the self-consciousness, intensity, variations, and delays of passion, together with its climax rising to disaster—not its sudden flaring. Consider our literature. The happiness of lovers stirs our feelings only on account of the unhappiness which lies in wait for it. We must feel that life is imperilled, and also feel the hostile realities that drive happiness away into some beyond. What moves us is not its presence, but its nostalgia and recollection. Presence is inexpressible and has no perceptible duration; it can only be a *moment* of grace—as in the duet of Don Giovanni and Zerlina. Otherwise we lapse into a picture-postcard idyll. Happy love has no history— *in European literature.* And a love that is not mutual cannot pass for a true love. The outstanding find made by European poets, what distinguishes them first and foremost among the writers of the world, what most profoundly expresses the European obsession by suffering as a way to understanding, is the secret of the Tristan myth; passionate love at once shared and fought against, anxious for a happiness it rejects, and magnified in its own disaster—*unhappy mutual love.*

Let us pause at this description of the myth.

The love is *mutual* in the sense that Tristan and Iseult "love one another," or, at least, believe that they do. Certainly their mutual fidelity is exemplary. But *unhappiness*

---

[1] On this alliance Hegel was able to ground a general explanation of the human mind, and also of human history.

comes in, because the love which "dominates" them is not a love of each for the other as that other really is. They love one another, but each loves the other *from the standpoint of self and not from the other's standpoint*. Their unhappiness thus originates in a false reciprocity, which disguises a twin narcissism. So much is this so that at times there pierces through their excessive passion a kind of hatred of the beloved. Long before Freud and modern psychology Wagner saw this. "By me chosen, lost by me!" Isolde sings in her frantic love. And the sailor's opening song from the mast-head predicts the inevitable fate of them both:

> Westward sweeps the eye, eastward on we fly.
> The wind so wild blows homeward now:
> my Irish child, where tarriest thou?
> Sighs from thy heart ascending,
> help to our sails are lending!
> Sigh, ah sigh, wind so wild!
> Sigh, ah sigh now, my child!
> O Irish maid, thou wayward, winsome maid!

Their passion is twice unhappy in that it flees from both reality and the Norm of Day. The essential unhappiness of this love is that what they desire they have not yet had —this is Death—and that what they had is now being lost—the enjoyment of life. And yet, far from this loss being felt as privation, the couple imagine that they are now more fully alive than ever and are more than ever living dangerously and magnificently. The approach of death acts as a goad to sensuality. In the full sense of the verb, it aggravates desire. Sometimes even, it aggravates desire to the point of turning this into a wish to kill either the beloved or oneself, or to founder in a twin downrush.

> Hear now my will, ye craven winds! [*Isolde begins by singing*]
> come forth to strife and stress of the storm!
> to turbulent tempests' clamour and fury!
> Drive from her dreams this slumbering sea;
> wake from the depths all her envious greed!
> Destroy now this insolent ship,
> let its wreck be sunk in her waves!
> All that hath life and breath upon it,
> I leave to you winds as your prize!

Drawn to a death remote from the life that has been spur-
ring them on, the lovers are doomed to become the
voluptuous prey of conflicting forces that will cast both
into the same headlong swoon. For they can never be
united till, bereft of all hope and of all possible love, they
reach the heart of utter obstruction and experience the
supreme exaltation which is destroyed in being fulfilled.

12

Old Tune So Full of Sadness

I n summarizing the Romance from an objective standpoint, we were led to detect in it a number of contradictions; and in supposing that the author really intended to illustrate how the rule of chivalry conflicted
with feudal custom we were led to see how these contradictions came about. Thereupon we set out to find the
real theme of the legend. The author sides with the rule
of chivalry, and in doing so betrays a sense of story-
telling. This in turn betrays a hankering after love for
its own sake, which implies a secret quest of the obstruction that shall foster love. But this quest is only the
disguise of a love for obstruction *per se*. Now, it
turns out that the ultimate obstacle is death, and at the
close of the tale death is revealed as having been the
real end, what passion has yearned after from the beginning, the avenging of a fate that, having been suffered, is
now at last redeemed.

Although the secrets disclosed by an analysis of the
myth are of considerable import, the inward private assurances of what is their nature are likely to be rejected
by our ordinary consciousness. My description has necessarily had to follow the meanderings of the internal logic
of the Romance, and I realize that its dryness may seem
vaguely damaging. I shall be consoled if the results are
correct. With proof to the contrary I shall be ready to

admit that some of the conjectures are questionable. It remains that my interpretation has enabled us to come upon some fundamental relations where they were in process of being formed, and that these relations subtend our fate. In so far as *passionate love* endows the myth with a new youth through its effect upon our own lives, it is henceforth impossible to overlook how it stands for a radical condemnation of *marriage*. The ending of the myth shows that passion is an *askesis*,[1] and that as such it is all the more effectively in opposition to earthly life that it takes the form of desire, and that, as desire, it simulates fate.

Incidentally, I have mentioned that such a love is profoundly connected with our liking for *war*.

Furthermore, if passion and the need of passion are indeed aspects of our Western way of coming to understand, we must consider—at least interrogatively—the existence of one more relation, which may ultimately turn out to be the most fundamental of all. We must ask ourselves if to understand through suffering is not the capital feature as well as the daring element in our most self-conscious *mysticism*. The two passions—the erotic (in a higher sense) and the mystical—speak one same language, whether because either is cause or effect of the other or because they have had a common origin—and perhaps both sound to our ears the same "old tune so full of sadness" which Wagner's drama orchestrates:

> That strain that asked, that asks me still,
> what fate for me was chosen . . .
> what fate for me?
> The olden ditty once more tells me:
> 'tis yearning and dying!

Thanks to a "physiognomical" examination of the shape and structure of the Romance, I have succeeded in setting forth the original content of the myth in all its harsh

---

[1] The word *"ascése,"* though not included in standard dictionaries, has lately become very popular with French religious writers. The word is a French adaptation of the Greek ἄσκησις = exercise, training, practice. It serves to indicate a religious preparation and training. The author is anxious to emphasize the severity and deprivation involved. Being a neologism, it will here be rendered throughout by "askesis"—Translator.

and noble purity. Two ways now beckon—one leading
back to the historical and religious background of the
myth, the other down from the myth to our own time.
Let us take each way in turn without presuppositions.
Here and there I shall pause to verify this or that clearly
localized origin or this or that unforeseen consequence
of the *relations* which have now been laid bare.

Book II

THE RELIGIOUS ORIGINS

1

The Natural and Sacred "Obstruction"

People are all more or less materialists today, for they are the heirs of the nineteenth century. They need only be shown some crude mimicry of "mental" events in nature or in instinct, and they will fancy that the "mental" has been explained. *It is whatever is lower that we take to be more real.* The superstition of our time expresses itself in a mania for equating the sublime with the trivial and for quaintly mistaking a merely necessary condition for a sufficient cause. The mania usurps the name of "scientific integrity," and is defended on the ground that it emancipates the mind from delusions about "spirit." Yet it is difficult to see how there can be any emancipation in "explaining" Dostoievsky by epilepsy or Nietzsche by syphilis. To deny the existence of mind is a curious way of ensuring its freedom. But however much I protest beforehand, no sooner do I admit that in instinct and sex there are spontaneous reactions analogous in some respects to those occurring in the passion of the Tristan myth than many people will suppose that this settles the matter so far as I am concerned. They are bound to think that the *obstruction* which has so often cropped up in the course of my analysis of the myth is something altogether natural. To delay pleasure is the most elementary of the wiles of desire; and man is "so made" as sometimes to subject himself to a semi-instinctive continence for the benefit of the species. Lycurgus, the Spartan legislator, required newly married husbands to remain continent for a considerable time. Plutarch says [1] his reason was that "it kept their bodies in strength and better state, to bring forth children," and that "it continued also in both parties a still burning love and a newe desire of the one to the

[1] North's translation.

61

other." Likewise feudal chivalry, it will be said, looked upon chastity as an instinctive obstacle to the assertion of instinct, and extolled it in order that warriors might be the better fitted to show valour.

But it is only in relation to life that discipline of this sort can have any value; not in relation to the mind. Such discipline yields to its own success; it aims at nothing ulterior. The eugenics of Lycurgus were in no way ascetic; on the contrary, he aimed at the better propagation of the species. The processes which secure the perpetuation of life cannot be anything more than the physiological *concomitant* of the reactions of passion. Of course, passion has to make use of the body and to obey its laws. But to recognize in what the laws of the body consist does nothing to explain, for example, why Tristan loves as he does. In fact, the recognition serves but to render more conspicuous the presence of some additional and "alien" factor, a factor having the power to make instinct turn away from its natural goal and to transform desire into *limitless* aspiration, into something, that is to say, which does not serve, and indeed operates against, biological ends. The same can be said of suggestions that the motives of behaviour characteristic of the Romance originated in the sacred customs and taboos of primitive peoples. Nothing is easier than to connect the distant *quest* of a bride with the custom of nuptial abduction observed among exogamic tribes, and to imagine that *prowess* was encouraged because it was an undisguised sublimation of much older customs inspired by nature in order to achieve biological selection. Even the *longing for death* can be assimilated to *the death instinct* that Freud and the latest biologists refer to.

But nothing in all this will explain the belated appearance of the myth, still less its localization in European history. Antiquity has left no record of an experience akin to the love of Tristan and Iseult. It is well known that the Greeks and Romans looked on love as a sickness— the expression is Menander's—whenever it went, no matter how little, beyond the sensual pleasure which was considered to be its natural expression. Plutarch calls love "a frenzy." "Some have believed it was a madness. . . . Thus those who are in love must be forgiven as though ill." We are thus led to ask whence arose the glorification of passion, which is precisely that feature of the Romance which we find moving. To speak of a deflexion of instinct is to say nothing, inasmuch as what we want to know is indeed how the deflexion was caused.

2

Eros, or Boundless Desire

Plato, alike in the *Phaedrus* and in the *Symposium*, speaks of a frenzy that, spreading from the body infects the spirit with malignant humours. This is not love as he commends it. But there is, he says, another kind of frenzy or delirium which is neither conceived nor born in a man's soul except by the inspiration of heaven. It is alien to us, its spell is wrought from without; it is a transport, an infinite rapture away from reason and natural sense. It is therefore to be called *enthusiasm*, a word which actually means "possessed by a god," for the frenzy not only is of heavenly origin, but culminates at its highest in a new attainment of the divine.

Such is Platonic love.[1] It is "a divine delirium," a transport of the soul, a madness and supreme sanity both. A lover with his beloved becomes "as if in heaven"; for love is the way that ascends by degrees of ecstasy to the one source of all that exists, remote from bodies and matter, remote from what divides and distinguishes, and beyond the misfortune of being a self and even in love itself a pair.

---

[1] I am, of course, aware that Socrates is made to say in the *Phaedrus* that the greatest satisfaction of the lover comes, not from physical fulfilment, but from consciousness of the joint attainment by lover and beloved of self-mastery; and in the *Symposium* that erotic passion at its highest is a delight in beauty of every kind, so that the lover who has ascended high enough will descry the supreme, eternal, self-same, and perfect beauty, the reality and substance of that in which everything else called beauty is a participant. But I am concerned above all with what European culture generally has preserved of Plato.

Eros is complete Desire, luminous Aspiration, the primitive religious soaring carried to its loftiest pitch, to the extreme exigency of purity which is also the extreme exigency of Unity. But absolute unity must be the negation of the present human being in his suffering multiplicity. The supreme soaring of desire ends in non-desire. The erotic process introduces into life an element foreign to the diastole and systole of sexual attraction—a desire that never relapses, that nothing can satisfy, that even rejects and flees the temptation to obtain its fulfilment in the world, because its demand is to embrace no less than the All. It is *infinite transcendence*, man's rise into his god. And this rise is *without return*.

Little has so far been discovered about the antecedents of Platonism, but they are certainly Iranian and Orphic. And through Plotinus the Platonic doctrine of love was transmitted to the medieval world. That is how the East came to brood over our lives and hence to stir up some very ancient memories. For from the depths of the West the voices of Celtic filids and bards arose in answer. It was perhaps an echo, or some ancestral harmony—all our races come from the East—or perhaps human nature is given everywhere and at all times to divinizing its Desire. I cannot pronounce upon the theory according to which the most ancient of Celtic myths are akin to the Greek—the quest of the Holy Grail being regarded as another form of the quest of the Golden Fleece, the Pythagorean theories of reincarnation as another version of druidical beliefs about immortality. But, whatever that theory may be worth, recent investigation has detected general convergences in support of the view that the religious beliefs of East and West had a common source.

The Celts spread over Europe from the Atlantic to the Black Sea long before the Romans embarked upon their conquests. But the Celts were not a nation. They were loosely held together by a civilization or culture which had its spiritual centre in the sacerdotal college of the druids. The college had not emanated from small tribes; it was "a kind of international institution" and served every people of Celtic race from the remote corners of Britain and Ireland across to Italy and Asia Minor. The travels and meetings of druids "cemented the union of

Celtic peoples and their feeling of being related." [1]
The druids were grouped in brotherhoods, and had very
wide powers. They were soothsayers, magicians, medi-
cine-men, priests, and teachers all in one. They set nothing down in writing, but by word of mouth, in gnomic
verses, they taught pupils for whom the course of instruction lasted twenty years [2].

The sacerdotal college of the druids was not unique.
Iranian magi, Indian brahmans, Roman pontiffs and
flamens, have been credited with identical institutions;
and that "flamen" is the same name as "brahman" indicates that the functions of each of these various kinds of
priests were fundamentally akin. [3]

However, as regards the Celts, there is no doubt that
they believed in a life after death. They pictured that life
to themselves as one filled with adventure—very like the
life led on earth, but purified. They even supposed that
some of their heroes were enabled *to return* from the
hereafter, and under other names to mingle with the
living. It is through this central doctrine of soul survival
that the Celts are akin to the Greeks. But every doctrine
of immortality implies a tragic preoccupation with death.
The Celts, according to Hubert, [4] "certainly elaborated a
metaphysic of death. They had meditated on death a
great deal. It had grown into a familar companion, *whose
disturbing nature,* however, *they deliberately disguised."*
And Hubert remarks further that in Celtic mythology
"the notion of death is found to predominate over all
things, and *everything discloses it."* These statements in-
vite juxtaposition with what I have said above about the
Tristan myth, which both veils and expresses a longing
for death.

Celtic gods, furthermore, formed two opposite sets,
light and *dark.* It is important to stress this fundamental
dualism in the religion of the druids. For that is where
Iranian, Gnostic and Hindu myths converge upon the

[1] H. Hubert, *Les Celtes* (Paris, 1932), II, pp. 227, 229, 274.
The best general study of Celtic civilization, history and archaeol-
ogy.

[2] H. d'Arbois de Jurainville, *Cours de littérature celtique,*
I, pp. 1-65.

[3] J. Vendryès, *Mémoires de la société linguistique,* XX, 6, 265.

[4] H. Hubert, op. cit., I, p. 18, and II, p. 328.

basic religion of Europe. From India to the shores of the Atlantic, though in the most varied forms, there is expressed the same mystery of Day and Night and the same mystery of the *fatal* struggle going on between them inside men's breasts. There is a god of uncreated and timeless Light, and there is a god of Darkness, the author of evil, who holds sway over all visible Creation. Centuries before Manes appeared, this opposition had already been established in Indo-European mythologies. The Iranian couple formed by Ahura Mazda and Ahriman is the classic instance.

Of direct interest for our purpose, Woman in the eyes of the druids was a being divine and prophetic. She is typified by the Germanic Velleda, who in Chateaubriand's *Martyrs* appears by night to a Roman general lost in reverie. "Do you know," she says to him, "that I am a sprite?" Eros has taken the guise of Woman, and symbolizes both the other world and the nostalgia which makes us despise earthly joys. But the symbol is ambiguous, since it tends to mingle sexual attraction with *eternal* desire. The Essylt mentioned in sacred legends as being both "an object of contemplation and a mystic vision" stirred up a yearning for what lies beyond embodied forms. Although she was beautiful and desirable for herself, it was her nature to vanish. "The Eternal feminine leads us away," Goethe said, and "Woman is man's goal," according to Novalis.

Thus the yearning for Light was symbolized by the nocturnal attraction of sex. In the eyes of the flesh, uncreated broad Day was but Night, even as our day corresponded for the god dwelling beyond the stars to the realm of Dispater, the Father of Shadows. There is a kinship here with the yearning *to founder* shown by the Wagnerian Tristan, although in the case of that particular Tristan he yearns to founder only in order that he may rise again into a Heaven of Light. The "Night" he sings of is Uncreated Day. And his passion is the cult of Eros—the desire that despises Venus even when in the throes of sensuality and he imagines he is in love with an actual fellow being. There has been too much talk about Nirvana and Buddhism in connexion with Wagner's opera. The pagan background of the West was more than ample for the needs of a magician who wished to brew his lovepotion with active ingredients. For that matter, it is significant that the original Celtic cult should have survived both the Roman conquest and the Germanic invasions. "The Gallo-Romans were mostly Celts in disguise, so that after the Germanic invasions Celtic fashions and inclinations reappeared in Gaul." [1] Both Romanesque art and the Romance languages witness to the wealth of the Celtic inheritance. Later on, it was thanks to the monks in Britain and Ireland—the two countries where the bardic legends had been preserved, and preserved, as it happens, by the clergy—that Europe was evangelized and brought back to the study of letters. This carries us to the threshold of the period in which the Tristan myth sprang up.

However, closer to us than either Plato or the druids, a kind of Indo-European unity may be seen looming out like a watermark upon the background of medieval heresies. As early as the third century, there spread over the geographical and historical area that is bounded by India on the one hand and by Britain on the other, a religion that syncretized all the myths of Night and Day, a religion which had been elaborated first in Persia and then by the Gnostic and Orphic sects. This religion actually spread underground, and it is known as Manichaeism. The very difficulty there is today in describing it must be held to indicate something of its deepest nature and the extent of its human importance. For one thing, everywhere the authorities and orthodoxies persecuted it with incredible violence. It was pretended to see in it the gravest of social perils. Its followers were slaughtered, its writings scattered and burned, so that the evidence on which it has been judged originated most often from its foes. The doctrine of the Persian prophet Manes assumed forms that varied widely according to what beliefs were already established among the peoples to whom it spread—Christians, Buddhists, or Mohammedans. In a Manichaean hymn recently retrieved and translated, Jesus, Manes, Ormuzd, and Sakyamuni are invoked one after the other, and finally so is Zardusht—that is to say, Zarathustra or Zoroaster. And there is reason to suppose, furthermore, that the existence of Celtic survivals in the French area of Languedoc provided certain

---

[1] Hubert, op. cit., I, p. 20. In the same way, the Gallic gods were given Latin names, but were not otherwise altered.

Manichaean sects with a particularly favourable soil.

For the understanding of what is to follow, two points in particular need to be stressed.

1. The fundamental dogma of all Manichaean sects is that the soul is divine or angelic, and is *imprisoned* in created forms—in terrestrial matter, which is Night. In the hymn called *The Soul's Fate*, a disciple of the saviour Manes causes his spiritual self to lament:

> I came out of light and the gods.
> Here in exile am I from them kept apart.
>
> .   .   .   .   .
>
> I am a god, of the gods I was born.
> But now I am made to know pain.

The soul's impulse to seek the Light has a kinship with the "reminiscence of Beauty" referred to in the Platonic dialogues, and also with the nostalgia felt by the Celtic hero when, having come back to earth from heaven, he recalls the existence of the isle where the immortals dwell. But the impulse is constantly being checked by the jealousy of Venus (who, in the hymn just quoted, goes by the name of Dibat). Even after a lover has become possessed by the yearning for light, Venus wants him to remain within dark matter. Hence there ensues the struggle between sexual love and Love, and it is a struggle displaying the fundamental *anguish* felt by fallen angels while confined in bodies all too human.

2. It has recently been shown [1]—and this is very important for what we are seeking to find out—that the structure of the Manichaean faith was "*in essence lyrical.*" In other words, the nature of this faith made it unamenable to rational, impersonal, and "objective" exposition. Actually, it could only come to be held in being experienced, and the experience of it was one of combined dread and enthusiasm—that is to say, of invasion by the divine—which is essentially poetic. The cosmogony and theogony of this faith became "true" for a believer only when certitude was induced by his recital

---

[1] H. Corbin, "Pour l'hymnologie manichéenne" (*Yggdrasil*, Aug. 1937).

of a *psalm*. So Tristan, it will be recalled, cannot state his secret, only sing it.

Every dualistic—let us say, every Manichaean—interpretation of the universe holds the fact of being alive in the body to be the absolute woe, the woe embracing all other woes; and death it holds to be the *ultimate* good, whereby the sin of birth is redeemed and human souls return into the One of luminous indistinction. We may already attain to Light while here below through a gradual ascent which is achieved in the progressive death of a deliberate *askesis*. But the goal and the end of the spirit is also the end of limited life, of physical life obscured by immediate multiplicity. Eros, object of our supreme Desire, intensifies all our desires only in order to offer them up in sacrifice. The fulfilment of Love is the denial of any particular terrestrial love, and its Bliss of any particular terrestrial bliss. *From the standpoint of life*, it is this Love which is the absolute woe.

There we have the broad Eastern and Western background of paganism out of which the Tristan myth sprang. It has now to be asked how indeed the myth should have come out of this background; what prohibitions and perils compelled this doctrine to put on veils and no longer to proclaim itself except in deceptive symbols, no longer to allure us except by means of the spell and secret incantation of a myth.

3

Agape, or Christian Love

The Gospel according to Saint John opens as follows: "In the beginning was the Word, and the Word was with God, and the word was God. . . . In Him was life; and the life was the light of men. And the light shineth in darkness; and the darkness comprehended it not." This might seem to be another expression of the eternal and relentless dualism according to which terrestrial

Night and transcendent Day are irrevocably hostile to one another. But no. The Gospel continues:

"And the Word was made flesh, and dwelt among us, (and we beheld his glory, the glory as of the only begotten of the Father,) full of grace and truth."

The incarnation of the Word in the world—and of Light in Darkness—is the astounding event whereby we are delivered from the woe of being alive. And this event, in being the centre of the whole of Christianity, is the focus of that Christian love which in Scripture is called *agap*e.

The event is unique, and not to be believed "naturally." That the Incarnation occurred is the radical negation of every kind of *religion*—the ultimate offence, not only to our reason, which is unable to countenance the absurd running together of the infinite and the finite, but also and especially to any natural religious disposition. Every known religion tends *to sublimate* man, and culminates in condemning his "finite" life. Our desires are intensified and sublimated by the god Eros through being embraced in a single Desire whereby they are abolished. The final goal of the process is to attain what is not life—the death of the body. Night and Day being incompatible, and men being deemed creatures of Night, men can only achieve salvation by ceasing to be, by being "lost" in the bosom of the divine. But in Christianity, thanks to its dogma of the incarnation of the Christ in Jesus, this process is completely inverted. Death, from being the last *term*, is become the first condition. What the Gospel calls dying to self is the *beginning* of a new *life* already *here below*—not the soul's flight out of the world, but its return in force into the midst of the world. It is an immediate re-creation, a reassertion of life—not of course of the old life, and not of an ideal life, but of our present life now repossessed by the Spirit. God—the real God—has been made man—a real man. Darkness has "comprehended" the light in the person of Jesus Christ. And every man born of woman who *believes* this is born again of the spirit here and now—dead to himself and dead to the world in so far as self and the world are sinful, but restored to himself and to the world in so far as the Spirit wants to save them.

Thereupon to love is no longer to flee and persistently to reject the act of love. Love now still begins beyond death, but from that beyond it returns to life. And, in being thus converted, love brings forth our *neighbour*. Eros had treated a fellow-creature as but an illusory excuse and occasion for taking fire; and forthwith this creature had had to be given up, for the intention was ever to burn more fiercely, to burn to death! Individual beings were but so many defects and eclipsings of the one and only Being; and as such none was susceptible of being really loved. Salvation lay *hereafter,* and a religious-minded person forsook the creatures from whom his god had turned away. But the Christian God has not forsaken us. He alone, among all gods known to us, has not turned away. Quite the contrary, *"He first loved us"*—loved us as we are and with our limitations; and these He even went so far as to put on, making Himself as one of us. In thus putting on, though without sin and without self-division, the garment of sinful and manifold men, the Love of God has opened an entirely new way to us—the way of *holiness*. And the way is the contrary of the sublimation that had been an illusory flight out of the concreteness of life. To love according to this new way is a positive act and an act of transformation. Eros had pursued infinite becoming. Christian love is obedience in the present. For to love God is *to obey* God, Who has commanded us to love one another. *To love your enemies* is to shed selfishness and the desirous and anxious self; it means the death of the solitary human being, but it also means the birth of our neighbour. In reply to the ironical question: "Who is my neighbour?" Jesus answered: "Whoever has need of you." From that moment every human relation has been given a new *direction* in being given a new *meaning*.

The symbol of Love is no longer the infinite *passion* of a soul in quest of light, but the *marriage* of Christ and the Church. And in this way human love itself has been transformed. Whereas, according to the doctrines of mystical paganism, human love was sublimated so thoroughly as to be made into a god even while it was being dedicated to death, Christianity has restored human love to its proper status, and in this status has hallowed it by means of marriage. Such a love, being understood according to the image of Christ's love for His Church (Ephesians, v. 25), is able to be truly mutual. For its object, from having been the actual notion of love and the exquisite and fatal branding of love ("It is better,"

Saint Paul says, "to marry than to burn") has become the other *as he or she really is*. And, in spite of the hindrance of sin, human love is a happy love, since already here below it can by obedience attain to the fullness of its own status.

When pursued to its logical extreme, the dualism of Night and Day had resulted, *from the standpoint of life,* in the ultimate misfortune—death. Christianity is a fatal misfortune only for the man who is parted from God, but it is a newly creative and blessed misfortune *already in this life* for the believer who "takes the cup of salvation."

4

East and West

It is the duty of a writer who refers to East and West in any but a geographical sense to define his terms. By "East" I mean in this book an attitude of the human mind which has reached its highest and purest expression in the direction of Asia; this mystical attitude is dualistic as regards the world and monistic as regards fulfilment. "Eastern" *askesis* is directed to negation of the Many and to absorption into the One; it looks to a *complete fusion* with a god, or, lacking a god (as in the case of Buddhism), with the universal One of Being. All that assumes the availability of a Wisdom, of a technique of progressive illumination—as with Yoga, for example—an *ascent* for the individual towards that Unity in which he will be lost. By "West" I mean a religious attitude which actually reached us from the Near East, but has been supreme solely in the West. According to this attitude, God and man are divided by a fundamental abyss—or, as Kierkegaard calls it, by "an infinite qualitative difference." This attitude accordingly does not look to any absorption or union in substance; but only to a communion, the model of which is the *marriage* of the Church and her Lord. And that assumes a sudden illumination or conversion, a *descent* of Grace, from God to man. No doubt the "Western" attitude has often been found in the East, and *vice versa*. But that is immaterial.

Now Eros, it will be recalled, requires union—that is, the complete absorption of the essence of individuals into the god. The existence of distinct individuals is considered to be a grievous error, and their part is to rise progressively till they are dissolved in the divine perfection. Let not a man attach himself to his fellow-creatures, for they are devoid of all excellence, and in so far as they are particular individuals they merely represent so many deficiencies of Being. There is no such thing as our neighbour. And the intensification of love must be at the same time a lover's *askesis,* whereby he will eventually escape out of life.

Agape, on the contrary, is not directed to a union that can only occur after life is over. "God is in heaven, and thou art on earth." And thy fate is being decided here below. Sin consists not in having been born, but in having lost God by becoming independent. And God is not to be found again by means of a limitless *elevation* of desire. However much our eros may be sublimated, it can never cease to be self. Orthodox Christianity allows no room either to illusion or to human optimism. But that does not mean that it condemns us to despair.

For we have had the Good Tidings—the tidings that God is seeking us. And He finds us whenever we hearken to His voice, and answer by obeying Him. God seeks us, and He has found us, thanks to His Son Who came *down* as far as us. The Incarnation is the historic sign of a renewed creation, wherein a believer is reinstated thanks to his very act of faith. Thereupon, forgiven and hallowed—that is to say, reconciled—he is still a man; there has been no divinization—but he no longer lives for himself alone. "Thou shalt love the Lord thy God, and thy neighbour as thyself." It is in loving his neighbour that a Christian is fulfilled and truly loves himself.

Agape brings no fusion or ecstatic dissolving of the self in God. The divine love is the *beginning* of a new life, a life created by the act of communion. And for a real communion there are certainly required two participants, each present to the other. It is thus that each is the other's neighbour. And since *agape* is alone in recognizing the existence of our neighbour—*Eros* failing to do so—and is the love of this neighbour, not as an excuse for self-exaltation, but as an acceptance of him or her in the whole concrete reality of his or her affliction and hope, it seems legitimate to infer that the kind of love called *passion* must have arisen usually among peoples who adored Eros, and that, on the contrary, Christian peoples—historically speaking, the inhabitants of the Western Continent of Europe—must have remained strangers to passion, or at least must have found it incredible. But history compels us to acknowledge that exactly the opposite has happened.

In the East,[1] and also in the Greece of Plato, human love has usually been regarded as mere pleasure and physical enjoyment. Not only has passion—in the tragic and painful sense of the word—seldom been met with there, but also and especially it has been despised in the eyes of current morals and treated as a sickness or frenzy. "Some think it is a madness," Plutarch says. In the West, on the contrary, it was marriage which in the twelfth century became an object of contempt, and passion that was glorified precisely because it is preposterous, inflicts suffering upon its victims, and wreaks havoc alike in the world and in the self.

As a result of identifying the religious components whose presence we had detected in the myth, we find ourselves confronted by a flagrant contradiction between doctrine and manners. Perhaps it is this very contradiction that can account for the myth.

---

[1] And by the "East" I mean a certain kind of attitude to both the whole of life and the world which was characteristic chiefly not of Persia, Islam, Arabia, or Judaism, which are directly connected with Western religious cycles, but of India, China, Tibet, Japan, and so on. The Chinese have married young, unions being arranged by the parents, and for them the problem of love does not arise. "The attitude of a European, who wonders all his life: 'Is it love or not? Do I really love this woman, or is it affection that I feel for her? Do I love God or do I merely want to love God? Am I in love with her or am I in love with love?'—to a Chinese psychiatrist that attitude might well appear as symptomatic of insanity. We are mad without knowing it. Our whole life is founded upon passion, and we want peace and tranquillity! I am myself the maddest of all madmen, alas! But at least now I know it." So writes Leo Ferrero in his book, *Désespoirs*.

5

Reaction to Christianity in European Manners

I offer the following scheme for the sake of clarity.

	Doctrine	*Theoretical Application*	*Historical Fulfilment*
Paganism	Mystical union (Blissful divine love)	Woeful human love	Hedonism; passion rare and despised
Christianity	Communion (but no union of essence)	Love of our Neighbour (Blissful marriage)	Painful clashes, intense passion

Psychologically, the paradoxes of this scheme are pretty easily accounted for. Neither during Plato's own lifetime nor in the course of the ensuing few centuries did Platonism become popular; it remained an esoteric wisdom. Esoteric likewise to some extent were the Celtic mysteries, and the Manichaean entirely so. Thereupon, Christianity triumphed. Under Constantine and under the Carolingian emperors its doctrines became the apanage of princes and ruling caste, who forced them upon all the peoples of the West. This, of course, meant the repression of the old pagan beliefs, which became the hope and refuge of natural inclinations frowned upon and not disposed of by the new rule. In the eyes of the Ancients, marriage, for example, was a utilitarian institution of limited purpose. If not adultery as understood today, at least concubinage was allowed by custom, for slaves could be both used and abused.[1] But Christian marriage, inasmuch as it is a sacrament, imposed on the natural man a constancy which he found unbearable. Any one compulsorily converted came under the restraints of the Christian code, but lacked the support of any actual faith. Inevitably the barbarian blood of such people must have rebelled, and they were all disposed to welcome a revival of the pagan mysteries in Catholic guise, since this brought a promise of "emancipation." Hence it was that the secret doctrines of which we have been investigating the antecedents had no real hold on the West except during the centuries they were banned by official Christianity. So it was that passionate love—a terrestrial form of the cult of Eros—came to invade the psyche of those members of the leading caste who had only simulated conversion and felt the marriage rule as a restriction. Yet devotion to a god who was anathema to the Church could not be avowed in the light of day. It took esoteric forms and flourished in the guise of secret heresies more or less orthodox in appearance. At the beginning of the twelfth century these heresies spread quickly. On the one hand, they wormed their way among the clergy, and a little later were manifested in many subtle and complicated ways in the great mystical revival. On the other hand, they drew a ready response out of the depths of the spirit of the age. They were able to penetrate the feudal world, which was not invariably aware of the source and mystic significance of a set of values it treated as fashionable and which it adapted to the purposes of its own amusement. Before long a religion that rejected the Incarnation as something too materialistic had itself taken on a materialist tinge!

It has been typical of the West as regards religion to keep the letter while betraying the spirit. Here is one instance. Plato linked Love and Beauty, although what he called Beauty was above all the intellectual essence of uncreated perfection—the form of all excellence. According to José Ortega y Gasset,[2] "it is impossible to tell to what deep levels of the Western mind Platonic

---

[1] In Roman law, slaves were not persons: *Persona est sui iuris; servus non est persona.*

[2] *Über die Liebe* (Berlin, 1933).

notions have penetrated. The simplest sort of person regularly employs expressions and betrays views which are derived from Plato." But such a person distorts these expressions and views in a direction suited to his Western nature; and it is in this way that popular Platonism has led us into a grievous error—the error of supposing that love is first and foremost a matter of *physical* beauty, when, actually, this beauty is but an attribute bestowed by a lover on the chosen object of his love. Daily experience shows well enough that "love beautifies its object" and that "official" beauty is no pledge of being loved. But the degenerate Platonism by which we are obsessed blinds us to the reality of the object as it is according to *its own* truth—or else renders it little likeable. And it sends us in pursuit of chimeras that exist only inside ourselves. It may well be asked why an error due to misunderstanding Plato should have succeeded so well and have endured invincibly. The error awakens obscure responses in every human being's heart, and in particular in the heart of every European. We have seen that as far back as the Celts, the druidical cult turned Woman into a prophetic being, "the eternal feminine" and "man's goal"; in this way it sought to materialize the divine urge and to endow it with a corporeal hypostasis. Moreover, Freud has now made us aware that a man's "type of woman," that image which he bears graven upon his heart and instinctively turns into a definition of feminine beauty, may be but a "mother fixation" haunting the recesses of his memory.

Assuming that we have now distinguished the causes of the curious contradiction between teaching and manners that grows visible in the twelfth century, it becomes possible to formulate a preliminary inference. *The cultivation of passionate love began in Europe as a reaction to Christianity (and in particular to its doctrine of marriage) by people whose spirit, whether naturally or by inheritance, was still pagan.*

But this would be mere theory and highly disputable were it not that we are in a position to trace the historical ways and means to the rebirth of Eros. We have already settled on a date. The earliest passionate lovers whose story has reached us are Abélard and Héloïse, who met for the first time in 1118! And it is in the middle of this same century that love was first recognized and encouraged as a passion worth cultivating. Passionate love was then given a name which has since become familiar. It was called *cortezia*, or courtly love.

6

Courtly Love: Troubadours and Cathars

That all European poetry has come out of the Provençal poetry written in the twelfth century by the troubadours of Languedoc is now accepted on every side. This poetry magnified unhappy love. M. Charles Albert Cingria remarks:[1]

"Between the eleventh and twelfth centuries, poetry—whether Hungarian, or Spanish, Portuguese, German, Sicilian, Tuscan, Genoese, Pisan, Picard, Champagne, Flemish, English, etc.—was at first Languedoc; which is to say, that the poet, who had to be a troubadour, was compelled to speak the troubadour language which was never other than Provençal.

"The whole of the Occitanian, Petrarchian, and Dantesque lyric has but a single theme—love; and not happy, crowned, and satisfied love (the sight of which yields nothing), but on the contrary love perpetually unsatisfied—and but two characters: a poet reiterating his plaint eight hundred, nine hundred, a thousand times; and a fair lady who ever says 'No.' "

No European poetry has been more profoundly *rhetorical*, not only in its verbal and musical forms, but also—paradoxical as it may seem—in its actual inspiration, which it obtained from a fixed system of rules which was codified as the *leys d' amor*. But it is likewise true that no rhetoric has been more productive of high-flown fervour. What it quickens with noble emotion is love outside marriage; for marriage implies no more than a phys-

[1] *Mesures*, No. 2 (Paris, 1937). The Provençal mentioned there was in reality the dialect of the county of Toulouse.

ical union, but "Amor"—the supreme Eros—is the transport of the soul upwards to ultimate union with light, something far beyond any love attainable in this life. That is why Love now implies chastity. "E d'amor mou castitaz," sang the Toulouse troubadour, Guilhem Montanhagol. "Out of love comes chastity." Love further implies a ritual—the ritual of *domnei* or *donnoi*, love's vassalage. It is by the beauty of his musical homage that a poet wins his *lady*. On his knee he swears eternal constancy to her, as knights swore fealty to their suzerain. He receives from her a golden ring and a chaste kiss on his brow. Thereupon the "lovers" are bound by the rules of *cortezia*: secrecy, patience, and moderation—the last not being altogether synonymous with chastity, but meaning rather restraint. . . . And especially a man has to be the *servente* of a woman.

Whence came this notion of a love "perpetually unsatisfied" and whence too that of singing with plaintive enthusiasm the praises of "a fair lady who ever says 'No?'" And how is it that such consummate poesy was at hand ready to serve the new passion? The miraculous character of the twin birth cannot be two greatly stressed. Within no more than about twenty years there were established together, on the one hand, a vision of woman entirely at variance with traditional manners—woman was set *above man*, and became his nostalgic ideal—and on the other hand, a new but fully developed poetry of an extremely complex and refined character—a poetry equally unknown to Antiquity, and to the few centuries of Romanic literary vigour that had followed the Carolingian Renaissance. Either both these things "dropped out of the sky"—that is to say, medieval society was suddenly and collectively inspired with them—or else they had some definite historical cause. On the first assumption, we must ask why the inspiration came at that particular time and in that particular area; and on the second assumption, why the historical cause should have remained a mystery ever since. The most curious feature of the business is that whenever the most serious authorities happen to refer to it they betray that they are at a loss and at once determine to say nothing.

It is generally recognized today that both Provençal poetry and the notion of love which informs its themes, far from being accounted for by conditions prevailing at the time, seem to have been in flat contradiction to them. "Evidently," according to M. Jeanroy,[1] "the poetry did not reflect the actual state of affairs, for the position allotted to woman in feudal institutions of the South was quite as lowly and dependent as in those of the North." If it is thus "evident" that the troubadours were not depicting the conditions around them, they must have obtained their notion of love from *elsewhere*. The same must be true, for that matter, of their art, their poetic technique. "An extremely original creation," M. Jeanroy writes, notwithstanding that each poet when he takes them singly he reproaches with having displayed no originality of any kind and with having merely refined on forms already fixed and on commonplaces. Yet one of them at least must have *created* the forms! Yet whenever some historian ventures on a theory of how courtly rhetoric came into being, the authorities turn on him with biting irony. Sismondi attributed the origins of emotional mysticism to the Arabs: his theory was disdainfully rejected as monstrous.[2] Diez discerned resemblances in the rhythms and pauses of Arab and Provençal lyric poetry: we are told he must not be taken seriously. Brinkmann and others suggested that Latin poetry of the eleventh and twelfth centuries may have provided models: but this, it is said, cannot be listened to, because the troubadours, it seems, were not sufficiently educated to have been aware of this poetry. Thus, no matter what explanation is offered, the authorities are apparently determined to pooh-pooh any attempt to give a meaning to what they have devoted their lives to studying. It is true that Wechssler, in a famous book,[3] supposed everything was going to be cleared up when he announced that he had found underlying Provençal poetry certain *religious* influences, of a neo-Platonist and debased Christian nature. But he was at once stigmatized "a doctrinaire"—the most damaging of insults—and several Frenchmen implied that as he was both a professor and a German he was hardly fitted to form an opinion

[1] A. Jeanroy, Introduction to *Anthologie des Troubadours* (Paris, 1927).

[2] A. Jeanroy, op. cit., I, p. 69.

[3] E. Wechssler, *Das Kulturproblem des Minnesangs* (Halle, 1909).

on a matter connected with the limpid and elegant genius of Southern France.

We thus have, on the one hand, a queer historical phenomenon, and, on the other hand, very learned refutations of whatever may claim to account for it. One professor writes: "To look upon those love songs which form three-fourths of Provençal poetry as being a faithful reflection of reality is quite as impossible as to regard them as being a bundle of set phrases devoid of meaning." No doubt. But thereupon the professor declares that as "a scrupulous historian" he takes care not to commit himself. That amounts to saying that the lyric poetry of courtly love, with which he is concerned, remains for him, till he learns to the contrary, "a bundle of set phrases devoid of meaning." Excellent "material," it is true, for a self-respecting philologist who does not intend to force a text, even by means of the least attempt to understand it.

For my part, I cannot rest content with such a scrupulous attitude. I cannot believe that the troubadours were so simple as merely to repeat forms picked up anyhow. Following E. Aroux and Péladan,[1] I wonder if the clue to the secret of all this poetry is not to be sought nearer at hand than any one has so far looked for it—much nearer, on the spot, and in the environment of the poets. I do not mean the purely "social" environment in the modern sense, but in the religious atmosphere which happened to determine the formal behaviour—including the social usages—of that environment.

One great historical event stands out in the Provençal twelfth century. Simultaneously with the lyrical surge of the *domnei*, and in the same provinces and among the same classes, there also arose a great heresy. Historians have declared that the Catharist religion was as powerful a menace to the Church as Arianism had been earlier. It has even been asserted that, notwithstanding the bloody Albigensian crusade, or on account of it, this religion won millions of secret converts in Europe during the thirteenth century and afterwards up to the Reformation.

---

[1] Eugéne Aroux, *Dante, pasteur de l'église albigeoise de Florence* (1856); Joséphine Péladan, *Le Secret des troubadours* (1906).

The exact origin of the Heresy can be attributed to the Neo-Manichaean sects of Asia Minor and to the Bogomil churches of Dalmatia and Bulgaria. The Pure or Cathars [1] were affiliated with the great Gnostic streams that flowed across the first millenary of Christianity. It is well known that the Gnosis, like the doctrine of Mani (or Manes), thrust down its roots into the dualist religion of Persia. What was the Catharist doctrine? For a long time it went on being repeated that "nobody would ever know," and this for the good reason that the Inquisition had burned all the liturgical books and doctrinal treatises of the Heresy, and that the only surviving testimony consisted of the answers of the accused during interrogation, these, however, having probably been extorted by the judges and deformed by the clerks who wrote them down. Actually, the discovery and publication in 1939 of a theological work of the Cathars—late, it is true—the *Book of the Two Principles*,[2] coming on top of the restoration of the New Testament and of rituals used by the Heretics,[3] enables us at the present day to understand generally and in a number of variations what were the dogmas of the "Church of Love," as the Heresy is sometimes called, although known mostly as the Albigensian heresy.[4]

Underlying the attitude of the Cathars, or, more generally, underlying Dualism, there has ever been, alike in the most various religions and in the minds of millions of individual men, the problem of Evil—evil as the spiritually-minded man experiences it in the world—and of course that problem is one always tragically present. To the problem of Evil Christianity offers an answer at once

---

[1] "Cathar" is from the Greek καθαρὸς, spotless.

[2] Liber *de duobus Principiis*, A. Dondaine, O.P., editor (Rome, 1939).

[3] Cf. Döllinger's publication, *The Secret Supper* (Munich, 1890).

[4] Three important works on Catharism have appeared recently. They are: Déodat Roché, *Etudes manichéennes et cathares* (1952); René Nelli, Charles Bru, Canon de Lagger, D. Roché, L. Sommariva, *Le Catharisme* (1953); Arno Borst, *Die Katharer* (1953). The third is in many respects in opposition to the other two, but all three, taken together, throw a strong light on the precise nature of the Heresy as well as on its evolution and complexities.

dialectical and paradoxical. It is an answer summed up in the two words "Freedom" and "Grace." More pessimistic and more solidly logical, Dualism declares Good and Evil to exist in absolute heterogeneity. There are two worlds, and two creations. In effect, God is Love, but the world is evil. Hence God cannot be the creator of the world, of its darkness, and of the sin which coils itself about us. His creation was first spiritual and then one of souls. It was completed and also perverted in the material order by the Rebel Angel, the Great Arrogant, the Demiurge—that is to say, by Lucifer or Satan. The latter tempted the Souls or Angels, saying "It is better to be down below, where you will be able to do both good and evil, than up above, where God allows you only to do good." [1] The better to seduce Souls, Lucifer showed them "a woman of dazzling beauty, who inflamed them with desire." Then he left heaven with her, in order to descend into matter and into sensible manifestation. The Angel-Souls, having followed Satan and the woman of dazzling beauty, were ensnared in material bodies even though these were and remained *foreign* to them. (This notion strikes me as throwing light upon a fundamental human sentiment or feeling, one that is still met with nowadays.) A soul is then parted from its spirit, which remains in heaven. Tempted by the prospect of freedom, a soul actually becomes the prisoner of a body with terrestrial appetites and subject to the laws of procreation and death. But Christ came among us to show the way back to the Light. The Dualist Christ, like that of the Gnostics and of Manes, was not really incarnated; he but took the appearance of a man. Such is the great Docetist heresy ("Docetist," from the Greek δόκησις apparition) which, from Marcion to our own day, expresses our quite "natural" refusal to countenance the scandal of a Man-God. The Cathars therefore rejected the dogma of the Incarnation, and *a fortiori* its Roman translation in the sacrament of the mass. They replaced it with a supper of brotherhood which symbolized purely spiritual events. They also rejected baptism by water, and recognized only baptism by the consolatory Spirit:

---

[1] Cf. the Catharist Prayer quoted by Döllinger. It should be noted that man's freedom, the faculty to do either evil *or* good, would thus have originated not in God but in the Devil.

the *consolamentum* was the major rite of their Church. It was given at initiation ceremonies to brethren who undertook to renounce the world and solemnly promised to devote themselves to God alone, never to lie or take an oath, never to kill, or eat of, an animal, and finally ever *to abstain, if married, from all contact with a wife*. It seems that initiation was preceded by a fast of forty days,[1] and that another of the same length followed. (Later, in the thirteenth century, the ritual fast or *endura* was to result in the voluntary death of some of the Pure, death for the love of God, the consummation of supreme detachment from any material law.) The *consolamentum* was administered by bishops, and included the imposition of hands, amid a circle of the Pure, and then the Kiss of Peace was exchanged by the brethren. Thereupon, the fresh initiate became an object of veneration for ordinary believers who had not yet been "consoled"; he was entitled to their "salute"—that is to say, to three "bows."

I have mentioned the part assigned to Woman as the Devil's lure to draw souls down into bodies. In return— one might say, in order to get even—a feminine principle, held to have pre-existed material creation, occupied in Catharism an analogous part to that of the Sophia-Pistis of Gnosticism. To the woman who was instrumental in the perdition of souls there corresponded Maria, symbol of the pure saving Light, intact (immaterial) Mother of Jesus, and (it would seem) the all-gentle Judge of released spirits.

The Manichaeans had for centuries the same sacraments as the Cathars; the laying on of hands, the Kiss of Peace, and the veneration of the Elect (or Pure). It is important here to mention that Manichaean veneration is addressed to the "Form of Light," and that this represents in every man *his own spirit* (which has stayed in heaven, beyond terrestrial manifestation) and welcomes the homage of his soul by a salute and a kiss. Hell

---

[1] The number forty is archetypal. Jesus was forty days in the wilderness. The Hebrews wandered for forty years between Egypt and the Promised Land. The Flood was brought about by a rainfall that lasted forty days. In Buddhist Tantrism the "service" of the Woman is broken up into trials or ordeals of forty days, etc., etc. Forty is the number for an ordeal or trial.

being the prison of matter, Lucifer, the Rebel Angel, can reign there only for the length of *time* that the "error" of souls persists. At the end of the cycle of their ordeals—comprising for men who have not yet been illumined several lives, physical and other—creation will return to the unity of the Original Spirit, the sinners borne off by Satan will be saved, and Satan himself will once again bow in obedience to the Most High.

Catharist dualism issues in an eschatological monism, whereas our Christian orthodoxy, inasmuch as it decrees the eternal damnation of the Devil and of hardened sinners, becomes ultimately dualistic, even though, contrary to Manichaeism, it professes the idea of a single creation, accomplished entirely at the hands of the Deity, and one that began by being entirely good. There is a final feature to be noted. As with so many eastern religions and sects—Jainists, Buddhists, Essenes, and Gnostic Christians—the Catharist Church consisted of two groups: the Perfect (*perfecti*),[1] who had received the *consolamentum*, and the mere Believers (*credentes* or *imperfecti*). The latter alone were allowed to marry and to go on living in a world which the Pure condemned, and this without having to comply with all the precepts of esoteric morality: bodily mortifications, contempt for creation, the severance of all worldly ties.

Saint Bernard of Clairvaux, quoted by Rahn, was able to say of the Cathars, notwithstanding that he fought them with all his might: "No sermons are more thoroughly Christian than theirs, and their morals are pure." His testimonial makes up to some extent for the slanders of the Inquisition. It is nevertheless odd to find a saint describing as "Christian" a form of preaching in which several of the fundamental dogmas of his church were rejected. As for the purity of the morals of the Cathars, it has just been shown that they professed beliefs entirely contrary to those upon which true Christian morality is based. *The condemnation of the flesh, which is now viewed by some as characteristically Christian, is in fact of Manichaean and "heretical" origin.* For it must be

[1] Incidentally, the name "Perfect" is to be found nowhere but in the records of the Inquisition. The term "Goodmen" (or, more simply, "Christians") seems to have been used by the Cathars themselves, and "Perfect" seems to have been ironical.

borne in mind that when Saint Paul speaks of the "flesh"
he means not the physical body but the *whole* of the
unbelieving man—body, mind, faculties, and desires—
and hence his *soul* too.

The Albigensian crusade, led by the Abbot of Citeaux
at the beginning of the thirteenth century, resulted in
the destruction of the towns inhabited by the Cathars, in
the burning of their books, the slaughter and burning of
the mass of the people who loved them, and the viola-
tion of their sanctuaries and supreme High Place, the
famous Castle of Montségur. The highly refined civilization of which they were the austere and secret spirit
was brutally devastated. Nevertheless, to that culture and
its fundamental doctrines we still pay tribute. We are its
debtors, as I hope to show, far more than we realize.

7

Heresy and Poetry

Should the troubadours be regarded as having been
Believers of the Catharist Church and the bards of
its heresy? This view, which I shall call the maximum
view in contrast to the one which I feel I myself am
authorized to adopt,[1] was put forward by a succession of
venturous spirits such as Otto Rahn, and, in my opinion,
they damaged it by trying to make it too plain at a historical rather than a spiritual level. Yet it is a view
singularly irritating and stimulating, for it seems as impossible to reject as to accept, as impossible to demonstrate as to deny utterly, and this is due to the very
essence of the phenomenon that it seeks to account for
—an affair both historical and archetypal, both psychical
and mystical, both concrete and symbolic, or, if you prefer, literary and religious.

The data are roughly as follows. On the one hand, the

[1] It is set forth on page 107 and is discussed at greater length
in Chapter 10.

Catharist heresy and courtly love developed simultaneously in the twelfth century and also coincĭded spatially
in the south of France.[1] How suppose that the two
movements were entirely unconnected? For them not to
have entered into relations would surely be the strangest
thing of all! But, on the other hand, and weighting the
opposite side of the scales, how could there be a connexion between those sombre Cathars, whose asceticism
compelled them to shun all contact with the opposite
sex,[2] and the bright troubadours, joyful and up to any
folly, who turned love, the spring, dawn, flowery gardens,
and the Lady, all into song? Our modern rationalism is
entirely at one with the Romanist scholars who declare
unanimously that Cathars and troubadours had nothing
in common! But the irrepressible intuition of those venturous spirits to whom I referred above answers, with
the approval of our common sense, "Show us, then,
how Cathars and troubadours were able to rub elbows
day after day, without making one another's acquaint-
ance, and how they could live in two completely water-
tight worlds amid the great psychical revolution of the
twelfth century!" To refuse to understand the Heresy
and courtly love each by means of the other and with
but one movement of the mind looks very much like
refusing to understand each of them one by one.

What is there in favour of the "venturous" view?

Raimon V, Count of Toulouse and Suzerain of Languedoc, wrote in 1177: "The heresy has penetrated

---

[1] The first troubadour, William of Poitiers, died in 1127. The
earliest references to an *organized* and public Catharist Church
date from 1160. But already in 1145, according to Borst, Catharism
was found to have spread in Bulgaria and England! The name
appears that year in Germany and two years later in Languedoc.
Arno Borst infers that Catharism invaded Europe in a couple of
years! He is surprised. I do not believe it. Under other names, or
even without name, Catharism existed in people's minds much
earlier than "historical" texts. Its doctrines were condemned in
France as early as the eleventh century—at Orleans, in Poitou,
Périgord, and Aquitaine; that is to say—and let us not fail to
notice it—in the very places where the first troubadours appeared!

[2] This went so far as to prevent a Perfect from sitting on a
bench if a woman had recently left it. Yet many women of the
nobility were Cathars and the troubadours dedicated to them their
lays.

everywhere. It has sown discord in every family, dividing
husband from wife, son from father, a man's wife from
his mother. Even priests yield to the temptation. The
churches are abandoned and falling into ruin. . . . The
most important people on my estates have been cor-
rupted. The crowd has followed their example and has
given up the (Catholic) faith, so that I no longer dare to
undertake anything." How suggest that the troubadours
lived and sang in such a world as is pictured there
without caring what went on in the heads and hearts
of the noblemen on whose bounty they lived? In reply
to that question we are told that the first troubadours
were seen in Poitou and the Limousin while the Heresy
had its centre more to the southward—in the county of
Toulouse. But we find that the language which the troubadours of the Limousin employed from the beginning is
the language of the county of Toulouse! And the same
language was soon being used by troubadours in other
parts of Europe. It is also contended that the courts most
often named by troubadours as making them particularly
welcome were those of nobles who remained orthodox.
But that does not hold for all of them. Far from it, as
will be seen presently. Moreover, quite possibly the presence of troubadours at such courts is a sign of heretical
tendencies in them. Here is the beginning of a song by
Peire Vidal:

"My heart rejoices on account of the agreeable and
sweet renewal, and on account of the Castle of Fanjeaux,
which seems Paradise to me; for love and joy are confined there, as well as all that is due to honour, and
sincere and perfect courtesy."

Who would dare to say, or even to think for a moment, that those lines sound Catharist? Yet what is this
Castle of Fanjeaux? One of the mother-houses of the
Cathars! The most famous of heretical bishops, Guilabert
of Castres, directed it in person from 1193, and the
poem quoted above may be ascribed to about 1190. It
is in the same castle that Esclarmonde of Foix, the
highest of heretical ladies, received the *consolamentum!*
The second verse of Vidal's song speaks solely of the
ladies:

"I have no enemy however mortal whose true friend I
do not become if he speaks to me of the ladies and
does them honour and praise. And as I am not in the

midst of them, but am going to another country, I utter
my plaint, I sigh and I languish."

The reader may well wonder if Peire Vidal can be more
than an amusing gallant, a flatterer of the wealthy wom-
en who formed his "public." But the rest of the poem
is disturbing. He lists the houses in which he has been
made welcome and the places from which, alas! he has
to take leave so as to get to Provence: the castles of
Laurac, Gaillac, Saissac, and Montreal; the counties of
the Albigenses and of Carcasses, "where the knights and
women of the country are courtly," and he refers to
"Dame Louve, who has so completely conquered me that,
by God and my faith! her gentle laughter lingers in my
heart!" Now we happen to know that *every one* of those
castles was a well-known focus of the Heresy; that they
were even "Heretics' Houses" (convents of a kind); that
the counties named were notoriously Catharist; and that
the "Louve" is Countess Stéphanie, alias La Loba, who
belonged to a group of active heretics! The poem, entitled in a modern anthology in all innocence, "Thanks for
Gracious Moments of Hospitality," thus acquires the
unexpected character of a kind of pastoral letter! And yet
I read it over again and rub my eyes. Can this really be
an instance of "pure coincidences?" The doubt and the
question recur *ad infinitum*.

It is again a "pure coincidence," perhaps, that the
troubadours, like the Cathars, extolled (without always
practising) the virtue of chastity; that, like the Pure,
they received from their lady but a single kiss of initiation; that they distinguished two stages in the *domnei*
(the *pregaire,* or prayer, and the *entendaire*), as the
Church of Love distinguished between Believers and Perfect. The troubadours scoffed at the marriage bond which
the Cathars called the *iurata fornicatio*. They reviled the
clergy and the clergy's allies, the members of the feudal
caste. They liked best to lead the wandering life of the
Pure, who set off along the road in pairs. And in their
verse are expressions taken from Catharist liturgy.

It would be only too easy to go on finding similar
"coincidences." But what of the arguments on the other
side? Not all the troubadours, I shall be told, were supporters of the Heresy. A number ended their days in a
convent cell. No doubt. And, moreover, Folquet of Mar-
seilles turns out to have taken part in the Albigensian

crusade. But on that very account he was considered a traitor, and one day was brought before Pope Innocent III and charged with having caused the death of five hundred thousand persons. As far as that goes, even if it could be shown that certain troubadours in particular never suspected the existence of a close connexion between the themes of their poems and Catharist doctrine, that would not show that the *origin* of the poetry was not Catharist. The troubadours, it should be borne in mind, displayed an admirable unanimity in composing their *coblas* and their *sirventes*. They all obeyed the same rhetorical canon. It is easy enough for poetry—and possibly very beautiful poetry—to be written with commonplaces of the time and for the poet concerned not to suspect the source of those commonplaces. Beauty apart, is this not indeed usual? And if it is objected that the troubadours, in the poems that have come down to us, never refer to their beliefs, the obvious answer is that the Cathars had to promise, on initiation, never to betray their faith, no matter what kind of death might seem to be in store for them. Thus the records of the Inquisition contain not a single admission about the *minesola* (or *malisola* or again *manisola*), the highest initiation ceremony of the Pure. We should also give due weight to how often the Courts of Love discussed the question, "Can a knight be true to his lady?" For all the troubadours had to undergo the semblance of a "marriage" with the Church of Rome—they were clerks—while serving in their "thoughts" another Lady—the Church of Love. . . . Bernard Gui, in his *Manuel de l'Inquisiteur,* shows that although the Cathars venerated the Blessed Virgin, she was not, in their belief, a woman of flesh and blood, the Mother of Jesus, *but their Church.*

It will be said that some troubadours abjured the Heresy without giving up the *trobar.* But it would not astonish us at all to see a newly converted poet of today devote to the Virgin images which he had invented for the praise of others and had as his stock in hand. I shall be told that Peire of Auvergne did penance. But what better proof that he had been a heretic?

However, let us turn to the textual evidence, which

exposes the rhetoric in its sheer nudity and transparence. There is the theme that *death* is preferable to earthly rewards:

> Far more it pleaseth me to die
> Than easy mean delight to feel.
> For what will meanly satisfy
> Nor can nor ought to fire my zeal.

Thus Almeric de Belenoi. "What will meanly satisfy" would rid him of his desire were it not that the ill he cherishes is love without end, *joy d'amor,* the frenzy that prevails over all else.

> . . . in fact this wild desire
> Is bound to be my death, no matter if I stay
>   or go.
> For she who could deliver me, no pity will she
>   show.
>   . . . and this desire
> Although it hath from frenzy sprung, it certainly
>   prevails
> Above the others all.

If he does not wish to die yet, it is because he feels that he has not yet become detached from desire, and feels that he would be leaving his body out of despair—a "mortal sin"; it is also that he is still unaware

> how this may be his weal
> That ecstasy his soul shall softly steal.

Did not the Catharist doctrine require that life should be ended, "not out of weariness nor out of fear or pain, but in a state of utter detachment from nature?" [1]

Next here is the theme of *parting,* the leitmotiv of all courtly love:

[1] Déodat Roché, a living scholar intensely interested in Catharism (cf. his *Etudes manichéennes et cathares* (1952) and *Le Catharisme* (1938)), insists likewise that in the Catharist view there was a "danger of flying too swiftly up to heaven," and opposes Catharism to Buddhism on that truly capital point.

Heaven! How doth it thus befall
The farther off I am the more I long for her.

Then there is Guiraut de Bornheil, who prays to the *true* Light [1] as he waits for the dawn of terrestrial day —the dawn that is going to reunite him with his "copain" (or comrade) of the road—and hence of his trials in the world. We may wonder whether the two "copains" are not soul and body—the soul bound to the body, but hankering after spirit? And we may also remember that missionaries go forth in pairs.

> O high and glorious King, O Light and Brightness true!
> O God of Power, Lord, suppose it pleases you,
> Make my comrade welcome, and grant him all your aid.
> For him I have not seen since fell the night's dark shade,
>   And soon will come the dawn.

But by the time the troubadour reaches the end of his lay, has he betrayed his vows, or has he found in the bosom of night that true Light from which there must be no parting?

> Noble comrade mine, so happy am I where I stay,
> I never wish again to see the rise of dawn or day.
> The loveliest of maidens that a mother could e're bear
> I now hold closely in my arms, so I no longer care
>   What happens to the envious or the dawn.

The nightingale was cheerfully giving throat to the trill that later on, in the second act of *Tristan,* provided Wagner with Brengain's sublime cry:

> Habet acht! Habet acht!
> Schon weicht dem Tag die Nacht! [2]

But Tristan has his answer: "Ever hold us, O night!"

---

[1] When a troubadour uses the word "true" before any of the words, "God," "Light," "Faith," or "Church," it may be a sign of Catharism. The Cathars took care to speak the language of orthodoxy, adding that significant little qualification for the benefit of the initiate.

> [2] "Have a care! Have a care!
> Now Night gives way to Day!

There is a parallel in the beginning of another (anonymous) "Dawn": [1]

"In a garden, in a hawthorn nook, the lady has held her lover in her arms till the watchman cried: 'God! It's the dawn! How quickly it comes!' 'How I should like, my God, that night should not end, that my friend could stay by me, and that never the watchman called the rise of dawn! God, it's the dawn! How quickly it comes!'"
But in no poem is it clear whether the "Fair Lady who ever says "No!" is a woman or a symbol. The troubadours all swear that they will never betray the *secret* of their mighty passion, as if it were a faith, and one that had been imparted to them by initiation.

"Cease, I tell you, in the name of Love and in my own name, treacherous accusers, steeped in every kind of malice, cease asking who is she, and which her country, whether near or far. This I shall keep well hidden from you. I would rather perish than fail by so much as a word."

What "lady" could be worthy of such a sacrifice! And this cry of William of Poitiers:

By her alone shall I be saved!

Or this invocation by Uc de Saint-Circ of a "Dame sans merci":

"I do not wish God to aid me nor to give me joy and happiness except through you!"
If these are only rhetorical tropes, we must ask ourselves what attitude of mind produced them, and what kind of Love can have been their Platonic idea or form? In the song, "Du moindre tiers d'Amour"—the tierce love of woman—Guiraut de Calanson says of the two other tierce loves—the love of parents and heavenly love—

"To the second is suited nobility and thanks; and the first is so lofty that its powers hover above the sky."
This one-in-three love, this feminine principle ("amor" in Provençal is of the feminine gender), which Dante presently found "moving the sky and all the stars," seems

---

[1] "Dawns" were an accepted kind of poem. It will readily be understood how appropriate they were for the purposes of a vision of the world in which Day and Night were hostile to one another.

indeed to be the Divinity-in-itself of the great heterodox mystics, the God of before the Trinity mentioned both in the Gnosis and by Meister Eckhart; and, more exactly still, the "super-essential" God who, according to Bernard of Chartres (c. 1150!), "resides above the heavens" and, of whom "Noys"—the Greek *voûs*—is the intellectual and *feminine* emanation. Nothing else would produce the uncertainty, the sense of dubiousness, which we cannot fend off as we read these love poems. The poems are about a real woman [1]—the physical *pretext* is there—but as in the Song of Songs the tone is truly mystical. Scholars keep on saying that this indicates something "perfectly simple"—a fad for idealizing woman and natural love. But they do not say how the fad arose. Was it from some "idealizing humour?"

Consider the lay by Peire de Rogiers:

> Bitter, bitter my distress must be,
> And never, never must my heart give up
> Its great and overwhelming grief for her,
> Nor I be granted e'en a passing hope
> Of joy however sweet, however good.
> Great joy could acts of prowess bring to me.
> I'll do none; all I know to want is SHE.

And the cry of Bernart of Ventadour:

"She has taken my heart, she has taken my self, she has taken me from the world, and then she has slipped away from me, leaving me with only my desire and my parched heart!"

And next from Arnaut Daniel—a nobleman who turned wandering jongleur and whose poems, according to authorities on the Romance languages, are "devoid of thought"—are two verses which seem to me to possess the very demeanour of negative mysticism and to display its invariable metaphors.

"I love and seek her so eagerly that I believe the very violence of my desires for her would deprive me of all desire whatsoever could one lose aught by loving well.

[1] Generally referred to by a symbolic name or *senhal,* even as the Sufi mystics refer to God in their poems!

For her heart drowns mine in a never-diminishing flood. . . .

"I want neither the Roman Empire nor to be named its pope [and for a very good reason!], if I am not to be brought back to her for whom my heart is ablaze and cleft in twain. But if she has not solaced my anguish with a kiss before the New Year, she destroys me and I am damned."

The intuition which directs this inquiry must be followed to the extreme end. If the Lady is not simply the Church of Love of the Cathars (as Aroux and Péladan considered they were entitled to think) nor the Sophia Maria of the Gnostic heresies (the Feminine Principle of Divinity), why should she not be the *Anima*, or, more precisely, man's *spiritual* element, that which the soul imprisoned in his body desires with a nostalgic love that death alone can satisfy?

In the *Kephalaia* or Chapters of Manes,[1] Chapter Ten tells how the elect person who has renounced the world receives the imposition of hands (among the Cathars the *consolamentum*, usually given at the approach of death); how he thus sees that he is "ordained" in the Spirit of Light; how at the last, in the moment of death, the *Form of Light,* which is his spirit, appears to him and consoles him with a *kiss*; how his angel offers him its right hand and also *greets* him with the Kiss of Love; how finally the elect person venerates his own *Form of Light*, his *feminine Saviour*. Let us now recall that a troubadour lovesick with real love awaited from the Lady of his Thoughts— who was in essence unattainable, and put "in too lofty a place for him" [2]—no more than a single kiss, a single look, a single greeting. Geoffrey Rudel, after long being in

[1] Discovered at the Fayum in Egypt in 1930 and published by C. Schmidt at Stuttgart in 1935.

[2] It is well known that one of the set themes of courtly rhetoric is the complaint that one "loves in too lofty a place." Scholars tell us that the poor troubadour, of socially low extraction, as a rule, fell in with the wife of some high and mighty baron, who disdained him. No doubt that happened in a few cases. But it does not account for the same plaint being breathed in the poems of Alfonso of Aragon, a most powerful king. For him, obviously, no woman in *this* world was too high. The real question is why the poet chooses to cast his love so high and chooses the unattainable.

love with the image of a woman he has never seen, beholds her at last after a sea passage and dies in the arms
of the Countess of Tripoli as soon as she has bestowed
upon him a single kiss of peace and a greeting. That is a
legend, but a legend drawn from poems which unmistakably celebrate "faraway love." Other women are said to
have been "real." Were they indeed more substantial than
a psychical event?

Several writers have suggested that the *historical puzzle*
could be solved by supposing that the Heretical Church
was reduced to clandestine operation, and that the troubadours were its agents. From that puzzle we now pass to
the mystery of a strictly religious passion, which involves
a mystical view of man. That view in turn is strongly upheld by the very experience of the human spirit. Let us
see if, by going between the points and limiting oscillations of our inquiry, we can get to the reality which usually
lies intermediately, the reality of courtly lyric poetry, even
though, because intermediate, it is by so much less
"clear" and less "pure."

8

Objections

There is a risk that the importance of the conclusions
to which the two preceding chapters point will be judged by the number of objections to which those conclusions
give rise. I hope to gain from criticism, and I do not want
to repress it. But the reader will appreciate my dealing
with the doubts that have very likely come over him so
far and my trying to dispel them.

There are, I think, four objections, and they are as
follows:

1. The Religion of the Cathars is still imperfectly understood, and it is therefore at the very least premature
to assume that this religion was the source, or a chief
source, of courtly poems.

2. The troubadours never admitted being of this reli-

gion, and never stated that this religion was the subject of their poetry.

3. On the contrary, the love which they extol is but the idealization or sublimation of sexual desire.

4. Out of a confused mixture of Manichaean and Neo-Platonic doctrines operating upon a background of Celt-Iberian traditions it is difficult to see how there could have arisen a rhetoric as highly elaborate as that of the troubadours.

With those objections I shall deal seriatim.

1. A RELIGION IMPERFECTLY UNDERSTOOD

If the Catharist religion were not known at all, then the problem of courtly lyric poetry would remain completely obscure, as the authorities on Romance languages allow. For my part, I cannot regard as absurd a poetic and morality of love out of which were to come in later centuries the most splendid of Western literary works. Furthermore, certain points about Catharist rites and beliefs have now been established beyond dispute. The origins of the Heresy are Manichaean. When we recall what was said above (II, 2) about the *essentially lyrical* character of Manichaean dogmas in general, it emerges that any small piece of additional information about this or that qualification or alteration to which the dogmas were subject in the Southern Church would not weigh much either for or against what I am contending. *What should be looked for in courtly rhetoric is not rational or precise equivalences of the dogma*, but the lyrical and psalmodic development of the fundamental symbolism. Likewise, to take a modern example, the "Christian sentiment" which is discerned in the poetry of Baudelaire is not a term for term transposition of Catholic dogma. It is rather the manifestation of a certain and even of a definite sensibility which but for Catholic dogma could not be imagined, and to this are added elements of vocabulary and syntax which are unmistakably of liturgical origin. It is not going too far to suppose that the strains which we have noted in the work of the Provençal poets stand in a similar relation to Neo-Manichaeism.[1]

[1] It is also credible that in many cases the correspondences of Catharist doctrine with courtly poems are very close. In a study

For that matter, the heretical tonality of the set phrases and expressions in the rhetoric of courtly love becomes evident as soon as those phrases and expressions are compared with the clerical poetry of the period. A specialist as sceptical as Jeanroy does not fail to notice it. Writing of the abstract lyrical poetry of the troubadours of the thirteenth century and how it tends to fuse God and the Lady of Thoughts, he writes: "It will be said that these are but rhetorical figures without consequence. Nevertheless the question is: Are not the theories which the troubadours developed with their grave intentness at the antipodes of Christianity? They must have noticed it. And why in their poems is there no hint of that internal rift, of that *dissidio*, which renders some of Petrarch's verses so full of pathos?" [1]

2. THE TROUBADOURS KEEP THE SECRET

To the theory that the troubadours were secretly Cathars several recent writers have objected that no courtly poet ever gave away the show, even after being converted to Catholic orthodoxy. That is to attribute to a man of the twelfth century a form of consciousness which he could not possibly have. If we try to place ourselves in the medieval atmosphere, it becomes clear that the absence of any symbolical meaning in a poem would have been something far more offensive then than it can be now. To a medieval man every thing meant some other

---

of one of the last of the troubadours ("Peire Cardinal était-il hérétique?" in *Revue d'Histoire des Religions,* June 1938), Lucia Varga goes so far as to propose that some of the poems of the troubadours should be used as *sources* of the Heresy. In support, she quotes some verses by Peire Cardinal (or Cardenal) which reproduce the exact terms of a Catharist prayer published by Döllinger. For example, "Give me the power to love those that thou lovest" (Cardenal) and "Vouchsafe to us that we may love those that Thou lovest" (Prayer). But it must also be noticed that Peire Cardenal, a true Cathar, speaks reprovingly of the "courtesy" in a poem where he says: "I do not engage in stupid exploits. . . . I have got away from love." I shall return to the theme of the poets of courtly love being compelled to tack between the twofold condemnation pronounced upon sexual love by the Perfect and upon idealized but adulterous love by the Catholics.

[1] *Poésie lyrique des troubadours,* II, p. 306.

things as in dreams, and this without any translation into concepts on his part. That is to say, he had no need to formulate the meaning of the symbols he used nor to become fully conscious of them. He was innocent of the rationalism which causes people today to abstract and empty of all significant overtones the objects to which they attend.[1] One of the best historians of medieval manners, Huizinga, provides a pertinent instance of this in the behaviour of Suso the mystic: [2]

"Towards the end of the Middle Ages two factors dominate religious life: the extreme saturation of the religious atmosphere, and a marked tendency of thought to embody itself in images.

"Individual and social life, in all their manifestations, are imbued with the conceptions of faith. There is not an object or an action, however trivial, that is not constantly correlated with Christ or salvation. All thinking tends to religious interpretation of individual things; there is an enormous unfolding of religion in daily life. This spiritual wakefulness, however, results in a dangerous state of tension, for the presupposed transcendental feelings are sometimes dormant, and whenever this is the case, all that is meant to stimulate spiritual consciousness is reduced to appalling commonplace profanity, to a startling worldliness in other-worldly guise. . . .

"Even in the case of a sublime mystic like Henry Suso, the craving for hallowing every action in daily life verges in our eyes on the ridiculous. He is sublime when, following the usages of profane love, he celebrates New Year's Day and May Day by offering a wreath and a song to his betrothed, Eternal Wisdom, or when, out of reverence for the Holy Virgin, he renders homage to all womankind and walks in the mud to let a beggar-woman pass. But what are we to think of what follows? At table Suso eats three-quarters of an apple in the name of the Trinity and the remaining quarter in commemoration of "the love with which the heavenly Mother gave her tender child Jesus an apple to eat"; and for this reason he eats

---

[1] For example, in the Middle Ages a man was too "naïve" to be able to devote himself to any material he deemed absurd— that is, material which lacked a religous significance and a fixed position in the scheme of values he accepted.

[2] *The Waning of the Middle Ages,* op. cit., pp. 136–37.

the last quarter with the paring, as little boys do not peel their apples. After Christmas he does not eat it, for then the infant Jesus was too young to eat apples. He drinks in five draughts because of the five wounds of the Lord, but as blood and water flowed from the side of Christ, he takes his last draught twice. This is, indeed, pushing the sanctification of life to extremes."

Must it be held that this is a drop from symbol into allegory? Certainly, but carried to an evident excess. Huizinga remarks some pages later that the simple religious sense of the people did not need to have its faith intellectually justified; the visible image of holy things was enough to establish their reality. This shows that in the eyes of the initiated and in those of sympathizers with the Church of Love the "secret" of the troubadours served as a *symbolical witness*. In the ordinary way it could not occur to any one that the symbols were invalid unless expounded and accounted for in non-symbolical fashion.

A contrary objection had been raised. How is it that no converted Cathar ever gave away the troubadours as being propagators of the Heresy? That, however, is easily answered. Obviously the troubadours were not looked upon as either preachers or missionaries; at most as Believers, and more often as merely sympathetic and friendly. Anyhow, such distinctions were much less sharp than they are now. The troubadours, for the benefit of a public in which the majority favoured the Heresy, made up their lays about a kind of love which happened to correspond (and to respond) to a very difficult moral situation, the situation that had been produced both by the religious condemnation of sexuality by the Perfect and by a natural revolt against the orthodox conception of marriage which had recently been affirmed afresh in the Gregorian reform. They had accordingly to protect themselves on two flanks—against the severity of the Perfect and against the severity of Catholics.

Nevertheless, it is easy to understand that the peculiar position of heretics caused some poets to be very discreet in indicating that, apart from the habitual symbolism which spoke for itself, their work possessed an exact double meaning. Hence symbols were sometimes vehicles of allegory as well, and took on a cryptographic guise. This happened with the school of the *trobar clus,* to which I have already referred. While on the subject of this school, Jeanroy remarks: [1] "Another way [of "baffling the reader"] was to put a sacred notion into profane dress, and to apply to divine love phrases appropriated by custom to the expression of human love." He claims not "to be able to unravel" the causes of this "singular perversion of taste in a form of literature that had newly arisen." The troubadour Alegret has, however, declared significantly:

"My verse must seem nonsense to fools who cannot understand it in two ways. . . . If some one wishes to challenge this line, let him come forward, and I shall show how it was possible to put in two [variant, three] words with various meanings."

There is no reason to suppose that the troubadours engaged in this skilful confusing of the sense (entrebescar, the Provençals called it, meaning "to interweave") merely as a literary exercise for the purpose of "puzzling their hearers with conundrums." "I interweave words rare, dark and colourful, pensively pensive," Rambaut of Orange writes. And Marcabru says: "Wise beyond doubt I hold him who divines what each word in my song means." It is true that he adds—sally or precaution?— "Because I myself am hard put to it to light up my dark speech."

How far a troubadour himself understood the deep purport of his symbols is something, indeed, that cannot be determined. After all, the general run of human beings are very little conscious of using metaphors.[2] What I quoted above about the artless way in which medieval people accepted symbolism needs to be borne in mind. Symbols were not translatable into prosaic and rational concepts. The question has therefore only to be asked concerning the *double* allegorical meaning. Furthermore, all this poetry was being produced in an atmosphere highly charged with passion. The happenings recorded in contemporary chronicles are among the wildest and most *surréaliste* in the history of European manners. A jealous lord killed his wife's favourite troubadour, and had the dead man's heart served up to her on a dish. The lady

---

[1] Op. cit., II, p. 16.

[2] If some inarticulate man copies the letters he sends to his beloved out of a text-book, it does not follow that the expressions he uses do not seem to him to express his true and sincere emotion.

ate it without knowing what it was. Her lord having told her, "Sir," she said, "you have given me such a delicious dish that never shall I partake of any other"; and she threw herself out of the window of the keep. In an atmosphere where such events were possible, poets, it will be agreed, can have had no difficulty in "colouring" a symbolism originally dogmatic.

3. COURTLY LOVE IS BUT THE IDEALIZATION OF SEXUAL DESIRE

This is the most common view. Against it is the fact that medieval symbolism usually operated from high to low—from heaven to earth. That is enough to dispose of the modern theories to which the materialistic prejudice has given rise. But we must enter into detail. Against Wechssler,[1] who also insists that courtly lyrical poetry is an expression of the religious sentiment of the time,[2] Jeanroy writes:

"In these bold claims one error of fact is easily detected. It may be admitted that in time the lay was emptied of its initial content and became no more than a tissue of hollow set phrases. But from the beginning till the end of the twelfth century that was not so. In the poems of that period the expression of carnal desire is so strong and occasionally so brutal that it is really impossible to mistake the nature of the poets' aspirations."

If that was so we may wonder why the author is embarrassed and almost irritable upon having to admit how ambiguous are the expressions of courtesy and their mystical undertones. He says: "Unquestionably the religious ideas of a period generally influence the view taken of love, and so too the vocabulary of courtship is modelled on that of devotion. Once 'adore' had become a synonym of 'love,' that first metaphor led to many others." In the face of that passage, it is hard to understand why Jeanroy rejects without discussion Wechssler's writings, in which it is contended that the "theories of love-making in the Middle Ages are but a reflection of the religious ideas of the period." Why is he so anxious to maintain at all costs

[1] E. Wechssler, *Das Kulturproblem des Minnesangs,* 2 vols. (Halle, 1909), op. cit.

[2] But Catholic and not heretical.

that the poems of the troubadours contain "realistic" notations and exact descriptions of the beloved Lady when elsewhere the troubadours are reproached with having used only stereotyped epithets? Geoffrey Rudel, Prince of Blaye, states quite clearly that his Lady is a creation of his mind, and that she vanishes at dawn. Elsewhere it is "a faraway princess" that he says he wishes to love. Yet M. Jeanroy is disturbed to find in Rudel's poems "details that appear to plunge us into reality and that there is nothing to explain." Here is an instance which he gives: "I am in doubt on the subject of a certain thing and my heart is in suspense: it is that all that the brother refuses me I hear the sister grant to me." On the other hand, Rudel describes his Lady: her body is *"gras, delgat et gen."* [1] In the first sentence which Jeanroy interprets as yielding a biographical indication there is an evident mystical sense: "What the body denies me, the spirit grants" (That is one instance; there are still other meanings). And as for the "realistic" epithets that are taken to apply to a "real" Lady, epithets completely *identical* are to be found in thirty or so other poets! (It is not surprising that I forget which learned student of the period declared that it looked as though the poetry of the troubadours had been the work of a single author singing the praises of always *the same Lady!*) Where, then, is the "strong and brutal" expression of an obviously carnal desire to be found? Is it in the crudity of certain terms? But such crudity was common and natural in the days before middle-class puritanism. The contention is anachronistic.

Here instead is a document that supports the symbolical theory. In a poem on women Rambaut of Orange says that if you want to win them you should be brutal, "punch them on the nose" (this is crude enough, surely?), and force them, because that is what they like.

"As for me [he adds], I behave differently, because I do not care about loving. I do not want to be put to trouble for the sake of women, any more than if they were all my sisters; and so with women I am humble, obliging, frank and gentle, fond, respectful, and faithful. . . . I love nothing, except this ring, which is dear to me because it has been on a finger. . . . But I am going too far; stop,

[1] "Plump, delicate, and pretty."

tongue! Because to say too much is worse than mortal sin!"

This same Rambaut of Orange, however, wrote admirable poems in praise of his Lady; and we saw earlier that a *ring* (such as Tristan and Iseult exchange) was the symbol of a constancy which happened not to be that of the body. Let me also stress the important fact that the courtly virtues of humility, frankness, respect, and fidelity to one's Lady are being expressly connected here with a rejection of physical love. Moreover, we shall see later[1] that in Dante the images are the more passionate and "realistic" in proportion to Beatrice's progressive rise in the hierarchy of mystical abstraction, where she becomes first Philosophy, then Wisdom, and finally Divine Knowledge. And one more small fact is that in the twenty-sixth Canto of the *Purgatorio* two of the troubadours most ardent in praising the beauty of their Ladies, the Provençal Arnaut Daniel and the Tuscan Guido Guinicelli, are found in the sodomites' circle.[2]

But all this only compels us to recognize how complex is a problem of which I have so far deliberately stressed only one aspect, and that the most disputed. We have too long been supposing that *cortezia* was a mere idealization of the sexual instinct. At the same time it would be going too far to assert that the mystical ideal on which *cortezia* must have been founded was always and everywhere being invoked, *or that in itself it could have only one meaning*. Nearly always an emphasis on chastity is accompanied by lewd excess. Without stopping to consider the charges of debauchery often brought against the troubadours—little, actually, is known about their lives—I may recall that at the same time as the Gnostic sects con-

---

[1] Book IV.

[2] Perhaps this is the place to mention that a courtly knight often gave his Lady the masculine title of *mi dons* (*mi dominus*), and in Spain *senhor* (*not senhora*). Andalusian and Arab troubadours did the same, and the greatest, the supremely mystical, were notoriously homosexual. However, I incline to think that here again, at least to begin with, all was religious symbol as much as or more than it was the translation of human relations. The narcissism inherent in any so-called Platonic love involves on the sexual plane obvious deviations into which it would be difficult to deny that some troubadours were tempted.

temned creation, and in particular sexual attraction, they erected on their contempt a peculiarly licentious set of morals. For example, the Carpocratians forbade procreation, and also divinized the spermatic fluid.[1] It is quite probable that the Cathars were given to similar excesses, and especially that their poorly disciplined disciples, the troubadours, were. Horrifying charges on this score are to be found in the records of the Inquisition. But these are often contradictory. At times they state that the Cathars looked upon the most gross sensual indulgence as harmless, and at others that they condemned marriage and also sexual intercourse, whether legitimate or not. Similar charges, we should remember, have been brought against every new religion, not excepting primitive Christianity. It is fair to quote the opinion of a Dominican who had occasion to search the archives of the Holy Office and who writes thus about the Cathars of Italy or Patarini:

"In spite of my careful examination of the indictments drawn by our brethren, I have not found that "consoled" heretics were guilty in Tuscany of monstrous acts or that they ever indulged, particularly between men and women, in sensual excesses."

So far, then, the scheme which I put forward at the beginning of Chapter 5 needs to be qualified as follows. Although deflexions of passion—in the strict sense I have given to the word "passion"—have a religious and mystical inspiration, they unquestionably encourage the sexual instinct *by the very fact that they seek to transcend it.*

All this leads me to assert confidently now, however hesitant I may have felt at the outset, that courtly lyrical poetry was *at least inspired* by the mysticism of the Cathars. This may look like a moderate contention, but, once it is granted, I think it implies and explains a great deal more.

So that we may better imagine how this *process of inspiration and influence* came to operate, let me offer a present-day analogy. I think it may be laid down that the data concerning *Surréalisme* and the influence of Freud's

---

[1] Cf. the documents translated and expounded in Wolfgang Schultz, *Dokumente der Gnosis* (Jena, 1910), pp. 158–64.

theories on this movement are fully determined and also
are fully known (in the complete sense of "known") to
a number of persons now living. Let us suppose that
in the future our civilization has been destroyed, and
that at some date following its destruction a historian
seeks to establish some of its details. Certain *surréaliste*
poems have been found, and he is able to translate them
and ascribe to them their correct date. He is further aware
that more or less contemporaneously with *Surréalisme*
there flourished a particular school of psychiatry. But
no writings produced by this school survive. Fascism,
which acceded to power soon afterwards, destroyed every
one of them on the ground that they were Semitic.
Nevertheless, the historian knows, thanks to booklets
issued by adversaries of this school of psychiatry, that it
put forward an erotic theory of dreams. The *surréaliste*
poems that have been preserved and translated seem
meaningless, and are open to the reproach of monotony
—always containing the same set of erotic and blood-
thirsty images and the same intense rhetoric, and it looks
as if they must all have had one author, etc. But then
some persons come along and suggest that the poems
merely describe dreams, and that perhaps they *are* no
more than dreams that have been set down in writing. The
suggestion is treated with unconcealed scepticism by authorities on the twentieth century. Thereupon, a writer—
one of those people not to be taken seriously—offers
the theory that the whole of *Surréalisme* was produced
under the influence of pyscho-analysis, and in support
of this theory points to the coincidence of dates and
the similarity of basic themes. The authorities on the
twentieth century shrug their shoulders. "Establish your
theory by means of documents," they say. "You know
very well there aren't any." "In that case, better to steer
clear of coherent theories.

"Meanwhile, your common sense is enough to show
you—

"(*a*) That the little we know about psycho-analysis does
not entitle us to look upon this doctrine as having inspired documents we already possess. (It seems clear that
Freud was above all a scientist, that he had a theory of
libido, and that he was a determinist; whereas *Surréalisme*
was above all a literary movement; none of its surviving

poems contain the word 'libido'); and these poems all lean towards idealisms and impulsiveness.)

"(*b*) *That the Surréalistes* never *stated* in any poem that they were disciples of Freud.

"(*c*) That the free will they extol is something every psychoanalyst was bound to deny.

"(*d*) Finally, that it is by no means apparent how a science having for its aim the analysis and cure of neuroses could have inspired a rhetoric of insanity, which must have been a challenge to science in general and to the science of psycho-analysis in particular."

So, the future authorities on the twentieth century. It happens, however, that we—who are living in the twentieth century—know exactly how these improbable things actually occurred. We are aware that the men who promoted the *Surréaliste* movement had read Freud and that they looked on him with the greatest respect. We are aware that but for him their theories and their poesy would alike have been altogether different. We are aware that *Surréaliste* poets felt no need and had no opportunity of referring to the *libido* in their writings. We are further aware that it was owing to *an initial misunderstanding* of the precise significance of Freud's (determinist and positivist) doctrines that the poets were led to seize on these doctrines as the subject-matter of their poesy—a most important point if all this is treated as analogical with what I am putting forward about the troubadours. And finally we are aware that it was only necessary for a few leaders of the movement to read Freud, and that the disciples were content to imitate the rhetoric of their masters.

Moreover, thanks to this analogy, it can be understood how a doctrine acts on poets less as a direct influence than by permeating their *atmosphere*, so that its central dogmas stir up shocked feelings and produce both a wish to be "in the know" and a wish to seize opportunities of self-advantage. The work of the poets who are influenced will therefore display a good many mistakes, variations, and contradictions. Hence, supposing additional information about the exact nature of Freud's theories came to light in the future, far from providing authorities on the twentieth century with the confirmation they expected, it would only seem to contradict the theory of my mere "writer, one of those people not to be taken seriously." [1]

There remains the fourth objection—that, the rhetoric of the troubadours being highly elaborate, it is difficult to see how a confused mixture of Manichaean and Neo-Platonist doctrines operating upon a background of Celt-Iberian traditions could have given rise to it. This objection I have so far dealt with only indirectly and by passing allusion. It deserves a chapter to itself.

9

Arab Mystical Poetry

It happens that as early as the ninth century there occurred an equally "unlikely" fusion of Iranian Manichaeism, Neo-Platonism, and Mohammedanism in Arabia, and the fusion was reflected in a religious poetry employing erotic metaphors that are strikingly akin to those of courtly rhetoric. In the twelfth century the chief writers of this kind of poetry were al Hallaj, al Gazali, and Suhrawardi of Aleppo. All three were troubadours of supreme Love, of the Veiled Idea, which they treated as beloved object but also as symbol of a longing for the divine.

Suhrawardi, who died in 1191, supposed Plato—whom he knew at second-hand from Plotinus, Proclus, and the Athenian school—to be a successor of Zoroaster. Indeed, his Neo-Platonism displays marked Persian mythical features. In particular, the doctrines about an antithetical relation of the World of Light and the World of Darkness which he borrowed from the Zend-Avesta were those that had inspired Manes and that became the root of the Catharist faith. These doctrines—exactly as happened later with those of the Cathars—were transmuted into a chivalrous love rhetoric, the nature of which is indicated by the titles of two mystical treatises, *The Lovers' Famil-*

---

[1] *Eppur si muove!* He would nevertheless be right, and the recognized authorities on the twentieth century in his day wrong.

iar and *The Romance of the Seven Beauties*. Moreover, at the time these and other similar treatises appeared there arose in a section of Islam a theological controversy of the same kind as occurred a little later in the medieval world of the West. It is true that in the Mohammedan world the controversy was made more intricate by a denial that man is able to love God (as the evangelical summary of the Law commands him). According to Mohammedanism, a finite creature can only love what is finite. In order therefore to express that love of the divine which they believed themselves to be experiencing, Arab mystics of the twelfth century had to resort to symbols having a secret meaning.[1] But, apart from this peculiarity—not without parallel in the situation of courtly rhetoric—the problems set up by the poetry of the Near East and by that of the West are identical.

Orthodox Mohammedanism was no more able than Roman Catholicism to allow that there is in man an element which in being cultivated will bring about the fusion of individual souls with the Divinity. But it was precisely this potential union of Creator and creature that was being implied in the erotico-religious *language* of Arab mystic poetry. The symbolism employed by the poets caused them accordingly to be accused of holding a disguised Manichaeism, and the charge cost al Hallaj and Suhrawardi their lives.[2] There is something poignant in the discovery that the grounds of the controversy are those which reappear in the case of the troubadours, and, later on—as we shall see—in, *mutatis mutandis,* the case of the great Western mystics from Meister Eckhart to John of the Cross.

A brief account of the "courtly" themes that figure in poetic expositions of Arab mysticism will show how thoroughly the parallel holds both as regards inspiration and expression. Suhrawardi speaks of lovers as being *Brethren of the Truth*. This was a name given to all

---

[1] Thus praise of wine—wine being forbidden by the Prophet —became symbolical of the divine intoxication of love.

[2] According to Louis Massignon, *Passion de al Hallaj*, p. 161, the chief charge brought against him was in these terms: "To adore God from love alone is the crime of the Manichaeans. . . . These adore God with a *physical* love, through the magnetic attraction of iron to iron, and their particles of light are impelled like a magnet back towards the focus of light whence they came."

mystic lovers who were at one with their beloved in a
mutual idealization [1] and who came to form a community analogous to the Catharist Church of Love. Mystics
of the illuminative school of Suhrawardi were inspired by
Persian Manichaeism, and recently discovered documents
relating to this faith contain a fable about a lovely maiden
who awaits the true believer on the far side of the
Bridge of Sinvat. When he appears she says to him: "I
am thyself!" According to certain interpreters of troubadour mysticism, the Lady of Thoughts is no other than
the spiritual and angelical part of man—his true *self*.
This may help towards a fuller understanding of what
I have called "the narcissism of passion." [2]

The Lovers' Familiar is built upon an allegory of "The
Castle of the Soul" which has various floors and compart-
ments. In one compartment there is a feminine being
called The Veiled Idea. She possesses secrets that will assuage, and it is she who can impart magic. [3] Other allegorical characters in the Castle include Beauty, Desire
and Dread, the Well-Informed, the Tester, the Well-
Known—all of whom recall the *Roman de la Rose*. The
same chivalric symbolism is found in *The Romance of
the Seven Beauties,* the treatise in which Nizami of Ganja
describes the adventures of seven maidens attired in the
colours of the planets and who are visited by a knight-
king. The Castle of the Soul became a favourite symbol
for Ruysbroek and Saint Teresa. In a poem by the "Lovers' Sultan," Omar Ibn al Faridh—to take one among
dozens of instances—the author describes the terrible
passion holding him in thrall:

> My fellow-citizens, surprised at seeing me a slave, said:
>   "Why is this youth mad?"
> And what can they say of me except that I am con-
>   cerned with Nu'm?
> Indeed, yes, I am concerned with Nu'm.
> When Nu'm gratifies me with a glance, I mind not if
>   Su'da is unkind.

Nu'm is a conventional name for a man's beloved, and

[1] Henry Corbin, Introduction to *The Lovers' Familiar.*

[2] Book 1, Chapter 8, in connection with Tristan.

[3] The Celtic Essylt was also a magician, "an object of contemplation and a mystic vision."

here it means "God." The troubadours also gave to their Lady of Thoughts a conventional name or *senhal*; and authorities today have vainly striven to discover who are the historical persons such names refer to.

Both the *salutation* and the *salute* that the initiated wish to give on approaching the Sage, but that the latter considerately gives first, [1] are a constant poetic theme of the troubadours, and later of Dante, and eventually of Petrarch. All these poets attach extreme importance to the "salute" given by the Lady, and their doing so is easily understood if we bear in mind the two senses of *salutare*—namely, "to greet" and "to save."

Arab mystics all insist that the *secret* of divine Love must be kept. They constantly complain of prying persons (*râgib* or *wâchi*) who want to find out about the mysteries, but not to take part in them with a wholehearted faith. To somebody's hasty question: "What is Sufi-ism?" al Hallaj replies: "Do not turn on Us; see our finger which has already been stained with the blood of lovers." Moreover, the prying are suspected of evil intentions: it is they who give lovers away to the orthodox authorities. Likewise in most of the Provençal poems there are characters described as *losengiers*—backbiters, careless gossips, spies—upon whom the troubadours heap invective. Our learned commentators nowadays have been rather hard put to it to explain these inconvenient *losengiers*, and have sought to dispose of the problem thus presented by alleging that in the twelfth century lovers must set great store by keeping their affairs secret (whereby no doubt they differed from lovers in other periods!).

Then also the eulogy of a death due to love is the leit-motiv of Arab mystic poesy. Ibn al Faridh wrote:

> The repose of love is a weariness; its onset, a sickness; its end, death.
> For me, however, death through love is life; I give thanks to my Belovèd that she has held it out to me.
> Whoever does not die of his love is unable to live by it.

This is the very cry of Western mysticism, *but also* it is

[1] Suhrawardi, *The Rustling of Gabriel's Wing*.

that of Provençal poesy. Saint Teresa's ejaculatory prayer was "I die of not being able to die!" Al Hallaj wrote: "In killing me you shall make me live, because for me to die is to live and to live is but to die." Life is indeed the terrestrial day of beings in a contingent world, in the whirl of matter; but death is the Night of Illumination, the vanishing of illusory forms, the Soul's union with the Beloved, a communion with Absolute Being. Hence, for Arab mystics, it is Moses who symbolizes the greatest of Lovers, because in having declared on Sinai his wish *to see* God he is held to have expressed a wish for death. And it is easy to understand that the final stage of the illuminative way taken by Suhrawardi and Al Hallaj had to be religious martyrdom at the summit of *joy d'amor*.

"Al Hallaj went to execution laughing. I said to him: 'Master, why this?' He replied: 'Such is the coquetry of beauty as she draws her lovers to her.'"

Finally, it has been ascertained that so-called Platonic love was in honour among the members of a tribe enjoying a great prestige in the Arab world, the tribe of the Banu Ohdri whose members died of love owing to their persistent exaltation of chaste desire, in accordance with the words of the Koran: "He who loves, who abstains from all that is forbidden, who holds his love secret, and who dies of his secret, he dies a martyr." "Ohdri love" became all the way into Andalusia the name of that which was going to become Courtly Love, first in the south of France, and then in the north of that country, in readiness for *Tristan*. . . .

Can it be established that Arab poesy actually influenced *cortezia*? Renan wrote in 1863: "An abyss separates the form and spirit of Romance poetry from the form and spirit of Arab poetry." Another scholar, Dozy, his contemporary, declares that Arab influence upon the troubadours has not been established "and it will not be." Today his peremptory tone makes us smile. (How often has someone written that an abyss separates Cathars and troubadours and that my contention would never be established . . . !) From Baghdad to Andalusia Arab poetry is one, one in language and one thanks to continuous exchanges. Andalusia was contiguous to the Spanish dominions, whose dynasties were mingled with those of Languedoc and Poitou. By now the blooming of Andalusian lyricism in the tenth and eleventh centuries has become well known. The detailed prosody of the *zadjal* is that adopted by the first troubadour, William of Poitiers, in five of the eleven poems by him that have come down to us. To try to establish Andalusian influence upon the courtly poems is no longer needful.[1] And I could fill pages with passages from Arabs and Provençals about which our great specialists of "the abyss which separates" would possibly fail to guess whether they were penned north or south of the Pyrenees. The matter is settled. But now here is what I am concerned with.

There occurred during the twelfth century in Languedoc and in the Limousin one of the most extraordinary spiritual confluences of history. On the one hand, a strong Manichaean religious current, which had taken its rise in Persia, flowed through Asia Minor and the Balkans as far as Italy and France, bearing the esoteric doctrines of Maria Sophia and of love for the Form of Light. On the other hand, a highly refined rhetoric, with its set forms, themes, and characters, its ambiguities invariably recurring in the same places, and indeed its symbolism, pushes out from Irak and the Sufis, who were inclined alike to Platonism and Manichaeism, and reaches Arabic Spain, then, leaping over the Pyrenees, it comes in the south of France upon a society that seems to have but awaited its arrival in order to *state* what it had not dared and had not been able to avow either in the clerical tongue or in the common vernacular. Courtly lyrical poetry was the offspring of that encounter.

Thus it was that from the final confluence of the "heresies" of the spirit and those of desire, which had both come from the one East along either shore of the Civilizing Sea, there was born the great western model of the language of passion-love.

---

[1] Cf. the work of the American, A. R. Nykl, his translation of *The Dove's Necklace* by Ibn Hazm—an exposition of Arab courtly love—and his general survey, *Hispano-Arabic Poetry and Its Relations with the Old Provençal Troubadours* (Baltimore, 1946). V. also the writings of Louis Massignon, Henry Pérès, Emile Dermenghem, Menendez Pidal, Karl Appel, etc.

10

A General View of Courtliness

Returning after a long interval to the problems raised in the preceding pages, I feel the need of bringing together at this point a number of fresh considerations. I should like the reader to decide whether they invalidate or, on the contrary, enlarge—in order the better to substantiate—my original contentions (by which I stand), that between *cortezia* and the religious atmosphere of Catharism there was a deeply embedded bond.

It will very likely have been noticed that above I confined myself to *analogies* in order to suggest the possibility of relations between a form of mysticism, a religious notion, or simply a view of man, and a determinate lyrical form. I referred to the connexion between Sufi-ism and the courtly poems of the Arabs; I suggested how a century or more hence the Freudian influence on the school of *Surréalisme* in this present century might be disputed. As originally put forward, my contentions roused some vigorous criticism without invariably being fully grasped. [1] The criticism, plus the numerous discoveries made in the last fifteen years by authorities on courtly love, Catharism, and Manichaeism, as well, possibly, as the experiences I myself have had and my own

---

[1] It should be pointed out that the most virulent attempts made in print to confute me were directed far less against my contentions than against the single theory mentioned in Chapter 7 of this Book II—the theory of Rahn, Aroux, and Péladan, that the poems of the troubadours were a kind of secret language of Catharism. To dispose of that really excessive simplification it is enough to re-read Chapters 8 and 9. I feel that my critics are rather to be held responsible for it than I myself, although I did fall into some incautious statements. It is these, unfortunately, that most helped to ensure the success of the book with a public that read it hurriedly; something, however, not altogether unprecedented.

researches—all that brings me today to a conception of *cortezia* hardly less "historical" than the one I sketched above, but far more psychological. I pointed to one *factual* relation (places and dates that are identical whatever we think) between Cathars and troubadours. I ventured to say that this relation cannot be ignored, and that the absence of any connexion between the two sets of people would be more astonishing than no matter what theory—"serious" or "frivolous"—of the nature of the connexion. But I took care not to go into the actual detail of the "influence," as many historians go for whom the real is only established by means of written records. I shall now venture a little further, but in my own direction and not in theirs. I put forward no textual and "scientific" solution of the problem, based on documents, which would mean that, in the words of Karl Jaspers, "the question no longer pauses there where it runs into mystery but goes on stupidly to lose its point by extracting a reply." I should like instead to penetrate more deeply into the *problematical* character of Courtly Love, while at the same time treating it as definitely as possible, and to do this because I think the task vital for the West of the present day, and also for the moral and religious conduct of us all.

So I am going to set out a few facts as though they were traps. I shall avoid indicating any causal connexion, and shall refrain from expressing any conclusions that might be taken out of their context, keyless chords upon which hasty critics and readers might otherwise fasten in order to exclaim: "Proofs!" or "How true!"

1. *The Psychical Revolution of the Twelfth Century.*

A neo-Manichaean heresy, come from the Near East through Armenia and Bogomil Bulgaria—that of the Goodmen or Cathars, ascetics who condemned marriage but who founded a Church of Love in opposition to the Church of Rome [1]—swiftly spread over France from Rheims, and from the north of Italy pushed into Spain, and then spread all over Europe. Simultaneously other heterodox movements agitated people and clergy. They

---

[1] As the word AMOR is opposed to ROMA. The heretics held it against the Catholic Church that they had *inverted* the very name of God, which is Love.

were movements which sought to counter ambitious pre-
lates and the holy pomps of the Church by means of a
refined spiritualism, and they resulted in some cases in
the formulation more or less deliberately of premature
naturalistic and even materialistic doctrines. Their excesses might be said to illustrate in advance Pascal's well-
known saying that he who wants to play the angel behaves like a beast. But really those excesses betrayed
the revolutionary character of the problems which the
age threw up and its profound *inordinatio,* of which the
most holy saints and the most learned doctors underwent
and suffered the passion at least as much as they succeeded in transmuting it into theological virtues and truths.
At the level of theological speculation, Saint Bernard of
Clairvaux and Abélard were the poles of this drama in
the Church. But outside the Church and in its margins,
among the common people to whom such disputes appeared *remote and incomprehensible,* there were increasing oscillations. From Henry of Lausanne and Peter
of Bruys to Amaury of Bène and the Ortliebian Brothers in Strasbourg, all condemned marriage. Incidentally,
marriage had just been forbidden to priests by the
monkish Pope Gregory VII. Against this, many of the
heretical preachers professed that, as man is divine,
nothing done with his body—the devil's booty—can af-
fect the salvation of his soul. "No sin above the navel,"
one Dualist bishop declared in order to excuse the li-
cense which several sects either fostered or put up with.

An entirely new kind of poetry sprang up in the South
of France, the birthplace of Catharism. It extolled the
Lady of Thoughts, the Platonic Idea of a feminine principle, and the encouragement of Love contrary to marriage, and at the same time of chastity.

Saint Bernard of Clairvaux undertook a campaign
against Catharism, founded an orthodox ascetic order to
match that of the Goodmen or Perfect, and then set up in
opposition to *cortezia* the first really effectual form of
emotional mysticism in the West—that of the Divine Love.

Many commentaries on the Song of Songs were written
for the nuns of the earliest convents for women, from
the Abbey of Fontevrault—so near the home of the first
troubadour, Count William of Poitiers—to as far as the
Paraclete of Héloïse. This epithalamian mysticism is to

be found in Bernard of Clairvaux, Hugh of Saint Victor, and Abélard himself.

Héloïse and Abélard first experienced themselves and then described abundantly in courtly poems and in letters the first great novel of passion-love in our history.

Geoffrey Rudel died in the arms of the Countess of Tripoli, the "faraway princess" whom he had loved without ever having seen. And Joachim of Floris predicted the coming incarnation of the Holy Ghost in a woman.

All that occurred either in reality, or else in an imagination that informed reality, in the places and at the time in which the legend and the myth of mortal passion were joined—in the *Romance of Tristan*.

In order to counter this powerful and almost universal rise of Love and of the cult of Idealized Woman, the Church and clergy were bound to set up a belief and a worship which met the same profound desire, as this sprang up out of the communal spirit of the time. While the Church had to fall in with that desire, the Church had also to "convert" it and lead it into the strong stream of orthodoxy.[1] Hence the repeated attempts from the beginning of the twelfth century onwards to institute a worship of the Virgin. It is from that time that Mary has generally received the title of *Regina coeli,* and it is as a queen that from that time art has depicted her. *For the Lady of Thoughts of cortezia there was substituted Our Lady.* The monastic orders which were then being founded were retorts to the orders of chivalry. A monk was "a Knight of Mary." In 1140, at Lyons, the canons set up a Feast of the Immaculate Conception of Our Lady. Saint Bernard of Clairvaux vainly protested in a famous letter against "this new feast of which the custom of the Church knows nothing, which reason does not approve, and that tradition does not authorize . . . and which introduces Novelty, the sister of Superstition and the daughter of Inconstancy." And Saint Thomas Aquinas, a hundred years after, vainly wrote in as forthright a fashion as possible, "If Mary had been conceived without sin, she

[1] Which did not prevent the Church of Rome, in the person of Pope Innocent III, who dreamed of "the empire of the world" and could not stand the defection of Northern Italy and Languedoc, from launching in 1209 a Crusade against the Cathars—the first genocide or systematic massacre of a people recorded by our "Christian" western history.

would not have needed to be redeemed by Jesus Christ."
The worship of the Virgin responded to a vital necessity
for the Church while under threat and pressure. When
several centuries later the Papacy sanctioned that worship,
the latter, without waiting for the seal of dogma, had already triumphed in all the arts.

Finally, there is another trait which cannot be attached
laterally to the others. It is in the twelfth century that
there is attested in Europe a radical change in the game
of chess which had originated in India. Instead of four
kings which had dominated the game in its first form, a
Lady (or Queen) was made to take precedence over all
other pieces, save the King, and the latter was actually
reduced to the smallest possibility of real action, even
though he remained the final state and the consecrated
figure.

2. *Oedipus and the Gods.*

Freud calls Oedipan the complex set up in the unconscious by the aggressiveness of the son against the
father, who obstructs love of the mother, and by the sentiment of guilt which ensues. The weight of patriarchal
authority compels the son to conform socially and morally;
the weight of the interdict bound up with the mother
(i.e. with the feminine principle) inhibits love; all that
has to do with woman remains "impure." This complex
of Oedipan sentiments is all the more compelling where
the social structure is the more solid, the father's power
the more assured, and the god from whom the father has
received his authority is the more reverenced. But what
happens in society where the union principle is relaxed,
the economic power in the hands of the father is divided,
and the divine power itself is broken up, either into a
plurality of gods, as in Greece, or into a god and goddess
couple as in Egypt, or finally, as in Manichaeism, into a
beneficent God (who is pure spirit) and a demiurge (who
rules matter and the flesh)? The compulsion which
created the Oedipus complex weakens proportionately.
Hatred of the father is concentrated upon the demiurge
and his handiwork: matter, flesh, procreative sexuality—
the while a purified sentiment of adoration may be
formed from the Spirit-God. At the same time love of
woman is partially released. It can be avowed in the form
of a worship for the divine archetype of woman, *on condi-*

tion that this Mother-Goddess remains a virgin, and thus escapes from the interdict which is maintained as regards a woman in the flesh. Mystical union with this feminine divinity is then tantamount to participation in the legitimate power of the luminous God, a "divinization," or literally a liberating enthusiasm, which unifies a being and "consoles" it.

3. *An Illustration*

There occurred in France in the twelfth century a marked relaxation of the patriarchal and feudal bond. Property was divided equally among all sons, by a proceeding called *pariage.* Suzerains lost authority. There was a kind of advance Renaissance of individualism. The country was invaded by a dualist religion. Finally, there was that powerful rise of the cult of Love of which I have just recalled the evidences. We are thus confronted with an actualization (or epiphany in history) of the possibility which we imagined in the sub-section above on Oedipus.

If we try to portray to ourselves the psychical and ethical situation in which a man would have been in those days, we notice first of all that he was, willy-nilly, involved in the struggle which deeply divided society, and the powers, families, and even individuals within themselves—the struggle between Heresy, which was present everywhere,[1] and Roman orthodoxy, which had been badly battered. On the Catharist side, marriage and sexuality were condemned without remission by the Perfect or *Consoled,* but were allowed in the case of mere Believers—who were the immense majority of heretics. On the Catholic side, marriage was a sacrament and yet in fact based on material and social considerations; it was imposed on the parties regardless of their feelings. Meanwhile, the relaxation of authority and of the powers allowed, as we have seen, for a fresh possibility of letting woman in, though under cover of an idealization and even of a divinization of the feminine principle. This served but to emphasize the contradiction between the two ideals (themselves in conflict!) and the reality of experience. The natural psyche and natural sensuality both writhed

[1] Cf. above the words quoted from Raimon V, Count of Toulouse, pp. 87-88.

amid the converging attacks, the antithetical condemnations, the restraints both theoretical and practical, and the freedoms that were being very obscurely foreseen in their fascinating novelty. . . .

It was at the heart of such an inextricable situation, and as though resulting from the many confusions which that situation was bound to produce, that there appeared *cortezia,* a literary "religion" of chaste Love, of idealized woman and her particular "piety," *joy d'amor,* its detailed rites, the rhetoric of the troubadours, its morals of homage and service, its "theology" and theological disputes, its initiates, the troubadours, and its Believers—the vast public, both cultivated and not, that listened to them and ensured their social fame all over Europe. Thereupon we behold this religion of ennobling love extolled by *the same men* who persisted in holding sexuality for "ugly" and "low"; and often *the same* poet is found to have been both an enthusiastic adorer of the Lady whom he extols and exalts and a scorner of woman whom he disparages; only recall the lines of Marcabru or of Rambaut of Orange quoted above.[1]

Curiously enough, the troubadours in whom this dichotomy is to be observed did not complain of it! It looks as though they had found the secret of reconciling the irreconcilable in the course of living. They seem both to reflect and to be *overcoming* the division of consciousness (in turn productive of a bad conscience) in the vast mass of a society divided, as we have seen, not only between flesh and spirit, but also between heresy and orthodoxy, and in the very heart of the Heresy, between the exigencies of the Perfect and the actual life of the Believers. . . . Thereupon let me quote one of the most sensitive modern interpreters of *cortezia,* René Nelli. He writes:

"Nearly all the ladies of the Carcassès, of the Toulousain, of the Foix, and of the Albi region, were Believers, and were aware—although married—that marriage was condemned by their Church. Many troubadours were undoubtedly Cathars, or at least were pretty fully aware of the current of ideas that had been in the air for two hundred years. In any case, they sang their lays for castle ladies, *whose bad consciences had to be pacified by song,* and who exacted from them less the illusion of a sincere love than a *spiritual antipode* to marriage, a state into which they had been forced."

The same author adds that in his opinion, "there can be no question of taking the chastity thus simulated as being either a real habit or a reflection of manners"; it has to be taken simply as "a *religious* (and therefore ceremonious) tribute rendered by imperfection to perfection"—that is to say, by the troubadours and by unsettled Believers to the morality of the Perfect.

But what after all (some present-day sceptic will say) can be the concrete meaning of the chastity extolled by jongleurs? And how account for the swift success of an alleged morality which was yet so ambiguous in Languedoc, in North Italy, Rhenish Germany, the whole of Europe, where after all "religious" passions and theology did not occupy the best part of life, and had surely not suppressed every kind of *natural* impulsion? Since Rousseau the moderns have indeed supposed that there exists a kind of normal nature upon which the pseudo-problems of culture and religion came to be super-added. . . . This touching illusion may assist them in "living," but not in the understanding of their lives. For all, the whole lot of us, lead our lives of civilized people quite without suspecting that those lives are being led amid a strictly insensate confusion of religions never completely dead, and seldom altogether understood and practised; of moral teachings which once upon a time were mutually exclusive but now are superimposed upon one another, or else combined in the background of our elementary behaviour; of unsuspected complexes which, because unsuspected, are the more active; and of instincts inherited less from some animal nature than from customs entirely forgotten, customs which have turned into mental furrows or scars, that are unconscious, and, on that account, easily confused with instinct. They were once upon a time either cruel artifices, sacred rites or magical gestures, or again profound disciplines elaborated by some kind of mysticism remote alike in time and space.

4. *Technique of "Chastity."*

Beginning in the sixth century there spread rapidly over the whole of India—both among Hindus and among

Buddhists—a religious school or "fashion" the influence of which went on growing for centuries.

"From a formal standpoint, Tantrism looks like a new and triumphal manifestation of shaktism. The secret force (*Shakti*) which animates the Cosmos and sustains the gods (among whom come first Siva and Buddha) . . . is strongly personified; it is the Goddess, Wife and Mother. . . . Creative dynamism falls to the Goddess . . . worship is concentrated upon this cosmic feminine principle; meditation takes account of her 'powers,' and Shakti makes deliverance possible. . . . In certain Tantric sects woman herself becomes a sacred object, an incarnation of the Mother. The religious apotheosis of woman was in fact common to every mystical current in the Indian Middle Ages. . . . Tantrism is *par excellence a technique,* even though it is fundamentally a metaphysic and a form of mysticism. . . . Meditation 'wakens' certain occult forces, which slumber within every man, and these, once awakened, transform the human body into a mystical body." [1] The object of the Tantric Yoga ceremonial, with its control of breathing, repetition of *mantras* or holy forms of words, and its meditation on *mandalas* or images containing symbols of the world and of the gods—was to transcend the human state. Buddhist Tantrism had close analogies in Hindu Hathayoga, a technique for the control of the body and of vital energy. Certain postures (*mūdras*) described in Hathayoga were intended "to use as a means of divinization and hence in integration, final unification, the human function *par excellence,* that which determines indeed the incessant cycles of births and deaths—sexual function." [2]

Thus speaks Siva: [3] "For my devout followers, I am going to describe the gesture of Lightning (*vajroli mūdra*) which destroys the Darkness of the world and should be treated as the secret of secrets." The details in the text allude to a technique of the sexual act without consummation, for "he who keeps (or takes back) his seed into his body, what can he have to fear of death?" as it is said in one Upanishad. In Tantrism, *maithuna* (or

[1] Mircea Eliade, *Techniques du Yoga,* pp. 176 to 191.

[2] Op. cit., p. 199

[3] *Siva Samhita,* 4, 78–102. Cf. Alain Daniélou, *Yoga, The Method of Reintegration* (1949), pp. 45 seq.

ceremonial sexual union) was treated as a Yogi exercise.
But most of the texts in which it is described "are written in a language intentionally secret and obscure,
with double meanings, in which a state of consciousness is
referred to in erotic terms" [1]—or quite as well the other
way round. This is carried so far as to make the reader
"never certain whether *maithuna* is a real act or simply
an allegory." At all events, the object is the "supremely
great happiness . . . the joy of annihilation of the self."
And this "erotic beatitude," obtained by the stoppage not
of pleasure but of its physical effect, was resorted to as
an immediate experience for entering into the Nirvanic
state. The texts point out that "otherwise the devout person becomes the prey of the sad Karmic law, like any
voluptuary."

What about woman in all that? She remained the *object* of a form of worship. Regarded as "sole source of
joy and rest, the woman lover synthesizes the whole of
feminine nature: she is mother, sister, wife, daughter. . . ,
she is the way to salvation." [2] Thus Tantrism included
the "novelty" of "attempting the tran-substantiation of
the human body with the aid of an act which, in every
form of asceticism, symbolizes the state *par excellence*
of sin and death—i.e. the sexual act." [3] But this act was
invariably described as that of man. Woman remained
passive, impersonal, pure principle, without features and
without name.

One late mystical school of Tantrism, *Sahajiyā,* "expands the erotic ritual to astonishing proportions. . . .
Great importance is given to every kind of 'love' and
the ritual of *maithuna* is made the goal of a long and
difficult ascetic apprenticeship. . . . During a first period
of four months a neophyte has to *serve* a 'devout woman'
like a servant, sleeping in the same room with her, and
then at her feet. During a further four months, while continuing to wait on her as before, he sleeps in the same
bed and on the left side. During a third period of four
months he sleeps on the right side. Then the couple have

---

[1] Mircea Eliade, op. cit., pp. 205 seq. Sometimes there are
"as many as five equivalent meanings for one term."

[2] L. de la Vallée-Poussin, *Bouddhisme, études et matériaux*
(1898).

[3] Eliade, op. cit., pp. 210 and 212.

to sleep together embraced. And so on. Such prelimi-
naries are intended to ensure the 'autonomization' of
sensual pleasure, which is considered to be the sole
human experience that can bring about Nirvanic beatitude
and the subjection of the senses—in short, a seminal
stoppage." [1] Similar practices are prescribed in Taoism,
but with the intent of prolonging youth and life by econ-
omizing the vital principle rather than with the purpose of
winning spiritual freedom by the deification of the body.
Tantric "chastity" thus consisted of making love without
actually making it, of seeking mystical exaltation and
beatitude through a *She* who had to be "served" in a hu-
miliating posture, but with the preservation of that self-
mastery from which a lapse might result in an act of
procreation such as would cause the fall of the *Cavaliere
servente* or lover back into the fatal reality of Karma.

5. *The Joy of Love.*

In undeniable contrast to these mystical texts and this
abstruse psycho-physiological technique, I now quote
some lays of "light southern troubadours," either ama-
teurs and great lords or else needy jongleurs, whom authorities on the Romance languages unanimously term
pure "makers of rhetoric." [2] *"Of love I know that it
gives great joy to him who observes its laws,"* says the
earliest known troubadour, William, sixth Count of
Poitiers and ninth Duke of Aquitaine, who died in 1127.
Thus the Laws of Love were already as settled as a ritual
by the beginning of the twelfth century. They were Moderation, Service, Prowess, Long Expectation, Chastity,
Secrecy and Pity, and those virtues led to Joy, which
was the sign and guarantee of *Vray Amor* or True Love.

Here are Moderation and Patience: *"Of courtliness
may boast he who knows how to be moderate. . . . The
welfare of lovers consists in Joy, Patience, and Moderation. . . . I approve that my Lady should long make me
wait and that I should not have from her what she promised me"* (Marcabru). Here is Service of the Lady:

[1] Ibid.

[2] I apologize for quoting only *fragments* of lays, only words
of song! often poorly translated and shorn through this double
betrayal of any strictly poetic rhythmic beauty. It should be clearly understood that I put forward no more than stripped meanings.

"Take my life in homage, Beauty of hard pity, so long as you grant to me that by you I shall tend to heaven!" (Uc de Saint Circ). *"Each day I grow better and am purified, for I serve and reverence the most suave lady in the world"* (Arnaut Daniel). (Likewise the Arab troubadour, Ibn Dâvoud, wrote: "Submission to the beloved lady is the natural mark of a courtly man.") Here is Chastity: *"He who is disposed to love with sensual love goes to war with himself, for a fool after he has emptied his purpose cuts a poor figure* (Marcabru). *"Hearken! Its voice* (i.e. the voice of Love) *will seem gentle as the song of the lyre if only you cut off its tail"* (Marcabru).[1] Chastity was held to have the power to deliver from the tyranny of desire by carrying (courtly) Desire to the extreme: *"By excess of desire, I think I shall remove her from me, if nothing is to be lost by dint of loving well"* (Arnaut Daniel). (Likewise, Ibn Dâvoud extolled chastity for its power of "perpetuating desire").

It is at the height of (true) love and of its "joy" that Geoffrey Rudel feels the most "remote from guilty love" and from its "anguish." He goes further in liberation: the physical presence of the beloved was soon to become indifferent to him: *"I have a lady friend, but I do not know who she is, for never, by my faith! have I seen her . . . and I love her well. . . . No joy is so pleasing to me as the possession of that distant love."* Joy d'Amor was held not only to liberate a desire under the domination of Moderation and Prowess, but also to be a Fountain of Youth. *"I want to retain (my Lady) in order to refresh my heart and renew my body, so well that I cannot age. . . . He will live a hundred years who succeeds in possessing the joy of his love"* (William of Poitiers).

I have quoted only poets of the first or second generation of troubadours (c. 1120 to 1180). In the thirteenth century those of the last generation made explicit what it was their models had celebrated in song. *"It is no longer courtly love if it is materialized or if the Lady yields as reward,"* wrote Daude of Prades, although, however, he did not shrink from giving details of the erotic gestures which a lover might venture upon with his Lady. And Guiraut of Calanson:

---

[1] Note by Professor Jeanroy: "That is to say, if you succeed in suppressing the consequences."

"In the palace where she (the Lady) sits are five doors; he who can open the first two easily goes through the three others, but it is difficult for him to come out of them; he lives in the midst of joy, he who is able to remain. Access is by four very sweet degrees, but enters there no churl or lout; such folk are lodged in the outskirts, which occupy more than half of the world."

Guiraut Riquier, who is sometimes referred to as the last of the troubadours, made the following commentary on those lines: "The five doors are Desire, Prayer, Service, Kissing, and Doing, whereby Love perishes. The four degrees are honouring, dissimulating, serving well, and waiting patiently." [1] As for False Love, it was roundly turned upon by Marcabru and his successors and in terms which can be thought to enlighten us indirectly regarding the nature of true love or at least regarding certain aspects of it. And first of all, Marcabru says, *"it joins hands with the Devil, he who hatches False Love."* (And indeed is not the Devil the father of material creation and of procreation, in the Catharist view?) The foes of True Love are "murderers, traitors, simonists, enchanters, voluptuaries, usurers . . . deceiving husbands, false judges and false witnesses, false priests, false abbots, false women recluses and false men recluses." [2] They

---

[1] Cf. above (pp. 123–124) the description of Service according to the *Sahajiyā* school. Guiraut Riquier's interpretation is correct. That can be verified by reading this sentence by Aelius Donatus (fourth century) in his Commentary on Terence: *Quinque lineae sunt amoris, scilicet, visus, allocutio, tactus, osculum, coitus.* It should be noted that Desire corresponds to *visus*—the notorious first gaze which inflames—and Service to *tactus.* The theme of the five lines of love can be traced right through the Latin poetry of the Middle Ages down to the Renaissance, where it reappears in Clément Marot and Ronsard. The variations are very slight. But in 1510 Jean Lemaire de Belges wrote in his *Illustrations de Gaule:* "The noble poets say that five lines there are in loves . . . gazing, speaking, touching, kissing, and the last which is the most desired, and towards which all the others tend for their final resolution— it is that which out of decency is called the gift of mercy (reward)." The contrast with courtly love is plain. And no less is the meaning given to *mercy,* which a number of authors assimilate for their part to grace in the writings of the troubadours.

[2] The Catharists condemned war and every kind of murder, legal or other. In the place of *false* judges, *false* priests, *false* recluses, and of *deceiving* husbands, the Inquisitors of the follow-

are going to be destroyed, "subjected to every ruin," and tormented in hell.

"Noble Love has promised that it would be thus, there would be the lamentation of the despairing.

"Ah! noble Love, source of goodness, by whom the whole world is lit up, I cry unto thee pity. From these moaning clamourings defend me, for fear I may be detained over there (in hell); in every place I look upon myself as thy prisoner and, fortified and cheered by thee on all things, I hope that thou wilt be my guide."

Finally, in opposition to those troubadours who no doubt took too much advantage of the ambiguities provided for by the "service" of courtly love, Cercamon did not hesitate to dot the i's and cross the t's as he wrote: "Such troubadours, in mixing up truth and falsehood, corrupt lovers, women, and married couples. They tell you that Love goes sideways, and that that is why husbands grow jealous and ladies are in suspense. . . . These false suitors cause a great number to abandon Merit and drive Youth away from them."

Whatever "material" reality or absence of reality corresponded in those days to such details of language, there is no disputing the existence of Courtly Rhetoric and its system of virtues, sins, laudations, and interdicts. It is easily read about. That rhetoric went on to enable the romance writers of the North—those who produced the Arthurian cycle, about the Grail and about Tristan—to describe actions and dramas, and not merely to make song about what may still be thought, on the part of the troubadours of the South, to have been a pure sentimental phantasmagoria.

6. *Apology to Historians.*

I do not believe that "scientific" history so called can be a criterion of the realities which interest me in this book. Let it be affirmed on its behalf that such and such a connexion cannot be established in "The present state of our knowledge"—that is to say, remains unbelievable till further notice. I am in search of a meaning and hence of illustrative and illuminating analogies. And I do not

---

ing century could be counted upon to have read simply "judges," "priests," "recluses," and "husbands!"

in the least claim to be confirming any theory whatever in calling the reader's attention to certain "facts" which "serious science" now holds to have been "established." I merely think that those facts are of a kind to feed the imagination. Here are two such "facts" to muse upon.

The *Tantra Pancha* is a collection of Buddhist and Tantric tales which was translated from Sanscrit in the sixth century by a doctor of Chosroes I, king of Persia. From that country it progressed swiftly in the direction of Europe, thanks to a series of translations in Syriac, Arabic, Latin, Spanish, etc. In the seventeenth century it was read by La Fontaine in French. It had then been translated from the Persian and the Persian was based upon an old Arabic version. The periplus, *The Romance of Balaam and Jehoshaphat,* is even more astonishing. In its present form it is a story of the spiritual evolution which leads Jehoshaphat, an Indian prince, to discover and embrace Christianity, the mysteries of which are made known to him by the Goodman, Balaam. The version which has come down in Provençal from the fourteenth century, while orthodox in main outline, bears indisputable traces of Manichaeism. According to the French neo-Catharist school,[1] the twelfth-century heretics were acquainted with a version which had not been amended by the Catholics and which was nearer to the original. Whether or not that suggestion comes one of these days to be verified, the Manichaean origin of the romance is attested by fragments of its original wording in eighth-century Uigur, which were discovered in Eastern Turkestan. It is possible to trace the transformation of the Hindu names "Baghavan" and "Boddisattva" (Buddha) into "Balaam" and "Jehoshaphat" via the Arabic forms of "Balawhar va Budhâsaf" or "Yudhasaf."

There are innumerable instances of the relations that subsisted between the East and the medieval West. I have selected these two, for which there is incontrovertible evidence, because they refuse the modern prejudice according to which any communication held to have occurred between Tantrism or Buddhist Manichaeism and the heresies of the South of France must seem "highly fantastic and improbable."

Déodat Roché, René Nelli, etc.

7. *Instead of Definite Conclusions*

Courtly Love resembles adolescent love when this is yet chaste and hence all the more consuming. It also resembles the love celebrated by Arab poets, who were mostly homosexual, as were a number of the troubadours. Its terms of expression have been taken up and used by nearly every great mystic in the West. It seems to us to have declined at times down to sophisticated fiddle-faddle in the style of the small medieval courts. It can be entirely imaginary, and many people insist that it was nothing but a verbal tourney. But it can also be a vehicle of the detailed though ambiguous realities of an erotico-mystical discipline for which the recipes were in India, China, and the Near East. All that seems to me likely. It may all be "true" in the various senses of the word—simultaneously and in different says. It all helps to a better understanding of courtly love, even if courtly love is something that nothing rational will explain.

In concluding the kind of counter-inquiry which I have been carrying out, and taking into account the most sensible objections brought against my *minimum theory* by members of a variety of schools, I am brought back to a kind of spiral that rises over my earliest observations. Courtly love came into existence in the twelfth century during a complete revolution of the western *psyche*. It sprang up out of the same movement which forced upwards into the half light of our human consciousness, and into lyrical expression by the human spirit, the Feminine Principle of *Shakti,* the worship of Woman, of the Mother, and of the Virgin. It shared in the epiphany of the *Anima* which, to my mind, marked the reappearance in Western man of a symbolical East. What makes it intelligible to us today are its historical signs or marks—its literally congenital connexion with the Heresy of the Cathars, and both its surreptitious opposition and its overt opposition to the Christian conception of marriage. But it would leave us now indifferent had it not, after many avatars (the procession of which I am about to narrate), preserved in our own lives an intimate and ever renewed virulence.

11

From Courtly Love to Arthurian Romance

If now from the South of France we move to the North, we find that in the Arthurian romances—*Tristan, Lancelot* and the whole cycle—courtly love, and its rhetoric with many meanings, were transferred from song to narrative. It has been said that the first courtly novel was born from the contact of alien legends with the notion of courtesy. The alien legends in question were the ancient Celtic sacred mysteries (of which, as it happens, writers such as Béroul and Chrestien de Troyes were not more than half aware), mingled with bits of Greek mythology. How far the literatures of Southern and of Northern France were independent of one another has been the subject of prolonged controversy. Today it seems to be agreed that the poets of the Romanic South communicated their style and doctrine of love to the "story-tellers" of the Round Table cycle. And the course of the transmission may be traced in historical documents.

Eleanor of Aquitaine left her Court of Love—in the South of France, the region of the *langue d'oc*—in order to marry Louis the Seventh, who was king of France from 1137 to 1180; and then, in 1152, she married Henry, who two years later became king of England.[1] At each removal she took her troubadours with her. It is thanks to her and to them, among others, that the Anglo-Norman *trouvères* became possessed of the rules and secret of courtly love. Chrestien de Troyes says that both the matter and spirit of his romances were obtained from Countess Marie of Champagne, Eleanor's daughter. Chrestien wrote a Tristan romance, the MSS. of which have been lost. Béroul was a Norman, Thomas an English-

[1] Her son, Richard Coeur de Lion, the friend of the Gascon troubadours and himself a troubadour, was excommunicated by Rome.

man. And, reciprocally, the Tristan legend became known over a considerable part of Southern France. So rapid an interaction can be accounted for by the existence of a former connexion between the South of before the Cathars and the Gaelic and Britannic Celts. It was noted earlier that the religion of the druids—whence filids and bards derived their traditions—taught a dualistic view of the universe and made Woman into a symbol of the divine. Now, the Christian heresy of the Perfect drew certain features of its mythology from its Celt-Iberian background. It was only natural that in the hands of the poets of the North this mythology should have been invested with darker and more tragic colours. Taranis, god of the stormy sky, takes the place of Lug, god of the sunlit sky. And although the courtly doctrine picked up and revived former aboriginal traditions, it was nevertheless something that the trouvères had learned, not something they had grown up in. That is why they often misinterpret it.

For that matter, it is extremely difficult to bring out the causes or to estimate the precise bearing of their misunderstandings. Are they due to a defective initiation? Was the tradition imperfect? Or was there a heretical tendency within the Heresy itself, a more or less sincere attempt to get back to orthodoxy?[1] Or was it simply that there had been a "profanation" of courtly subject-matter which the trouvères seized upon none too scrupulously and directed to other ends than those of the troubadours? Pending some thorough research into the matter, let me point out that a number of the Britannic romances turn out to be more "Christian" and others to be more "barbarian" than the poems of the troubadours, and yet indisputably it is by those poems that all of them were inspired. We do not know if Chrestien de Troyes thoroughly grasped the rules of love which he was taught by Marie of Champagne. We do not know to what extent he *wished* to make his romances secret chronicles of the Church of Love,[2] or mere allegories of courtly morality and mysticism (as I now incline to believe). It is easy to see why there is an absence of written evi-

---

[1] Particularly in the case of Chrestien de Troyes.

[2] As has been supposed by Otto Rahn, Péladan, and Eugène Aroux.

dence here. Many interests must have joined forces to prevent the Heresy from being spread, and the Heresy on its side wished to remain esoteric. Obviously, however, Chrestien de Troyes distorts the meaning of the myths he recounts. In the Lancelot romance, which dates from about 1225, symbolism and allegory are obviously both present, however incongruous are the elucidations with which the author follows his account of each episode. One elucidation, however, deserves to be mentioned, because, notwithstanding the author's unawareness of what he was saying, its Catharist origin is clearly discernible. Lancelot, while wandering in the forest, reaches a place where the road forks. He hesitates between going left or right. Then, in spite of the warning given on a cross which appears in front of him, he goes to the left. Before long a knight in white armour rides up, throws him off his horse, and takes away his crown. The crestfallen Lancelot then meets a priest, to whom he makes confession. "I shall tell you the meaning of what has befallen you," the priest says. "The road to the right which you ignored at the fork was that of earthly chivalry, in which you have long triumphed: the road to the left was that of heavenly chivalry, which allows no killing of men or overcoming of champions by force of arms: it is the realm of spiritual things. And you bore with you on this road the crown of pride. That is why the knight overthrew you so easily; for he represented the very sin you had committed." [1]

After that literary historians are at liberty to talk about "incredible adventures," "easily contrived marvels," "touching ingenuousness," "primitive freshness," and so on. A little more penetration would lead us to see, on the contrary, that the real barbarism is displayed in our contemporary notion of the novel, which we are quite

---

[1] In another passage, the knights, having taken Holy Communion, give one another the Kiss of Peace, according to the Eastern rite, which the Cathars appear to have taken over.—Finally, M. Anitchkov has shown that the bridge which the Knights of the Grail have to cross is really the Sinvat Bridge of Manichaean mythology, a bridge thrown across an infernal river, and one that alone the *elect* are able to cross. "There is cause for describing the creative group of the Britannic material as Manichaeizing," Anitchkov writes (*Joachim de Flore*, p. 291), after having insisted on the Catharist influences apparent in all those romances.

content to take as a faked photograph of events without significance, whereas Arthurian romance was knit by an intimate *coherence* of which we no longer possess so much as an inkling. Actually, in these wonderful adventures nothing whatever is without its meaning; everything is symbol or delicate allegory; and only the ignorant stop short at the apparent puerility of the tale, this puerility being intended of course to conceal the underlying meaning from the superficial glances of the *uninformed*.

But even if the trouvères were inferior to the troubadours in mystical wisdom, their romances do not consist merely of *errors*. They dealt with a new theme, that of physical love, the theme of the fault. The writings of Chrestien de Troyes are not only love poems, as has so often been said; they are also genuine *novels*. For, unlike the Provençal poems, they take the trouble to describe the betrayals of love, instead of merely expressing the passionate surge in its mystical purity. The starting-point of both *Lancelot* and *Tristan* is a sin against courtly love—the physical possession of a real woman, and hence a "profanation" of love. It is owing to this initial fault on his part that Lancelot fails to find the Grail, and is humiliated countless times while wandering along the celestial way. He has chosen the earthly road, he has betrayed mystic Love, he is not one of the "Pure." Alone the "Pure"—true "savages" such as Bohort, Perceval, and Galahad—can be granted initiation. Clearly the account of his wanderings and of the penalties he suffers required the narrative form, not that of mere song. In *Tristan* the initial fault is painfully redeemed by the long penance which the lovers undergo. That is why the tale ends "well" from the standpoint of Catharist mysticism—that is to say, why it culminates in a double self-inflicted death.[1] Thus there are reasons of a spiritual nature to account for the elabora-

---

[1] In an analysis of the "erotic magic" of the Grail cycle (in *Lumière du Graal* (1951), a collection of twenty studies by various authors), René Nelli puts forward some observations which may usefully be set beside Chapter 10 of this Book II. He writes: "This erotic magic was inspired first of all by a belief that the female body displayed by its mere presence certain supernatural powers, the same that were attributed to the Grail. [The Grail rejuvenated those who contemplated it.] . . . It was also due to faith in an occult force which resulted from a repressed carnal

tion of a new literary style—the style of the novel—which
was to become truly literary, however, only later on,
when it became detached from the myth—by then provisionally exhausted—at the beginning of the seventeenth
century.

12

From Celtic Myths to Arthurian Romance

Tristan must seem the most thoroughly courtly of Arthurian romances because the epic element—the battles and schemings—is reduced to a minimum and the
tragic development of the religious doctrine alone determines the strong and elemental progress of the tale.
But *Tristan* is also the most "Arthurian" of courtly romances, because it incorporates religious and mythologi-
cal components that are plainly of Celtic origin to a
much greater extent than do the romances of the Round
Table, and in a way that renders these elements sharply
identifiable.

Hubert very truly says about Gaelic literature, that
"it contains matter derived from the religion of the Ancient Britons as by a miracle; for it arose in a Christian
country that had been first Romanized and then colo-
nized by the Irish." [1] Nevertheless, the miracle is attested
by a large number of the incidents exploited by Béroul

---

transport. . . . Pure love was understood to be one that remains
pure in perilous circumstances, though these be provoked, and that
applies the energy of this Desire to higher ends than copulation.
Pure love allowed every carnal contrivance save "the act." . . .
Retained love was indeed the internal motor of the Quest, which
bore all the characteristics of being an initiation into a Femininity
not to be seized by the carnal senses." The author seems to have
penetrated the "Tantric" quality of Courtly Love, more truly, I
think, as it is manifested in the Arthurian Cycle than it is in the
poems of the troubadours.

[1] H. Hubert, *Les Celtes*, II, p. 286.

and Thomas, incidents that it has only become possible
to account for thanks to the most recent archaeological
discoveries about the Celts. Actually, the religious matter has such vigorous poetic power that its survival is
easy enough to understand, even in a world which had
lost the druidical faith and forgotten the meaning of the
druidical mysteries.

The cycle of Irish legends contains many tales about
a journey which the hero undertakes to the country of
the dead. This hero—Bran, Cuchulinn, or Oisin—"*is attracted by a mysterious beauty*"; "he sets sail in a *magic ship*"; and he lands in a wonderful country. "In the
end he wearies of this land, and wants to return home.
It is in order to die." [1] This evidently is the source of
the wounded Tristan's first aimless sea journey which results in his finding the magic balm. Other situations in the
Tristan romance have fairly close prototypes in the
stories of the Irish cycle. For example, in the tragic idyll
of *Diarmaid and Grainne* the two lovers flee to the forest,
where the husband pursues them. In *Baile and Ailinn* the
lovers arrange to meet in a deserted spot, where death
has preceded them and prevents their coming together;
"for it had been predicted by the druids that they would
never meet in life, but that they would meet after death,
and then never be parted again."

It would be easy to note further similarities. But the
resemblance between certain features of behaviour is even
more striking. It will be remembered that Tristan is an
orphan and that he is brought up in the castle of his
uncle, King Mark. Now it frequently happened among
the Celts in the most remote times that children were
entrusted "to the care of a qualified person in some great
house, a house of men." They were taught there by a
druid, and were thus sheltered from women. "This institution, which is commonly given the Anglo-Norman
name of 'fosterage,' was retained in Celtic countries: we
find children being entrusted to foster-parents, of whose
family they became members, as is shown by the fact that
a certain number acquired the family name of their foster-
father. These foster-fathers were sought either among
members of the mother's family or among druids." [2]

[1] Hubert, op. cit., II, p. 298.

[2] Hubert, op. cit., II, pp. 243–44.

In the same way, Tristan, who is brought up by Mark, his maternal uncle, becomes by fosterage the king's "son." [1] The Celtic custom of a ritual gift, of exchanging ostentatory gifts with efforts to go one better (*potlatch*), figures also in *Tristan* and in the Romances of the Round Table. Many episodes begin with a "blank" promise made by the king to some damsel who has asked him for a gift, without saying of what. As a rule, the damsel wants some highly dangerous mission undertaken. "Tournaments," Hubert says,[2] "certainly formed part of this vast system of competition and of going one better." Further, it is well known that Celtic youths, on reaching puberty—that is, at the time they left the house of men— had to accomplish some feat—the killing of a stranger or some prowess of the chase—in order to win the right to marry. The battle with the Morholt in *Tristan* is the exact reproduction of that custom, although in the Romance there is no allusion to its sacred origin. All this renders Hubert's theory plausible—that Celtic mythology was transmitted to the courtly cycle, not through any properly religious channels, but by a more profane cult of heroes and of prowess, which had gradually replaced the gods and their worship in popular legend.

"Gaston Paris noted with acumen that the romance of Tristan and Iseult gives forth a peculiar note which is not heard again in medieval literature, and he accounted for this by the Celtic origin of the poems. It is through Tristan and through Arthur that the most limpid and precious part of the Celtic genius was incorporated in the European spirit."

Thus Hubert.[3] The "peculiar note" which Bédier has admirably reproduced in his modern transcription of the legend so unmistakably finds the path to our hearts that we can *isolate* the non-Celtic, and therefore courtly, element which was responsible in the twelfth century for the production of the myth. What differentiates an Irish legend from the legend told by Béroul and Thomas is that

---

[1] Psycho-analysts will not fail to look upon the unhappy affair of Tristan and Iseult as the consequence of an Oedipus complex. But foster-fathers sometimes had as many as fifty legal sons—so that the link was rather weak—and also, as many documents testify, incest was permitted among the Celts.

[2] Op. cit., II, p. 234.

[3] Op. cit., II, p. 336.

in the former what brings disaster is an entirely external *fate*, whereas in the latter it is a secret but unerring *wish* on the part of the two mystic lovers. In Celtic legends action and resolution are determined by an *epic* element, in courtly romances by an *internal tragedy*. Then also Celtic love—in spite of the religious sublimation of Woman by the druids—is above all sensual love.[1] The fact that in some legends this love is secretly at war with orthodox religious love, and is thus compelled to express itself in estoteric symbols, helps us to see how it came about that the Britannic background was so easily absorbed into the symbolism of the courtly romance. But the analogy remains theoretical, although it has doubtless encouraged the modern tendency to confuse Tristan's passion with mere sensuality.

A couple of quotations from Thomas, the most self-conscious of the authors of the five early versions of the legend, will be enough to show how original the courtly myth is. The cohesive principle which courtly mysticism gave to the religious, sociological or epic elements that had been inherited from the old Britannic background is expressed and *expounded* in a language astonishingly modern. The principle is that suffering considered as an *askesis* has to be loved—suffering is indeed the "beloved pain" of the troubadours. Tristan, on the night of his marriage to Iseult of the White Hand, faces the most cruel of struggles within himself, for he cannot decide to possess his wife.

"Ysolt as Blanches Mains he desired for her beauty and for her name Ysolt: for the beauty alone that was in her, he had not desired her if she had not the name Ysolt, nor for the name without the beauty. . . . Tristan would fain have vengeance; yet *for his malady he seeketh such vengeance as will double his torment*." [2] By the very fact that Iseult of the White Hand is now his wife, he must not and cannot any longer desire her.

---

[2] This is evidenced, for example, by *Tannhäuser*. The *Tannhäuser* of the sixteenth century is a late German adaptation of Hiberno-Scottish legends; it owes nothing whatever to courtly influence. The Montsalvat of the Chaste is replaced by the Venusberg!

[1] *The Romance of Tristan and Ysolt* by Thomas of Britain, translated by Roger Sherman Loomis (New York, 1931). M. de Rougemont's italics.

"An the good that he hath were not his, he had not despised it in his heart: but that which it behoveth him to have, he may not heartily love. If he might not have that he hath, he had longed to win it: he would think to find it better than his own: and *for this cause he may not love his own*. . . This befalleth many men: when they have some travail and anguish and great pain and distress, *such things they do to escape and deliver and avenge them as thereof cometh great harm*: often they do of purpose things whereof they endure sorrow. I have seen it betide unto many that when they may not have their desire or thing that they love, they strive unto their utmost power: of their distress they do such deeds whereby oft-times they double their grief. . . . Whosoever doth that he desireth not to do because that he may not have some good thing, doth his will despite his desire." [1] [*Encontre désir fait volier,* are Thomas's own words.]

A Celtic background of religious legends—which, as it happens, were at a very remote period common to both the Iberian South and its *langue d'oc* and to the Irish and Britannic North; customs of feudal chivalry; semblances of Christian orthodoxy; a sometimes very compliant sensuality; and, finally, the individual fancy of each of the poets—there, when all is said and done, are the materials thanks to which the heretical doctrine of Love (which was profoundly dualist in spirit, and probably Catharist in its immediate origin) underwent its transmutations. In this way was the Tristan myth born. I am far from intending to analyse the metamorphosis; it eludes us doubly, in being poetic and in being mystical. But we now know whence the myth came and whither it must lead. And perhaps we have gained an inkling—although this is something that could not be put into words —of how the myth may be enacted in an individual human life or embodied in a piece of imaginative literature.

[1] Ibid. M. de Rougemont's italics.

13

From Arthurian Romance to Wagner, via Gottfried of Strasbourg

The first time *the Myth was created anew,* out of a mind exceptionally conscious of the theological implications, was in the version by Gottfried of Strasbourg about the beginning of the thirteenth century. Gottfried was a clerk who read French—he often quotes lines from Thomas—and who was strongly moved by the controversies which had raged between Bernard of Clairvaux and the Cathars, and had also involved Abélard, the School of Chartres, and several heretics who came dangerously close to the Abbot of Cluny's "mysticism of the heart."

A theologian and a poet, and well aware of the significance of his preferences, Gottfried sets forth far better than his models the strictly religious importance of the Dualist Myth of Tristan. But also, and for the same reason, he discloses better than all the others a fundamental element in the Myth—a sensual fret and a "humanistic" pride that makes up for the fret. There is fret in it, because it depicts the sexual instinct being resented as a cruel fate and as a tyranny; there is pride, because the tyranny is imagined to become a divinizing force—setting man up against God—once it is decided to yield to it. (The paradox heralds Nietzsche's *amor fati.*) Whereas Béroul limits the action of the philtre to three years, and Thomas makes the "herb wine" symbolize the intoxication of love, Gottfried treats it as the seal of destiny—the sign of a blind force external to the persons concerned, and as an expression, too, of the goddess Minne's will. That goddess, I ought to say, is a revivescence of the Grandmother and comes out of mankind's most remote religions. But no sooner is the philtre drunk than it lifts its victims outside all moral bounds into a realm which can only be divine. Thus by the philtre those

139

who drink it are both shackled to sexuality—a law of life—and compelled to go beyond it, thanks to a liberating *hubris* which lifts them over the mortal threshold of duality and of personal differentiation. This second paradox is essentially Manichaean, and it may be said to subtend Gottfried's immense poem.

Gottfried copies Thomas, but also makes what he likes of him. He alters, and in altering causes the reader to sit up and attend; for what he alters are three decisive moments of the action.

(*a*) He somewhat ferociously throws into relief the unmistakably blasphemous nature of the episode of the Judgement by red-hot iron;

(*b*) For the Forest of Morrois he substitutes a "Grotto of Love"—the *Minnegrotte*— thanks to which he is able to compare the architecture of a Christian church with that of a temple.

(*c*) He decides that, instead of being nominal, the marriage of Tristan to Iseult of the White Hand shall be consummated.

His long unfinished poem—about 19,000 lines have come down to us, but the death of the lovers, though heralded, was never narrated—is alike more religious and more sensual than Béroul's and Thomas's. Above all, he declares and expounds what the Britons show without explanation and apparently without on their own part any astonishment. He thus develops and discloses the extent to which *Catharism* is latent in the anonymous legend.[1]

(*a*) The Judgement of God was a barbarian custom, but the Church recognized it in the twelfth century and had indeed just subjected to it some women in Cologne

[1] On this subject two large volumes published in 1953 should be consulted: Gottfried Weber, *Tristan und die Krise des Hochmittelalterlichen Weltbildes um 1200*. This infinitely detailed work (with exhausting repetitions) by a learned German philologist contains an abundance of "scientific proofs" of each point touched upon in the present chapter. I found no need of them in writing the first edition of my book, but certainly they do not harm! Over hundreds of pages Gottfried's religious convictions are compared with the doctrines of Augustine, Bernard, Hugh of Saint Victor, and Abélard, and the comparisons bring out strikingly how deeply Gottfried was a Cathar and how anti-Catholic (in a manner that, to my mind, foreshadows the Renaissance rather than Luther).

and Strasbourg who were legitimately accused of Catharism. The ordeal consisted in grasping with the bare hand
a red-hot iron bar. Only liars and perjurers were burned.
As I recalled above,[1] Iseult asks to be subjected to this
judgement when she is accused of betraying King Mark.
She invites the judgement out of excessive pride and in a
spirit of defiance. She swears that no man has ever held
her in his arms except the king, unless—and here she
laughs—she ought to count a poor pilgrim who has just
carried her ashore from a boat; and the poor pilgrim is
Tristan in disguise. The ordeal is a success. Gottfried
says:[2]

"It was thus manifest and proved that the most virtuous Christ swings to every wind like a weathercock and
takes any fold like a mere cloth. . . . He lends himself, and
can be adapted, to anything, according to the heart of
each, in behalf of sincerity as in behalf of cheating. . . .
He is ever what it is wanted he should be."

The allusion to the "heart" is unmistakably directed at
Bernard of Clairvaux, whose writings were so familiar to
the poet as in many places to be imitated by him in
their dialectical accounts of suffering, desire, and ecstasy,
with, however, inversion of the lessons to be drawn. For
the poet, the final ecstasy does not lead into the daylight of God, but into the nocturnal darkness of passion;
not to a human being's salvation but to his dissolution.
The passage cited above expresses a virulent resentment
at orthodox doctrines which "make Christ take any fold
like a mere cloth" and cause Him to sanction posteriorly
everything that, in the eyes of Gottfried himself and of
the heretics of his day, the "pure" Gospel and the Dualist Gnosis condemned—the world as manifested, the
flesh in general, and in the world the social order of the
time—feudal, clerical, and martial—and within that order, marriage.

(b) The *Minnegrotte* is pictured as a church, the poet
displaying a genuine understanding of liturgical symbolism
and of the beginnings of Gothic architecture. But for an
altar there is substituted a bed. The bed is consecrated
to the goddess Minne as the Catholic altar to Christ,
and on the bed the courtly sacrament takes place: the

---

[1] Book I, Chapter 4, above.
[2] Lines 15733–15747.

two lovers "communicate" in passion. Instead of the eucharistic miracle, instead of the transubstantiation of the material kinds and the divinization of him who receives these, flesh commingles with spirit in transcendental unity. Lovers, and not believers, are made divine by the "consummation" of the substance of Love. Whether this is spiritual or physical is left deliberately uncertain, and the uncertainty is, I feel, profoundly significant. And Love is opposed to the fervour of the Cluniacs in the same terms as Eros to Agape; and, I must add, is incompatible with that other sacrament which orthodoxy has "perverted" in adapting it to social and material ends—the sacrament of marriage joining two bodies even where there is no love between them, a sacrament which the Cathars never stopped attacking as *iurata fornicatio*. Moreover, it seems possible to identify in this episode of the *Minnegrotte* the dialectic which the great mystics were to resort to from the thirteenth to the seventeenth centuries. The three ways—purgative, illuminative, and unitive—are very plainly prefigured here, though inflected or inverted by Gottfried's dualist and even Gnostic convictions.[1]

(c) In being consummated, Tristan's marriage to the second Iseult establishes a parallel (which Thomas avoids) with the loveless marriages of Iseult the Fair to King Mark. Both are stigmatized as due to temporal and physiological necessity, as being part of *the exile of souls* held captive in their imprisoning bodies. Thomas voices with full Manichaean virulence the judgement of courtly moral teaching, which he regards as above the judgement of the Church and of his time, the Church and the time being both guilty in his eyes as in the eyes of all Cathars. But his pronouncement sets in a queer light the erotico-eucharistic "consummation" that he narrates as taking place in the *Minnegrotte*. In a Catharist view of the world, to make love without loving in accordance with courtliness (in this instance, courtliness is *Minne*), and to yield to a purely physical sensuality, is the supreme and

---

[1] Regarding Gottfried's Gnosticism, he seems to have believed, like the Carpocratians, that the *purgatio* of tyrannical instinct is only to be obtained by yielding to the instinct in the first place, with the intention, however, of attaining to the illuminative ecstasy that will bring about essential (though not epithalamian) union.

original sin. To love with pure passion, even without physical contact—the sword laid between a couple's bodies and the theme of partings—is the supreme virtue, and the true way to divinization. Between those two extremes, which the Myth illustrates against the psychical and religious background of the twelfth century, every kind of confusion about love is made more than possible —inevitable. We are still in the thick of the consequences now in the twentieth century; otherwise this book would be aimless. But it is possible to stick up landmarks.

Very obviously Gottfried of Strasbourg makes use of the "matter of Britain" as he likes, and turns the myth of Love-for-death into a Catharist legend with a freedom which may have cost him his life (we do not yet know whether it did or not). But it is equally plain that the framework of the tale, its plot and predominant topics, favoured the poet's intention in a way which should be termed really *congenital*. The myth of Tristan betrays itself, as much in its essence, its innermost structure, its progression and form, as in its teaching, to be fundamentally heretical and dualistic. Chance has no place here, nor is there occasion for any such suspension of judgement as some of our learned friends seem wont to mistake for "science."

Tristan is far more profoundly and indisputably Manichaean than the *Divine Comedy* is Thomist.

Nevertheless, Gottfried made the legend *explicit* in a new fashion that is big with consequences. He prefigured that betrayal of genius which Wagner effected six and a half centuries later. Even if we did not know that Wagner's source was Gottfried's poem, a textual comparison of the two works would make it obvious. The short, hurried, antithetical, and breathless lines of the second act of the opera are almost a pastiche of Gottfried.[1] The famous duet in which Tristan and Isolde mingle their names, deny their names, sing of surpassing the separate self, and time, space, and earthly calamity, is taken almost literally from different passages of the poem.[2] But what Wagner resurrected by means of mu-

---

[1] And it looks as though Gottfried first imitated Abélard's *sic et non*. The famous love affair between the Doctor and the Nun constantly haunted the author of the most theological version of *Tristan*.

[2] Here is just one instance. Cf. Gottfried, lines 18352 to 18357:

sic is, far more than the form, the philosophic and religious content of Gottfried's poem. The created world is the Devil's. Everything within his empire is under the sway of necessity: human bodies are doomed to experience desire, and the love philtre symbolizes the ineluctable tyranny which that means. Man is not free. He is determined by the Devil. But if he accepts his calamitous destiny *up to the death* which will free him from his body, he may attain to that fusion of two selves who will thereupon have ceased *to suffer* love and will enter upon Supreme Joy. What Wagner took from Gottfried is all that the Britons did not wish to say or did not know how to say, and were content to expound by means of narrated actions—the religious and heretical nostalgia for an escape out of this wicked world, the condemnation and simultaneous divinization of sensuality, the strivings of the soul to escape from the fundamental *inordinatio* of the period, and from the tragic contradiction between Good—which must be Love—and the Evil that is victorious over Good in the created world. In short, Wagner took from Gottfried his fundamental dualism. And that is how it is that his work still acts upon us, more insidiously and with greater fascination for our sensibility than Joseph Bédier's aesthetic restoration.

14

What Has Been Ascertained So Far

Allowing for the change of key which was effected in the poetic language of courtly love when this language passed from the South of the troubadours to the less civilized North of the trouvères, we can now realize that all our peregrinations finally lead to the masterpieces of Béroul, Thomas, and Gottfried of Strasbourg. The religions of Antiquity, some of the mystic systems of the Near East; the heresy thanks to which they

---

"*Tristan und Isot, ir und ich . . . niwan ein Tristan und ein Isot*"; and Wagner, Act II, 2, and all the last part of the scene: "*nicht mehr Tristan . . . nicht mehr Isolde!*"

were revived in the Languedoc, the reaction against that
heresy in the Western mind and in feudal custom—all
that resonates in a muffled way right through the myth.
We have thus been brought back to the *Romance of
Tristan*, having ascertained why it was necessarily written
at a particular time, the very time in which certain particular heretical traditions intersected, as it were, certain particular institutions whereby those traditions
stood condemned savagely; for that was the moment when
the heretical traditions were compelled to find expression
in equivocal symbols and to take on the form of a myth.

Taking these convergences in the aggregate, it becomes
possible to say that *the passionate love which the myth
celebrates actually became in the twelfth century—the moment when first it began to be cultivated—a religion in
the full sense of the word, and in particular a Christian
heresy historically determined.* Whereupon it may be
inferred (*a*) that the passion which novels and films have
now popularized is nothing else than *a lawless invasion
and flowing back* into our lives of a spiritual heresy the
key to which we have lost; and (*b*) that underlying the
modern breakdown of marriage is nothing less than a
struggle between two religious traditions, or, in other
words, a *decision* which almost always we reach unconsciously, in complete ignorance of the causes, ends, and
perils involved, and for the sake of a morality which, although still alive, we no longer know how to justify.

Moreover, passion and the passion myth are active in
many other ways than that in which our private lives are
affected.

Orthodox mysticism in Europe has been another passion, and its metaphorical language is at times curiously
akin to that of courtly love.

Considered chronologically, the great body of European
literature expresses nothing other than an increasing
secularizaton of the myth, or—as I would rather say—
successive "profanations" of its content and form.

Finally, *war* in Europe, and every one of the formal
modes of conducting it down to about 1914, kept pace
with the transformations of the myth, largely owing to
their chivalric origin, and perhaps for other reasons as
well.

Such are the matters to be dealt with in the Books that
follow.

Book III

PASSION AND MYSTICISM

1

How the Problem Stands

Attempts to account for mysticism have often consisted of saying that it is a deflexion of human love; which is but to say that it is a form of sexuality. My examination of the *Romance of Tristan* and of its historical sources has led me to reverse the relation. In this particular case it is fatal passion which has to be identified as a form of mysticism, more or less conscious and definite. That is, of course, no warrant for generalization; but at least it calls for the restatement of a problem which nineteenth-century materialism had thought itself qualified to settle to the detriment of mysticism. Very likely the problem is not one open to being solved simply and finally. But how it stands does require to be made clear.

Whether passion is being treated as a form of mysticism, or vice versa, the two are assumed to be in *some* relation. Possibly, however, the nature of language is what leads us to discern such connexions. It has long been recognized that the metaphors of love and mysticism are akin. But the closest similarities in vocabulary do not necessarily argue any likeness between the things that the words refer to. Thus up to a point we may be the victims of a verbal illusion—of a kind of protracted punning. Nevertheless, here is a problem that has to be faced. Let me indicate why.

In the first place, if passion involved no more than physiological factors the Tristan myth would be unintelligible. Sexual instincts are manifested as a hunger, and this hunger, like that for food, tends to obtain satisfaction at any cost. The more ravenous, the more indiscriminate it becomes. But the passion of the myth is compelled by its very nature to reject satisfaction. The more intense, the more it recoils from being assuaged.

149

This passion, therefore, is not a hunger, but a kind of drug which produces intoxication. It has recently been asserted that every drug-addict is a mystic unawares. But there can be no drugging, physical or moral, except by the effect of some *foreign* agent, which instinct, left to itself, would get rid of as quickly as possible. Animals do not get intoxicated.[1]

In the second place, and conversely, mysticism does not seem able by itself to account for passion. As soon as we suppose that it does, we see that this involves explaining why the most striking metaphors employed in mystical writing are drawn from the language of sexual love, and not, for example, from the vocabulary of breathing or nutrition; why what it has *invariably* been attempted to equate with mysticism should be sexual instincts, and this long before the advent of Freud and his school.

Such is the dilemma in which we are landed: if we try to treat passionate love as a mere matter of sex, it is evident that we then do not know what we are talking about. If conversely we seek to connect this love with anything *alien* to sex it will have queer results, as Schopenhauer might have said. Let us treat the problem as it is propounded by the myth, and as it must have appeared in the twelfth century. An actual instance—especially as it is a piece of literature produced *before* there arose the great wave of orthodox mysticism—supplies the best starting-point for an inquiry into how the "very queer results" arise.

2

"Tristan" as the Account of a Mystical Experience

As we have seen, the *Romance of Tristan* is in many respects a first "profanation" of courtly mysticism and of the doctrines which had inspired it—Neo-Plato-

[1] There is, it is true, *formica sanguinea,* an insect which keeps in its nest a parasite exuding a delicious sweat, and the presence

nism, Manichaeism, and Sufi-ism. The mythopoeic process was only too successful, either because Béroul and Thomas, or their forerunner, did not fathom at all points the unalloyed teaching of courtesy, or else because they were carried away by the ardour of narrative construction (in the modern and literary sense of the term), and wished to meet the inclinations of their audience, which consisted of people less civilized than were the inhabitants of the South. For what distinguishes the Romance is that its plot turns upon a *transgression* of the rules of courtly love, since the whole dramatic story proceeds from there having been adulterous intercourse. That is how it is a novel in the modern sense, not merely a poem. Yet, taking them together, and bearing in mind what provides the internal motive power of the action, most of the situations mark stages in a mystical career. There are "moments" in the pure tradition of the Cathars, and others can be connected with mystical experience in general as regards details which are identical among orthodox and heterodox alike, and also among the pagans—Persians, Arabs, and even Buddhists. It will not do therefore to suppose that we are dealing with some commonplace novel about adultery. Tristan is unfaithful to heresy, the mystic virtue of the Pure, which was a *virtue* also for the authors of the legend. The fault lies not in his being in love, but in his fulfilment of his love.

To compare two forms of mystical experience is a delicate and perilous task, and all the more so here for the fact that one of them is distorted by an epic superstructure. Nevertheless, let me suggest a rough parallel between what happens to Tristan and a properly mystical experience. If I lead a reader to rash inferences, I can repair the damage later. After being wounded in overcoming the Morholt, Tristan has himself put on board a boat with neither sail nor oar. He has only his sword and his harp. The boat is cast adrift, so that he may go in quest of the soothing balm which shall rid his blood of its poison. This is the very model of a yielding up to the influence of the supernatural at the beginning of a mystical experience. This is how a soul, fatally wounded by sin,

---

of the parasite ends by upsetting everything. This ant's pathological habit has been compared to dipsomania. So long as ants remain speechless, any theory is possible.

renounces rational and visible aids, and courts an unknown grace. Modern poetry supplies many accounts of this desperate but eloquent setting out at a venture, which, although then but a rudimentary form of the mystic quest, allows no ignoring of the lyre and symbolic sword—symbolic of a challenge to established society. Few no doubt of our latter-day poets have experienced a "fatal love." For some, the quest dwindles into a pleasant cruise from which they return with a manuscript ready for the press. Others distil a drug productive of picturesque visions. Nearly all give the secret away.

But Tristan has met love. At first he failed to recognize it. When King Mark—established authority—despatches him to bring back the faraway princess, he does not suspect that the mission is going to seal his own fate. Then occurs the irremediable mistake of drinking the *love-potion*. In analysing the content of the myth, I pointed out that, in being predestined, the error is tantamount to an alibi. The lovers insist that they have been in no way to blame for anything they have done, as their passion cannot be acknowledged either to society (which looks upon it as criminal) or to themselves (since it condemns them to die). That is the psychological aspect of their experience. But there is a religious aspect also. The irrevocable drinking of the potion, which appears at the time to be due to chance, but which looks afterwards as if everything had conspired to bring it about, symbolizes a soul's *election* by omnipotent Love, its being unexpectedly seized by its vocation as if in its own despite. Thereupon, with the drinking of the potion, Tristan (as Gottfried of Strasbourg says of Tristan's father) "entered upon another life." To quote Gottfried further: "His senses were as though delivered from all natural curbs, and his life was being consumed." The words perfectly confirm what I have described as passion in opposition to what is natural love.

In the ordinary way this first and crucial summons should open the way to fasting and self-mortification, and lead to an *endura*. But Tristan, carried away by the violent effect of the first revelation which may sometimes inflame the blood, transgresses the rule of the Pure. He obtains his symbolical kiss by force, and profanes it. Thereupon the powers of evil are let loose.

Sigh, ah sigh, wind so wild!
Sigh, ah sigh now, my child!
O Irish maid, thou wayward, winsome maid!

Thereupon a lifetime of penance is going to be required
in order to wipe out the sacrilege. But the fundamental
misfortune of this love is not only that the sin must be
redeemed. The *askesis* of self-redemption must also, and
above all, deliver a man from having been born into this
world of darkness and lead him to the state of final and
fortunate detachment in which he can undergo the deliberate death of the Perfect. Tristan's penance therefore has
a meaning entirely different from Christian repentance.
And although there are times in the Romance when
orthodoxy and heresy seem to get singularly mixed, such
indications leave one in no doubt regarding the predominant intention, an intention made unmistakable at
the last by the death of the two lovers in sombre splen-
dour. Every episode, moreover, points to this intention;
for example, that of the "harsh life" led by Tristan
and Iseult in the Forest of Morrois. In the *Roman en
prose*, "We have lost the world, and the world us," Iseult
laments; and Tristan answers: "If the whole world were
now with us, I should see but you alone." This must
indeed be an *endura*. The retreat in the forest symbolizes a period of fasting and self-mortification such as
we know that the Cathars underwent in order that
their faculties might be all absorbed in the exclusive contemplation of love.

A profound characteristic of passion—and also of
mysticism in general—may be discerned here. Later Novalis, a mystic devoted to Night and to a secret Light,
wrote: "The lover is alone with all that he loves." For
that matter, among many possible interpretations, it can
be held that his maxim states a purely psychological
piece of observation—that passion is by no means the
fuller life which it seems to be in the dreams of adoles-
cence, but is on the contrary a kind of naked and
denuding intensity; verily, a bitter destitution, the *impoverishment* of a mind being emptied of all diversity,
an obsession of the imagination by a single image. In
the face of the assertion of its power, the world dis-
solves; "the others" cease to be present; and there are no

longer either neighbours or duties, or binding ties, or earth or sky; one is alone with all that one loves. "We have lost the world and the world us." Such is ecstasy, a flight inward from all created things. How can we avoid calling to mind those "deserts" of the Dark Night described by Saint John of the Cross! "Put things far away, lover! My road is flight!" And several centuries before Novalis Saint Teresa of Avila declared that a soul when in ecstasy should feel "as though there were only God and itself in the world."

Are we entitled to compare religious geniuses of the first rank with a poem in which the mystical element is quite rudimentary? Admittedly, to do so would be blasphemy of a kind if the Romance were concerned with no more than a passion of sensual love. But everything points to our being on the *via mystica* of the Perfect. The difference from orthodox mysticism lies in the content of the spiritual states and the goal of those states, not in their form.[1] I shall return to this presently.

In the meanwhile, here is a further point of comparison. Spanish mystics have a well-known habit of insisting on

---

[1] Gottfried of Strasbourg's *Tristan* contains the following passage:

> It is not without reason
> That this hollow
> Has been put away in a wilderness.
> It means
> That the place of love
> Lies not in beaten ways
> Nor about our human dwellings.
> Love haunts the deserts.
> The road that leads to its retreat
> Is a hard and toilsome road.

Should it still be doubted what kind of love is being referred to, let me say that Gottfried admits having wandered in the desert himself, but without meeting the reward of his pains (he means that he has not become one of the Perfect).

> I have known the hollow
> When only eleven years old.
> But to Cornwall have I never been.

How could physical love be intended here? The last line shows clearly that the "hollow" is purely symbolical since it may exist elsewhere than in Cornwall. Possibly "Cornwall" stands for a temple or grotto of the heretics.

an account of what they *suffer*. Saint John of the Cross
says in *La Noche oscura:* [1]

"So brilliant and pure is the light of contemplation that
when this Divine light assails the soul, in order to expel
its impurity, the soul feels itself to be so impure and
miserable that it believes God to be against it, and
thinks that it has set itself up against God. This causes
it so much grief and pain (because it now believes that
God has cast it away) that one of the greatest trials
which Job felt when God sent him this experience, was
as follows, when he said: 'Why hast thou set me opposite to thee, and I am become burdensome to myself?'"
The saint does not refer to bodily or moral pains arising
from the mortification of senses and will, but to the
soul suffering separation and rejection while its love is
most ardent. A hundred pages could be quoted in which
there recurs the same lament of the soul about feeling
deserted by the divine and being overwhelmingly an-
guished; about "the sense of a deep void . . . of a cruel
death to the three kinds of goods that may assuage the
soul—temporal, natural, and spiritual goods"; and about
"the feeling of rejection which counts among the sternest
ordeals of the state of purification."

Tristan is but an adulterated and sometimes ambiguous expression of courtly mysticism. In interpreting
some of those situations in the Romance which seem
most thoroughly "mystical," it is wise, if we do not
wish to go seriously astray, to set out from human love
and by way of sublimation—not in the opposite direction, from divine Love to metaphors, as we need to do
when dealing with the great orthodox mystics. Bearing
this in mind, we may trace in the myth more than one
aspect of the sufferings undergone in mystical experience.
It will be recalled how the troubadour laments:

> Heaven! How doth it thus befall?
> The farther off I am the more I long for her.

And, indeed, never does love thrill Tristan so wildly as
when he is parted from his "lady." This can be accounted
for by elementary psychology, but the point here is that

---

[1] Saint John of the Cross, *Complete Works*, translated by E.
Allison Peers (London, 1934), I, p. 407. *The Dark Night of the
Soul*, II, v.

it represents the anguish undergone in a purifying *askesis*.
We have seen that in the Romance the repeated *partings*
of the lovers answer to an altogether internal necessity
of their passion. Iseult is a woman beloved, but she is
also more than this: she is symbol of luminous Love.
When Tristan wanders far away from her, his love for
her waxes, and the more he loves her the more he is
afflicted. But, of course, by now we are aware that the
real purpose of the partings is to produce suffering.
This brings us back to mysticism from the other end, so
to speak. The more Tristan loves, the more he wants to
be parted from the beloved. This means that the more
he loves, the more he wants to be rejected by love. So
strongly does he want to be rejected that he comes to
doubt Iseult's "love" for him, treats her like an adversary,
and commits himself to a "blank" marriage with the other
Iseult—the other "faith," the other Church, whose communion he has to decline!

Only in one passage of the Romance does orthodoxy
for a moment have the better part. When the effect of the
love-potion has at last worn off, Tristan and Iseult go
to visit the hermit Ogrin in his cell. This results in a
meeting between one who endures for the sake of his
God and the lovers who endure for the sake of another
Love. It is then that they repent—for the first and last
time. Iseult is to go back to her legal husband—heresy
is to return to the bosom of the Church. But as the king
draws near with his escort of barons, the lovers exchange a ring of everlasting fidelity and secrecy. Submission is but simulated. And presently in demanding the
ordeal of the red-hot iron the queen is seeking to avenge
herself upon the king's God, whom this ordeal dupes
twice.

However external and a matter of form these correspondences may be, they cannot fairly be dismissed as
mere coincidences. But if the forms are the same, it remains to be seen in what respect the matter differs and
how the matter can ever have come to be treated as
identical in both cases. It might all be regarded as a gross
confusion of Creator and creature, in the Romance; a
case, according to the text-books, of the famous "divinization of woman." Supposing Iseult had been merely a
beautiful woman—as subsequent centuries were to think
—the mystic similitudes which I have set forth would

belong to the order of language, and specially to metaphor. I shall not try to deny that aspect of the question.
It will have consideration. But I believe that there is a
good deal more. For if there were not, then the whole
religious background of the legend would have to be
either denied or neglected, notwithstanding the historical
evidence. As regards the meaning of the myth, we should
be brought back to zero and the Romance would not be a
courtly novel; or else, again, courtly love would cease to
be what it actually was, and would set itself to resemble
what our men of learning imagine it was. That is as good
as to say that we can understand nothing about nothing.
Once again, the matter in question is the *passion*
of love, and not love purely profane and natural. What,
it seems to me, lies at the heart of the antithesis between
the two forms of mysticism is that the Romance deals, not
merely with profane and natural love, but with *passionate* love. Orthodox mysticism brings about a "spiritual
marriage" of God and the individual soul already in this
life, whereas the heretical looks to union and complete
fusion, and this only after the demise of the body. In
the eyes of the Cathars, this world was past all possible
redemption, and their belief implied in theory that profane love is absolute misfortune, an impossible and blam-
able attachment to an imperfect creature. In the eyes of
the Christian, on the other hand, divine love is a misfortune also, since man in his fallen state is unable to
love God fully in return, but it is a misfortune which
nevertheless creates man anew, and which, far from being
antagonistic to profane love, results in making this love
holy through marriage. Accordingly, the mystic lovers in
the Romance are compelled to pursue the *intensity* of
passion, not its fortunate appeasement. The keener their
passion, and the more it can detach them from created
things, the more readily do they feel that they are on the
way to attaining the death in *endura* which they desire.
But by Christian mystics, on the contrary, the reality of
the mystical state is subjected to the test of the deeds
and works that issue from it.[1] At least, such has been

---

[1] Saint Teresa says: "In order to please God, and in order to
receive great benefits from Him, these benefits must—such is His
will—pass *through the hands* of holy mankind in whom, as He
Himself has said, He finds His satisfaction." Meister Eckhart did
not see this, but cf. Chapter 3 below.

the constant intention of those mystics who concentrated
their prayers upon the truly incarnated Christ. The Perfect, however, did not believe in the Incarnation, and
could not be aware of the *return* of the soul to a life
renewed. "I die of not being able to die," Saint Teresa
says; but she means that she is not able to die to the old
life enough to become alive in the new, and thus to obey
without anguish.

I see nothing in *Tristan* to recall the "rejection of gifts"
which is spoken of by Eckhart and Saint John of the
Cross. The lovers now and then complain of their passion and curse the fatal potion which has been the cause
of their terrible sufferings. "*Amor par force les demeine.*"
But ultimately it is complete passion that they accept
like a *last* revelation in death. So with their attitude to
creatures. They are not going to *meet* them again after
having passed through their passion and its *askesis*. They
are unaware of that movement of *return to the world*
so characteristic of Christianity. Saint John of the Cross
also has experienced perfect detachment. "When the passions are mortified, the soul receives no more nourishment from creatures; and in that way is filled with obscurity, and is deprived of the objects which the passions were presenting to it." (*Noche oscura, III.*) (The
passage can certainly bear comparison with that admirable
cry by Bernart of Ventadour: "She has taken my heart,
she has taken my self, she has taken from me the world,
and then she has eluded me, leaving me with only my
desire and my parched heart.") Beyond that state,
Saint John of the Cross experienced complete viduity, in
which not only the world and his neighbour, and love
with its object, but even the *desire* of love, seem to escape
at the height of the exaltation. "Empty of all cov-
etousness, nothing impels upward and nothing draws
downward." (*Maxims.*) The troubadour Arnaut Daniel
also refers to the "excess of desire" which takes away
"all desire." But the theopathic state does not lead Saint
John of the Cross to condemn creatures. Meister Eckhart—who is, perhaps mistakenly, held to be a Platonist
—has the ability to say in magnificent terms that the
pure soul is the place of redemption for creatures who
have lost their nature through sin. "All creatures pass
from their life to their being. All creatures bear themselves into my reason so as to be within me reasonable.

I alone, I bring all creatures to God." That is the movement which is lacking theoretically in any kind of mysticism based on the luminous Eros.

Where the two forms of mysticism differ most is as regards *humility*. And there again the key to the antithesis lies in the mystery of the Incarnation. The Romance is steeped in the Celtic atmosphere of knightly *pride*. The high deeds which Tristan performs are inspired by a desire to be valiant. Like all passionate people, he foolhardily revels in the sense of power which comes over him in moments of peril. Hence ultimately he grows to want danger for its own sake, to want to experience passion for a never-ending passion, and to desire an irrevocable death. At this extreme, prowess appears as the material sign of a process of *divinization*. True mystics, on the contrary, are the very essence of prudence, rigour, and clear-sighted obedience. If "death is my gain," it is because "Christ is my life" and because Christ was incarnated—that is, came down to us. That is why a Christian does not fall into the delusion of supposing that death for the sake of love can transfigure him; instead he accepts the limitations of his terrestrial vocation. "Nothing impels him upward, nothing draws him downward," Saint John of the Cross said, and this *"because he places himself at the centre of his humility."*

3

Curious but Inevitable Transpositions

The whole of European poetry has come out of courtly love and out of the Arthurian romances derived from this love. That is why our poetry employs a pseudo-mystical vocabulary, from which, quite unaware of what they are doing, persons in love still draw today their most commonplace metaphors. Yet even as the romantic myth had made use of a stock of imagery, names, and situations taken out of the accumulations left by Celtic religion—that is to say, a religion already dead—so

our literature and our passions now ignorantly and
pervertedly employ a terminology which mysticism alone
invested with a valid meaning.

More than once the ambiguous character of the myth
has caused us to hesitate in the presence of this or that
episode. Was it a case of profane love—according to the
letter of the Romance—or of a symbol of the luminous
Eros, or even a symbol of the Church of Love? It is thus
understandable that a reader unaware of the mysteries
should almost unavoidably be brought in consequence to
transpose into profane life all these too carefully veiled
allegories. The process is easily imagined. Saint Augustine
wrote this prayer: "And behold, thou wert within me,
and I out of myself, when I made search for thee!"
He was addressing God, eternal love. But suppose that a
troubadour—one of the Geoffrey Rudels—should have
expressed the same prayer while pretending to address it
to his Lady. The lover, accustomed to mystical metaphors,
which he interprets with their profane meaning, is tempted
to see in the same phrase an expression of the passion
which he loves: the passion that is tasted and savoured
for its own sake, in a kind of indifference to its living
and external object. So we saw above that Tristan does
not love Iseult in her reality but to the extent that she
revives *in him* the delightful cautery of desire. Passionate
love tends to grow like the exaltation of a kind of narcissism.

Once the mysteries had been forgotten, it was inevitable that readers of the Romance should interpret its
too skilful allegories as applying to profane life. The
modern mind has supposed that the transposition thus
effected—after the twelfth century—could serve as a
primary datum. It has supposed that it could "explain"
the higher by the lower—unalloyed mysticism by human
passion. And so it founded a new "science," which was
based on the study of language in general and on the
similarity of metaphors in particular. But where did the
metaphors originate? In a kind of mysticism which, as
I have shown, was disguised, persecuted, and then forgotten. So thoroughly was it forgotten as heresy and so
completely did it pass into everyday use through poetry
that the Christian mystics took up its metaphors as if
these had been *natural*. And we today have done likewise, and so have our men of learning. The "science"

is therefore valid on condition the signs are changed in every one of its statements. For instance, where the science speaks of mysticism as having resulted from a sublimation of instinct, it is enough to change the direction of the relation stated, and to write: The "instinct" in question is the result of the profanation of an early form of mysticism.

But the modern mind is so reluctant to accept this conversion that I had better go further into the mechanism of the transpositions, and even recognize the validity of some of the current objections. For after all has not mysticism, it will be said, been open in at least one tendency, to every kind of confusion? Was it not first the mystics who took advantage of the language of the pagan Eros?

4

Orthodox Mystics and the Language of Passion

The central event in the world from the standpoint of every kind of religious life that is Christian in content and in form must be the Incarnation. To shift however little from this centre involves the double peril of humanism and idealism. The Catharist heresy idealized the whole of the Gospel, and treated love in all its forms as a leap out of the created world. The craving for this flight into the divine—or enthusiasm—and for this ultimately impracticable transgression of human limitations, was bound to find expression, and thereby to betray itself fatally, through the magnification in divine terms of sexual love. Conversely, the most "Christocentric" mystics have had a propensity to address God in the language of human feeling—the language of sexual attraction, of hunger and thirst, and of the will. This is a magnification in human terms of the love of God.

In this way we become aware of the two great streams into which all mysticism divides. They are seldom met with pure in a particular work. Even in writings the most truly representative of one or the other, both may nearly always be discerned, if only as temptation coincides in a believer with the will to obedience. Historically speaking, it is not very easy to isolate either. But theologically the position is clear. The first stream is that of *unitive mysticism,* which aims at a complete *fusion* of the soul with the divine. The second stream may be called *epithalamian mysticism,* which aims at the *marriage* of a soul to God, and which therefore implicitly maintains an essential distinction between creature and Creator.

It will make for clearness, while avoiding an excessive simplification, if I take a few individual examples—the only examples worth while in this domain.[1] We thereby shall obtain some insight into the cause of the curious fact *that the misuse of the language of love by religious writers must be linked, from a historical standpoint, with the orthodox stream.*

The first example I take from Rudolf Otto, who in his book *West-Östliche Mystik* [2] first compares the founder of German mysticism in the fourteenth century, Meister Eckhart, with the Hindu mystic Sankara, and then contrasts them. The interesting thing for my present purpose is that Otto distinguishes East and West by calling these two forms of mysticism respectively eros and agape, rather in the way I have done above.[3] Sankara, according to Otto, rejects the world and condemns it beyond appeal. *Nirvana,* Sankara said, cannot accept *sansara,* which is life in its diversity and infinite flux. Eckhart, on the contrary, discerns the presence of God in every creature, so that through the soul of a believer all creatures "pass from their existence into their being." It has been possible for Otto to carry out his comparison, because in the Middle Ages in Europe there existed a mystical tradition akin to Sankara's. It was, Otto says,[4]

---

[1] For indeed generalizations are nowhere more misleading than in connection with the mystics. In *St. Jean de la Croix et l'expérience mystique* (Paris, 2nd ed., 1931), Jean Baruzi admirably remarks on page 613 that if we attempted to take a general view of the various forms of mysticism known to us, "the mystical experience would seem homogeneous only in so far as it is commonplace and in so far as we failed to apprehend its nature."

[2] Gotha, 1929.   [3] Book II, Chapter 4.

[4] *Mysticism East and West,* translated by Bertha L. Bracey and Richenda C. Payne (New York and London, 1932), p. 212.

"a mysticism of exaggerated emotion where the 'I' and the 'Thou' flow together in a unity of intoxicated feeling. Eckhart knows nothing of such emotional orgies or such a 'pathological' love (as Kant calls it). For him love is not eros but the Christian virtue of agápe, strong as death but no paroxysm, inward but of deep humility, at once active in willing and doing as Kant's 'practical' love.

"Here Eckhart differs completely from Plotinus, though he is always represented as his pupil. Plotinus also is the publisher of a mystical love, but his love is throughout not Christian agápe, but the Greek eros, which is enjoyment, and enjoyment of a sensual and supersensual beauty arising from an aesthetic experience almost unknown to Eckhart. In its finest sublimation it still bears within it something of the eros of Plato's Symposium: that great Daemon, which is purified into a divine passion out of the ardor of procreation, yet even then still retains a sublimated element of the original passion."

For Eckhart, the true mystic way is not that which ascends from an emotional state in order to reach supreme union at the summit of a love ecstasy. "Minne einigt nicht," he writes, "Sie einigt wohl an einem Werk, nicht an einem Wesen." [1]

"Rather the 'at-one-ment' [i.e. union] [Otto continues] is itself the condition and the first ground of the possibility of true agápe. Nor has his agápe anything in common with the Platonic or Plotinian eros, but it is the pure Christian emotion in its elemental chastity and simplicity without exaggeraton or admixture." [2]

And from this union results "confidence, faith, surrender, service."

Indeed, I myself feel that it is a communion rather than a union; for, as Eckhart expresses it elsewhere,[3] when "the soul escapes from its nature, its being and its life, and is born into the Divinity, no distinction remains

---

[1] "Love does not unify; it unites all right in act, never to an essence."

[2] Op. cit., p. 213.

[3] At the end of the sermon, *Nisi granum frumenti*. It must be admitted that there is an elusive ambiguity about Eckhart's use of the word "union" (*Einung*), and yet it would seem clear enough from the passage I quote here that Otto is right and that he believed in no essential fusion.

but this: the Divinity is still God, and the soul is still a soul." The spiritual act of love is initial, not final. A Christian holds that to die to self is the beginning of a more real life here below, not the ruin of the world. Moreover, Otto quotes a further passage from Eckhart which does not refer to union, but to an equality of the soul with God. "Und diese Gleichheit aus dem Einen in das Eine mit dem Einen ist Quelle und Ursprung der aufblühenden glühenden Liebe." [1] Otto finds this passage to confirm how for Eckhart "the proper expression of the feeling of at-one-ness is not a mystical *pleasure,* but agápe, a love of a kind which neither Plotinus nor Sankara mentions or knows." [2]

It would thus seem that Otto succeeds in plainly defining two *poles* of universal mysticism, and that the East (Sankara, Plato, Plotinus) differs from the West (here typified by Eckhart) in the very way I have been saying that Catharist mysticism is to be distinguished from the Christian doctrine of love. But Eckhart, it must be recognized, did not dwell in the odour of sanctity. The Avignon pope, John XXII, in a bull issued in 1329, went the length of condemning several of his theses. Among these the tenth is stated in the bull to read as follows:

"We become completely changed into God and are converted into Him even as the bread is changed into the body of Christ in the sacrament: I am thus changed into Him because He Himself makes me become His. Unity and not similitude. By the living God, it is true that there is then no longer any distinction." As extracted from Eckhart's writings, this thesis seems expressly to contradict Otto's interpretation. It puts Meister Eckhart in the Eastern camp, making out that his mysticism aspires after an *essential* union and so is heretical.

One certainty is that Meister Eckhart is the dialectician *par excellence* and that it is only too easy to extract from his writings the most contradictory truths. Of his work it has proved possible to say that "negation and

[1] "And this identity out of the One into the One with the One is fount and source of a flowering glowing love."

[2] Op. cit., p. 214.

affirmation together form the truth. One is not true without the other, and one is inconceivable except in relation to the other. Affirmation and negation are inseparable, being but two aspects of one truth." [1] It is no less significant to notice that Flemish mystics vigorously attacked Eckhart's writings on those very heads regarding which he seems to Otto to have been orthodox—essential union and the neglect of works. Every one must stand to the East of somebody else, and Meister Eckhart evidently represented the heresy I am calling "eastern" in the opinion of Ruysbroek. Ruysbroek, in his *Book of the Twelve Beguines,* refers to Eckhart—who had been his own master—and to Eckhart's faithful disciples as "those false prophets" who "imagine that they partake of God by their nature." "These persons who want to be not only God's equals, but God Himself, are more wicked and diabolical than Lucifer and his satellites." And again: "They will neither learn, nor know, nor will, nor love, nor thank, nor extol, nor desire, nor possess. . . . That is what they call the perfect poverty of the spirit. . . . But those who are born of the Holy Ghost and sing his praises, practise every virtue. They know and love; they seek; they find. . . ." In short, they act.

It is evident that Ruysbroek accuses Eckhart of Quietism. He puts forward against him a kind of activism of love. He himself did not believe that all distinction between the soul and God can be abolished. The soul cannot train itself to partake of the Divine, but only to resemble God. It can behold God in the *mirror* of a spirit that has been entirely purified. "We contemplate what we are and are what we contemplate; for our essence, without losing any of its proper personality, is united to the divine truth which respects the distinction." And again, "The abyss separating us from God is one," he says, "which we perceive in the secret places of the self. It is essential distance."

This brings me to the point I wish to set forth. If the soul is able to achieve essential union with God, then the soul's love of God is a happy love. It may be expected to display no need of the vocabulary of passion, and this is indeed what history shows. "I fancy," the Abbé

---

[1] B. Groethuysen in *Hermes* (Paris, July, 1937).

Paquier writes,[1] "that the Eckhartian mystics never resort to the language of human love." On the contrary, if it is believed, in accordance with Christian orthodoxy, that the soul cannot achieve essential union with God, the soul's love of God becomes, in the strictest sense, an *unhappy mutual love*. It may then be expected to express itself in passionate language, in the vocabulary of the Catharist heresy as this has become "profaned" by literature and been taken over by human passions. For the rhetoric of the Heresy is the best fitted to describe and communicate the altogether ineffable nature of the emotion experienced. Here again the documentary evidence supports and makes clear the apparent paradoxes of my outline. It is Ruysbroek who, with his doctrine of an essential distinction, introduces into the writings of the mystics of the North the "epithalamian" vocabulary.

"Here then the irresistible desire has come [he says]. To compel oneself continually to seize what cannot be seized. . . . And the object of this desire can be neither given up nor seized.[2] To give it up is unbearable, to retain it impossible. Silence itself lacks the strength to grasp it in its hands."

Ruysbroek pours into his glowing style all the metaphors of passionate love. He speaks of being submerged in love, of swooning away, of embraces and of hurricanes of eagerness, of the fire of love that burns the soul day and night, of orgies of love, overflowing delights, of being intoxicated with love, and of love's bruisings. "He has drunk up my spirit and my heart," Ruysbroek causes one of his beguines to say in referring to Christ. "I have become lost in his mouth," another says. And a third declares: "Oh, to drink in the glances of love and to be engulfed in them intoxicated!"

In the thirteenth century the Franciscan mystics sup-

[1] Cit. apud Baruzi, *St. Jean de la Croix,* p. 642. The absence of "epithalamian" expressions may possibly serve as a criterion for deciding whether or not a given mystic believed in essential union, and in that case Abbé Paquier's remark goes against Otto's contention: we are led to put Eckhart among the heretics. Obviously I am simplifying matters, but the question is one worth examining closely.

[2] One of the troubadours says: "Love neither forsakes me nor can it well take me."

ply a no less striking instance of the use of courtly terminology. Saint Francis himself, it is well known, learned French in his youth, and delighted in French tales of chivalry. He dreamed of becoming "the finest knight in the world." It will be remembered that he began his ministry by removing his clothes in the presence of the bishop and of a great crowd assembled in the main square of Assisi. When he was quite naked, he said to his richly attired father that henceforth his only father would be God. The bishop threw his cloak over Francis, who fled into the countryside declaiming verses in French in a loud voice. He felt that the utter destitution of his body had made it the humble servant of his soul. Thereupon there was nothing to hamper his ascent towards the Supreme Good. Remembering the French romances he had read, Francis made Poverty his "Lady," and deemed it an honour to be her "knight."

The Franciscan wandering knights spread over Italy as the troubadours had spread over the South of France. They were to be met with on the roads and in market places, and from village to castle. The poems of Jacopone da Todi—"God's jongleur"—the lauds of his imitators, the letters of Saint Catherine of Siena, the Book of the Blessed Angela di Foligno, and the many tales of the Fioretti,[1] show that the rhetoric of the troubadours and of the courtly romances was the direct inspiration of the Franciscan poetic impulse, which in turn deeply influenced the mystical vocabulary of subsequent centuries.

"Remember, O creature, that thy nature partaketh of the angels. Dost thou tarry in this mud, and thou shalt have to stay for ever in darkness."

So one of the lauds attributed to Jacopone da Todi and his followers; and the suggestion in this passage that men are in some way angels disturbingly recalls the doctrine of the Cathars. Other lauds, while obviously more Catholic in their inspiration, are for that reason only the more "erotic" and "courtly" in phraseology. For example:

"My heart melteth like ice on fire when I straitly embrace my Lord, and cry: 'The love of Love consumeth me, I am united with Love, intoxicated by love.'

[1] Saint Francis called Friar Giles "a paladin of the Round Table," and the saint's *miracles*—such as the conversion of the Gubbio wolf—occurred in the same circumstances as did the feats of *prowess* of the wandering knights.

"In flames I burn and languish, crying: 'In living I die, and in dying I live. Yet do I not love, but am athirst for love; I hunger to be united with Love.'" [1]

5

Courtly Rhetoric in Spanish Mysticism

If now we turn to the writings of the great Spanish mystics of the sixteenth century, Saint Teresa and Saint John of the Cross, we find them employing the whole rhetoric of courtly love, even its most delicate shades of expression. Here are the chief topics common alike to the troubadours and to these orthodox mystics:

"To die of not being able to die." [2]

The "sweet cautery."

"Love's dart" that wounds but does not kill.

The "salute" of love.

Passion that sets one apart from the world and other beings.

Passion that renders every other kind of love colourless.

To complain of an ill that is yet prized more than every joy and worldly good.

To deplore that words should betray an "ineffable" emotion which nevertheless demands to be avowed.

Love as a purifying emotion that drives away all vile thoughts.

The substitution of the will of love for the real will.

The "struggle of love" in which it is needful to be defeated.

The symbolism of "castles" as havens of love.

---

[1] From *Ciascun amante,* described as "a dance of mystic love."

[2] This famous exclamation of Saint Teresa's was inspired by the Franciscan Angela di Foligno, who said: "I die of a desire to die!"

The symbolism of the "mirror" for imperfect love reflecting perfecting love.

The "stolen heart," the "ravished understanding," the "rape of love."

Love treated as an ultimate "understanding" (*conoscenza* in Provençal).

All this kind of thing has led the materialistic psychologist—from Voltaire to Freud—to declare with odd assurance, and purely on verbal grounds, that mystics are the victims of a sexual aberration. And, as is well known, the views put forth by the learned in the nineteenth century have now become the prepossessions of the vulgar. However, not only is the materialistic attitude to mysticism clearly more indicative of an obsession in those who cling to it than enlightening about mysticism itself, but also it is an attitude based upon an error at once historical and psychological. For (*a*) the language of passion, as the mystics employ it, has not been to begin with the language of the senses and of nature, but the rhetoric of a kind of *askesis* exemplified by the twelfth-century heresy of Southern France; and (*b*) geniuses such as Saint John of the Cross and Saint Teresa must have been more alive than any one else to the perils of "spiritual luxuriousness" (the expression is Saint John's), and both speak of it so freely that in their case the usual suspicion of an "inhibition" must be meaningless.

These two points deserve to be elaborated. In the first place, it needs to be insisted that the language of the mystics is not open to being confused with the profound nature of the experiences they underwent. J. Baruzi writes of Saint Teresa that "the source of many of her images has been traced, but it is not so easy to find the origins of the psychological language in which she undoubtedly most truly expressed her nature." All mystics, and Saint Teresa as much as any of them, complain of a want of new words (*nuevas palabras*) with which to praise the works of God as they experience these in spirit. Their silence is *truer* than their speech. The only thing I wish to do here is to consider the *inherited material* of their literary vocabulary.

To confine myself to an instance which is at one and the same time the most celebrated, the best known, and that which has most strikingly misled the authorities,

the fact is that Saint Teresa constantly employs and even
refines upon courtly rhetoric. Is this a matter of literary
influence? Of some underground heretical connexion? Or
even of an independent re-creation which might be partly
accounted for on the lines of remarks made in the
preceding chapter? "How can we tell," Baruzi says,
"whether some of the images which John of the Cross
takes from the Song of Songs were extracted directly from
the Biblical poem or were not at the same time images
which he rediscovered and, so to speak, verified for himself, because they expressed a newly experienced delight?" [1] These are questions which I do not believe any
one is equipped to settle. The best informed specialists
hesitate over attributing to very famous—and, as it happens, orthodox—mystics, such as Ruysbroek or Saint
Teresa, the originating of the actual terminology used by
Saint John of the Cross. As regards Saint Teresa, however, we may trace unmistakable sources. The fondness
shown by the mystics for the romances of chivalry has
often been pointed out. Saint Teresa in her girlhood doted
upon them.[2] It seems even that she once thought of
writing a romance herself in collaboration with her brother
Rodriguez. It is also well known that the religious writings which were her intellectual nourishment were all the
work of authors strongly imbued with courtly and chivalric rhetoric. M. Gaston Etchegoyen says:[3]

"The noble language of *Amadis of Gaul*, its erotic metaphors, and its subtle refinements, are found also in Francisco de Ossuna and Bernardino de Laredo [writers whom
Saint Teresa made her master] as well as in the *Excla-
maciones* and the *Castillo interior*.

"In Spain the authors of romances of chivalry display
the same realism as those of treatises on mysticism, sac-
rificing a sense of the marvellous in favour of a more
familiar and moving intimacy, as they tend to treat the
human and the divine on one plane, either by *contemplat-
ing the divine from a secular standpoint or by giving
the human a divine interpretation*.

"Above all, courtly and divine love encourage one an-

---

[1] Op. cit., p. 343.

[2] Vide her *Vida*, chap. II.

[3] *L'Amour divin: essai sur les sources de sainte Thérèse* (Paris,
1923), Part IV.

other to a like heroic notion of moral obligation, of action, and of faith. Amadis of Gaul and Saint Teresa could both have taken for their motto: 'To love in order to act.' [Although courtly love, in its pristine purity, loved in order to suffer, in order 'to endure'.]

"A fusion of divine and courtly love was effected, not in the feeble extravagances of the romances of mystic chivalry, but by the twelfth-century troubadours of Provence. The most fecund material in their doctrine, and in their symbolism and terminology, was taken over by mysticism in the thirteenth century, thanks to St. Francis of Assisi.

"Considering St. Teresa alone, we see that the romances of chivalry had a psychological influence upon her, and also a literary influence which is chiefly evident in the warlike symbolism of the *Castillo interior*."

What an extraordinary return and incorporation of heresy by means of a rhetoric devised by heretics for use against the Church, and which the Church, thanks to the saints, eventually wrested from them! Let me summarize the stages of the process. The heresy of the Perfect is brought down from Eros to Venus and is carried the length of kinship with a poetry of love apparently altogether secular; the confusions that this involves flatter natural desires, so that little by little the heresy vanishes from before the eyes of the worldly whom the deceptive charms of art have taken in, and they treat the language as simply poetry. Finally, first a hundred and then another three hundred years later, nobody remembers that the garment was ever meant to cover anything but nature, and Christian mysticism comes along in order to make it into a cloak for Agape!

The partiality of the Christian mystics for the terminology of passion has generally been interpreted psychologically according to the materialistic superstition.[1] Everything possible—and indeed rather more than everything possible—has been attributed to a "deflexion" of sexual instinct. On the whole, the nineteenth century never felt greater self-satisfaction than when equating the superior with the inferior, the mental with the material, and the significant with the insignificant. It called this "explaining." There is no need to demonstrate that most

---

[1] Cf. the writings of Max Nordau, Krafft-Ebing, Murisier, Leuba, Freud, etc.

of the time it was merely casting its critical sense to the winds. But I may remark that its propensity in this direction may well testify to some deep *resentment* of poetry and indeed of all creative—and hence venturesome —activity of the mind.

But it is desirable to insist further, that for men of the sixteenth century erotic language was more innocent than it is in our eyes. We are the neurosis victims, heirs of a bourgeois form of Puritanism that has come down to us from a disbelieving nineteenth century. Saint John of the Cross, who described in a remarkable page of psychological penetration the moves of a flesh attracted by the beginnings of mystic exaltation (*Noche oscura,* I, v. 3), exaggerates no more than he dissimulates the relative gravity of such incidents. To recite at this point the formulas of "sublimation" and "inhibition" is simply to refuse to understand what one is talking about. Where is the inhibition, where the censorship, in Saint Teresa's writing to a religious who has complained of experiencing an emotion of the senses each time he enters upon prayer, "I find that this is indifferent to prayer, and that it is best to pay no attention whatever to it." So, Saint John of the Cross, replying to one of his brothers, who could not communicate without experiencing sexual emotion, and who, accordingly, had been commanded not to communicate more than once a year, advises him not to be upset about it, to receive the sacrament each week, whatever happens—and the brother is cured, because he no longer fears excessively. If we are required to say anything further about psycho-analysis, let us not fail to notice that Saint John of the Cross plays here the part of a doctor, not that of a neurotic.

"It will perhaps seem to you [writes Saint Teresa] that some of the things to be met with in the Song of Songs might have been put differently. Considering our grossness, I should not be surprised if that came to your mind. I have even heard some persons told that they should avoid hearing them. O God! how great is our wretchedness! It befalls us as it befalls those venomous animals which change into poison everything they eat."

From the formal comparison of the *writings* of Eckhart with those of Ruysbroek, Saint Teresa and Saint John of the Cross, we may now infer that metaphors borrowed from current language by the mystics have a character in close relation to their doctrine of union or to their faith in the Incarnation. Ruysbroek, Saint Teresa, and Saint John of the Cross are very distinctly "Christocentric." Everything in their minds sets out from the drama of the division which sin opened between man and his Creator; all ends in moments of active communion in Grace, and that is what they call "marriage"—the communion of the elect soul with Christ the Church's bridegroom. But the way of the *parted* man is passion—and passion is everywhere in their writings, whereas it is absent from those of Eckhart.

That is why orthodox mysticism—the kind least suspect of equivocal partiality—was led *by the very object of its faith* to use, and at times to abuse, the language of passionate love. A use and an abuse into which modern psychology was bound to read meanings agreeable to its doctrine, but meanings that seem to me to be controverted by history.

6

A Note on Metaphor

However, the matter may be carried further. It is possible to say: "Let us grant that the language of passion was derived from a courtly literature, itself produced in the atmosphere of a certain heresy. Did not this heresy in turn arise out of sublimated physiological proclivities?" *Historically,* the question has nothing to go on; and yet theoretically the objection is possible and even inevitable. But to ask if "mind" or "matter" is the ultimate *cause* of phenomena involving both is like asking: "Which came first, the hen or the egg?" For example, we are quite unable to tell whether the language of mysticism resulted from a materialization of the spiritual—in which event the latter would be a first cause—or on the contrary from a sublimation of physiological phenomena—in which case these phenomena must underlie what is being expressed. But one thing is certain: we are confronted with two factors which never exist singly. That should content everybody, although in fact it contents no one.

Metaphor, indeed, affords another instance of that eagerness of the contemporary mind to settle a question in favour of whatever is lower. We speak of a *bitter* taste, and also of a *bitter* pain. This everybody is ready to explain by saying that to speak of a bitter pain is to use a metaphor and to give the epithet a figurative sense. The *real* meaning of the word "bitter" is made a physical sensation, which is thus held to have preceded any mental one. Very possibly, but actually we do not know. It is impossible for anybody who thinks that the physical came first to give *reasons* for his opinion. Nobody has found out that the "material" meaning of every word has actually preceded the "mental" meaning. The opinion that it has is merely based on a presumption—that the physical is *more true and more real* than the mental, and hence that the physical is at the foundation of all things and is the principle of all *explanation*.

The mechanics of this presumption have been set forth and criticized by Dr. Minkowski and Arnaud Dandieu [1] both pertinently and with subtlety. According to these writers, literal and figurative meanings cannot be subordinated to one another, because both express in their respective departments an indivisible reality, which is more profound than, and also anterior to, either its sensorial or mental aspects. How could we otherwise explain that one and the same word serves to denote such diverse things? Actually, a pain may be no less bitter than the taste of salt, and what we denote by the same word in each case is a way of being affected —whether by the senses or by thought—in the wholeness of our existence. Likewise with our metaphors of love. People nowadays do not hesitate to argue as follows: "*Love* means to me sexual attraction. Saint Teresa everlastingly talks of love. Ergo, she was not only a mystic, but an erotomaniac unawares." But we have seen that Saint Teresa was unaware of nothing, and that, on

---

[1] E. Minkowski, *Vers une Cosmologie* (Paris, 1936), chapter on metaphor, and Arnaud Dandieu and R. Aron, *La Révolution nécessaire* (Paris, 1931), chapter on Marcel Proust.

the contrary, "passionate" lovers may be mystics unawares. The arguments cancel out. We know nothing of primal origins. What we have been able to distinguish is the interplay of the two factors in historical evolution. Let me sum it up again, for clarity.

Our language of passion comes down to us from the rhetoric of the troubadours. It was a supremely ambiguous rhetoric. Its symbols of sexual attraction were the product of Manichaean dogmatics. But little by little, as it was gradually separated from the religion in which it originated, it passed into manners, and became part of the common language. Now, a mystic who wishes to describe his ineffable experiences is compelled to resort to metaphor. He takes his metaphors wherever he comes upon them, and as they already are, although he can, of course, inflect their meaning. Beginning with the twelfth century, the current metaphors became those of courtly rhetoric. If the mystics adopted them unhesitatingly, it was not in the least that they were "sublimating" sensual passions; they used them, because the habitual form of expressing such passions—which had themselves been given substance by another kind of mysticism—suited the expression of the spiritual love which they were experiencing. The form of expression was the more appropriate to describing the "unhappy" relations which a soul entertained with its God, that the form had been the more thoroughly humanized, i.e. was detached from the heresy. For the heresy had assumed the possibility of union between God and soul, which implied divine felicity and the unhappiness of every human love; whereas orthodoxy assumes that union is impossible, which implies divine unhappiness and renders human love possible within its own limits. It follows that what is the language of human passion according to the heresy corresponds to the language of divine passion according to orthodoxy. There has thus been a continuous interaction, and it is altogether arbitrary to isolate this or that moment and set it up in the guise of a primary *datum*.

7

The Mystic Deliverance

The time has come for us to be arbitrary in this way and to decide the question in favour of the mental—that is to say, in favour of the primacy of mind. Whether arbitrary *ante* or *post rem*—and in this case there is no real difference—the decision can nevertheless be justified by arguments. In the first place, it seems to me that the language of passion can be accounted for on the view that mind comes before matter because it expresses, not the triumph of nature over mind,[1] but an encroachment of mind over instinct. "There is love whenever desire is so great as to go beyond the confines of natural love," the troubadour Guido Calvacanti declared in the thirteenth century; and it is in his transcending the confines of instinct that man is set up as mind. This is alone what enables human beings to speak. For language offers the possibility of lying *as much as* the possibility of stating what is. Animals cannot lie; they are unable to state what instinct does not supply; they cannot go beyond necessity or beyond satisfaction. But passion—the love of love—is, on the contrary, an urge going beyond instinct and thereby it *gives* instinct *the lie*. In such circumstances the lie can only be uttered by mind.[2]

Secondly, if Saint John of the Cross, and even

[1] As is implied in such an everyday expression as "blinded by passion" or "madly in love."

[2] How deeply are statement and lying bound together in passionate love! Indeed, the will to expression, the will to self-description, as if in order to obtain a more intense self-enjoyment, is typical of all passion. And it also implies the conviction that other people must fail to understand, and that if they question or accuse us they must be lied to for the sake of preserving the very essence of passion.

176

Ruysbroek and Saint Francis, obviously appeared later than the moment at which passionate love flowered into consciousness, this moment is in turn later than the pseudo-Christian mysticism of the Cathars.

And, thirdly, it has probably been a mistake to suppose that the proposition, "Every erotomaniac is a mystic unawares," can be countered by the statement, "Or the other way round." The *epigoni* of the great mystics may sometimes seem to us as if they had been erotomaniacs unawares.[1] Nevertheless, erotomania is unquestionably a kind of drugged state, and everything goes to show that Eckhart, Ruysbroek, Teresa, and John of the Cross were the exact opposite of any drug-taker. For a drug-taker is the victim not of his passion but of the material means which he employs in order to obtain his transports. Although a drug-taker's passion may have originated in a conscious or unconscious desire to escape from an intolerable terrestrial confinement, it remains that he is first and foremost the slave of his drug. Psychologically speaking, he is a fallen being, whose senses are deadened, whose mind has become clouded, and who ends up in idiocy. But the great mystics, on the contrary, urge the need of pushing beyond the trance stage and of reaching a clarity of mind ever purer and more daring, and even of verifying the high gifts of grace by means of their repercussions *in everyday life*. Saint Teresa deemed good only those visions that impelled her to act better and to love more. Above all, the great mystics are agreed in seeing at the summit of their ascent the attainment of a sovereign freedom of the soul. Saint John of the Cross and Meister Eckhart say in different words the same thing: a mystic should strive after attaining a state in which he is able "to forgo his gift" and to desire it no longer for its own sake. In spiritual marriage, according to John of the Cross, a soul comes to love God without any longer *feeling* its love. It might seem as if this were a state of perfect indifference; actually, it is the perfect state of hard-won poise and of immediately active understanding. On the far side of trances and *askesis*, the mystic experience culminates

---

[1] Especially the female *epigoni,* such as Marguerite Marie Alacoque in the seventeenth century, who so vividly describes the nuptial bed and what takes place in it!

in a state of the most thorough "disintoxication" of the soul and of the utmost self-possession. And only then does *marriage* become possible, meaning as it must, not the enjoyment of eros, but the fecundity of agape.

Thus ultimately orthodox mysticism stands forth as the highest way of purgation and as the most effective discipline for transcending passionate love, even when in a sublimated form. The cycle of Christian *askesis* leads the soul back to happy obedience, to acceptance of creature limitations, albeit with a spirit renewed and a freedom regained.

8

The Twilight of Passionate Love

It is the dogma of the Incarnation that radically distinguishes orthodox mysticism from heretical. It is that dogma which gives an altogether different meaning to the word "love" in the two cases.

The Catharist heretics set up Darkness against Light, as is done in the Gospel according to Saint John. But the Word of Light did not, in their view, put on the form of Darkness; it was not "made flesh." They did not want the perfect Light to communicate itself to us through life. (They did not believe in the humanity of Christ.) They wanted to go straight to Love by means of love, and from Darkness into Light without transition. Thus were they bound to founder, as Icarus foundered. (He who would go to God without passing through Christ is going to the Devil, said Luther energetically.) They felt that Darkness is a mystery of the Light, the final secret of which Light alone knows.[1] But they did not know that Darkness is the Anger of God—called forth by our rebellion—and not the work of an obscure demiurge. (Such at least in the biblical doctrine. Refusing to be taught by

---

[1] Karl Jaspers has magnificently expressed the final assumption of Darkness by the Light in his *Philosophie*.

the Light in this life and by means of "matter," misunderstanding an Agape that sanctifies creatures, and so ignorant of the true nature of what they held to be sin, they ran the risk of being irremediably lost in sin precisely when they thought they were escaping from it.

And hence it came about that there was a fatal confusion between the divinizing Eros and that Eros which is the captive of instinct. Hence it came about that the "enthusiastic" passion, the *joy d'amor* of the troubadours, was fated to issue in unhappy human passion. This impossible love left in men's hearts an unforgettable cautery, a truly devouring ardour, a thirst which death alone could quench: they suffered "the torture of love" and set themselves to loving it for its own sake.

The passion of the Perfect called for a divinizing death. The thirst which it put into men's hearts when they were without faith, but had been overwhelmed by the fiery poetry, drove them to seek in death no more than the supreme thrill. And likewise, the love of the Lady became, as soon as it was no longer a symbol of union with uncreated Light, the symbol of an impossible union with woman; retaining from its mystical origin an indefinable divine element, falsely transcendent, an illusion of the liberating glory of which suffering remained the sign! Thus occurred a tragic reversal. To surpass oneself to the extent of union with the transcendent, when the goal is no longer the Light, and while ignorant of the "way," is to cast oneself down into Darkness. The surpassing thereupon is no more than an exaltation of narcissism. It is intended to achieve not *liberation* from the senses, but a painful *intensity* of sentiment. Intoxication by the spirit.

The history of passionate love in all great literature from the thirteenth century down to our own day is the history of the descent of the courtly myth into "profane" life, the account of the more and more desperate attempts of Eros to take the place of mystical transcendence by means of emotional intensity. But magniloquent or plaintive, the tropes of its passionate discourse and the hues of its rhetoric can never attain to more than the glow of a resurgent twilight and the promise of a phantom bliss.

Book IV

THE MYTH IN LITERATURE

1

Of the Influence of Literature on Conduct

It will now be seen what sin is and how sin proceeds. It is when human will turns from God in order to be a will unto itself, that it arouses its own ardour and burns with its own affection, an ardour which is proper to it and has nothing in common with the ardour that is divine.—JAKOB BOEHME.

In a general way it is difficult *to check* the actual influence of the arts upon the everyday life of a period. Does music refine manners? And what may be the effect of painting? Architecture, it is true, produces dwellings, but the fact does not constitute its character as art. So with this or that philosophy. Very different, however, is the situation of a literature which may be shown historically to have bestowed its vocabulary upon passion. If literature can boast of having affected the manners of Europe, it is certainly due to our myth. More accurately, it is due to the rhetoric of the myth, as inherited from Provençal love. There is no need to attribute to sounds and words any magical power over our conduct. The adoption of certain linguistic conventions naturally involves and fosters the rise of the latent feelings most apt to be expressed in this way. That is the sense in which it may be said, following La Rochefoucauld, that few people would fall in love had they never heard of love.

Passion and expression are not really separable. Passion comes to birth in that powerful impetus of the mind which also brings language into existence. So soon as passion goes beyond instinct and becomes truly itself, it tends to self-description, either in order to justify or intensify its being, or else simply in order to keep *going*. In this sphere, tracing the process is easy. The emotions first experienced by an upper class and then through imitation by the masses are literary creations in the sense that a given rhetoric is the sufficient condition for them to be *avowed* and hence for them to be made conscious. In the absence of this rhetoric, the emotions would no doubt still exist, but accidentally, lacking recognition, and they would be treated as unmentionable and contraband peculiarities. But it has invariably happened that the putting into circulation of a new rhetoric caused neglected potentialities of the heart suddenly to become profusely actualized. The publication of *Werther,* for example, led to a wave of suicides. Rousseau made the whole of the French court take to drinking milk. Chateaubriand's *René* filled several generations with melancholy. This is because in order to admire nature unadorned, to adopt a certain gloomy mien, or even to commit suicide, it is necessary to be able "to explain," either to oneself or to others, what one is feeling. The more a man is given to sentiment, the more likely is he to be wordy and to speak well. Likewise, the more passionate a man is, the more likely is he to reinvent the tropes of the rhetoric, to rediscover their *necessity,* and to shape himself spontaneously according to the notion of the "sublime" which these tropes have indelibly impressed upon us.

That is why it will be easy enough to mark the stages of the transformation undergone by the courtly myth in the *morals* of the peoples of Europe. It can be taken for granted that, except of course for certain delays and simplifications, these stages have kept pace with the *literary* transformations to which over the same lapse of time the myth was being subjected. In describing the sweep of classical mysticism, I was able to note the moment at which the myth was incorporated. The sweep was an ascending one, and led to a release through a snapping of the spell. Literature, on the contrary, is the way downward to manners. Hence it is the popularization of the myth—or better still, its "profanation" [1]—that I am now going to survey.

---

[1] This word I am invariably using in the two senses of "sacrilege" and of "secularization."

2

The Two Roses

T he best starting-point is supplied by the *Roman de la Rose,* written between 1237 and 1280, about a century after Béroul and Thomas had produced their versions of *Tristan.* The Albigensian crusade had devastated the courtly civilization of Languedoc and scattered the last of the troubadours. What happened to the tradition of Love? It seems clear that as early as the middle third of the century the heretics—now being hunted by the Church and dispersed all over Europe—forsook giving literary expression to their "religion." Likewise Catharism was henceforth to be buried in the deep and dumb layers of the people, whose social life precluded noble ceremonial, so that the magnificent symbols of the great age of feudalism were no longer available. The apparent silence, however, did not halt its progress. The Church of Love was reproduced in countless sects more or less secret and more or less revolutionary, and their close similarity of feature testifies to a common origin and to a tradition faithfully preserved. In fact, all these sects denied the dogma of the Trinity—at least in its orthodox form; all evinced a high-flown spirituality; all professed a doctrine of "radiant joy;" all were anti-clerical, cultivated poverty and vegetarianism, and displayed an egalitarian spirit, extending in some instances to complete communism. Presently these same features were being displayed all together among the Brethren of the Free Spirit and the Rhenish Ortliebians—who were perhaps in touch with the Waldenses, neighbours of the Cathars—and not only among the Waldenses themselves, but also among the disciples of Joachim of Floris, among the beguines and beghards of the Low Countries, the English Lollards, the Moravian Brethren (if not among the Hussites); and, further, among the heretics of the Reformed Churches—Schwenckfeldt, Weigel, the Anabaptists and the Mennonites. Luther, Calvin, and Zwingli fought these dissenters with the same violence that Rome had employed against its own sectarians. But they could not and did not wish to wipe them out entirely. Nowadays Mennonite communities in which Russian strains have mingled—Dukhobors and Khlystis—exist as far afield as Canada and Paraguay. Their notion of love has not changed.

But before the middle of the fourteenth century courtly literature had turned into simply a means of expression—a rhetoric. This rhetoric tended automatically *to idealize* the profane objects it dealt with. As soon as this tendency made itself felt, it excited, as it was bound to do, a so-called "realistic" reaction. The double movement finds its illustrious witnesses in the *Roman de la Rose,* which was written in two parts, each by a different author. The first part, produced in about 1237, was the work of Guillaume de Lorris; the second part, by Jean de Meung, was finished before 1280.

The Rose of Guillaume de Lorris is love of the ideal woman, by now a real woman and yet inaccessible in her garden frosted over with allegories. Danger, Male-Bouche, and Shame defend Bel Accueil from the boldness of suitors. The *obstacle* to the union of love is figured by a necessity that is now moral and no longer in the least religious. The lover has to deserve his reward, not by any mystical *askesis,* but by a refinement of mind. Jean de Meung, on the other hand, looks upon the Rose as no more than sensual pleasure. A most outspoken realism supersedes Lorris's fiddle-faddle; Platonism gives place to an apology of sensual enjoyment, and emotional fervour to cynicism. The Rose is won by main force. Nature triumphs over Mind; and reason over passion.

Each of the two parts of the Romance had its own progeny. Lorris led to Dante—who perhaps translated him —and on to Petrarch and much further, down to the allegorical novels of the seventeenth century and to *La Nouvelle Héloïse* in the eighteenth. From Jean de Meung the ancient tradition, according to which passion is to be rejected as "a sickness of the soul," was transmitted to the lower levels of French literature—to *gauloiserie* and the schools of broad Gallic jokes, to controversial rationalism, and to a curiously exacerbated misogyny, naturalism, and man's reduction to sex. All this has simply been pagan man's normal way of defending himself against the myth of unhappy love. Perhaps in effect his attitude has not been so very different from the realistic Christian vision. That, however, is a matter to which I shall return.

3

Sicily, Italy, Beatrice, and Symbols

In about the year 1200 Rambaut de Vaqueiras, a troubadour of Languedoc, exchanged some verses with the powerful Marchese Alberto Malaspina. It would seem clear that at this time similar exchanges—call them "literary" if you like—kept the South of France in touch with Lombardy and Venetia. Once again, the map of the influence exerted by the troubadours coincides with the map of heresy. A little later the Franciscan movement arose out of a like conjunction of the "spiritualists"—this time, inside the Church—and the poets. Meanwhile, around Palermo, where Frederick the Second held court, there blossomed the so-called Sicilian School. To what extent this courtly poesy of the South was inspired by the troubadours is still obscure. Only one Provençal poet is known to have appeared at the Sicilian court, and Frederick was a persecutor of heresy. It may also be wondered how far the Sicilians still had "intelligence of Love." Was all they had preserved of the *trobar clus* simply the trick of baffling the reader? There is a temptation to think so, in view of the way Dante and his friend Cavalcanti attacked their master, Guittone d'Arezzo, and mocked his disciples, calling them "sectarians of ignorance, blind men claiming to distinguish colours, geese striving to rival eagles."

When Dante comes upon Bonagiunta da Lucca in Purgatory he takes the opportunity of expounding the *dolce stil nuovo*. This was the artful and caressing style in which the Northern School had reacted against the influence of such indefatigable imitators as Bonagiun-

ta. It was novel, but at the same time a return to
sound tradition. Its striking feature was its *conscious*
renovation of the symbolical vocabulary of the troubadours. The style into which the Sicilians had fallen was
a dubiously allegorical one. In treating the Lady as a
real woman, they addressed her with a conventional and
frigid amorousness. Dante, Cavalcanti, and still others,
favoured more spontaneity, more of the ardour of a
wooer; but they were nevertheless aware that the Lady
was entirely symbolical. Indeed, they were not only
aware of it; they said so—and this was their novelty. For
such was the paradoxical secret of courtly love; stilted
and inanimate when addressed to woman, it became all
ardent sincerity as soon as it was directed to the Wisdom of Love. Dante is never more passionate than when
Philosophy is the theme of his song, unless it is when
Philosophy has turned into Holy Science. This sincerity
was an unmistakable legacy of the troubadours; and quite
the opposite of what somebody today would imagine. In
the *Convivio* Dante speaks of it as a secret needing to
be veiled in "a lovely deceit." This the Cathars had well
understood. But it should be borne in mind that they
never said so.

It is because Dante and his friends felt that they must
define their art that, better than any one else, these
Italian poets enable us to pierce the real mystery of the
troubadours; rather in the way the seven colours of the
spectrum can be distinguished at dusk whereas in broad
day they form but a single luminousness the very strength
of which precludes analysis. It is at this stage of poetry
that the themes mingled by the *trobar* in the artless trans-
parency of his symbolism become evident. Jacopo da
Lentino, last of the Sicilians, utters the following plaint:

"Oft doth my heart die, and more cruelly than by a
natural death, for your sake, Lady, whom it desires and
loves more than self. . . .

"I have within me a fire that I feel will never be put
out. . . . How is it that this fire consumeth me not?"
Dante too says: [1]

"Love, that discourseth to me in my mind yearningly
of my lady, moveth many a time such things with me
anent her that my intellect loses its way among them.

[1] Canzone III.

"His discourse soundeth so sweetly that the soul that heareth him and feeleth, must cry: 'Oh me! that I have not power to tell that which I hear of my lady.'"

And the symbolical meaning of the Lady can no longer be in doubt when Guido Guinicelli refers to her as the source of "our faith":

"There goeth she along the road, so filled with nobility and grace that she puts down the pride of him to whom she giveth greeting, and, be he not already of our faith, she doth bring him to it."

Dante, moreover, can have been no blasphemer when in the *Vita nuova*[1] he penned that verse with its sublime beginning, *"Angelo chiama in divino intelletto"*;

"An angel crieth in its divine intelligence and saith: 'Lord, in the world a marvel is displayed in act, emanating from a soul that shineth after as here on high. Heaven, that hath no other lack than to possess her, craveth her of its Lord and every saint entreateth the grace.' Pity alone defendeth our cause; for God speaketh, intending my lady: 'Beloved mine, now suffer in peace that your hope be, so long as it pleaseth me, there where is one who looketh to losing her and who in Hell shall say to the damned: "I have beheld the hope of the blessed."'"

Can he have been referring to Beatrice as a woman? Is it her presence as such that the saints entreat and that is the hope of the blessed? Or is she the Holy Ghost in the act of upholding His Church with the charity of Christ—Pity—till every soul shall have been able to attain to the New Life?[2] What must seem like blasphemy here below is that the ambiguity is still maintained. That is how there arose a discussion between Orlandi and Cavalcanti about the meaning of their words. "Is this Love life or death?" the first boldly inquired. "The power of love often produceth death. . . . There is love whenever desire is so great as to go beyond the confines of natural love. . . . As it is not due to quality, it perpetually reflects its own

---

[1] XIX, pp. 34–47, in Dent's edition.

[2] Beatrice certainly existed, and Dante certainly loved her. Hence here we have a *sublimation*, the opposite of what happened in the case of the troubadours. Beatrice becomes in turn Philosophy, Wisdom, and the Holy Science that shows the way into Paradise and makes intelligible its mysteries.

effect. It is not a pleasure, but a contemplation." There can be no doubt about it. Love is mystic passion. But the part played by natural love in the heavenly prospect still needed to be made clear. This was done by Davanzati, when, in a little fable written towards the end of the thirteenth century, he described the real nature of the Love he praises and insisted that it is perilous to stop short at the terrestrial forms which are merely its image. He says:

"As a tigress assuageth her cruel pangs by gazing into a mirror wherein seemingly is the image of the whelps she hath been seeking—thanks to this pleasure the hunter is forgotten, and she tarrieth there, and goeth not in pursuit—so he whom love hath penetrated draws in life from beholding his lady, for 'tis thus he doth assuage his heavy affliction. . . . But the lady hath not a kind heart; the day passeth and his hopes are unfulfilled."

Here, unmistakably, the Lady with the unkind heart is a woman who turns Love to her own advantage. In a moral bestiary belonging to the same period I find the same fable with this ending:

"I trow this beast is ourselves. Her whelps whereof a hunter hath despoiled her are our virtues; and the hunter is the Devil, who maketh us to see that which is not. 'Tis thus that many have perished because they put off going after the Lord."

The moment was approaching when poets would yield to the spell of the mirror and of profaned rhetoric. Petrarch allowed himself to be snared by "that which is not," but the image of his Laura, who, as he later lamented, detained him over long from "going after the Lord."

4

Petrarch, the Converted Rhetor

Chè mortal cosa amar con tanta fede,
Quanta a Dio sol per debito conviensi.

"Everybody—even the man on some small rock washed by the sea—is aware that the world has witnessed one superlative lover and that this lover was Petrarch. Best of all, it is true. . . . What do we mean by a man *simply* in love? This is nothing of the kind. Petrarch was in love extraordinarily, blazingly, like a very sun." [1]
That is the astonishing thing about Petrarch, that in his describing his memorable passion the symbols of the troubadours were quickened for the first time by an entirely pagan breath! Pagan, and not in the least heretical! Petrarch stands at the antipodes not only of Dante, but also of the rhetors whom Dante attacked. The "secret" I spoke of just now had evaporated. It was no longer effective. The language of Love had at length become the rhetoric of the human heart. For reasons given above (Book III), this "radical profanation" was bound to produce the kind of poetry most suited to serve orthodox mysticism, and it was indeed from this poetry that the mystics in due course drew their finest metaphors. The temptation was irresistible, and a few examples—chosen almost haphazard—will show why.
Here is Petrarch's sonnet on the first anniversary of his love for Laura:

And still I bless the day, the hour, the place,[2]
When first so high mine eyes I dared to rear;
And say, "Fond heart, thy gratitude declare,
That then thou had'st the privilege to gaze.
'Twas she inspired the tender thought of love
Which points to heaven, and teaches to despise

[1] C.A. Cingria, *Pétrarque* (Lausanne, 1932).
[2] Sonetto XIII. Translations by Francis Wrangham.

The earthly vanities that others prize: [1]
She gave the soul's light grace, which to the skies
Bids thee straight onward in the right path move;
Whence bouy'd by hope e'en now I soar to worlds
    above."

Where Petrarch excels is in taking Tristan's harp [2] and
in plucking from it the wail of the "esquisite anguish,"
the cherished ill, the delight that is consuming him.

O vivid lustre! of power absolute
O'er all my being—source of that delight
By which consumed I sink, a willing prey. [3]

Oh breathing death! yet ill I joy to feel! [4]
Unsanction'd thus to rule, oh! whence thy art?

Without a helm, upon a swelling sea,
I feel my fragile bark the wind's poor sport. [5]

We have already met with this bark—on board which,
like Tristan, Petrarch has taken his harp with him—and
we have also met the "sway" which he laments while
aware that he has willed it fatalistically.

And thus my martyrdom no limit knows,
A thousand deaths and lives each day I feel. [6]

[1] Saint Teresa says: "These graces are accompanied, so far as
the mind is concerned, by a complete detachment from creatures.
One then feels far more of a stranger to worldly affairs."

[2] He was acquainted with the Romance and quotes it a number
of times. for example, in the *Trionfo d'amore,* he says:
    Here be the erring knights in ancient scrolls,
    Lancelot, Tristram, and the vulgar souls
    That wait on these.

[3] Canzone LXXII. Translation by Lady Dacre.

[4] Saint Teresa says: "It is a martyrdom at once exquisite and
cruel."

[5] Sonetto CXXXII. Translation by Susan Wollaston.

[6] Sonetto CLXIV. Translation by R. G. Macgregor. Saint Teresa says: "The soul . . . would fain have its anguish never end."
Again: "Once the soul is put to this torture, it would fain pass
thus the whole of the life remaining to it."

Elsewhere he speaks of Laura as his "beloved enemy," and his lament recalls that of Tristan when giving up Iseult so that she may return to her husband.

> O cruel absence! why
> Didst thou remove me from the menaced woes? [1]

For when Laura is near her eyes

> inflaming with a light divine
> So burn my heart, I dare no more repine. [2]

But here again woman, whether absent or present, is never but the *occasion* for a torment he cherishes above all else:

> I know to follow while I flee my fire:
> I freeze when present; absent, my desire
> Is hot. [3]

All romantic love is summed up in this last line. And how much better does Petrarch dissect the nature of the melancholy than it ever was to be by its most self-conscious victims when in due course it became the *mal du siècle!*

"Often am I assailed by other passions [he says elsewhere,] [6] but their assaults are short and passing. At times, however, this ill invades me with an obstinacy that grips and torments me for days and nights on end. The ordeal affords me no ray of light nor tremor of life; it is an infernal night and a cruel death. And yet—here is what may well be called the height of woe!—I feed on these particular pains and sufferings with a kind of delight so poignant that if I am snatched away from them it is against my will." [5]

[1] Sonetto CCLIV. Translation by R. G. Macgregor.

[2] *Trionfo d'amore.* Translation by Anna Hume. Saint John of the Cross says: "O sweet cautery!" And cf. his meditation on this line in *The Living Flame of Love.*

[3] Idem.

[4] *Secretum meum* (*De Contemptu mundi*).

[5] Saint Teresa says: "From this desire which fills the whole soul as in a flash, there arises a pain uplifting the soul above itself and above all created things. The soul but yearns to die in this solitude. If it is then addressed, and although it may strive with all its strength to give answer, its efforts are defeated. Try as it may, it cannot snatch itself out of this solitude."

And Saint Augustine, with whom on this occasion Petrarch supposes himself to be having a dialogue, is made to reply:

"Thou knowest full well what ails thee. Presently thou shalt learn its cause. Tell me: Why art thou so sad? Is it really the way of things in the world? A bodily pain? Some unjust stroke of fortune?" Petrarch says: "Nothing in particular of the kind."

He was experiencing in advance of the age of romanticism what Chateaubriand, in a memorable phrase, called "the vagueness of the passions." And here is the summons to death:

> Loose me from forth my darksome prison here,
> That to so glorious life the passage bars.[1]

The "infernal night" has been changed into Day; the "cruel death" into a new Life. And in order that passion shall not lack a touch of the sublime, here also is divinization. Petrarch asks how he can possibly go on living while parted from his lady.

> Love's answer soon the truth forgotten shows—
> "This high pure privilege true lovers claim,
> Who from mere human feelings franchised are." [2]

Then there was his famous ascent of Mount Ventoux, which gave him much food for thought. And above all there was the Black Death, which ravaged Europe in 1348, and reminded him that his "human qualities" bound him to a pitiful state of being. In the *Song of the Great Plague*—a matchless masterpiece of self-examination—he says:

> Ceaseless I think, and in each wasting thought [3]
> So strong a pity for myself appears
> That often it has brought
> My harass'd heart to new yet natural tears;
> Seeing each day my end of life draw nigh,
> Instant in pray'r, I ask of God the wings

---

[1] Sonetto LXXII. Translation by Lady Dacre.

[2] Sonetto XV. Translation by R. G. Macgregor. Saint Teresa says: "How great the sway of a soul uplifted by God Himself to this height, from which it surveys all things but is bound by none!"

[3] Canzone CCLXIV. Translation by R. G. Macgregor.

With which the spirit springs,
Freed from its mortal coil, to bliss on high;
But nothing to this hour, pray'r, tear, or sigh,
Whatever man could do, my hopes sustain.

"Take up at length, wisely take up your part:
Tear ev'ry root of pleasure from your heart,
Which ne'er can make it blest."

Too long has he pinned his hopes to "the false and fugitive sweetness" of an idealized love.

For o'er my heart from time to time I feel
A subtle scorn, a lively anguish steal,
Whence ev'ry hidden thought,
Where all may see, upon my brow is writ.
For with such faith on mortal things to dote,
As unto God alone is just and fit.
Disgraces worst the prize who covets most.

But how shall he tear out of his heart this blaspheming love, this demented desire?

Passion, whose strength I now from habit feel
So great that it would dare with death itself to deal.

The very self-awareness betrayed in such a cry—a cry giving away the ultimate secret of the courtly myth—is the sign that a man has been touched by grace. What can tear out the vain hope is a single-minded faith in forgiveness. And at last converted expectation discovers that to which it is really looking:

"It lifts you now to hope more blest and sweet,
Uplooking to that heaven around your head,
Immortal, glorious spread.
If but a glance, a brief word, an old song,
Had here such power to charm.
Your eager passion, glad of its own harm,
How far 'twill then exceed if now the joy so strong."

5

The Inverted Ideal of "Gauloiserie"

To impose a style on the life of the passions—that dream of the whole of the pagan Middle Ages tormented by Christian law—such is the secret wish that was to give rise to the myth. But inevitably the faith "unto God alone just and fit" was confused with doting on "mortal things." And it was this confusion, not orthodox doctrine, which set up the tragic antithesis between body and soul. The poesy of *cortezia* had received its inspiration from the Eastern (monasticism hails from the East) and heretical disposition to asceticism shown by the Perfect. Clearly, then, it is this that little by little, by means of a literature of idealization, infected the ruling class of medieval society. There was bound to be a reaction in the direction of "realism"; and, as it happens, this reaction was strongest in the middle class. Its beginnings are visible quite early in the twelfth century, in the very hey-day of courtly love. The glorification of wanton indulgence was carried to the same extreme as the glorification of chastity. *Fabliau* contended with poem; shamelessness with idealism. The *Débat de l'âme et du corps*, which belongs to this period, is the first witness to a struggle that the doctrine of Christian marriage was supposed to resolve. A soul just parted from its body assails its erstwhile companion with bitter reproaches, alleging that if it is condemned to damnation the body is to blame. But the body retorts with a *tu quoque* (which has some justification!). So, keeping up their belated recriminations, the two go forward together into everlasting torment.

It was the growing resentment by the body displayed here that inspired the *fabliaux*, and they met with tremendous success—their readers frequently being the same persons who enjoyed reading idealizing romances. The fabliaux were ribald anecdotes hawked about all

196

over medieval Europe and retold with countless variations. They heralded the comic novel, which in turn
heralded the novel of manners, which heralded the controversial naturalism of much of the fiction of the nineteenth century. But it does not seem to me that these successive literary styles were engendered in a direct line.
More closely than with its predecessors, each step
in the movement towards a fiction that should be "true
to life" was connected with a corresponding step in the
movement towards a refined artificiality; and hence progression was impelled by a reaction. Charles Sorel was
the product of *L'Astreé*,[1] not of the fabliaux; Marivaux's novel *Marianne* [2] was the product of Marivaux's
own comedies, not of Sorel; and Zola, the product of the
decay of romanticism as much as, if not much more than,
of Balzac—who, in Zola's day, passed for a realist.

To return to the thirteenth century, perhaps we have
not hitherto sufficiently understood how the sensuous
and often pornographic style of the fabliaux betrays an
absence of realism identical, when all is said and done,
with that of the idealizing courtly epics. I believe that
gauloiserie—I mean, the ribaldry and salaciousness of the
fabliaux—expresses an attitude which is simply the inversion of Petrarch's. A passage from Huizinga [3] should
make this clear.

"French authors like to oppose 'l'esprit gaulois' to the
conventions of courtly love, as the natural conception
and expression opposed to the artificial. Now the former
is no less a fiction than the latter. Erotic thought never
acquires literary value save by some process of transfiguration of complex and painful reality into illusionary
forms. The whole genre of *Les Cent Nouvelles Nouvelles*
and the loose song, with its wilful neglect of all the nat-

---

[1] *L'Astrée* is a pastoral romance by Honoré d'Urfé, the first
parts of which appeared in 1610 and the last part—posthumously
—in 1627. M. de Rougemont's point here is shown in the fact that
Charles Sorel (1597–1674) wrote a novel of adventure, *Histoire
comique de Francion* (1622), with the deliberate object of destroying the vogue of the pastoral romance in France at that time,
and that, on finding that *L'Astrée* was still extremely popular, he
went on to publish a mock pastoral entitled *Le Berger extravagant*
(1627).—Translator.

[2] Published from 1731 to 1741.

[3] *The Waning of the Middle Ages,* op. cit., p. 99.

ural and social complications of love, with its indulgence towards the lies and egotism of sexual life, and its vision of a never-ending lust, implies, no less than the screwed-up system of courtly love, an attempt to substitute for reality the dream of a happier life. It is once more the aspiration towards the life sublime, but this time viewed from the animal side. It is an ideal all the same, even though it be that of unchastity."

This underlying connexion between *gauloiserie* and an over-refined treatment of love is brought to the surface in a thirteenth-century satire called *L'Evangile des femmes*—a sequence of quatrains, the first three lines of each extolling woman in the courtly manner and the last being brutally depreciatory. Another indication of the connexion is the fact that if chivalry made a mock of marriage from above, *gauloiserie* was undermining it from below. The procedure adopted by the latter is well indicated in the *Dit de Chiceface*. Chiceface is a fabulous monster who feeds only on women who keep their marriage vows and he is terribly emaciated. But his comrade Bigorne, whose diet consists exclusively of submissive husbands, is the very barrel of a fellow.

There should also be noted the attitude taken up by the clergy while these two opposite but interrelated tendencies—both begotten by the myth—were making their way in literature. It was Canon Petrarch who gave the example. His later poems are devoted to eulogy of the Virgin—Our Lady in contrast to "my" Lady—but with no forsaking on that account of the customary vocabulary of courtly poesy.[1] Dante may be said to have avenged the troubadours aforetime by putting the "Knights of Mary" in hell. These knights were Italian monks who were also known as "Jolly Knights," because, although they had enlisted under the leadership of a saint, they led dissolute lives.

---

[1] According to A. Jeanroy, op. cit., II, p. 130, no poem devoted solely to the Virgin is known to exist earlier than the second third of the thirteenth century.

6

The Later History of Chivalry
Down to Cervantes

The influence exercised by Arthurian romance throughout the thirteenth, fourteenth, and fifteenth centuries is attested by hundreds of texts. It was an influence that spread over the same area as that of the troubadours—that is to say, over the whole of Europe. The German *Minnesänger* were nurtured on Catharist legends; and for that matter all they did was to adapt the tales of Chrestien de Troyes from the French. The Romance of *Tristan* was translated into every language of the West. Malory's prose version in the *Morte Darthur* dates from the end of the fifteenth century. Dante looked on the epic and romantic cycle of Northern France as a model for all narrative prose, and Brunetto Latini included in his *Rhetoric* a portrait of the ideal woman which had been extracted from *Tristan*. Countless imitations were produced as far afield as Norway, Russia, Hungary, and the Hispanic lands; and the most instructive examples of these in the fifteenth and sixteenth centuries are the tales of *Amadis* in Portuguese, in Spanish, and finally in French.

It is remarkable, but doubtless not surprising, that the authors of some of these imitations were brought to rediscover the original meaning of the mystical legends, although, owing either to caution or to lack of penetration, they only made use of a thoroughly Catholic mythology —something, as we have seen, that could hardly be in harmony with the original intention. In 1554 there was published in Spain a book by Hyeronimo de Sempere entitled flamboyantly *Libro de Cavalleria celestial del pié de la rosa fragrante*. In this Christ is given the guise of the Lion Knight; Satan, of the Serpent Knight; John the Baptist, of the Desert Knight; and the Apostles are turned into the twelve Knights of the Round Table.

Manichaeistic esoterism, ever latent in Arthurian romance, reappears as a filigree within such symbols.

Cervantes does not name the numerous romances of "heavenly chivalry" which were being found thrilling in his day.[1] In *Don Quixote* he is concerned merely to discredit romances of secular adventure. This neglect on his part remains puzzling. It tells in favour of the theory that he was aware of the true meaning of courtly literature, and mocked his contemporaries with a sense of desperation for clinging to an illusion of which they had lost the key. On this theory, the character Don Quixote was ridiculous only because he wished to undergo an *askesis* for which he had not received initiation and to follow a way of life for which the times were altogether out of joint. The Roman Church had triumphed. The best thing was to be on the winning side, together with the decent and realistic Sancho Panza.

7

"Romeo and Juliet" and then Milton

Yet Rome had not triumphed everywhere. In one island her power was still disputed—the island home of the last of the bards. In Cornwall and in Scotland the traditions of the bards were still alive when James Macpherson published in 1765 his so-called *Works of Ossian*.[2] In Ireland they survive to this day. I must forgo touching upon the problem of the extent to which English literature, both popular and learned, is connected with this background of Celtic legend. But it is significant to find at the end of the seventeenth century a sound scholar such as Robert Kirk, the theologian and humanist, writ-

---

[1] I have already mentioned the influence of this literature on Saint Teresa and on the Spanish mystics in general.

[2] Although Morven and Selma, it has been established, are names Macpherson himself invented, Ossianic ballads really did exist in Scotland in the eighteenth century.—Translator.

ing a treatise on sprites which bears no trace of either scepticism or irony.

We know almost nothing about Shakespeare—but he has left us *A Midsummer Night's Dream*. It has been alleged that he was a Roman Catholic—but *Romeo and Juliet* is the one courtly tragedy, as well as the most magnificent resuscitation of the myth that the world was to be given till Wagner wrote and composed his *Tristan*. So long as the life and even the identity of Shakespeare remain matters of speculation, it is futile to inquire whether or not he was privy to the secret traditions of the troubadours. But it may be noted that Verona was a main centre of Catharism in Italy. According to the monk, Ranieri Saccone—for seventeen years a heretic— Verona contained nearly five hundred Perfect, not to mention the far more numerous Believers. It is quite likely that the legends of those days preserved some memory of the violent struggles between Patarenes and orthodox in that city.

In the margin of the religious disputes of the sixteenth century, which caused the ancient heresies to be wrapped in an ever greater darkness, the tragedy of the *Veronese Lovers* tears aside the veil for an instant and leaves in our eyes the negative record of a flash, "the black Sun of Melancholy." Sprung up out of the depths of a spirit avid of transfiguring torments, out of the abysmal night in which the lightning flash of love plays now and then on features motionless and fascinating—that *our own self* of horror and divinity to which the most splendid poems of Europe are addressed—resurrected all of a sudden in its full stature, as though stunned by its provocative youth and drunk with rhetoric, on the threshold of the Mantuan tomb here once again the myth stands forth in the glow of a torch which is being held aloft by Romeo.

Juliet rests, put to sleep by the potion. The son of Montague enters, and he speaks.

How oft when men are at the point of death,
Haue they beene merrie? Which their Keepers call
A lightning before death. Oh how may I
Call this a lightning? O my Loue, my Wife,
Death that hath suckt the honey of thy breath,
Hath had no power yet vpon thy Beautie.

Thou art not conquer'd; Beauties ensigne yet
Is Crymson in thy lips, and in thy cheekes,
And Deaths pale flaggs not aduanced there.

>   . . . Ah deare Juliet:
> Why art thou yet so faire? I will belieue,
> Shall I belieue? that vnsubstantiall death is amorous?
> And that the leane abhorred Monster keepes
> Thee here in darke to be his Paramour?
> For feare of that, I still will stay with thee,
> And neuer from this Pallace of dym night
> Depart againe: heere, here will I remaine,
> With Wormes that are thy Chambermaides: O here
> Will I set up my euerlasting rest:
> And shake the yoke of inauspicious starres
> From this world-wearied flesh: Eyes looke your last,
> Armes take your last embrace: And lips, O you
> The doores of breath, seale with a righteous kisse
> A dateless bargaine to ingrossing death:
> Come bitter conduct, come vnsauoury guide,
> Thou desperate Pilot, now at once run on
> The dashing Rocks, thy Sea-sick wearie Barke:
> Here's to my Loue.
>
>   *(Drinks.)*
>   O true Appothecary:
> Thy drugs are quicke. Thus with a kisse I die.

Death's *consolamentum* has sealed the one kind of marriage that Eros was ever able to wish for. Once more there comes a profane "dawn," and once more the world goes on again. Restored to his strict reign, the Prince declares:

> A glooming peace this morning with it brings. . . .
> Go hence, to haue more talke of these sad things.

There is no doubt that Milton, although a Puritan, underwent the influence of Cabalistic doctrines, and anything less "spiritualizing" it is impossible to imagine. But does not the revolt of the Puritans against the monarchy and the bishops who had turned worldly remind us of the rebellion of the Pure against feudalism and the clergy?

Two poems that Milton wrote in youth—*L'Allegro* and *Il Penseroso*—describe the antagonism of Light and Darkness, and the necessary choice which at that time he had not yet made. (Indeed, he never did choose, or at least chose with such reservations as to leave it impossible to determine more closely than he wished in which direction.) Even before embracing the cause of the Puritans, Milton, searching for an epic theme, had sometimes turned over in his mind the Celtic legend of Arthur and the Knights of the Round Table. In *Il Penseroso*, after he has hailed black Melancholy, he turns to the "sad Virgin" and bids her the soul of Orpheus to sing, or else to call up him that left half-told the story of Canace's husband,

> That own'd the vertuous Ring and Glass,

and also "great bards" who

> In sage and solemn tunes have sung,
> Of Turneys and of Trophies hung;
> Of Forests, and inchantments drear,
> Where more is meant than meets the ear.

Milton, when preparing his *History of Britain*, studied the Arthurian chronicle and its legends. In *De Doctrina christiana* he attacked—to quote a recent French commentator [1]—"the creative power of God, and also the dogmas of the Trinity and the Incarnation; and he repudiated traditional theological definitions which could not be supported from the Bible." Even if we set aside this last feature, which, after all, links Milton with the Reformation, is this not the one and same heresy that everywhere and at all times appears as the mainspring of the grand lyrical poetry of passion?

As for Milton's "materialism," it does not contradict a "courtly" doctrine of love as much as might be supposed. Between a monism assimilating mind to matter, or vice versa, and a dualism which condemns matter in the name of mind, there is a gap which the history of Gnostic and Manichaean sects shows to be not unbridgeable, especially on the ethical plane. Idealism and materialism have important presuppositions in common. Extreme licentiousness sometimes goes hand in hand with

---

[1] Floris Delattre, *Milton* (Introduction to *L'Allegro*, to *Il Penseroso*, and to *Samson Agonistes*) (1937).

an extreme and fanatical chastity. And Milton's negation of death leads him into inferences similar to those expressed by the Cathars. Like them, Milton thinks that a good will issues from intellectual principles, and that a good will can purge us of evil desires—of sensual leanings, the major sin. And Fludd, his master in occultism, taught that light is the divine substance.

It remains that Milton's theories are more "rational" and are open to a more practical social application than those of the heretics of Southern France. (He looks on marriage, for example, as "a remedy for incontinence.") Hence these theories did not foster such excessive confusions of the carnal with the spiritual as had previously not failed to occur among Neo-Manichaean sects.

8

"L'Astrée," or from the Mystical to the Psychological

The history of what happened to the myth in the Romance in the seventeenth century can, alas! be summed up in a sentence. Its mystical element was degraded into pure psychology. The Romance was given over to an excessively refined literature. Honoré d'Urfé, La Calprenède, Gomberville, and Georges de Scudéry, together with his sister Madeleine, had none of them the remotest notion of the esoteric meaning of the chivalry of legend. The symbolical nature of the subjects that they dealt with afresh merely induced them to write interminable novels à clef. Polexandre is Louis XIII, Cyrus is the Great Condé, Diane is Maria of Medecis, and so on. The incidents remained the "annoyances" that love meets with, but the obstacle to the satisfaction of love was no longer the secret and metaphysical wish for death of Tristan; it became that fad of the ruling class, a point of honour. It is the heroine who is the more cunning in the invention of excuses for parting. She delights too in terrifying her chivalrous suitor; and in Gomberville's novel Polexandre roams like one possessed over the five continents to make amends for whatever may have been the cause of a single angry glance from his mistress. In the end he is still uncertain whether this "queen of the unattainable Island" is not going to have him beheaded. But, as a rule, the tales finish up with a wedding. Foreseen on the first page, the wedding is delayed till the ten thousandth when the author is a star performer in his line. The happy ending was first introduced in the allegorical novel of the seventeenth century. The genuine courtly romance culminated in death; it dissolved into an elevation outside the world. Now there was a general desire that everything should be tidied up; society had to be in the right, and hence the endings of novels became a return to something essentially alien to romance—happiness.

In *L'Astrée* the great tragic themes of the myth reappear as no more than melancholy echoes. No doubt there are the twelve laws of Love, ingeniously contrived partings, a eulogy of chastity, and even challenges to a death of release. But the stark and elemental interactions of *Tristan* have dwindled into mere coquetting, and the struggle between Night and Day has become but the play of twilight. No longer does the drawn sword lie between the two lovers; instead Céladon places there a gilt globe tied with his shepherdess's favour. And here is something that sums up all the rest. In the fifth and final volume, the despairing Céladon summons death, and Astrée, on her side, also feels that there is only one way out. Together they go to the Fountain of Truth, which is guarded by lions and unicorns, and ask for an end to be put to their ills. According to the oracle, the spell put upon the fountain will only be broken at the death of the most constant lover and of the most constant mistress. (Incidentally, this recalls the way the lovers in *Tristan* seek forgiveness on the score that the effects of the love-potion have been beyond their control.) Céladon takes his courage in both hands and advances. But thereupon, *mirabile dictu!* the lions and unicorns set to devouring one another, the sky grows dark, thunder roars, and the Genie of Love appears in order to make known that after all the spell is broken. Astrée and Céladon have fainted—a metaphorical death—and are carried to the dwelling of the druid Adamas, where they revive; and presently they get married.

It is customary to declare the prodigious success of *L'Astrée* unaccountable. And yet its charms are not unequal to those of our recent French novels of fancy and enchantment. And the psychology of French writers has not ceased to delight in allegorical elegance; witness Jean Giraudoux. La Fontaine doted on *L'Astrée*, and declared it "exquisite." Its scene is laid on the banks of the little river Lignon, north of Saint Etienne, and Rousseau went there specially from Lyons in order to seek out the shade of Diane and Silvandre. It is true that the two characters were entirely unknown to the landlady at his inn. She told him that the neighbourhood possessed excellent blacksmiths, and that its wrought iron work was deservedly reputed. "The good woman," he notes with disappointment, "must have taken me for a locksmith's apprentice."

Actually, I feel quite capable of undertaking the eulogy of *L'Astrée*. From the standpoint of literary *art,* it is an achievement of capital importance. Never have the resources of a more highly accomplished rhetoric been harmonized to such a degree. One cannot imagine a novel being better written; or more severely regulated in its progress by the laws of an unerring aesthetic. The use of "constant characters"—shepherd, shepherdess, fickle youth, coquette, bold lover, and so on—guarantees exactitude, and I may even say, veracity, to the interplay of emotion. Here it is art and not "life" that directs matters. We are in the presence of a creation of the mind, and not of a confusion of cloudy reflections, of more or less damaging admissions, and undeserved bits of luck (as novels are today). In a word *L'Astrée* is a real *oeuvre.* It presupposes the mastery of one's craft and twenty-five years of attentive effort. The literary snobbery that made it a success was more enlightened than ours.

But also the fact that the book has such finish allows us to put a plain question: What is the actual success of literary effort worth? If we recall the primitive myth, every theme of which *L'Astrée* takes up afresh, it strikes us that in Urfé's book the tragic is degraded to emotion, and fate into a piece of fictional machinery. All is turned into moralizing and aiming to please. Are we to suppose that the most admirable literature, by reason of its very impeccability, is simply a *by-product* of the mystic systems that bring forms and myths into existence?

And that in order to flower and to be fulfilled in a work of art, literature would seem to require the provisional drying up of the deep springs that have watered it? Is it not for that reason that literature, however strongly it may indulge the passions of the heart, offers practically no resistance to attacks from a realistic mind and from what is called civic sense—as appears in our own day? Whereas mystic systems and religions draw an added vigour from the confutations and mockery that may be strewn in their path?

A decree of the semi-official Boileau—his short *Dialogue sur les héros de roman*—was enough to condemn to silence and neglect—even in our text-books today—both the fiction of spells and enchantments engendered by *L'Astrée* and its parasite, the comic novel.[1] Only one more flame, a flame tenuous and pure, was going to be lit—Madame de Lafayette's *La Princesse de Clèves*. In this novel of unhappy love, death is given the mild form of a voluntary parting, and in place of chivalry we have virtue, a virtue which sides in the end with the world.

9

Corneille, or Giving Battle to the Myth

It was in the French classical drama—and therefore the heart of an intolerant order—that passion most strikingly scored its revenge. Corneille's *La Place royale* is a distinctly unkind play. Alidor, in love with Angélique as she with him, "is disturbed by a love that attaches him too closely," and so he tries to arrange that his mistress shall fall into the arms of his friend Cléandre. Whence it is commonly imagined that Corneille

---

[1] Sorel's *Berger extravagant* [mentioned above, p. 197, note.—Translator] repeats in the key of burlesque, alias "realism," all the artificial situations of *L'Astrée*. Likewise Scarron's *Roman comique* (1662), etc.

was the first writer to represent passion being controlled, if not by morality, at least by reason. This would mean that he was the first writer to escape from the domination of the myth, and the matter is accordingly worth examining. Here is how Alidor complains in Act I:

'Tis surfeit of her love oppresses me like doom.
Did she grow cool a moment, I should escape my gloom.
Some touch of jealousy, one look of irritation—
At once I could subdue my mad infatuation.
But she is without fault, and more perfect than she
Is the attachment fond that she displays to me.
By such intentions sweet is all she does impelled
That I'm o'erwhelmed with favours till my peace lies felled.

There is no need to go on. These opening lines are enough to rouse our suspicions. What! Happiness he declares to be fatal to his peace, and were only Angélique unfaithful to him that would cure him of his love! This Alidor must be a queer monster! Let us say rather that what he is trying his best to conceal is all too obvious. He too is a lover who yearns to burn! But his yearning he can only admit by asserting its opposite; for he appears on the stage of history at a period when a yearning for misfortune has become difficult to avow. "I blush to suffer grievous ills that I lament," he declares presently. Thus shame is what inspires his deceit. Actually, he suffers from the absence of any *obstacle* between the too fond Angélique and himself. The game he wants to play is short of a King Mark. He is in the situation of Tristan and Iseult at the end of their three years in the Forest, when Tristan was able to renew the obstacle by restoring the queen to her husband. Alidor has to invent a rival. Thwarted in the gratification of his yearning by the lack of anything that can part him from Angélique, but ashamed to admit how that lack causes him to suffer, he thinks of deploring that he should be fettered *too closely* by her fidelity, when actually he despairs of being fettered closely enough. In proclaiming a need to be free he expresses a deep-seated wish to be in such a position as no longer to want any freedom whatever. This is the position in which he would be the moment Angélique gave the least sign of escaping from him. But he is artful, as the following passage from the play shows:

> CLÉANDRE. Was ever lover glowing with an ardour
> Such as to complain that he was being
> lov'd too much?
>
> ALIDOR.   What! Can you then suppose I am so
> commonplace that vulgar feelings I'd
> contentedly embrace?

His manner is haughty; let us be on our guard. It is a sign that he is about to indulge in more deceit. He continues:

> 'Tis mad to be the slave of what has us in thrall,
> And mad to feed with love what's not at beck and call.
> I hate its forcing me; hence firmly I'm intending
> To keep my expectations on my will depending.
> Free of ardour's bondage, 'tis my ambition bold
> That as I please I'll warm, and as I please grow cold.

The passage may erroneously be regarded as typical of Corneille: will-power triumphs over passion. But even if we were unaware of the existence of the myth, the remainder of the comedy would show us that Alidor's real desire is exactly the opposite of what he thus haughtily contends that it is. " 'Tis mad to be the slave of what has us in thrall" really means: "It is only worth while becoming the slave of what holds us completely in thrall —what, in eluding us, causes our ardour to glow ever more intensely—for that is what would truly *please* us." The last six words, "and as I please grow cold," are simply a piece of rhetorical artifice intended to persuade the reader, or Cléandre, or Corneille himself, that freedom is desired, whereas what is wished for is obviously "ardour"—and no subservient ardour either.

Let me repeat that it is easy to be taken in. Corneille does his best to ensure that we shall be. In the dedication of the play to some unidentified person, he says:

"It is from you I have learned that a decent man's love should always spring up at the bidding of his will; that love should never be where it might also not be; that if nevertheless this happens, it is a tyranny the yoke of

which must be thrown off; and, lastly, that a person beloved is under far greater obligation to our love when this
results from our choice and her qualities than when it
arises from a blind attraction and is compelled by some
inherent disposition we are unable to fight against. . . .
Nothing is a gift unless it might also be withheld from
us."

This is good, and well put. But do not let us overlook
that to refuse obedience to inexorable compulsion and to
give only with the freedom that makes a gift worth while
were two things inculcated by courtly love as fundamental; they were made requisite in one of the *leys
d'amor*. Moreover, there was an ulterior motive in re-
quiring them; it was believed that they would tell against
marriage. In spite of themselves, Alidor and the Angélique, whose fidelity he deplores, are in a situation
equivalent to the married state; and he wants to escape
from this situation not owing to love of freedom, as he
alleges, but owing to love of passion. He says:

> Whatever be the cost, my chains must be struck off,
> For fear that union could my self-control corrode,
> And turn a love by force into a love I owed.

This is most faithfully the language of courtly love. But
we must note a curious contradiction. To begin with,
Alidor declares that he wants peace; but now he expresses a fear of marriage on the ground that peace is
precisely what it would bring to him.

> Let me give her offence and thus stir up her hate.
> As long as o'er her heart my sway I have retained
> Desir'd recovery can never be attained.

His desire of recovery—let us read: "desire to be on fire"
and therefore a fear of recovery—is satisfied in Act V.
Later on, in an *Examination* of the play, Corneille rec-
ognizes this, at the same time as he necessarily simulates
surprise at it.

"This fondness for peace [he writes] does not prevent Alidor from showing in the fifth act that he is still
passionately attached to this mistress, notwithstanding
his having resolved to be rid of her, and notwithstanding
the betrayals he has inflicted upon her, *so that it seems as*

*if he only begins to love her once he has given her cause
to hate him."*
Here is a clean breast of the matter. But from the
purely psychological aspect in which Corneille views it, he
is bound to overlook the significance of the *myth* that
directs Alidor's behaviour, and in the end he decides very
feebly that Alidor is simply guilty of a logical fallacy.
"This displays," he says, "an unevenness of conduct that
is vicious."

Corneille's blindness regarding his real intention should
not astonish us, even though this intention is so perfectly
carried out. The centre of the myth of unhappy love is,
as we have seen, a passion that cannot be admitted.
Corneille's originality lies in having sought to attack and
deny this passion by which he was sustained, and to
attack and deny the myth that he reinvented in his two
most splendid tragedies, *Polyeucte* and *Le Cid*. He wished
to preserve at least the *principle* of freedom—that is, the
principle of the human person—without however sacri-
ficing to it the delightful and tormenting effects of the
irresistible "love-potion"—here metaphorical. Better still,
he made the wish to be free a highly effective instrument of the passion which it claimed to cure. Hence
the unparalleled tension of these "dramas of duty," as
those incapable of liking them will ever go on calling
them.

10

Racine, or the Myth Unloosed

In relation to the myth, the antithesis in which Racine
and Corneille are usually placed amounts to this—
that Racine sets out from the assumption that the love-
potion divests those who have drunk it of every shred of
responsibility—"C'est Vénus tout entière à sa proye
attachée" [1]—whereas Corneille insists on treating the

---

[1] *Phèdre*, Act I, iii. The heroine is avowing her passion for
her stepson, and describes herself as the personification of Venus
intently ravening her prey.

potion as "a tyranny the yoke of which must be thrown off." That is how it happens that there is a voluptuous harmony in the one and a dialectical tension in the other, the former allowing himself to be carried along by the stream, the latter battling against it even as it sweeps him along (or the better to feel himself being swept along).

An *invitus invitam* [1] being the subject of *Bérénice,* this play may be described as a plot from Antiquity being interpreted by a "modern" who bears in mind the courtly notion of unhappy returned love. The *invitus invitam* thus becomes the very expression of the myth. But Racine, in his early plays, accommodates the scope of the myth to the proportions of an excessively "allowable" psychology.

"I have not [he says] gone so far as to make Berenice kill herself, as Dido did, because Berenice and Titus had not given one another the ultimate pledges which Dido exchanged with Aeneas, and hence unlike Dido she was under no obligation to renounce life." Obviously the "plea" being opposed here to the passion of Darkness is artificial and weak.

"A tragedy [Racine continues] need not necessarily include bloodshed and death; it is enough that the action should be lofty, the characters heroic, and *the passions excited in it,* and that pervading the whole there should be that majestic sadness wherein all the enjoyment of tragedy resides."

But the "majestic sadness" referred to is only half the myth—its diurnal aspect and its moral reflection in our lives as finite creatures. There is lacking the nocturnal aspect and its mystic flowering in the infinite life of Darkness. There is lacking what might symmetrically be called "that majestic delight wherein all the pain of Romance resides." For in order to reach this other aspect, or even to become aware of it, he would have had to go as far as death, the death he deems unnecessary. Contrary to received opinion, the much extolled classical sense of decency involves a metaphysical impoverishment which en-

---

[1] "Titus, who passionately loved Berenice, and even, so it was supposed, had promised to marry her, sent her away from Rome, *against her will and against his own,* soon after he had succeeded to the purple of the empire."—Suetonius, as adapted by Racine in the preface to *Bérénice.*

genders confusions of incalculable effect. For, after all, let Racine's "sadness" be as "majestic" as you please, inasmuch as it is self-confined and implies neither a beyond nor any reversal of plot into joy, and inasmuch, further, as it is accepted for what it is in the world of day and nevertheless is called "enjoyment," I do not see how it can ever be more than a *morosa delectatio*.

No doubt we are entitled to dispute the ultimate truth of the mystical (Manichaean) belief at the root of the passion myth. None the less, it must be admitted that the belief endows the drama and the ordeals of the lovers with a grandiose justification. If the lovers are infatuated with obstacle and with their consequent anguish, that is because the obstacle is death in disguise and because death is the pledge of their transfiguration, of the moment in which what has hitherto been Darkness will be revealed as absolute Light. But Racine, in failing to go the length of death, constrains both us and himself to savour an essentially dubious sadness. The Eros of *cortezia* claimed to release men from the life of matter by way of death; and Christian Agape aims at sanctifying life itself. But Racine, in being content to represent "passions excited" and to produce the "sadness" in which he invites us to find an indefinite "enjoyment," betrays a rather morbid acceptance of the defeat of mind and of the resignation of the senses. At this stage Racine's work is already hinting that his surrender to the *mal du siècle*—that is to say, to the secularization of passion—can only lead him into Jansenism; for Jansenism is the kind of morose mortification—self-punishment, Freud calls it—most appropriate to the romantic temperament. But his conversion could never have occurred had it not been for a crisis in which he himself became aware of the true character of his frenzy. *Phèdre* makes not only a decisive moment in the poet's life, but also one in the transformations which the myth underwent in the course of European history.

11

"Phèdre" or "Punishing" the Myth

The death-theme is omitted from *Bérénice* by the operation of a moral "censorship" of unmistakably Christian origin. At this stage Racine neither can be, nor does he wish to be, entirely clear-sighted. For then he would be compelled to reject that which he dares cherish only in his innermost heart without admitting to himself that he is cherishing it. But the shock of a passion which he conceived for some woman—very likely, the actress Champmeslé—together with the first stirrings of a real faith, drove him—as if in his own despite and more wholeheartedly than he had foreseen—to the limits of avowal.

In *Phèdre* death gets its own back. Yes, Racine was now aware that it is necessary for a tragedy to include bloodshed and death if it is about passionate love. However, he did not want death to be a transfiguration. He was now siding with day, and death could be no more than the penalty for his previous protracted indulgence. Passion, his own passion, is what he punishes when consigning the daughter of Minos to death, and passion is also his victim. Under cover of the ancient story, Racine penalizes himself twice over. First, by making the obstruction incest—that is to say, an impediment there is no admitting any wish to overcome. Public inclination—to which Racine was invariably very attentive—continued to side with Tristan against King Mark, with the seducer against the deceived husband; but it could never have sided with an incestuous couple. Secondly, Racine penalizes himself at second-hand by refusing to allow that Hippolytus shall return Phaedra's passion. *Phèdre* was written for Marie Champmeslé, who played the queen; and Hippolytus is Racine—Racine as he now wished himself to be: insensitive to the fatal spell. Identifying Phaedra with the woman he loved, he scored over

the object of his passion, and convinced himself that
this passion was to be condemned *beyond appeal*.

But, as I have said, Racine at the time he wrote
Phèdre was in the thick of a crisis and still undecided
regarding its resolution. Hence the profound duplicity of
the play. The moral law, the law of day which Racine
wished to obey henceforth, compelled him to make the
young prince insensitive to Phaedra's love. Her love is
therefore termed "incestuous," although she is only Hippolytus's step-mother. At the same time, the old Adam,
the natural Racine, sought to evade this rigorous law,
which, in banning incest, makes passion impossible. He
did so by causing Hippolytus to be in love with Aricia;
for she, as will be seen, is Phaedra in disguise. It is a
highly subtle device.

"As regards the character of Hippolytus [Racine
writes in the preface to *Phèdre*], I had noticed in the
Ancients that Euripides was reproached with having represented him as a philosopher free of all imperfection:
so that the death of this young prince aroused far more
indignation than pity. I thought I ought to give him
some frailty *which should render him a little guilty towards his father*, without however depriving him of any
of that magnanimity thanks to which he spares Phaedra's
honour, and allows himself to be oppressed without ac-
cusing her. *I call 'frailty' the passion that he feels against
his will for Aricia, who is daughter and sister of his
father's mortal enemies.*"

So Aricia in the play is "the love forbidden by the
Father"—a veiled substitute for incestuous love. [1]

Pyscho-analysis has recently made us familiar with more
cunning subterfuges! But it is not incest, it is passion, that
interests and involves Racine. The other means he hit
upon of referring to it in voluptuous terms, even while
submitting to its being condemned, was that of the unim-
peachable argument of the love-potion. Here, as in the
myth, "Destiny" is made to relieve both the author and
those who love of all responsibility.

---

[1] Hippolytus, referring to Aricia in Act I, asks:
        Shall I espouse
    Her rights against my sire, rashly provoke
    His wrath?
The translations are by R. B. Boswell (1890).

> The gods, dear prince, if once your hour is come,
> Care little for the reasons that should guide us.[1]

These are not gods that Corneille would have worshipped!
Nor would he have allowed that gods can be deceived,
nor that a fault can be laid at their door.

> The gods will bear me witness,
> Who have within my veins kindled this fire.[2]

And here is the waiting-woman Oenone who speaks to
Phaedra in the same strain as the waiting-woman Brengain speaks to Isolde:

> You love. We cannot conquer destiny.
> You were drawn on as by a fatal charm.[3]

I spoke of "duplicity," but this is so thoroughly essential
to the play, producing as it does the very crisis from
which the play issues, that to blame the author would
be foolish. *Phèdre* had to be. The myth had to be
brought up into the light. There had to be this painful
upthrust on the part of the yearning for death as it first
sought its self-release by means of an impossible avowal,
then held back, and finally attained to self-confession in
the very moment of renunciation—keeping pace with the
motion of the queen on three occasions.[4] All this had
to be, in order that passionate love might finally succumb
to the Norm of Light. For in *Phèdre* terrestrial day, for
the first time since the rise of the myth in the twelfth
century, triumphs over the death of the woman lover,
thus reversing the whole of the interaction in both *Tristan*
and *Romeo and Juliet*.

> Death from mine eyes veiling the light of heav'n,
> Restores its purity that they defiled.

> She dies, my Lord!

---

[1] *Phèdre*, Act I, i.   [2] Act II, v.   [3] Act IV, vi.

[4] The confession to the Nurse in Act I; that in Act II to Hippolytus: "Hé bien, connoy donc Phèdre et toute sa fureur!";
and the avowal made to Theseus in Act V.

> Would that the memory
> Of her disgraceful deed could perish with her! [1]

In spite of everything, in spite even of this last touch that Racine made into a piece of deceit, I believe he must have been sincere when in the preface to *Phèdre* he wrote:

"This I can vouch for, that I never wrote a tragedy in which virtue was more plainly exhibited than it is here. The least faults are severely *punished*. The mere notion of a crime is regarded with as much horror as a crime itself. *The frailties of love are treated as real weaknesses.* Passions are brought before the eye only in order to show how much disorder they cause."

This is far removed from the intention of "exciting passions" in order to gratify a desire for "majestic sadness." It is within sight of Port-Royal. (Racine was educated in the principal Jansenist center at Port-Royal, but broke with his masters over his love of the theatre.—Ed.)

Racine, like Petrarch, belonged to the race of troubadours who betray Love for love. Nearly all of them ended up in religion. But let us notice: a religion of retreat—perhaps as a final insult to intolerable day.

12

Eclipse of the Myth

In spite of Corneille and in spite of Racine up to *Phèdre,* the end of the French seventeenth century suffered from, or rather benefited by—whichever you like —a first eclipse of the myth alike in manners and in philosophy. The ordering—not to say, the drilling—of feudal society by the King-State involved somewhat far-reaching changes in emotional relations and in customs. Marriage became once again the basic institution, and reached a point of stability at which it was with difficulty

---

[1] Act V, vii.

to be made to remain in subsequent centuries, and which in previous centuries had not been known. An "alliance" between two families was negotiated with as much formality as one by diplomatists. If the parties happened to have a real or fancied inclination for one another, this merely added an element of exquisite perfection and of agreeable luxury to the arrangement—an ultimate touch of whimsicality amounting almost to insolence. (In the eighteenth century it quickly came to be considered bad taste.) Suitability of rank and a matching of "qualities" were the perfect standards of a satisfactory marriage, curiously like the custom of China. Indeed, it was in the "rational" seventeenth century that European manners became severed from religious beliefs, even as Confucius considers they should be, and, although the change apparently attracted no notice, were made to conform to the current laws of reason, and hence to ignore the Christian absolute. No longer the unforeseeable effects of grace, but "worth," decided that there should be a union, and it was "worth" alone which rendered "agreeable" a prospective partner whose pros and cons had been ingeniously weighed. Such was the triumph of Jesuitic morality. Emotion was imprisoned in the showy contrivances of the classical baroque. For that matter, the analytic treatment of passion by such writers as Descartes, its conversion to clearly distinct psychological categories and to rational hierarchies of qualities, worthiness, and faculties, must of necessity have brought about the dissolution of the myth and the arrest of its original impetus. For the sway of the myth is not asserted but there where precisely all moral categories vanish—beyond Good and Evil, in *transports*, and in the transgression of the sphere within which morality is valid.

The case of Spinoza would deserve a chapter to itself, but his influence on manners only made itself felt two centuries after him, when the *Sturm und Drang* philosophers had translated him into German for the benefit of poets, and these had translated him to metaphors for the benefit of an emotional middle class. The ultimate result was to produce chatter about the divinity of countryside impressions on a Sunday. Spinoza defines love as "joy accompanied by the idea of an external cause." [1] The defini-

---

[1] *Ethics*, Book III, def. 6.

tion is accurate in a single instance, the only instance this mystic considers—when the external cause is a God with whom our soul may identify itself.[1] But Spinoza disregards the existence of *obstruction*. Actually, our human passions are always connected with antagonistic passions, our love with hate, and our pleasures with our pains. Between joy and its external cause there is invariably some gap and some obstruction—society, sin, virtue, the body, the separate self. Hence arises the ardour of passion. And hence it is that the wish for complete union is indissolubly linked with a wish for the death that brings release. It is because passion cannot exist without pain that passion makes our ruin seem desirable to us. When the Portuguese nun Mariana Alcaforado wrote to the man who had seduced her, she said: "I give thanks to you from my innermost heart for the despair into which you have cast me; I despise the peace in which I lived before knowing you. Adieu! Love me, then, for ever, and go on making me suffer the cruellest torments!" Towards the end of the eighteenth century, another woman, Julie de Lespinasse wrote: "I love you as one ought to love—with despair!"

But till the advent of Rousseau the eighteenth century in France was indeed a period of total eclipse for the dark Sun of Melancholy. The "points" and "worthiness" which the rakes of the Regency and of the reign of Louis the Fifteenth considered "civil" were no longer in any sense moral, but intellectual and physical. When the distinction between mind and body took the place of the separation of mind from believing soul, the result was to divide a human being into intelligence and sex. Actually, with every obstruction removed, passion was without impetus. And it became the fashion to talk of *passionnettes* or little passions. The god of Love was no longer an adamant destiny but a cheeky child. Hardly anything was forbidden. Of the natural obstruction of modesty enough was retained for the needs of the rhetoric of desire, but no longer even enough for the needs of that of love. "A fine virtue," Madame d'Epinay said, "that has to be attached with pins!" (I fancy that those pins

[1] This supports what was said earlier in connexion with Eckhart. Unitive mysticism is unaware of divine *passion*.

were not mentioned by chance: "Love *points* you," the rhetoric said. A little later blood was going to flow under the Terror; but we are for the moment only at "war in lace cuffs.")

Yet this century of sensuality was not that of sensual health, if it was thought to cure it of the myth. "The women of our time do not love with the heart; they love with the head," said Abbé Galiani. "An old blind *débauchée* of wit," wrote Horace Walpole in a letter, and thereby gave perhaps the best description of feminine Don-Juanism. For it is woman who dreamed of Don Juan, and although there were Richelieus and Casanovas to incarnate the dream I am less sure of their reality than of that of the desire which created them. That desire was well viewed by the Goncourt Brothers in their classical book on woman in the eighteenth century. "Instead of giving her the satisfactions of sensual love and settling her down to voluptuousness, love fills her with anxieties, drives her from one trial to another, from one attempt to another, shaking in front of her as she goes step by step into shame the temptation of spiritual corruptions, a *falsehood about ideals,* the elusive caprice of dreams of debauchery."

"A falsehood about ideals" sums up indeed whatever cynical reaction the myth may have given rise to. I have mentioned more than one example. The eighteenth century was too polished to allow *gauloiserie*: it replaced that by an *affectation* of voluptuous facility. In the sally that all love amounts to no more than the touching of two skins I see less the affirmation of an inhuman materialism than a proof of the secret persistence of the myth in the hearts of the men of the eighteenth century. A modicum of amorous illusion and diffused idealism had to subsist for Chamfort to have considered it *piquant* to note down the maxim and to have published it. It could still astonish. It was no more—and was destined never to become more—than an inverted idealism.

13

Don Juan and the Marquis de Sade

If we shut our eyes after gazing at a white statue we shall have the image of a black. In the same way, the eclipse of the myth conjured up the exact opposite of Tristan. If Don Juan, historically speaking, is no invention of the eighteenth century, the period nevertheless played in relation to this character the very part assigned in Manichaean doctrine to Lucifer as regards Creation. The period gave shape to Tirso de Molina's (Don Juan) *Tenorio,* and endowed the hero of that play with two thoroughly typical features—*noirceur* and *rascality.* Nothing could be more directly the reverse of the twin virtues of chivalrous love—candour and courtesy!

The way in which the mystical character of Don Juan stirs the emotions of women and fascinates the minds of some men is to be accounted for, I fancy, by his *infinitely contradictory* nature. Don Juan is at one and the same time sheer spontaneity of instinct and sheer mind aflutter over the sea of possibility. He is constant inconstancy, and also the constant quest of the one woman whom desire in its untiring self-deception is never able to find. He is the insolent avidity of a youth renewed at every fresh encounter, and he is also the hidden weakness of an inability to possess, because devoid of enough *being* ever *to have.* Let me be content with taking the dramatic Don Juan as an inverted reflection of Tristan, and in Mozart's *Don Giovanni* rather than in Molière's *Don Juan*; for the latter, in my opinion, is by far the less significant.[1]

The contrast occurs first in the external demeanour and movement of the two characters. Don Giovanni seems always to be riding the high horse, and always to be poised in readiness to leap forward again whenever

[1] It may be mentioned incidentally that at its original production in the seventeenth century Molière's play had no success.

he chances to have halted in his progress. But Tristan walks on to the stage with the somnambulistic deliberation of one hypnotized by some object of wonderful and inexhaustible value. The former possessed a thousand and three women,[1] the latter only one. But it is the man of many who is poor, whereas in a single being infinitely possessed there is concentrated the wide world. Tristan can forgo the world—because he loves! But Don Giovanni, although incessantly loved, is never able to love in return. Hence his anxiety and his agitated wanderings. Don Giovanni seeks in the act of love a voluptuous profanation. By remaining chaste, Tristan wishes to achieve a divinizing "prowess." Don Giovanni's line is rape, and no sooner has he scored than he surrenders the field and flees. But the rule of courtly love made of rape the crime of crimes, a felony for which there is no remission; and of homage a pledge unto death. Don Giovanni, however, likes crime for its own sake, and in that way subjects himself to the morality which he transgresses. In order to enjoy abusing it, he has the greatest need of its existence. Tristan, instead, considers that he is freed from the play of rules, from sins and virtues, having been granted the grace of a virtue which transcends both the world and the Law. In sum, the antithesis is as follows— Don Giovanni is the demon of unalloyed immanence, a prisoner of worldly appearances, and the martyr of a more and more deceptive and despicable sensation, whereas Tristan is the prisoner of a realm lying beyond night and day and the martyr of a *rapture* which is transformed at death into unalloyed bliss. It may also be noted that if, when the Commander holds out his hand in the last act, Don Giovanni jokes, laughs loudly, and provokes death, he thereby redeems in a supreme act of defiance the base deeds that would have dishonoured a true knight; but Tristan, sad and brave, never surrenders his pride till luminous death is at hand.

I see the two to have only one feature in common. Both appear sword in hand.

From about the time Louis the Fourteenth died in

---

[1] In Spain alone, and plus 1,062 in other countries!—Translator.

1715 till Louis the Sixteenth ascended the throne in 1774, Don Juan reigned over the dreams of a French aristocracy that had gradually fallen from feudal heroism. The Duke of Richelieu and the Duke of Lauzun on the topmost social rungs, Bezenval and Casanova at the level of the rascally adventurer—such were the paragons who took the place of the ideal destroyed in the preceding century. The repression of the myth by an all-embracing irony and the applauded triumph of "felons" soon excited some curious reactions. Amid so much pliancy, so much intellectual and sensual refinement, so much satiation, one most profound human need was left ungratified—the need of suffering. If the body social encourages this need, it grows enfeebled, as is shown by the waning of the Middle Ages; but if the body social remains unconscious of this need or imagines that the need can be ridiculed, it quickly dries up and grows enervated. Thereupon the mind proceeds to invent in the guise of acts of cruelty the sufferings it has forbidden the heart to undergo. Kindness is a stranger to those who have not suffered: their fancies lose all vital touch and all capacity for being in sympathy. Woman in the eyes of men of the eighteenth century was merely "an object." At one extreme there had been the ideal woman, the unalloyed symbol of a Love drawing love away beyond visible forms; at the other there was now woman as a mere means to pleasure, the more or less agreeable instrument of a sensation which kept men self-isolated.

I distinguish in the contradiction between Don Juan and Tristan, in the intolerable tension of a mind that experiences this contradiction for itself, because susceptible to sensuality and desirous of the courtly idea, the basis for the writings of the Marquis de Sade and the very motives of his rebellion. Sade admired the poetry of Petrarch, as he remarks in his *Crimes de l'amour*. The admiration had been traditional in his family ever since his direct ancestor, Hugues de Sade, married Petrarch's lady, Laure de Noves.[1] Petrarch seems to have been simply unaware of the existence of either desire or bodies; unaware of the reality of "an object." Sade, a product

---

[1] Abbé de Sade, the Marquis's uncle, is the author of *Remarques sur les premiers poètes français et les troubadours,* and of three (anonymous) volumes of Memoirs of Petrarch.

224 LOVE IN THE WESTERN WORLD

of the eighteenth century, was only too conscious of its
monotonous tyranny. What Petrarch ignored was the
physical obstruction upon which a lover has to get his
own back. Yet the object is only too unmistakably there:
it is the means to pleasure, and pleasure is a doom. How
be released from it except by excess, since all excess
issues from the mind! Nothing could be more icily rational than the countless "voluptuous" inventions of the
Marquis's rage. Where pleasure is, there must suffering
be; and suffering is the sign of a redemption. We are
purified by evil; let us sin then to the utmost so as to
destroy it by subjecting it to tortures which will nevertheless afford us some pleasure, and this will be part of
our *askesis*! A dialectical frenzy seized Sade. Only murder
can restore freedom, and it must be the murder of the
beloved, inasmuch as loving is what fetters us. Only one's
love can be really killed, for one's love alone is *sovereign*.
The crime of an impure love will redeem purity.

With this key in hand, let us now consider a passage
from *La Philosophie du boudoir,* in which Dolmancé
puts forward a moral defence of murder.

"What! [he says] An ambitious *sovereign* shall be
able to destroy as he likes and without scruple the foes
that hamper the execution of his schemes for achieving
greatness! *Cruel, arbitrary and imperious laws* shall likewise murder in every century millions of human beings!
And yet weak and unfortunate private persons such as
ourselves shall not be allowed to sacrifice a single being
to our *revenge* or to our caprice? Could anything be more
barbarous or more ridiculously queer? And should we not,
under cover of the most profound mystery, avenge ourselves *abundantly* for this absurdity?" [Italics mine.]
Had the Marquis de Sade been asked what were the inner
motives of his weird moral professions, no doubt he would
have taken refuge in a cold-blooded prolixity. But every
one of his arguments is transparent. They all mean the
exact opposite of what they say literally.[1] His glorification of sex is a continual and deliberate profanation of

---

[1] "Sade wrote *Juliette ou les Malheurs de la vertu* (1791), and
then *Justine ou les Prospérités du vice*. It is the exact opposite
(and therefore, according to psycho-analysis, the exact opposite
of this opposite, and so on) of *Remedies for One and the Other
Fortune* by Petrarch," C. A. Cingria remarks in his *Pétrarque*.

the profaned eighteenth-century morality. It is the act of
an atheist taking "the negative way" (because he despairs of unloosing his bonds), and therefore challenging
love to manifest itself by killing the criminal.[1] For
only thus could release be obtained—according to the
faith of the troubadours.

14

La Nouvelle Héloïse

Brought up in the Genevan countryside, Rousseau escaped the influence of urban Don Juanism; but he
was unable to steer clear of a literature to which his
temperament responded very deeply. This literature may
be called Petrarchism. Strictly speaking, Rousseau's novel
is not a resuscitation of the primitive Tristan myth. It

---

[1] The above analysis of the sadistic crime has been strikingly
supported in two remarkable studies by Pierre Klossowski: "Le
Mal et la Négation d'autrui dans la philosophie de D. A. F. de
Sade" (*Recherches philosophiques* (Paris), IV, 1934–45) and
"Temps et aggressivité" (ibid., V, 1935–36). The author considers that Sade looked upon evil as the only element in nature.
In *La Nouvelle Justine* there occurs this passage: 'Yes, I hold nature in abhorrence; and this is because I am only too well aware
that I detest it. Apprised of its horrible secrets, I have taken a
kind of pleasure in copying its dark wickedness." Hence the sadistic desire to obtain release from the tyranny of sex through excesses of debauchery.
Another truly Manichaean attack on Creation is as follows:
"The life principle in every being is no other than the death principle. We take in both at one and the same time and nourish them
within us." But if life and created nature are but dark wickedness and cruelty, it becomes necessary to obtain release from them
by exceeding this cruelty and wickedness. And there is but the
alternative to be cruel either to ourselves or to others. Sade chose
others. He preferred to be a criminal rather than a victim. Hence
the Sadistic conscience is the antithesis of the romantic conscience.
The romantic—Petrarch—punishes himself in order to preserve
the beloved, whereas Sade sought to kill the beloved.

lacks the savage violence of the legend, and, still more markedly, the esoteric background. What Rousseau resuscitated was the spiritual state originally brought into existence by imitators of the troubadours through their "secularization" of a doctrine that they were aware of only as a profane rhetoric. This spiritual state is *acedia* —the happy melancholy cultivated by Petrarch, the Vaucluse hermit. The analytic summaries added by a zealous editor to the third edition of the novel contain situations such as the *leys de cortezia* allowed for. Rousseau puts the *Canzoniere* into prose, and makes them rather middle-class in the process.[1] Honoré d'Urfé had turned courtesy into a profane casuistry. Rousseau made of it a kind of refined pietism. Here again the deterioration is obvious.

The Héloïse who lived in the twelfth century[2] and whose letters to Abélard have been preserved is far closer to Iseult, Juliet, and Mlle de Lespinasse than to Julie d'Étanges, the heroine of Rousseau's novel. And, in spite of his magnificent name, there is nothing either mystical or chivalrous about Saint-Preux, the hero. Moreover, although the novel ends with death, it is only after passion has been renounced; and the death of Julie is Christian—as far as Rousseau is able to make it so. In a

---

[1] A quotation here, an allusion there, show that Rousseau was well acquainted with Petrarch, the real inventor of a feeling for nature and of the poetry of solitude.

[2] Let me repeat that the famous love of Abélard and Héloïse is the *first historical example* of the kind of passion dealt with in these pages. In the Latin *Funerary Hymn* for Héloïse—composed perhaps by herself—the woman lover beseeches as follows:

    Relieve me of my cross,
    Lead me to the light,
    And give my soul release!

Whereupon the chorus of nuns sings:

    Let them have respite from their labour,
    And from their painful love!
    Union for those who dwell in heaven they besought,
    Even now are they in sanctuary with the Saviour.

Abélard returned this passion rather poorly. But his extremely heretical theology is akin on essential matters to the spiritual doctrine of the Cathars. And in his *Lamentations* he gives voice to the same loud cry as romanticism and Tristan: *Amoris impulsio, culpae iustificatio.*

letter to his publisher, by the way, he insists at length
on his own Protestantism and that of his characters;
but without impugning his sincerity, it may be suspected
that his "Calvinism" concentrated on the Supreme Being
as easily as it seemed to overlook Christ. All this does
not prevent me from confessing a very lively liking for
the style of the novel. In this respect, indeed, *La Nouvelle
Héloïse* is the only novel comparable to *L'Astrée*.
Its clear-sighted psychology, too, there are serious grounds
for admiring. Moral "Rousseauism" is being hastily
judged when we attribute to the author the beliefs of his
characters. If Rousseau was the first to describe such
errors, it was because he had suffered from them more
than most people and was the more strongly resolved to
get away from them. But the moral of the story is commonly overlooked, and the tone, the emotional content,
and a certain complaisance such as the romantic style
fosters, are all that we notice. Evidently Rousseau was
no more taken in by the "religion" of love than Petrarch
had been at the end of his life. Once Julie is married
and she analyses the past common to her lover and herself,[1] there could not be a piece of closer reasoning,
albeit feminine, than she employs in tracking down the
deliberate confusion of Eros with Agape.

"Virtue is so essential to our hearts that when once
true virtue has been forsaken we fashion another to our
own liking, and hold to it perhaps the more strongly
for having chosen it ourselves."

Yet there is good reason for believing that the atmosphere of *La Nouvelle Héloïse,* so fresh to the
eighteenth century, had a power of contagion which the
moral of the story was quite unable to weaken. And it
is in this contagious power that the myth unquestionably
reappears—enfeebled, ashamed, and embarrassed, but,
thanks to an indefinable funereal shudder, recognizable
enough through the veil of virtuous tears. Hardly has
Saint-Preux had his "expectations" fulfilled than [2] he
begins gloomily to doubt.

"No [he says], it is not those transports that I
most regret. Ah, no! Take away if you must those intoxi-
cating favours for which I would lay down my life a

---

[1] Part III, Letter XVIII.
[2] Part I, Letter LV.

thousand times, but *give me back everything else, all that has a thousand times obliterated them.* Give me back that close union of soul. . . . Julie, please tell me: can it be that previously I did not love you, or is it that I now love you no longer? What a doubt!"

The ambiguity of his sigh frightens him, and yet he goes on to admit with a kind of vexation which he barely conceals, "My feelings for you have become more calm, it is true, but also more affectionate, and, moreover, of a different kind. . . . The sweetness of friendship moderates the frenzy of love." The Tristan part of him comes to life once he has been guilty of the "fault" of possessing the beloved, and it would readily forgo the "calm sweetness" he speaks of. He too has wanted to burn, and to keep his desire unsatisfied. He too is going to invent fresh and altogether gratuitious *obstructions*—excuses for parting and situations voluptuously hopeless. That is why there is the insistence—painful and, coming at this moment, somewhat overdone, I feel—on the plebeian origins of Saint-Preux, which are held to exclude all possibility of a legal union. That is why, too, social prejudice is assimilated to the exigencies of a virtue declared to be religious *ad hoc*. But the unavowable motives of the confusion are readily discernible. In the twelfth century chastity was ordained by courtly love; now chastity has become a middle-class custom. But, whether one or the other is being deferred to, what is really at work is the myth. In the letter already quoted, where Julie recalls the trials they have had together, she also describes as a "holy ardour" the chaste love that ravished them—notwithstanding that as such it was already open to being condemned—but "a crime," "horrors," "corruption," are the names she gives to this same love when she considers that stage of it which began with the gift of her physical self. Clearly, the fault they care about is the infringement of *cortezia*, not the infringement of the middle-class virtue which they all too often invoke. I might go on: the exegesis of *Tristan* could easily be repeated for *La Nouvelle Héloïse*. In both, obstruction produces the same interaction. There is, however, this decisive difference: Rousseau ends with marriage—that is to say, with the triumph of the world as sanctified by Christianity—whereas the legend glorified in death the complete dissolution of terrestrial ties.

15

German Romanticism

The state of mind of the lovers in *La Nouvelle Héloïse* is sentimental, not mystical. [1] Yet it was by taking this state of mind as a starting-point that romanticism set out to recover a primitive mysticism with which it was unacquainted, but the sacred and fatal power of which it grew aware of in flashes.

I have traced the gradual degradation of the myth as it passed from Thomas's *Tristan* via Petrarch and *L'Astrée* down to French classical tragedy. Little by little it was made humane and broken up into components less and less mysterious. Finally Racine felled it, though not before he had suffered a most grievous wound in the course of his struggles with the dark angel. Then Don Juan sprang on the stage, and from Molière to Mozart the myth underwent a major eclipse. But with the appearance of Rousseau's novel, which was produced on the margin, so to speak, of the eighteenth century, we are launched upon a new journey, a journey over the same road, but in the opposite direction. Via *Werther* —a retort to the *Héloïse*, which, in ending far more badly, is closer to the original model—we come to Jean Paul, Hölderlin, and Novalis. Amid the commotion of the French Revolution, the Terror, and the ensuing European wars, it became possible to make certain admissions and a certain kind of suffering was enabled to proclaim its true nature. For the first time, the worship of Darkness and of Death rose up into the field of lyric *awareness*. Hardly had Napoleon been overcome than Europe was invaded by a more insidious tyranny,

[1] It may be Rousseau's fault, or more likely that of the poetical movement known as Symbolism, but nowadays many ladies imagine that "mystical" means "sentimental"—stained glass, blue shadows, arpeggios, mental somnolence, sensual reverie!

which lasted till the day Wagner caused the myth all at once to stand forth to its full height and charged with its full virulence. Music alone could utter the unutterable, and music forced the final secret of *Tristan*.

It is not my intention to enumerate the countless manifestations of the myth in European literature, chiefly in recent times. I wish only to mark the stages of its alterations, and to resolve some merely apparent contradictions. There is no need to bring forward every piece of evidence for the statement that without exception all the German romantics revived the courtly theme, the theme of unhappy mutual love.[1] Even if the quotation of a few selected passages, which I shall leave to speak for themselves, looks like special pleading —because agreeing so perfectly with my account of the myth—these passages will prove more eloquent than any commentary.

Here is a letter to Hölderlin from his Diotima:

"Last evening I reflected for a long time about passion. No doubt *the passion of supreme love is never fulfilled here below*! Be sure to understand my feeling: to seek *this* satisfaction would be madness. *To die together*! (But silence! That seems like over-excitement, and yet it is so true!) Such is the only fulfilment. But we have sacred duties in this lower world. We are left with nothing but the most perfect confidence in one another and faith in that all-powerful divinity of Love which, though invisible, will go on guiding us for ever and will for ever strengthen our union." [2]

I quote from the private diary of Novalis:

"It occurred to me while seated on the tomb [of his betrothed] that my death could provide mankind with an example of everlasting fidelity, and in a way establish that it is possible to love as I have loved. . . .

"When pain is being shunned, that is a sign that one no longer wants love. Whoever loves must everlastingly remain aware of the surrounding void, and keep the

---

[1] In 1808 A. W. von Schlegel began a modernized version of *Tristan*. Many others—among them Rückert (1788–1866), Immermann (1796–1840), Platen (1796–1835)—followed suit with poems or poetic dramas. Platen's poem begins: "He whose eyes have once beheld beauty is already marked out for death."

[2] Italics in the original.

wound open. May God grant that I shall preserve this pain which is exquisitely dear to me. . . .

"Our vows were not exchanged for this world."

And here are some of the maxims of Novalis:

"All passions end like a tragedy. Whatever is finite ends in death. All poetry has a tragic element.

"A union formed even unto death is a marriage bestowing on each a companion for Night. It is in death that love is sweetest. Death appears to one still alive as a nuptial night, the heart of sweet mysteries.

"The intoxication of the senses may be related to love as sleep is to life. It is not the better part, and a man of strength must always prefer waking to sleeping."

The following two passages strike a truly Manichaean note:

"We must keep God and Nature apart. God has nothing to do with Nature: He is its goal, the substance in which it must eventually be harmonized.

"We are spirits that have come out of God; we are divine seed. One day we shall become even as our Father Himself."[1]

Hymnen an die Nacht renew the theme of the "Dawn" poems of the troubadours. Dark Eros beseeches that morning shall not be born again:

"May thy spiritual fire devour my body; may I be closely united with thee in an ethereal embrace, and then may our nuptial night endure for ever and ever."

And there might be quoted all those works of Tieck's in which love is termed "a sickness of desire, a divine apathy." [2] To extol a death undergone deliberately for the sake of love and in order to be absorbed into the divine—such was the deep religious purpose of the new Albigensian heresy called German romanticism. Death

---

[1] The painter Otto Runge had a Manichaean view of the world also. In a vast undertaking which he projected, "The Four Seasons," he intended to depict the four seasons of the spirit—Morning, infinite illumination of the universe; Day, infinite form of the created; Evening, infinite negation of existence at the beginning of the universe; Night, infinite depths of the knowledge of God, the Absolute Existence.

[2] Tieck in *Sternbald* tells the story of the troubadour Geoffrey Rudel, and in *Phantasus* and elsewhere dwells at length on the characteristics of courtly love.

is the ideal goal of "lofty men" in Jean Paul's *Die unsichtbare Loge*. In Novalis death blends with love. Kleist made of it "the one fulfilment" possible for "a supreme passionate love" to which the body would not lend itself. But poets were not alone in succumbing to the appeal of a nocturnal other world; a philosopher such as Schubert speculated on the *Nachteseite* of existence. Fichte himself defines a love in-essence-impossible—the true love that rejects any object whatever in order that it may launch into the infinite. He says it is "a desire for something altogether *unknown,* the existence of which is disclosed solely by the need of it, by a discomfort, and by a void that is in search of whatever will fill it, but that remains unaware of whence fulfilment may come." Hoffman voices an identical view when he names this *unknown* something "poetry."

"And now [he says] there shoots up, like a pure celestial flame giving out warmth and light but not burning, all the ineffable felicity of the higher life, born in the innermost recesses of the soul. The spirit puts out a thousand feelers, every one vibrating with desire. It weaves its net around *her* who has appeared, and she is his . . . *and she is never his,* for the thirst of his aspiration is ever slakeless."

In German romanticism the Western mind set out again on the venture previously undertaken by the unitive mystics; it adopted the old heresy of passion and sought to achieve the ideal transgression of all limitations and the negation of the world through extreme desire. On every side the scattered components of the myth reappeared and came together ready for Wagner, who, in fashioning them into a final synthesis, was the one and only poet who dared exhibit the myth for what it is. We should not be surprised to find that the first poem inspired by recollection of the Cathars and Catharist mysticism is the work of a most thorough-going romantic—Lenau's epic *Die Albigenser.* The following lines from this poem form a kind of profession of faith of that "new religion" dreamed of by Novalis and his friends:

> The age of Christ, now screened from us by God,
> This age also will pass.
> The New Alliance will be broken;

And then our God we shall behold as Spirit:
There shall be celebrated the Alliance Everlasting.
Spirit is God! That almighty cry will go resounding
Like joyful thunder through the springtime night!

16

The Myth Withdraws into the Human Breast

The intimate rhythm of German romanticism, the diastole and systole of its heart, are enthusiasm and metaphysical melancholy. It is the abysmal dialectic of the Manichaean heresy and the perpetual reversal of day into Darkness and of night into Light. The same impulse which bears a soul towards the light and divine unity, is, when considered from the standpoint of this world, no more than an impulse towards death and essential separation. Such is the tragical character of transcendental Irony, the perpetual motion of romanticism, the passion that ruins without respite all the objects which it is able to conceive and which it desires—nature, the beloved, the self—all that is not uncreated Unity and dissolution beyond return. But the enthusiasm is real; it is the *endieusement* of the troubadours, the *endiosada* of the Spanish mystics, *joy d'amor* in the dionysiac delirium. Out of it spurt perpetually, at the supreme point of elevation, extravagant fantasies. There is romantic gaiety as there is being moved and melted: moments of relaxation between two contradictory transports, returns to the world.

It is such a moment of queer joy, born of metaphysical irony, that French romanticism lacks. In this romanticism the data are the same, but the rhythm is less ample and the mind goes too swiftly to the point. France, during the Revolution and Empire, had no energy to spare for speculation in the realms of the spirit: it had no "new religion," no romantic philosophers,[1] little or no meta-

---

[1] Not till a century later did one appear—Bergson, the disciple of Schelling.

physics and little or no fancy—that superabundance of a
mind uplifted by its own drama. French romanticism
failed to get beyond the sphere of individual psychology.
It thus gained in lucidity, and hence, within its narrower
purview, was brought more swiftly·than the Germans to
mournful conclusions.

Certainly André Chénier is being a true romantic as
he describes

L'enthousiasme errant, fils de la pâle Nuit.

And Chateaubriand's famous invocation, "Arise swiftly,
longed-for tempests, that are to bear René away into
the expanses of another life!" is an unalloyed chant of
the passion of Darkness. But there was no mystic dawn
on the spiritual horizon, nor true joy of love at the
summit of those transports. The self was never transcended. It recoiled from the final illusion of a cosmic
release. It fell back, disenchanted, upon the analysis of
its own sadness and clear-sighted ineffectuality. French
romanticism was over-ripened; it was disillusioned, and—
I am tempted to say—too exact. By the side of it, Jean
Paul and Novalis cut callow figures. The attraction of
death among the Germans stimulates the sweetness of
being alive; perhaps this is because a German is more
simple and more strongly assured of the reality of another world. A French romantic has been the poorer
for remaining an eloquent sceptic, and on account of
his fear of seeming ingenuous and of the prolific vul-
garity in which the most truly German poets deliberately
revel notwithstanding their nostalgia! [1] Chateaubriand's
René amuses himself one day by dropping willow leaves
one by one into a stream and endowing with an idea each
leaf that the stream carries away. He watches intently for
the accidents of which his leaves are in danger. The reader feels he is reading some German poet, and expects
that the world's treasure will presently be exhibited. But
swiftly the eighteenth-century Frenchman grows aware
of how he is behaving and thinks it ridiculous. "So

---

[1] Cf. the portrait in Novalis's diary of Sophie von Kühn, his
former betrothed, who died at sixteen. He recalls her favorite
dishes and notes that she liked wine. A Frenchman shrugs his
shoulders at such childishness.

this is the depth of puerility to which man's magnificent mind can sink!" The "magnificent mind" therefore ends up with an epigram: "And yet it is true that many a man will bind his fate to things of such small worth as my willow leaves." (The remainder of the admirable paragraph will repay reading down to the famous invocation, "Arise, longed-for tempests! Come, Auster!" [1])

To the unintentional rationalists that the French romantics were, to the atheists who did not manage to believe in their most consoling fancies, love could not long be "the ineffable felicity of the superior life" that E. T. A. Hoffman called it; but rather that "taciturn and ever threatened" love that is the subject of Alfred de Vigny's most splendid verse. The absence of a naïve interest in the quotidian forms of life facilitated detachment of mind and the abstract purification of sentiment. Beings and things—their pretexts—once pierced by a disillusioned gaze, were quickly no longer genuine obstacles. And the myth, deprived of its external shapes, became what it is in essence—a voluptuous destruction of the self by the self. "We have learned better without having experienced enjoyment," René says; "there are still desires and men have no more illusions. . . . Men live with a full heart in an empty world." Thereupon woman herself ceased to be the indispensable symbol of the nostalgia of passion. In Sénancour's *Obermann* the "obstacle" is entirely within; it consists of the duality of a self unable to achieve either vindication or dissolution, unable to attain either self-possession or possession by another.

We knew that Tristan did not love Iseult for herself, but only on account of the love of Love of which her beauty gave him the image. He, however, did not know this, and his passion was naïve and strong. René, and Obermann still more, are unable even to believe in the image; they have grasped that the drama takes place inside them, between the intolerable laws of finite ter-

---

[1] In connexion with Chateaubriand's invocation, the Song of Songs says: "Awake, O north wind; and come, thou south; blow upon my garden, that spices thereof may flow out;" and Cantico XXVI by Saint John of the Cross runs:
Come, South Wind, that awakenest love,
Blow through my garden,
And let its odours flow.

restrial existence and the desire after a transgression of
our limits, fatal but divinizing.

Few, however, were the French romantics who attained to this bold, arid, and exact self-knowledge, which
is closer to negative mysticism than might be supposed.
Most of them reverted in time to the illusions of human
love, without being able to recapture the vigourous simplicity of the myth. They refined amazingly on the traditional "pretexts" for the parting of lovers: from *Le Lys
dans la vallée*—the most ingenuous—to *Adolphe*—the
most fully conscious—the "pretext" is sometimes marriage and honour, or social duty, or virtue, or the lover's
melancholic secret or some religious scruple, or, lastly,
avowed narcissism. The myth became progressively
more thoroughly internal, while the obstacle invoked
crumbled and dissolved in sceptical criticism, and while
moral rules degenerated and all vestiges of a "sacred"
element vanished from social life.

17

Stendhal, or the Fiasco of the Sublime

A man of the eighteenth century who had received
the mark of romanticism, and moving, moreover, in a highly sceptical world, Stendhal provides the
perfect example for an analysis of the profanation of
the myth.

Here was a man whom the need of passion tormented;
he had discovered in his "soul"—that is to say, in a
yearning after the sublime—the void spoken of by Fichte,
the insatiable call of the unknown, of the Unknown Woman that alone will fill this void. To love passionately
would be indeed to live! He imagined quite sincerely that
his longing was physical (and trotted out his own little
materialistic explanation of it). Had he been told that
what he felt was but the impress of the myth upon his
mind, a habit inherited from European culture, and in
particular from literature, he would have roared with

laughter; for he was convinced that mysticism and religion were dead. But he had to admit that his desire for passion, that even passion itself in the world he lived in, were frowned upon alike by reason and by the prevailing scepticism. Hence the need he experienced of justifying that need. Hence his famous treatise, *De l'Amour* (1822). The opening words of the preface betray that it is a controversial work.

"Although dealing with love, this little book is not a novel, and above all contains none of the distractions of a novel. It is simply an accurate and scientific treatise on a type of madness which is very rare in France." [1] And to this madness Stendhal gives the name of "passion-love."

He declares that there are four kinds of love—passion-love, sympathy-love, sensual love, and vanity-love. It is only the first which finds grace in his eyes. He accounts for it by means of the crystallization theory. "I call 'crystallization' that process of the mind which discovers fresh perfections in its beloved object at every turn of events." Thus in the salt mines of Hallein, near Salzburg, if a bough stripped of its leaves is dropped into the depths of a disused working, it is picked out two or three months later "with a vast number of spangled shifting, glittering diamonds." On this theory, falling in love is to endow a woman with perfections she does not in the least possess. And why do we do this? Because we need to love, and because the only thing that can be loved is beauty. In more simple language, crystallization is the process by which a man idealizes the woman he loves.

I believe it was Ortega y Gasset [2] who first pointed out that this famous theory makes passionate love a mere *error*. "Not that passion is held to err often," Ortega adds, "but that it is deemed to be in itself an error. . . . Stendhal's case is pretty obvious: he did not truly love, and, above all, he never was truly loved." Tristan loved, Don Juan was loved; but a man who had nothing in common with the former except nostalgia and nothing in common with the latter except inconstancy was led to describe love as "a soul-sickness"—in the

---

[1] Translation by Vyvyan Holland (London, 1928).

[2] *Uber die Liebe,* op. cit.

pure tradition of Antiquity, except for his saying that in being afflicted with this sickness he felt happy. Thus, in *De l'Amour,* Stendhal is a doctor studying in his own person the symptoms and progress of a malady he does not consider likely to be fatal. The whole difference between his "crystallization" and the idealization of *cortezia* lies in this—that Stendhal is aware that there must be a de-crystallization, the return to a state in which the beloved will be viewed as she actually is. In his conviction, the antidote to the love-potion is inconstancy. Tragedy is being turned into farce.

One feature of his book strikes me: the description is admirably vivacious, accurate, and at times profound, but it is completely pessimistic, inasmuch as he is dealing with an error and is disconsolate when freed from it. Whence comes a pessimism incompatible with the view of life which he had elaborated for himself? That is the question he never asks himself. He notes, it is true:

"Pleasure does not leave half the impression that pain does, and in the second place, apart from this drawback in the amount of emotion produced, *sympathy* is only excited about half as much by a picture of happiness as it is by one of misfortune."

And again:

"A soul made for passion feels in the first place that this happy life [marriage] *irks him,* and perhaps, also, that it only gives him commonplace ideas."

A little further on he says:

"There are very few moral afflictions in life that are not rendered precious by the *emotion* which they excite."

That is something true. We like pain, and happiness does rather bore us. You find it quite natural? And yet a Hindu or a Chinese is astonished. A resurrected citizen of classical Greece would be none the less so. How have we acquired this odd like and dislike? Are they not contrary to nature? Once again Stendhal does not ask, not being in a position to answer. As a crude materialist—the crude are the best: they are the most straightforward—he boldly suppresses the whole problem, thanks to his theory of crystallization, his theory of an error. In his opinion, passion is to be accounted for by an error propitious to desire. "This phenomenon," he says, "arises from the promptings of Nature which urge us to enjoy ourselves and which drive the blood to the head." There you are! A man's faculties become clouded, and they set to "crystallizing." But it is not explained how instinct decides to commit the error requisite for this crafty process—I mean, instinct alone, left to itself.

Like Ortega y Gasset, I think that Stendhal's explanation is inaccurate in the first place as regards the facts. There is one love which, far from going astray, is alone able to recognize in the beloved his or her real though hidden virtues. Secondly, his solution seems of the verbal type. For to say that passion is an error—as it may be sometimes—does not explain how the error arises. Neither instinct nor nature is in the habit of going wrong in that way. If an error occurs, it must be due to the mind. The truth is that Stendhal fell victim to a spiritual experience that went beyond what his materialistic beliefs could cope with. Yet he was a contented victim; and that is why he did not push his inquiry further. His book *De l'Amour* really bears witness to the dread which invaded his self-analytic mind in the presence of the myth—not that he actually wished for release from this myth, but that he had lost the clue to understanding it.

However, it must not be supposed that Stendhal in the course of his inquiry did not more than once "get hot." He devotes two long chapters to love in Provence in the twelfth century, and he reproduces in an appendix the rules of courtly love.[1] "A singular civilization," he says. And then he ponders for a bit. It looks as if he must suspect something. But no. "I could quote," he goes on, "twenty anecdotes to show the prevalence in the Provence of that time of *an amiable and witty gallantry between the two sexes conducted on strict principles of justice. . . .*" And in the next chapter he of course does not fail to quote all twenty anecdotes.

[1] François Raynouard (1761–1836) and Claude Fauriel (1772–1844) had recently brought about a revival of medieval studies in France.

18

Wagner, or Completion

Now fades the world with all its glamours
Life in holiest loving, ne'er more to awaken
Truest, deepest soul's desire.

The man who put that into *Tristan und Isolde* knew that
passion is something more than an error. He understood
that it is one of the fundamental decisions open to a
human being, a choice exercised in favour of Death if
Death is release from a world under the sway of evil.
But the boldness shown in *Tristan und Isolde* is of a
kind that is only put up with owing to a complete misunderstanding, a misunderstanding which, in being built
up and maintained by a sort of social consensus, is
tantamount to a blindness at once obstinate and unconscious. The assertion has so often been made by qualified
persons that in the end the world has come to believe
that Wagner is dealing with sensual desire. In the face
of all the flagrant evidence to the contrary which the
opera affords, the belief is significant. It indicates the
social necessity of myths, of deceits which society puts
forth in self-defence out of a wish to preserve the established forms of its organization, even while the individuals
of whom it consists surrender semi-consciously (and under cover of withstanding them) to the passions that
threaten its ruin.

In writing *Tristan,* Wagner transgressed the taboo. He
said everything—admitted everything, not only in the
words of his poem, but still more in the notes of his
score. He sang of the Darkness of the dissolution of forms
and beings, of the release of desire, of desire become
anathema, and of the tremendously plaintive and blessed
twilit glory of the spirit after it has been rescued at the
price of a fatal wound inflicted on the body. But the
malevolent content of the message had to be denied in

240

order to be admitted. At all costs the content had to be travestied, and given some tolerable interpretation according to common sense. The overwhelming mystery of Darkness and of the destruction of our bodies was declared to be the "sublimation" of a poor secret of broad day—the attraction of the sexes, the purely animal law which the body obeys; what society needs in order to procreate and to consolidate itself, what the middle class needs in order to feel life. That this was done so quickly does not testify to any exceptional social vitality; rather the operation was facilitated by the frivolousness of the ordinary theatre-going public, by its clumsy sentimentality, and—frankly—its wonderful ability not to hear what is being sung. Hence Wagner's *Tristan* can be revived with impunity before audiences who feel stirred in complete security, so strong is the widespread certainty that *nobody will credit its message.*

The drama opens with a monumental evocation of the pride, and the barbarous and sometimes even criminal violence, of feudal honour. Isolde wishes to avenge the affront she has suffered. The potion she gives to Tristan is intended to bring about his death, but a death disallowed by Love, a death in accordance with the laws of day and of revenge—brutal, accidental, and devoid of mystical significance. The highest Minne, however, causes Brengain to make a mistake that can preserve Love. For the death-potion she substitutes the drink of initiation. Hence the one embrace which conjoins Tristan and Isolde as soon as they have drunk is the solitary kiss of the Catharist sacrament, the *consolamentum* of the Pure! From that moment the laws of day, hate, honour, and revenge, lose all power over their hearts. The initiated pair enter the nocturnal world of ecstatic release. And day, coming back with the royal procession and its discordant flourish of trumpets, is unable to recapture them. At the end of the ordeal which it compels them to undergo—this is their passion—they have already foreseen the *other* death, the death that will alone fulfill their love.

The second act is the passion song of souls imprisoned in material forms. When every obstacle has been overcome, and the lovers are alone together in the dark, carnal desire still stands between them. They are together, and yet they are two. The "und" of *Tristan und*

Isolde is there to indicate their duality as creatures. Here music alone can convey the certitude and substance of their twin nostalgia for one-ness; music alone can harmonize the plaint of the two voices, and make of it a single plaint in which there is already being sounded the reality of an ineffable other world of expectation. That is why the leitmotiv of the love duet is already that of death.

Once again day returns. The treacherous Melot [1] wounds Tristan. But by now passion has triumphed. It wrests away the apparent victory of day. The wound through which life flows out is passion's pledge of a supreme recovery—that recovery of which the dying Isolde sings once she has cast herself upon Tristan's corpse in an ecstasy of the "highest bliss of being."

Initiation, passion, fatal fulfilment—the three mystic moments to which Wagner, with a genius for simplification, saw that he could reduce the three acts of the drama, express the profound significance of the myth, a significance kept out of sight even in the medieval legends by a host of epic and picturesque detail. Nevertheless, the art form adopted by Wagner renews the possibility of "misunderstanding." The story of Tristan *had* now to be in the form of an opera for two reasons connected with the very essence of the myth. Even as the sin of the first man, and of each man, brings time into the world; and even as the transgression of the rules of chaste love by the legendary lovers turned the poetic lay of the troubadours into a novel [2]—so the powers of day, when brought forward in the first act, introduce struggle and duration, the elements of drama. But a play does not allow everything to be stated, for the religion of passion is "in essence lyrical." Hence *music* alone is equal to conveying the transcendental interaction, the wildly contradictory and contrapuntal character of the passion of Darkness, which is the summons to uncreated Light. European music has been defined as the emotional harmony of opposites—in musical terminology, counterpoint. It is the expression of a painful duality, which, al-

---

[1] Melot is the informer, a character constantly figuring in courtly poems. The troubadours called him the *losengier*.

[2] Cf. Book II, Chapter 11, p. 130. A novel is a poem which no longer expresses a moment, but duration.

though permanent at the level of life, vanishes in the luminous grace beyond physical death. Now, a play completed by music is an opera. Hence it is not by chance that both the Tristan myth and the Don Juan myth have received full expression only in operatic form. If Mozart and Wagner have produced the masterpieces of musical drama, it is thanks to a previous affinity that links this form of artistic expression with the subject each of them took. Music alone speaks worthily of tragedy, of whom she is mother and daughter.

However, in the case of *Tristan* the plastic share in a stage production comes to raise a new obstruction to the direct apprehending of the myth. Actors, the costumes they wear, and the scenery,[1] all keep attention focused on reality, demand the presence of "day," and fatally contradict the profound significance of the action. So long as our eyes are fixed on the stage, we are at the mercy of terrestrial shapes—and ridiculous at that. There, all too visibly before us, are a fat woman and a mighty warrior who are both being a prey to the anguish of desire. But let us shut our eyes, and at once the play is illuminated. The orchestra describes broadly the extent of an entirely internal tragedy. The melodies in their distressing morbidity disclose a world in which carnal desire has become no more than an ultimate and impure apathy of souls in process of curing themselves of life. Only the sorrowful lighting of the third act—the yellowish obsession of the fevered—is able to give to my *eyes* the profound sense that the lovers are being exiled into ecstasy. Because artificial and over-crude, this lighting successfully heralds the extinction of day and shows that dawn has already become no more than a dusk vainly intensified.

Another critical commonplace—incidentally quite at

[1] Especially the realistic scenery which producers insist on using—the decoration of the tent aboard ship in Act I, the painted ivy on the walls of the castle in Act II. This is precisely where extremely simple, abstract, metaphysical, dreamlike, scenery is called for, and not Tristan's interminable gesticulations while breathless on his couch and Isolde hampered by her veils. [*Note* of 1954: The new scenic production of *Tristan* at Bayreuth, which is the work of Wieland Wagner, fulfils the hope which I expressed in the first version of this book. It is now possible to sit through the second act with one's eyes open.]

variance with the one according to which *Tristan* is a glorification of sensual desire—is about Schopenhauer's alleged influence over Wagner. Whatever Nietzsche and even Wagner himself may have thought, it seems to me that this influence is greatly exaggerated. A composer of Wagner's calibre does not put "ideas" to music. No doubt he obtained out of Schopenhauer some phrases which he used in his poem, and an intellectual coherence that justified his giving the action certain internal movements—that is all, and it is not of great interest. About the *askesis,* the negation of the created world, the identification of sexual attraction with a will-to-live that clouds the understanding—all the mystical element that has rashly been called Buddhist, Wagner did not need to be taught. It is because he carried it pulsating within his own breast that he was the first to discover the evidence of it in the symbols of the Minnesänger, in the Manichaean legend of Parzival, and underlying the Christian imagery of the Holy Grail —that sacred stone of Persians and Cathars, that cup used by Gwyon,[1] the Celtic divinity.

That Wagner restored the mislaid significance of the legend in all its virulence is no contention I am trying to get accepted; it is what the words and music of the opera amply make evident. It is through this opera that the myth was completed. But such an "end" bears two contradictory meanings—like most terms in the vocabulary of existence, since they are used of beings in a position to act, not of inanimate things. "Completion" means that a being, a myth, or a work has been fully expressed; it also means death. Hence, once "completed" by Wagner, the myth had lived. *Vixit* Tristan!

And there began the era of its phantoms.

---

[1] Gwyon (whence "guyon" meaning "guide" in Old French) means the Führer who has in his custody the secrets of initiation with a divinizing voice.

19

The Myth Is Popularized

The myth took *the way of poetry*.

Edgar Allan Poe begot Baudelaire, who begot *Symbolisme*, which begot mandragora, disembodied women, *jeunes Parques*, hardly feminized appearances of "leakages"—as one speaks of leakages of water—fissures in reality, flights into dreams. The tradition became enfeebled, intellectualized, sophisticated. The way was decidedly too narrow for a man to enter upon it wholeheartedly, and in fact taking this way was delegated to some detached human *faculties*.

The myth also took *the way of the novel*.

But this way soon opened on to a crowded main road, such as people stroll along on Sundays to watch the fine big cars go by and to complain of the speeding. Balzac's *Le Lys dans la vallée*, Constant's *Adolphe*, Fromentin's *Dominique*, Flaubert's *Madame Bovary*, Zola's *Thérèse Raquin*, André Gide's *La Porte étroite*, Proust's *Un Amour de Swann*, are successive French steps in psychological dissociation, in the degradation of the external "obstacle," and in the conscious admission (which, because conscious, is alien to romance) that this is in its nature exclusively intimate and subjective—a nature religious in the case of Gide, quasi-physiological in that of Proust. Parallel to these steps are D'Annunzio's *Trionfo della Morte*—admirable as a commentary on Wagner—Tolstoy's *Anna Karenina*, and most of the great Victorian novels, especially *Tess of the D'Urbervilles* and *Jude the Obscure*; and in our own time the Platonistic novels of Charles Morgan.

But, following Wagner, masterpieces became less significant of the descent of the myth into manners than have been mass-produced novels, popular stage successes, and, above all, films. The real tragic element in our period has been diffused in mediocrity. Thereupon to be truly serious implies an understanding, and the rejection or acceptance, of what moves or stirs the masses—an understanding of the broad anonymous rivers that sweep detached individuals along with a force the mind still finds it repugnant to gauge. The process whereby our literature, whether middle-class or "proletarian," has come to consist mainly of novels, and of love stories at that, corresponds precisely to an invasion of the contemporary mind by the now completely profaned content of the myth. The myth, indeed, must cease to be the real thing once its sacred framework is removed and the mystic secret which it both divulged and veiled is vulgarized and popularized. The *claim to passion* put forward by the romantics thereupon becomes a vague yearning after affluent surroundings and exotic adventures, such as a low grade of melodramatic novel can satisfy symbolically. That this no longer has any kind of valid meaning is evident as soon as we realize how impossible it is for the readers of these novels to imagine a mystic reality, an *askesis,* or any effort on the part of the mind to throw off its sensual fetters; and yet courtly passion had no other purpose, its language no other key. Purpose and key have been lost and forgotten; and passion, although the need of it still disturbs us, is now a mere sickness of instinct, seldom fatal, usually poisonous and depressing, and quite as degraded and degrading in comparison with the Tristan myth as the consequences of dipsomania, for example, must be in comparison with the divine intoxication described in the poetry of the Arab mystics.

The drama has been more instructive. During the Second Empire the French middle class made a last attempt to accommodate within its social framework the lawless workings of the passion. For the passion survived any form of mysticism, thanks ambiguously to romanticism. Heredity—or whatever went by the name—transmitted the attenuated virus of the love-potion; literary culture kept alive, at least in a portion of youth, the want of a nostalgic cautery; and all this made up a complex which was taken to be "nature" itself, although it represented only a psychological, and perhaps only a physiological, remainder. The attempt to normalize passion for the middle class, by re-creating a form of conventional expression which would be acceptable to the social order, was shown in the French drama from Alexandre Dumas to Henry Bataille. The "eternal triangle," which served as a model for most French playwrights down to 1914, simply reduces the Tristan myth to proportions suitable for modern society. King Mark is become the Cuckold; Tristan, the junior lead or gigolo; and Iseult, the idle, dissatisfied wife who reads novels. Here again two moralities confront one another. The felon barons of the legend are now the supporters of the established order. They defend middle-class marriage, the laws of inheritance, convention, and a settled state of affairs. They side with the husband, and are therefore slightly ridiculous. But it is the other morality which invariably triumphs—even though at the price of a pistol shot. This is romantic morality, holding the claims of love to be indefeasible and implying the superiority from a "spiritual" standpoint of mistress over wife. As for the love-potion, an alibi for responsibility, it is now romantically called "irresistible passion," and the supporters of the established order wisely lump belief in it with whatever they contemptuously refer to as a "literary" attitude. Eventually even, it was no longer attempted to dispute that the distillation of the old love-potion obtains encouragement from its victims. Proust, for example, devotes hundreds of pages to a minute analysis of the way this encouragement operates and of the unconscious stratagems to which it resorts.[1]

I have called all this recent literature middle class. Indeed, because its trend is invariably against the middle class, it has had the effect of contributing to the stability of the established order. Literature is thus employed—unconsciously, of course—to ensure that the subversive desires of the individual mind shall be volatilized in sensual reverie. It is true that the morality of marriage comes off rather badly, but that does not matter, since the middle class is well aware that the institution is no longer grounded in morality or religion, but rests upon financial foundations—prospects of inheritance, dowries, the social position of each party, business connexions, and so on.

There is thus a wish *to enjoy* the myth as *cheaply* as possible; and this wish is expressed with complete artlessness in sentimental films.

[1] See in particular *Un Amour de Swann*.

Art has seldom worked in a more artificial and rhetorical convention than it did in American film studios during the early nineteen twenties. It was then that the happy ending had its heyday. Every plot had to lead up to a final lingering kiss against a background of roses or rich hangings. The convention was faithful to the myth in the last stage of the latter's downfall. It allowed the complete fusion of two contradictory wishes—the wish that nothing shall be settled and the wish that everything shall be settled, the one romantic, the other middle-class. The profound satisfaction which spectators unfailingly find in a happy ending must be due precisely to its resolving the contradiction of their double wishfulness. For there can be no love story unless love meets with opposition. There is accordingly an abundance of obstructions to the fulfilment of love, and it does not matter how farfetched they are, because the wish for romanticism renders the spectator impervious to the straining of his credibility. For an hour or two, accordingly, the story can rebound, and we be full of heartfelt suspense, which is what we want. But the obstruction of love must ultimately mean death and a renunciation of terrestrial goods. This we no longer want once we have grown aware of what it is. A plot-maker has therefore to devise the suppression of any obstacle at some point earlier than death, and the result is the ending which novels and films commonly have. Yet the ending must also possess a "poetical" atmosphere that will conceal the bump back into everyday life, and that will also, as compensation for the way romanticism has been disappointed, fill the middle-class citizen and his wife with a sense of relief. Hence in the modern drama, in the popular novel, and in the films which incessantly resort to the triangular plot, the tragic idealism of the primitive myth has turned into a rather vulgar nostalgia, the idealization of tame desires; and, moreover, these desires are being redirected towards worldly enjoyments, which means that in relation to courtly love they are being completely inverted.

The *religion* of the troubadours lent itself to a very cunning indulgence of *instinct*, instinct being excited by the very insistence on denying it. The equivocal character of the mystical phraseology of heresy thereupon brought into being as early as the thirteenth century a profane rhetoric of passion. And it is the spread of this phraseology in the novel (and in the drama) that in the course of the last hundred years has caused instinct to become the real basis of a rhetoric, the tropes of which now give it a semblance of ideality.

20

The Glorification of Instinct

As the Rose of Guillaume de Lorris was countered by Jean de Meung's, and as Petrarch's crystalline rhetoric was countered by Boccaccio's sensual phantasmagoria, so romanticism has brought about in our day a revolt that its leaders would like to think "primitive." The object of idealization is no longer feeling, but instinct. I have in mind a school of Anglo-American novelists in revolt against middle-class Puritanism—a school including D. H. Lawrence, Erskine Caldwell, and their disciples or imitators. These writers seem to be saying in effect:

"We have had enough of being made to suffer for ideas, for ideals, for idealized and perverted little hypocrisies which no longer take anybody in. You made woman into a kind of divinity—coquettish, cruel, and vampiric. Your fatal women, your adulterous women, and your women made arid by virtue, have emptied life of all delight for us. We shall get our own back on them. Woman is first and foremost a female. We are going to make her drag herself to the domineering male on her belly.[1] Instead of singing of courtesy, we shall praise the cunning of animal desire, the complete obsession of the mind by sex. And our vast bestial innocence will rid us of your liking for sin, which is but a disease of the procreative instinct. What you call morality is what makes us nasty, gloomy, and shameful. What you call dirt can purify us. Your taboos are sacrileges on the real divinity, which is Life. And life is instinct released from mind, a great solar power that crushes and magnifies the prolific man, the magnificent unleashed bully."

[1] There is an incident of this kind in Caldwell's *Tobacco Road*.

One of these prophets has even gone the length of saying: "I want to be as vital as a cow."

Possibly this new mystic doctrine of "Life" has inspired some fine literary work, but it also has a political aspect. In curiously identical guise, it is met with at the origin of a movement no longer needing to be either examined or convicted. This movement has called itself National Socialism, Fascism, or Communism, according to the doctrinal and economic excuses it has employed in order to seize power. It denies the next world, not so as to suppress the gods, but so as to use their thunder by deifying the here-below. To be divested of moral personality and merged again in the cosmic flux of instinct remains a *theoretical* aspiration for the bards of solar primitiveness; but the *practice* cannot mislead us for a moment. There are no magnificent bullies, only bullies. The idea of beauty, which Lawrence supposed was still firmly operative, is the legacy of a bankrupt period: it is a debt nobody *there* is prepared to honour. The totalitarian ruling caste is not going to consider itself accountable to a Platonic "spirit" that it looks upon as being to blame for all the trouble and as having already paid for this with its life. So much is quite obvious.

It is no less obvious that when under pretence of destroying whatever is artificial—idealizing rhetoric, the mystical ethics of "perfection"—people seek to swamp themselves in the primitive flood of instinct, in whatever is primeval, formless, and foul, they may imagine they are recapturing real life, but actually they are letting themselves be swept away by a torrent of *waste-matter* pouring from the disintegration of the ancient culture and its myths. Moreover, there is nothing truly primitive about men today. The existence of what the current jargon calls heredity, and the Church original sin, means that we have irrevocably lost all direct touch with our origins. To plunge down below our moral rules is, therefore, not to abolish their restraints; it is to yield to an insanity from which wild animals would recoil. The mistake lies in supposing that "the real thing," the longing for which has now become an obsession, is there to be found. It is not lying in wait for us on the far side of a surrender to enervated instinct and resentful flesh. It is not hidden, but lost. The only way to recover it is by building it up afresh, thanks to an effort that shall go against passion—that is to say, by some action, a putting in order, a purification, that will bring us back to the sober mean. Truly to act in this respect is not to escape out of a world deemed diabolical; it is not to kill this hampering body. But neither is it to fire a revolver at spirit on the ground that spirit has deceived us.[1] To act is indeed to accept the conditions we have been given in the conflict between the spirit and the flesh; it is to strive to surmount the two antagonistic powers, not through their destruction, but by uniting them. Let the spirit come to the aid of the flesh and so recover the support of the flesh, and let the flesh submit to the spirit and thus recover peace. There lies the way.

The Eros of death and the Eros of life—each conjures up the other, and each has no true end or ending but the other, which it has been striving to destroy! And so everlastingly till all life and all spirit shall have been consumed. Such is the pursuit undertaken by the man who mistakes himself for a god. It is the last of the motions of passion, and the exasperation of this motion we call war.

21

The Spread of Passion into Every Sphere

The *social function* of the sacred myth of courtly love in the twelfth century was to order and purify the lawless forces of passion. Its transcendental mysticism secretly directed the yearnings of distressed mankind to the next world, and concentrated them there. No doubt it was a heresy, but a peaceful one, and in some respects productive of a civilizing stability. But its being opposed to the propagation of the species and to war was enough to cause society to persecute it. It was the Roman Church that carried fire and the sword to the provinces which

---

[1] A Nazi officer is reported to have said: "Every time I hear the word 'Geist' [spirit] I slip the safety-catch of my revolver."

had been won for the Heresy. In destroying the material shape of this religion, the Church doomed it to spread in a form more dubious and perhaps more dangerous. Tracked down, repressed, and disorganized, heresy soon underwent a thousand distortions. The disorders which it had encouraged in spite of itself, the glorification of human love that was the inversion of its doctrine, its language both essentially and opportunely equivocal, and also open to every kind of abuse—all this was bound to defy the judges of the Inquisition, and then to invade the European mind even where still orthodox, and finally, by a kind of irony, to bestow its passionate rhetoric upon the mysticism of the highest saints.

When myths lose their esoteric character and their sacred purpose they take literary form. The courtly myth was peculiarly fitted to do this, since the only way of stating it had been in terms of human love, which were given a mystical sense. Once this mystical sense had vanished, there remained a rhetoric which could express our natural instincts, but not without distorting them imperceptibly in the direction of another world; and this other world, in growing more and more mysterious, answered the need of idealization which the human mind had acquired from a mystical understanding first condemned, then lost. This was the opportunity of European literature, and this alone will account for the sway which literature has exercised from that moment all the way down to our own time, first over the upper classes alone, later over the masses as well—a sway unique in the history of civilizations.

Nevertheless, when the dark forces had been deprived of their sacred element, the classical style sought to impose *an art form* upon these obscure powers deprived of their sacred form. Romanticism supervened to attack these ritualistic vestiges. Hence, at the end of the eighteenth century, there occurred the magnification of all that the Tristan myth, and later its literary substitutes, had been intended *to contain*. The middle-class nineteenth century witnessed the spread into the profane mind of a "death instinct" which had long been repressed in the unconscious, or else directed at its source into the channels of an aristocratic art. And when the framework of society burst—under a pressure exerted from quite another quarter—the content of the myth poured out over everyday life. We were unable to understand this diluted elevation of love. We supposed it to be a new springtime of instinct, a revival of the dionysiac forces which a so-called Christianity had persecuted. The whole of modern literature took up the hymn of "liberation." Why, then, did literature strike such a melancholy note? How is it that the novel—which for the first thirty years of this century outdistanced all other literary forms—has resulted in no more than a shifting and slippery analysis of human doubts and human emptiness? There can be no doubt that by 1930 the novel had run dry of all its sap, and could only recover an ephemeral virulence by putting itself at the service of partisan mystic systems. Does this mean the end of romanticism?

The spectacle afforded by contemporary manners does not allow that to be inferred. The present breakdown of middle-class marriage is a delayed triumph—perverted, if you like, but nevertheless a triumph—for a profaned passion. But far outside marriage and the realm of sex properly so called, the content of the myth together with its phantoms have now invaded other spheres. Politics, the class war, national feeling—everything nowadays is an excuse for "passion" and is already being magnified into this or that "mystic doctrine." The reason for this is that we have grown incapable of giving up anything for the sake of something better, incapable of regulating our desires, of understanding their character and object, and of keeping their vagaries within bounds. We can no longer express ourselves figuratively.

The last surviving formalities of love were swept away by the war of 1914, and I would emphasize the symbolical fact that we have stopped making formal declarations of love at the very time we have allowed wars to begin without any declaration either. We are returning to the age of abduction and rape, though minus the ritual that has surrounded such violence in Polynesia The gradual profanation of the myth, its conversion into rhetoric, and in turn the dissolving of the rhetoric together with the thorough popularization of its content, can be traced step by step in a sphere at first sight entirely alien to what we have been examining—in the gradual transformation of European warfare and its methods.

Book V

LOVE AND WAR

1

How They Are Similar

From desire to death via *passion*—such has been the road taken by European romanticism; and we are all taking this road to the extent that we accept—unconsciously, of course—a whole set of manners and customs for which the symbols were devised in courtly mysticism. And, as I have said, passion means suffering. Therefore, inasmuch as our notion of love enfolds our notion of woman, it is linked with a theory of the *fruitfulness of suffering* which encourages or obscurely justifies in the recesses of the Western mind a liking for war.

This peculiar connexion between a certain view of woman and the European conception of war has had profound consequences for morality, education, and politics. In order to deal with the subject in a manner commensurate to its importance, it would be necessary, not only to have a thorough grasp of the matters so far touched upon in these pages, but also to have thoroughly mastered military theory, and to be acquainted with what psychological research has collected in the course of the last half-century or so regarding "the fighting instinct" and its relation to the sexual instinct. But in this field an examination of *formal modes* is no less instructive than an inquiry into *causes,* and it is certainly less deceptive. There is no need, for example, to invoke Freudian theories in order to see that the war instinct and eroticism are fundamentally allied: it is so perfectly *obvious* from the common figurative use of language. Let me then consider some similarities in the practice of the *arts* of love and war from the twelfth century down to the present day. I must not be taken, however, to be presupposing that the transformation of the myth has necessarily been prior to the transformation of warfare, or vice versa.

2

The Warlike Language of Love

Already in Antiquity poets used warlike metaphors in order to describe the effects of natural love. The god of love is an *archer* who shoots *fatal arrows*. Woman *surrenders* to man, and he *conquers* her because he is the better warrior. The Trojan War was fought for the possession of a woman. And one of the oldest novels we possess—Heliodorus's *Theagenes and Chariclea,* written in the third century—already refers to the *"battles of love"* and to the "delightful *defeat"* suffered by the man who *"falls under the unerring shafts"* of Eros. Plutarch makes it clear that the sexual morals of the Lacedaemonians were determined by their military requirements. The eugenics of Lycurgus, and his detailed laws concerning the relations of husband and wife, had no other aim than to ensure the aggressive vigour of the soldiery.

All this confirms the natural—that is to say, the physiological—connexion between the sexual and fighting instincts. But it would be idle to seek any kinship between the *tactics* of the Ancients and their notion of love. The two fields remained under quite distinct rules, and offered no ground for comparison. But this has not been true in Western Europe since the twelfth and thirteenth centuries. The language of love was then enriched with phrases and expressions which had unmistakably been borrowed from the art of giving battle and from contemporary military tactics. It is no longer a question of the more or less dim awareness of a common origin, but truly of a close similarity of detail. A lover *besieged* his lady. He delivered *amorous assaults* on her virtue. He *pressed her closely*. He *pursued* her. He sought to *overcome* the final *defences* of her modesty, and *to take them by surprise*. In the end the lady *surrendered to his mercy*. And thereupon, by a curious inversion typical enough of courtesy, he became the lady's *prisoner* as well as her *conqueror*. He became a *vassal* of this *suzerain,* in accordance with the laws of feudal warfare, as if it had been he who suffered defeat.[1] It only remained for him to give proofs of his *valour*. So much for polite language. But slang, both military and civil, was rich in words and phrases which were rendered even more significant by their coarseness. And when firearms came into use, they gave rise to countless jokes of *double entendre*. Writers, indeed, delighted to take advantage of the resemblance, for it provided them with an inexhaustible rhetorical topic.

"O, all too fortunate captain [Brantôme writes],[2] who at the front and in the towns hath fought and killed so many men who were the foes of God! And O, more and more fortunate still, you who hath fought and overcome in many other assaults and bouts such a lovely Lady under the banners of your bed!"

It is not surprising that, once such metaphors had become *commonplace,* mystical writers should have employed them and transposed them—in the way I have described earlier [3]—to the key of divine love. Francisco de Ossuna—who was steeped in courtly rhetoric and was one of Saint Teresa's favourite authors—writes in his *Ley de Amor*:

"Do not believe that the battle of love is like other fights in which the clamour and fury of an appalling war prevail on either side; for love fights only by means of caresses and threatens only with tender words. Its arrows and blows are gifts and blessings. Its encounter is a most effective promise. Sighs make up its artillery. Its taking possession is an embrace. Its slaughter consists of giving one's life for the beloved."

It was shown earlier that courtly rhetoric began by expressing the struggle between Day and Night. The part played by *Death* is of capital importance: it marked the defeat of the world and the victory of the life of light. Love and death were connected by *askesis*, as instinct

---

[1] The German for "defeat" is *Niederlage,* which literally means "in the position of being on the ground, of lying under." The French, in saying "avoir le dessous" for "having the worst of it," also invoke the sense of "under." The *Roman de la Rose,* it may be noted at the same time, uses the symbol of a besieged tower and speaks of "securing allies in the stronghold."

[2] *Rodomontades espagnoles.*   [3] Book III, above.

connects desire and war. But neither the religious origin
nor the physiological kinship of the fighting and procreative instincts was enough to determine the *exact* use
of warlike phrases in European erotic literature. What
does account for everything is that there existed in the
Middle Ages a rule actually applicable to the arts of
both love and war—the rule called chivalry.

3

Chivalry: A Rule of Love and War

"To formalize love," according to J. Huizinga,[1] "is
the supreme realization of the aspiration to the life
beautiful." He is describing the ideals of medieval society.

"To formalize love [he says again] is a social necessity, a need that is the more imperious as life is more
ferocious. Love has to be elevated to the level of a rite.
The overflowing violence of passion demands it. Only by
constructing a system of forms and rules for the vehement
emotions can barbarity be escaped. The brutality and
the licence of the lower classes were always fervently, but
never very efficiently, repressed by the Church. The
aristocracy would feel less dependent on religious admo-
nition, because they had a piece of culture of their
own from which to draw their standards of conduct,
namely, courtesy."
I need not recall that courtesy not only owed nothing to
the Church, but went against ecclesiastical morality. This
in itself should be enough to bring about the revision of
many opinions about the spiritual unity of the Middle
Ages! But if courtly morality did not succeed in trans-
forming the private behaviour of the upper classes, who
continued "astonishingly rough," at least it played the
part of an ideal that made externals very handsome. It

---

[1] *The Waning* of *the Middle Ages,* op. cit., p. 96. I cannot
speak too highly of this admirable work.

triumphed in literature, and succeeded, moreover, in impressing itself upon the most violent reality of the period—I mean, war. At no other time has an *ars amandi* given birth to an *ars bellandi*.

It is not only in the detailed rules of personal combat that the effect of the ideal of chivalry was evident, but also in the fighting of battles, and even in politics. Military formality came to be treated as if it had a kind of religious validity. Men often allowed themselves to be killed in order not to infringe absurd rules. Froissart asserts that the "Knights of the Star had to swear never to fly more than four acres from the battlefield, through which rule soon afterwards more than ninety of them lost their lives." [1] Likewise, the requirements of strategy might be sacrificed to aesthetics or courtly honour.

"Some days before the battle of Agincourt [Huizinga says] [2] the king of England, on his way to meet the French army, one evening passed by mistake by the village which the foragers of his army had fixed upon as night quarters. . . . The king, 'as the chief guardian of the very laudable ceremonies of honour,' had just published an order, according to which knights, while reconnoitring, had to take off their coat-armour, because their honour would not suffer knights to retreat, when accoutred for battle. Now, the king himself had put on his coat-armour, and so, having passed it by, he could not return to the village mentioned. He therefore passed the night in the place he had reached, and also made the vanguard advance accordingly."

There are countless instances where a futile carnage resulted from the attempt to fulfil at great peril vows of an overweening arrogance. Indeed, danger was what knights courted for its own sake, even as on other occasions they showed themselves prompt with excuses for not keeping their word. Courtly casuistry furnished excellent excuses of this kind. It not only ruled morality and law, but also regulated ceremonials, tournaments, hunting, and especially love. Honoré Bonet's *L'Arbre des batailles* is a treatise on the laws of war, which discusses with the help of biblical texts and articles of canon law such questions as: "If in the course of the fighting a knight loses a piece of armour he has borrowed, does he have to

[1] Ibid., p. 86.   [2] Ibid., pp. 86–87.

make it good?" "Is it allowable to fight a battle on a holy day?" "Is it better to fight after a meal or fasting?" "In what circumstances is it legitimate for a prisoner of war to escape?"

As for the political aims inspired by the notion of chivalry, they were chiefly—again according to Huizinga —to fight for a universal peace which a union of kings was expected to preserve once it had been won, and to conquer Jerusalem and expel the Turks. Both these aims were chimerical, and nothing shows better how the courtly ideal was in flat contradiction with the "stern reality" of the age. It represented a pole of attraction for thwarted spiritual aspirations. It was a form of romantic escape at the same time as a brake applied to instinct. The detailed formality of war was devised to check the violent impulses of feudal blood, even as the cult of chastity among the troubadours was intended to check the erotic excitement of the twelfth century. "Two attitudes to life were formed, so to speak, side by side in the medieval mind—one, pious and ascetic, attracted all moral sentiment; the other, spurred on by a sensuality given over to the devil went to the opposite extreme. According as one or the other was in the ascendant, there arose a saint or a sinner; but on the whole they balanced one another, though not without now and then a wide swing of the scales."

4

Tournaments, or the Myth in Action

There was, however, one place where the erotic and fighting instincts were in almost perfect harmony with the ideal courtly rule. This was the strictly circumscribed area of the lists where tournaments were held. There the frenzy of the blood had full play, even though it was under the aegis of a sacred ceremonial and subject to symbolical restraints. A tournament was the sporting equivalent of the mythical function of *Tristan,* as this function has been defined in these pages. Passion was to be expressed with all its strength, but also to be veiled religiously so that it might be acceptable to social opinion. A tournament was a physical representation of the myth.

"Literature did not suffice [Huizinga says] [1] for the almost insatiable needs of the romantic imagination of the age. Some more active form of expression was required. Dramatic art might have supplied it, but the medieval drama in the real sense of the word treated love matters only exceptionally; sacred subjects were its substance. There was, however, another form of representation, namely, noble sports, tourneys and jousts. Sportive struggles always and everywhere contain a strong dramatic element and an erotic element. In the medieval tournament these two elements had so much got the upper hand that its character of a contest of force and courage had been almost obliterated by its romantic purport. With its bizarre accoutrements and pompous staging, its poetical illusion and pathos, it filled the place of the drama of a later age." [2]

Nothing seems to me better able to place us in the dreamlike atmosphere of the *Romance of Tristan* than the accounts of tourneys in Chastellain's chronicles and the memoirs of Olivier de La Marche, both men having been historiographers of the gorgeous and chivalric Duchy of Burgundy in the fifteenth century. They succeed in uniting love and death in an artificial and symbolical landscape pervaded by a lofty sadness.

"The hero who serves for love, this is [to quote Huizinga again] [3] the primary and invariable motif from which erotic fantasy will always start. It is a sensuality transformed into the craving for self-sacrifice, into the desire of the male . . . to suffer and to bleed

---

[1] Ibid., pp. 68–69.

[2] The dramatic function of tournaments may possibly have been one source of modern tragedy. For this tragedy came into being at the very moment tournaments went out of fashion, in a time when their warlike, sporting, and theatrical components were breaking up. In that case, tragedy might be regarded as an "action" deprived of the *physical* danger implicit in a tournament, but on that account giving all the greater satisfaction to a need of sentimental and spiritual emotion.

[3] Ibid., p. 67.

for his lady-love. The expression and the satisfaction of desire, from having both seemed unattainable, were transmuted into something loftier—a heroic action undertaken for the sake of love. Death thereupon became the only alternative to the fulfilment of desire, and in any event release seemed assured."

The ceremonial of the tournaments drew its inspiration from the romances of the Round Table. A Passage of Arms of the fifteenth century is based on a fictitious chivalrous adventure connected with an artificial scene called "The Fountain of Tears."

"A fountain is expressly constructed, and beside it a pavilion, where during a whole year a lady is to reside (in effigy, be it understood), holding a unicorn which bears three shields. The first day of each month knights come to touch the shields, in this way to pledge themselves for a combat of which the 'Chapters' of the Passage of Arms lay down the rules. They will find horses in readiness, for the shields have to be touched on horseback. . . .

"The knight should be unknown. He is called 'le blanc chevalier,' 'le chevalier mesconnu,' or he wears the crest of Lancelot or Palamedes. The shields of the Fount of Tears are white, violet, and black, and overspread with white tears." [1]

The erotic factor in tournaments is also shown by the custom according to which a knight carried—like Lancelot—the veil or a fragment of the dress of his lady, and sometimes after the lists handed this to her stained with his blood.

"The Church was openly hostile to tournaments; it repeatedly prohibited them, and there is no doubt that the fear of the passionate character of this noble game, and of the abuses resulting from it, had a great share in this hostility." [2]

However, when tournaments reached the height of their vogue, it was a sign that chivalry had begun to decline. At the beginning of the fifteenth century—about the time of the Battle of Agincourt—new brutalities drove it into literature, entertainments, and symbolical games. The fifteenth century witnessed the appearance of the foot-

[1] Ibid., p. 72.   [2] Ibid., p. 71.

soldier; and less than a hundred years later the lanz-knechts introduced from the East the use of the drum. "Its hypnotic and discordant beat symbolized the transition from chivalry to the modern art of war. It was a step in the mechanization of warfare." And finally chivalry was killed by the invention of artillery. "There is an irony of fate in the fact that Jacques de Lalaing, prototype of the Hainault pattern knight of the fifteenth century, should have been killed by a cannon ball."

Yet the formalities of war and of courtly love had given European customs an impress that did not fade till the present century. The notion of personal valour and of the warlike feats represented by the duel and by prowess (the single-handed combat between two leaders); the notion of regulating the conduct of battles according to a quasi-sacred etiquette; the view that military life must be ascetic (long fasts before the ordeal of battle), rules for settling who should be the victor (he, for example, who spent the night on the battlefield), and finally the close parallel between erotic and military symbolism— all that never ceased to determine the modes of making war throughout the ensuing ages. So that any alteration in military tactics may be looked upon as related to an alteration in the notions of love, or vice versa.

5

Cannon and Condottieri

"Italy had at no time enjoyed a state of such compleat prosperity and repose as in the year 1490; and some time before and after. The people also had taken advantage of this halcyon season, and been busied in cultivating all their lands, as well as mountains and valleys; and being under no foreign influence, but governed by their own princes. Italy not only abounded with inhabitants and riches, but grew renowned for the grandeur and magnificence of her sovereigns, for the splendor of many noble and beautiful cities; for the seat and majesty of religion, and for a number of great men of distinguished abilities in the administration of public affairs, and of excellent accomplishments in all the sciences and in every noble art. She had also no small share of military glory according to the knowledge and practice of arms in those days."[1]

The military glory had been obtained by *condottieri*. Professional soldiers in the service of princes and popes, the *condottieri* were much less given to making war than to ensuring that war did not take a toll of lives. They were not only adventurers, but skilled diplomatists and astute traders. They knew the price of a soldier. The essence of their tactical practice was to make prisoners and to disorganize the enemy's forces. Sometimes—and this was their supreme achievement—they succeeded in defeating the foe in a truly overwhelming manner: they robbed him of all his strength by buying up his entire army. Only when this was not possible did they have to fight. But, according to Machiavelli, in those days there was nothing dangerous about a battle.

"Fighting invariably takes place on horseback, the soldiers being protected by arms and assured of preserving their lives if taken prisoner. . . . The lives of the defeated are nearly always spared. They do not remain prisoners for long, and their release is obtained very easily. A town may rebel a score of times; it is never destroyed. The inhabitants retain the whole of their property; all they have to fear is that they will be made to pay a levy."

In its own field—then deemed inferior—this art of war was the expression of a culture admirably humane, of a profound "civilization," the opposite of a "militarization." In Burckhardt's phrase, the State had become a work of art. War itself had grown civilized, to the full extent that such a paradoxical statement can be true. Duels between commanders were in honour, and were enough to bring a campaign to a close. For that matter, these duels were no longer a submission to the "judgement of God," but the triumph of one personality over another. The use of fire-arms was deplored as being incompatible with human dignity; and the condottiere Paolo Vitelli put out the eyes and cut off the hands of some *schiop-*

---

[1] Francesco Guicciardini, *Storia d'Italia;* translation by Austin Parke Goddard, 1763.

pettieri of the enemy, who had been captured, because it seemed to him infamous that a gallant and perhaps noble knight should have been wounded by a common, despised foot-soldier. Love had undergone a similar alteration.

Burckhardt lays stress [1] on the way in which marriages were arranged without fuss, with short engagements, and how a husband's claim on his wife's fidelity was never asserted as strictly as in northern climes. Women of the upper class were as well educated as the men, and enjoyed full moral equality, at a time when exactly the opposite was the case in France and the Empire. And if war had turned into diplomacy in the highest quarters and had become venal in practice, the same was true of love. Courtesans could play a leading part in social life, very much as the hetaerae of Ancient Greece had done. The most famous among them were remarkable for being highly cultivated; they wrote and recited verse, played musical instruments, and were excellent conversationalists. This paganizing of the life of sex marked a considerable decline in the influence of *cortezia* and a depreciation of the tragic myth. The Platonism in vogue at the small ducal courts, and so well described by Cardinal Bembo and by Baldassare Castiglione (in the dialogues of his *Libro del Cortegiano*), was really, in a refined and thoroughly hedonistic form, a liking for social functions. It was then that "courtesy" acquired its modern meaning of politeness and good breeding. The view that life was evil had become a thing of the past. And "the death instinct" had apparently been neutralized.

It was upon this happy, immoral, and entirely peace-loving [2] Italy that the French troops of Charles the Eighth presently descended. The roar of *thirty-six brass cannon* spread panic through the peninsula as if this roar had been the signal of the end of the world. Charles brought with him into Italy, Guicciardini says, "the seeds

---

[1] J. Burckhardt, *The Civilization of Italy in the Renaissance* (London and Vienna, 1937).

[2] It is only fair to recall that killing was very common. But murder remained an individual affair. In the present militarized world, on the other hand, the individual is deprived of this means of venting his passions, it having become the prerogative of the community. Cf. the passage quoted from the Marquis de Sade, above, p. 224.

of innumerable calamities, horrible events, and changes in all scenes of affairs. For from this passage derived their origin not only changes of states, but also new fashions, new and bloody ways of making war, and diseases unknown till those days." The peace and concord that had hitherto prevailed in the land were so upset that it was afterwards impossible to restore order and quiet. Not that the Italians had been unaware of the use of artillery, but they despised all these new engines, as I have already mentioned, and as is shown by Ariosto's invective on fire-arms. The French, Guicciardini continues,

". . . brought a much handier engine made of brass called cannon, which they charged with heavy iron balls. . . . They were planted against the walls of a town with such speed, the space between the shots was so little, and the balls flew so quick, and were impelled with such force, that as much execution was done in a few hours as formerly in Italy in the like number of days. These rather diabolical than human instruments were used not only in sieges, but also in the field."

Another thing that terrified the Italians was that whereas in the militia of the *condottieri* "many of their men at arms, being a mixture of peasants, people in low life, and subjects of different potentates, . . . they were generally persons that had neither natural nor acquired parts to enable them to act gallantly," the French forces appeared in the form of a *national army*.

"The men at arms were almost all subjects of France, and not of the mean sort, but gentlemen and noblemen." The officers "lay under no temptation to go into another service either to gratify ambition or avarice."

It was seen that there must now be great slaughter, and indeed at the Battle of Rapallo, which practically opened the campaign, ". . . there were killed, in fighting and in the pursuit, above a hundred men; doubtless a great slaughter, if we consider the manner of fighting in Italy in those days."

And this was no more than a beginning! Burckhardt says that the devastation wrought by the French seemed trifling in comparison with what was done a little later by the Spaniards, "in whom perhaps a strain of non-western blood, or perhaps familiarity with the sights provided by the Inquisition, let loose diabolical instincts." Artillery and the massacre of civilians! Modern warfare had come into being. Little by little this warfare was going to transform the inspired and magnificent knights into troops disciplined and uniform. The transformation was going to result in our own day in abolishing every vestige of the passion for making war, as gradually men serving machines became themselves machines and felt neither anger nor pity while performing a few automatic movements intended to deal death at a distance.

6

Classic Warfare

In the seventeenth and eighteenth centuries the main effort of the men of war was directed to controlling the mechanical monster in order that as many as possible of the humane features of warfare might be preserved. It was not possible to give up technical inventions—artillery and fortifications. But at least the *rules* of tactics and strategy could be so multiplied as to allow the intellect and the "valour" of the commanders to retain a semblance of supremacy among the factors entering into the struggle. Chivalry stood for an attempt to endow instinct with a kind of correct deportment. Warfare in the classical age of Western Europe was conducted with great formality because there was a wish to preserve and renew this correct deportment, notwithstanding the advent of inhuman factors. Following the desolation left by the Thirty Years' War, there was a desire to keep expenditure within bounds—men cost dear!—and to avoid alarming a population so thoroughly as to render recruitment impossible.

Vauban turned siege into a kind of mental operation carried out in stages, and these stages, it has been well said, were rather like the five acts of a French classical tragedy.

"It is at this period that war did indeed become the equivalent of a game of chess. When, following a series of

complex manoeuvres, one of the two adversaries had lost
or won several pawns—towns or fortresses—there
came the great battle. Standing on some hilltop, from
which he could survey the whole field, the entire chess-
board, a marshal skilfully caused his splendid regiments
to advance or retreat. Check and mate, the loser put his
pawns away: the regiments marched off to winter quarters, and everybody went about his business pending the
next game or campaign." [1]

It may be inferred that every time war has recovered
the aspect of a *game,* this was because society wished to
reintroduce the passion myth into its culture—that is to
say, wished to confine a lawless force within a framework
and give it a ritual form of manifesting itself. This is
what actually happened in the seventeenth century, as
may be seen from the chapters on *L'Astrée* and on
French classical tragedy in Book IV, above.

"Here matter was being made mental, so as to determine the behaviour of the fighters, who, after all, are
living and thinking beings." So wrote Foch about war in
the eighteenth century.[2] It is a curious remark, but it
is based on a passage in Von der Goltz, which is worth
quoting:

"The mistake made by generals who can only follow
rules is that they look upon the aim of war as being to
carry out neatly organized manoeuvres and not to wipe
out the forces of the enemy. The military world has
invariably fallen into this mistake whenever it has neglected the natural trend of things and the influence of
the heart on human resolution, and has abandoned the
plain and simple notion underlying the laws of war—
that matter must be made mental."

The statement is typical of the attitude of mind that
made its appearance with the French Revolution—at a
time, that is to say, when collective *instincts* and catastrophic *passions* were being let loose. The two modern
strategists I have quoted do in fact blame the generals of
Louis the Fourteenth and Louis the Fifteenth, of Queen

---

[1] J. Boulenger, *Le Grand siècle* (Paris, 1915).

[2] Ferdinand Foch, *Les Principes de la guerre* (Paris, 1929).
This is a new edition. The first appeared in 1903, and was trans-
lated by Hilaire Belloc under the title, *The Principles of War*
(London, 1918).

Anne and Frederick the Great, for having sought to carry
on war at the price of getting as few men killed as possible. Yet this was the supreme achievement of a civilization whose whole aim was the regulation and ordering of
Nature, matter, and the determinism of both, according
to the laws of human reason and of personal benefit. It
may have been an illusory aim, but without it no civilization and no culture are possible. Racine, too, as I have
recalled, was at one time of the opinion that it is possible to construct a tragedy without using crime as the
chief ingredient.

The classical age may be summed up in its refusal to
see any nobility in disaster. It recognized, not only that
war and passion were inevitable evils, but also that they
were desired. Nevertheless, it placed the greatness of man
in his ability to limit their effect and to make them serve
other ends; I may even say—in his ability to subordinate
them to the civilian art of diplomacy. Louis the Fourteenth was wont to engage in war over legal and personal
questions unconnected with national honour. The war of
the Spanish Succession was a quarrel between a husband
and his father-in-law over the payment of a stipulated
dowry. And in this same age marriage was negotiated
upon similar considerations—reciprocal advantages, suitable social rank, landed estates or financial substance.
Passion no longer played any part in it whatsoever.

As far as that goes, love itself was about to become a
matter of tactics. It was to lose its dramatic halo.

7

Fighting in Lace Cuffs

The eighteenth century affords the best illustration of
the resemblance between love and war, as a few
indications are enough to show. Don Juan succeeded
to Tristan; perverse sensuality to fatal passion. And at
the same time war was "profaned": in place of Judge-
ments of God and in place of sacred chivalry, ascetic,

bloody, and barded with iron, there arose a crafty diplomacy and an army commanded by courtiers in lace cuffs, who, since they were libertines, did not intend to jeopardize the refinements of life.

The epic legends, and likewise the romances of the Round Table, abound in accounts of incredible slaughter. A knight depended for his fame on the number of enemies he had transfixed, the number of heads he had cut off. If possible, he had to cleave a man in two at a single stroke of his sword. The ferocious exaggerations in these tales show plainly enough what actually excited the passion of men and women in the Middle Ages. Glory be to blood! But in the eighteenth century it was considered a famous feat to have reduced an invested town at the price of only three dead on both sides. A skilled art was in honour. Marshal de Saxe wrote: "I do not favour battles, particularly at the beginning of a war. I am sure a good general can make war *all his life* and not be compelled to fight one." If, after all, there had to be hand-to-hand fighting, it was not in anything less than a pitched battle or a proper siege; and the tradition of chivalry in its wildest and most lofty aspect recovered a last moment of prestige. Behold the great Condé in his plumed hat prancing up and down among the enemy's troops, like the true hero of *L'Astrée* that he was! And what supreme civility in the face of death at Fontenoy! [1]

But it was John Law, the Scot who was commissioner-general of finance in France during the minority of Louis the Fifteenth, who achieved the complete "profanation" of war and of its sacred passion. He was in favour of reverting to the methods of the *condottieri,* although no doubt unaware that these had forestalled him.

"Victory [he wrote] [2] always falls to the side having the last crown. France keeps up an army costing 100 millions a year, which means two milliards every twen-

---

[1] When the head of the English column was fifty paces from the French lines, the officers on either side saluted, and Lord Hay, a captain of the Guards, called out: "Tell your men to fire!" But, "No, sir, you shall have the honour," replied the Comte d'Auteroche. The first volley mowed down the French. —Translator.

[2] *Œuvres* (Paris, 1934).

ty years. We are not at war for more than five out of
these twenty years, and this war, moreover, puts us
back at least one milliard. It thus costs us three milliards in order to make war for five years. Lasting
success being uncertain, what is the consequence? That
with plenty of luck, we may expect to destroy 150,000
of the enemy by fire, sword, flood, famine, fatigue, and
disease. Thus the destruction, either directly or indirectly, of one German soldier costs us 20,000 livres, to
say nothing of the losses suffered by our own population, losses which are only repaired at the end of
twenty-five years. Instead of all this costly, clumsy, and
dangerous paraphernalia, would it not be much better to
save money by buying up the enemy's army whenever
occasion arose? An Englishman has reckoned that a
man is worth £480. That is a topmost figure and
they are not all so dear, as everybody knows; but at
least we should save half our cash and the whole of our
population, for in return for our money we should get
an extra man, whereas under the present system we lose
the man we had without being able to employ the
other whom we destroy at such cost."

The Goncourt Brothers have admirably discerned the
fundamental identity of what occurred in love and war
during the eighteenth century. This is how they described
the "tactics" of the roués of the period:

"It is this warfare and this game of love that perhaps
disclose the most profound characteristics of the century, its most hidden devices, and—quite unexpected in
the French temperament—something like a genius for
duplicity. What nameless great diplomatists and great
politicians, more ingenious than Cardinal Dubois, more
insinuating than Cardinal Bernis, were numbered among
the little group of men who made the seduction of a
woman the centre of their thoughts and the main business of their lives! . . . What schemings worthy of a
novelist or strategist did they not engage in! Not one of
them ever undertook a woman without having first made
what is called a *plan,* without having given the night to
walking up and down and studying the stronghold. . . .
And the attack once launched, they remained to the end
the same astounding actors, very much like the books of
the period, in which no single emotion is not given as ei-

ther feigned or dissimulated. 'Neglect nothing,' was the motto of one of them." [1]

The motto would have been appropriate to a general, but it was one unfortunately which leaders like Soubise [2] never forgot except on the battlefield.

8

Revolutionary War

Between Rousseau and German romanticism—that is to say, between the first reawakening of the myth and the fullness of its tempestuous maturity—there occurred the French Revolution and the campaigns of Bonaparte. Into war there returned catastrophic passion.

From a strictly military standpoint, what novelty was contributed by the Revolution? "An outburst of passion never before equalled," is the answer given by Foch. According to him, the heresy of the old school had been to seek to make war into an *exact science* when it is really *a terrible and passionate drama*. Everybody knows, of course, that an explosion of sentimentality preceded and accompanied the Revolution, an event passionate far more than—in the strict sense of the world—political. With the murder of the king—a deed which in a primitive society would have had a sacred and ritualistic significance—the violence that had long been pinned down by the classical formality of warfare became once again something at once horrifying and alluring. It was

[1] E. and J. de Goncourt, *Les Femmes au XVIIIe siècle* (Paris, 1864).

[2] Frederick the Great defeated Soubise at Rossbach in Saxony in 1757. This gave rise to a popular song in Paris, the first verse being:

> Soubise dit, la lanterne à la main,
> J'ai beau chercher; où diable est mon armée?
> Elle était pourtant là, hier matin,
> Me l'a-t-on prise, ou l'aurais-je égarée?
> —Translator.

the cult and blood-spilling mystery that gave rise to a new form of community—the Nation. *And a Nation requires that passion shall be translated to the level of the people as a whole.* Actually, it is easier to feel that this happened then to give an account of it. Every passion, it may be objected, presupposes the existence of *two* beings, and it is therefore difficult to see, if passion was taken over by a Nation, to whom the Nation then addressed itself. Let us remember, however, that the passion of love is at bottom narcissism, the lover's self-magnification, far more than it is a relation with the beloved. Tristan wanted the branding of love more than he wanted the possession of Iseult. For he believed that the intense and devouring flame of passion would make him divine; and, as Wagner grasped, the equal of the world.

> Eyes with joy are blinded . . .
> I myself am the world.

Passion requires that the *self* shall become greater than all things, as solitary and powerful as God. Without knowing it, passion also requires that beyond its apotheosis death shall indeed be the end of all things.

And nationalist ardour too is a self-elevation, a narcissistic love on the part of the collective Self. No doubt, its relation with others is seldom averred to be love; nearly always hate is what first appears, and what is proclaimed. But hate of the other is likewise always present in the transports of passionate love. There has thus occurred no more than a shift of emphasis. And what does national passion require? The elevation of collective might can only lead to the following dilemma: either the triumph of imperialism—of the ambition to become the equal of the whole world—or the people next door strongly object, and there ensues war. Now it is to be noticed that a nation undergoing the early surges of its passion seldom recoils from war, even if that war must be hopeless. A nation thus unconsciously expresses a readiness to court the risk of death, and even to meet death, rather than surrender its passion. "Liberty or death," the Jacobins yelled, at a time when the forces of the enemy seemed to be twenty times as strong as their own, and when therefore "liberty" and "death" were words very near to having one and the same meaning.

Thus Nation and War are connected as Love and Death are connected. And from this point onwards nationalism has been the predominant factor in war. "Whoever writes upon strategy and tactics should confine himself to expounding a *national* strategy and tactics, for these alone can be of use to the nation for whom he writes." Thus General von der Goltz, a follower of Clausewitz. And Clausewitz constantly asserted that the Prussian theory of war must be based on the experience gained in the French Revolutionary and Napoleonic campaigns. The Battle of Valmy was a victory of passion over "exact science." It was to the cry of "Long live the Nation!" that the Sans-culottes repulsed an allied army still bent on conducting operations on "classic" lines. It will be recalled that Goethe, after witnessing the battle, said: "On this field and on this day a new era begins in the history of the world." To this famous pronouncement Foch adds:

"Truly enough a new era had begun, the era of national wars that are fought *under no restraints whatever,* because a nation throws all its resources into the struggle, because the aim of these wars is not to safeguard some dynastic claim, but to defeat or propagate philosophical ideas and intangible advantages, because these wars are staked upon feelings and passions, elemental forces never enlisted before."

There is a certain parallel between the love affairs of Bonaparte and then Napoleon on the one hand, and, on the other, his campaigns in Italy and Austria. One kind of battle such as he engaged in corresponds to his conquest of Josephine—a bold stroke delivered by the weaker adversary, who hurls the whole of his forces against one decisive spot, and bluffs. Another kind of battle corresponds to his dynastic marriage with the Archduchess Marie Louise—and this was a big affair destined to find a place in the text-books: Wagram, for example, where military science, having assumed rhetorical proportions, was combined with an overwhelming and violent element of surprise. Possibly the defeat at Waterloo was due to an excessive parade of military science, possibly to the fact that by then national-revolutionary dash was exhausted. Certainly, at any rate, Napoleon was the first to take the passion factor into account each time he gave battle. That is why a general whom he had just defeated in Italy was heard to exclaim: "It is incredible how this fellow Bonaparte ignores the most elementary rules of war!"

9

National War

Beginning with the French Revolution, "the hearts of the soldiery" became part of the armoury of battle, and, as Foch puts it, war grew "fierce and tragic." This does not mean that it thereupon became possible for any individual soldier to decide a war, provided he was sufficiently heroic; only that the collective emotions came into play—what one may dare call the passionate might of the Nation. The romantic poets had a notable share in the wars of emancipation which Prussia fought against Napoleon. And the essentially passionate philosophies of thinkers like Fichte and Hegel were the earliest reinforcements of German nationalism. That is why the wars of the nineteenth century became more and more bloody. It was no longer rival interests that came into conflict, but antagonistic "religions." And, unlike interests, religions do not compromise; instead they exact a heroic death. At all times religious wars have been by far the most violent.

And yet, although this is true as regards the first three-quarters of the century, and above all of the period from 1848 to 1870, following the latter date national passions were provisionally appeased, and for forty years they gave place to capitalistic and commercial enterprise. Violence was still resorted to in the name of the Nation, but material advantages were undoubtedly what ruled. Foch insists on this very well in his *Principes de la guerre*.

"War [he says] became national in the first instance for the sake of winning and securing the independence of peoples—that of the French in 1792–93, of the Spaniards in 1804–14, of the Russians in 1812, of the Germans in 1813, and of Europe in 1814. At this stage it produced those glorious and powerful displays of popular passion known as Valmy, Saragossa, Tarancón, Moscow, and Leipzig.

"War then went on being national for the sake of winning *unity of races* or *nationality*. This is what the Italians and the Prussians claimed to be fighting for in 1866 and 1870. In its name also the king of Prussia, after he had become German emperor, put forward a title to the German provinces of Austria.

"But if war is still national today [1903], it is for the sake of securing economic benefits and profitable trade agreements.

"After having been the violent means whereby peoples wrested a place in the world for themselves which made them into nations, war has become the means to which they still resort in order to enrich themselves."

"Trade follows the flag." The colonial era was the last period of "peace" that Europe can be said to have deserved. I have already pointed out[1] that in manners and in literature this era was characterized by a final attempt to mythologize passion. The reaction does not bear comparison with chivalry (although its social purpose was the same), because it was adapted to the present scale of society. What now inspired convention and the formality of our behaviour was no longer any spiritual principle, but calculations of private advantage, which cannot supply the community with a stout armature. The very Nation being invoked had lost its romantic prestige: the flag protected the interests of the State, not the passions or honour of the best elements in the body social. And the office of the State was now no more than the honorific one of a board of directors; it made war in behalf of banks, as in the case of the conquest of Madagascar. In short, colonial warfare was but an extension of capitalistic competition in a form that laid a heavier burden on the country at large though not on the great business firms.

Towards the end of the nineteenth century love[2]

---

[1] Book IV, Chapter 19, above.

[2] I mean that abstract and striking thing, unreal but significant,

among the middle classes had become a most curious medley of nervous sentimentality and of regard for dividends and dowries, as it still is today in matrimonial advertisements. Pure sex, if it happened to intrude, could only cloud these petty schemings and mass-produced "noble sentiments," in the same way as a drop of water clouds absinthe. War likewise had become a compound into which entered, on the one hand, the working up of popular opinion—what was the *Revanche* for 1870-71 but a piece of national sentimentality?—on the other hand, the ambitions of business-men and financiers. The true warlike element had to provide for itself surreptitiously. War was growing middle-class. Blood was getting commercialized. Army men already seemed anomalous to the realists, and to women and idle gapers a kind of thrilling survival.[1] Yet it was being generally supposed that the tremendous potential of frenzy and slaughter which had been piled up in Europe as a result of the cultivation of passion for centuries could be disposed of without incurring havoc. The war of 1914 was a most impressive consequence of this disregard for the myth.

10

Total War

With the Battle of Verdun in 1916, which the Germans called the *Materialschlacht* or Battle of War Material, it must seem that the resemblance instituted by chivalry between the *modes* of love and war came to

the *average of typical expressions* of love in a given period—as unreal and as significant whether ugly or beautiful, whether at the end of the nineteenth century or during the famous century of Louis the Fourteenth, whether vicious or virtuous. There are signs which are not a particular period itself—every period contains some of everything—but which belong to one period rather than to another. That is all I mean.

[1] The attitude was that of democracies on the occasions when they grow excited over a royal wedding.

an end. No doubt it had always been the concrete aim of war to overcome the enemy's resistance by destroying his armed might.[1] But the nation it was sought to defeat was not thereby destroyed: all that collapsed were its defences. Victory was determined by pitched battles against a professional army, the investing of fortresses, the capture of a commander—in short, by a system of exact rules the application of which was in consequence an art. And the victor triumphed over what was *alive,* a country or a people, either of which could be an object of desire. The whole face of war was thus changed with the introduction of the material and inhuman methods employed at Verdun.

For as soon as war, from having been merely military, becomes a "total war," the destruction of armed resistance means the wiping out of the whole live might of the enemy—the workmen incorporated in factories, the mothers who are begetting future soldiers; in short, the whole of the "means of production," things and persons lumped together. War is no longer the rape, but the murder, of the hostile and coveted object of desire. Verdun, moreover, was but the preamble of this new kind of war; for there the process was confined to the methodical destruction of a million *soldiers,* and no civilians. But it was a *Kriegspiel* that allowed the final touches to be put to an instrument which is now able to operate on a far wider scale—against areas such as London, Paris, or Berlin; that is to say, not against cannon-fodder, but against the flesh and blood manufacturing the cannon— an instrument of obviously much more far-reaching effect.

The technique of dealing death from afar has no equivalent in any imaginable code of love. Total war eludes both man and instinct; it turns upon passion, its begetter. And it is this, not the scale of the massacres, that is new in the history of the world.

This suggests three remarks.

War arose *in the country*, and in connexion with fighting it has been customary down to the present time to speak of *campaigns* and of *fields*. But since 1914 we have witnessed the *urbanization* of war. The first Great War provided a large portion of the peasant masses of

[1] To force a woman's resistance by seducing her is peace; to do so by violating her is war.

Europe with their introduction to mechanical civilization. It was a kind of conducted tour of a World Exhibition of death-dealing arts and industries, with daily demonstrations upon live subjects.

The effect of this general enlistment of the mechanized means of destruction was *to neutralize the actual passion for war* in the hearts of fighting men. The assuaging of violence in bloodshed gave place to mass brutality, and rival hordes were hurled at one another, not by the impulse of passionate frenzy, but in obedience to the calculating brains of engineers. Henceforth, man was no more than the servant of matter; he himself became a material, and one that is more effective the less human it is in its individual reflexes. In this way, notwithstanding the drug-effect of propaganda, victory came to depend ultimately on the laws of mechanics rather than on the forecasts of psychology. The fighting instinct was thwarted. From 1914 to 1919 the explosion of sex which had usually accompanied huge armed struggles could only occur among civilians at the rear. In war, despite efforts in official quarters and on the part of certain popular writers and photographers to spread a high-flown sentimentality, a soldier's coming on leave was now simply the onrush of a male obsessed by an enforced continence that had lasted too long. Countless doctors and soldiers testified to the way in which a war of material was accompanied by a "sex disaster."[1] A widespread impotence—or at least its premonitory symptoms, chronic onanism and homosexuality—was the result vouched for by statistics of a sojourn of four years in the trenches. That is how it came about that presently for the first time there was a general revolt of soldiers against war,[2] because war, far from being an outlet for the passions, had become a kind of vast castration of Europe.

[1] Cf. *Sittengeschichte des Weltkriegs* (two vols., Vienna and Leipzig, 1930), the results of an inquiry by the late Magnus Hirschfeld and twelve other German doctors.

[2] The modern lanzknecht, realizing that this total war is the negation of the passion for war, embarked upon absurd adventures, which he sought precisely because they were absurd and inhuman. Cf. notably the novels of Ernst Jünger (*A Chronicle from the Trench Warfare of 1918* [London, 1930], etc.) and of Ernst von Salomon.

Total war thus implied the discarding of *every accepted mode* of fighting. Beginning with 1920, all the "diplomatic fuss" of ultimatums and "declarations" of war ceased to have currency. Hostilities were no longer brought solemnly to a close by the signing of treaties. The arbitrary distinction between open and fortified towns, civilians and soldiers, authorized and unauthorized means of destruction, all disappeared. It follows that the defeat of a country could no longer be symbolical or metaphorical—that is, be confined to certain agreed *signs*—but had actually to be its death. Here again we see that once the notion of rules is discarded, war can no longer be an act of rape between nations; it must be a sadistic crime, the possession of a dead victim, and hence in fact a *non-possession*. It can no longer exhibit a normal sexual instinct, or even the passion that employs and transcends this instinct, but only that—as we have seen —irresistible perversion of passion, the "castration complex."

11

The Transplanting of Passion into Politics

Games require to be played on an enclosed ground. When the field of war, from being such a ground —the lists decorated with symbols—became a bombardment sector, passion was ousted from it. And passion thereupon sought and found other means of expression. Moreover, it was driven to do so by as much as anything the weakening of private and moral powers of resistance and by the altered nature of war. On the one hand, manners in democratic countries have grown so flexible as not to tend any longer to set up absolute *obstructions* such as intensify passion. On the other hand, the totalitarian system of breaking in the young tended to banish from private life every kind of internal tragic experience and ambiguous emotion. Lawlessness in manners and authoritarian hygienics operated to roughly the same effect. The human need of passion was thwarted, whether hereditary or acquired through culture; its intimate and personal impulses were enfeebled by such regimentation.

Love between the wars became a curious medley of anxious intellectualism—a number of novels in the twenties depicted dread and the middle-class defiance of restrictions—and of materialism—what Germans called the *neue Sachlichkeit*. It was clearly recognized that romantic passion could no longer obtain the ingredients necessary to sustaining its myth, could no longer select means of resistance in the midst of an atmosphere charged with tempestuous and secret devotion. A pathological fear of falling in love in a simple, straightforward manner and of suffering "deceptions of the heart," together with a feverish hankering after "experiences," formed the "climate" of the chief novels in vogue. The unambiguous significance of this was that *the individual relations of the sexes had ceased to be the most appropriate theatre for passion to occur in*. Passion, it seemed, was being detached from its concomitant. We entered upon a period of wandering *libidos* in quest of new spheres of activity. The first to offer itself was that of politics.

The mass-politics practised since 1917 are simply an extension of total war by other means, if I may be allowed to convert Clausewitz's definition of war as "diplomacy carried on by other means." The political use made of the term "front" at once shows this. Moreover, a Totalitarian State is but the state of war being prolonged and renewed, and then made permanent, in a nation. But if total war abolished the merest possibility of passion, politics transferred individual passions to the level of the Collective Being. Everything that a totalitarian education withheld from individuals was heaped upon the personified Nation. It is the Nation (or the Party) that had passions. It is the Nation (or the Party) that took over the whole interplay of exciting obstructions, *askesis,* and the rush made unwittingly towards a heroic and therefore divinizing death. Whereas within and at the bottom personal problems were now sterilized, externally and on top the passionate potential was being intensified daily. Eugenics took control of the morality that concerns the citizens of a State, and eugenics are a rational negation of any kind of private "experience." Yet this only served to increase the tension of the whole, personified in the Nation. The Nation-State said to the Germans: "Beget children!"—and that was a negation of passion. But it also said to its neighbours: "There are too many of us within our frontiers. I must therefore have more territory!"—and this was a new passion. Hence all the tensions abolished at the bottom were heaped on the top. Unmistakably, when rival wills to power confront one another—and there were already *several* Totalitarian States!—they are bound to clash passionately. Each becomes for some other an *obstruction*. The real, tacit, and inevitable aim of the totalitarian elevation was therefore war, and war means *death*. Furthermore, as happened with passionate love, not only was this aim vigorously denied by those concerned, but also it actually was unconscious. Nobody dared to say, "I want war," any more than in passionate love the lovers said : "We want death." Nevertheless, everything being done hastened the attainment of this aim. And everything that was being excited could only find its true significance in war.

There is abundant evidence of this novel resemblance between politics and passion. The restraints which the State imposes in the name of the nation's greatness result in a collective *askesis*. The umbrageous susceptibility of Totalitarian Nations is the equivalent of a knight's honour. And, moreover, let me stress one striking feature. The masses respond to the dictator in a particular country *in the same way* as the women of that country respond to the tactics of suitors.

I wrote in 1938:

"Hitler's success with the German masses may seem surprising, but a non-German would be quite as much astonished by the kind of behaviour that pleases German women. The Latins woo a woman by turning her head with flattering talk, and it is likewise with a flood of flattering talk that French politicians woo their voters. Hitler is more rough and ready. He expresses anger and grievances in the same breath. He does not persuade; he casts a spell. Conjuring up destiny, he asserts that this destiny is himself. He thus releases the masses from responsibility for their conduct, and hence he rids them of any oppressive sense of moral guilt. The crowd surrenders to the dread saviour, and hails him as its liberator in the very moment he paralyses and possesses it. We should note that the popular term in Germany for getting married is *freien*, a verb which means literally 'to free.' " Hitler is presumably only too well aware of this.

" 'There is [he writes] [1] something so thoroughly feminine about the attitude and reactions of the great majority of the common people that its opinions and conduct are the result of feeling far more than of pure cogitation. The masses are not very susceptible to abstract ideas. On the other hand, they are easily gripped by an appeal to emotion. . . . In all ages the force that has launched the most violent revolutions has not been the announcement of some scientific idea which seized the crowd, but a fanaticism that stimulated it and an actual hysteria which infected it with wild enthusiasm.'

"Yes, this has been so 'in all ages.' But the novelty today is that this passionate influence over the masses described by Hitler is accompanied by a rationalizing influence over individuals. Furthermore, this influence is not obtained by some agitator, but by the Leader who incarnates the Nation. That is why the transference of passion from private to public life has resulted in an unprecedented concentration of power. It will need a superhuman Wagner to orchestrate the stupendous catastrophe of passion become totalitarian."

We are brought to the verge of a conclusion that I was far from foreseeing when I began this book. The gradual transformation which the European myth of passion underwent proves to have taken the same course alike in the history of methods of warfare and in the history of literature. And in both cases the transformation culminated in an aspect which receives too little notice—I mean, the dissolution of the *formal modes* instituted by chivalry. In literature "throwbacks" occur, but in the realm of war every change is irreversible; and it is in this realm that the need of providing a fresh solution first became evident. The answer of the twelfth century was courtly chivalry, with its romantic morality and myths. The answer of the seventeenth century is symbolized in French classical tragedy. The answer of the eighteenth was Don Juan's cynicism and rationalist irony. But romanticism

[1] *Mein Kampf.*

was no answer, unless—and this is possible—its eloquent surrender to the nocturnal forces of the myth is regarded as an ultimate attempt to enfeeble the myth by deliberate excess. However that may be, the defence was hardly proportionate to the peril simultaneously let loose. The anti-vital forces long dammed up by the myth then overflowed into the most various spheres, so that there followed a dissociation—using the word in the exact sense of a "severance of the bonds that hold society together."

And yet I feel that to allow all passion to be absorbed by the Nation can prove no more than an emergency measure. The menace may be held off for the time being, but it is also being made to weigh permanently upon the very lives of those peoples who have thus been formed into solid masses. No doubt the Totalitarian State is a newly devised *formal mode*, but one too vast, too rigid, and too geometrical for the complex lives of human beings, however militarized, to be successfully shaped and organized within its framework. Police measures do not constitute a culture, or slogans a morality. Between the artificial framework of great States and the everyday life of men and women, the gap is too wide, so that restlessness and uncertainty are greater than ever. Nothing is *really* settled.

It is possible that we shall have total atomic war, spiritual and moral disintegration, and the problem of passion together with the civilization that brought this problem into existence, will vanish in smoke. But it seems to me more likely that the problem will arise again in totalitarian countries even as it has never ceased to exercise us who belong to liberal societies. In the two concluding books of this work, accordingly, I treat the problem as still active. The first of them deals with a conflict in our manners between the myth and the institution of marriage; the second sums up an attitude which I put forward less as a final answer than as what I have chosen for myself.

Book VI

THE MYTH v. MARRIAGE

1

The Breakdown of Marriage

The Middle Ages had two rival moral systems—one upheld by Christianized society; the other the product of heretical courtesy. The first took marriage for granted, and even made it into a sacrament; the second promoted a set of values in the light of which—at any rate theoretically—marriage was a mistake. The attitude of each to adultery clearly indicates their mutual antagonism.

In the eyes of the Church, adultery was at one and the same time a sacrilege, a crime against the natural order, and a crime against the social order. For the sacrament conjoined in one and the same act two faithful souls, two bodies capable of begetting, and two juridical persons. It was therefore a sacrament that made holy the fundamental needs of both the species and the community. Whoever broke the triple undertaking given at the altar did not thereby become "interesting," but an object of pity or contempt. The Roman Catholic synthesis was intended to harmonize fire and water, as alike in Scripture and in the Fathers it was possible to find thoroughly contradictory theories regarding the holiness of procreation—the law of the species—and regarding the holiness of virginity—the law of the spirit. The Old Testament, for example, deems a numerous progeny the sign of election, whereas Saint Paul says that it is good for a man not to touch a woman, even if he also says that it is better to marry than to burn.

The heresy which was bound up from the beginning with the *cortezia* of the South of France condemned Catholic marriage on each of the three heads just mentioned. It denied that marriage was a *sacrament*, declaring its sacramental character to be established by no

single unambiguous text in the Gospel.[1] It declared procreation to be the work of the Prince of Darkness, the
Demiurge who, in its view, had created the visible world.
It sought to destroy a social order which could countenance and demand war as a manifestation of the collective will to live.[2] But the mainspring of its triple rejection of marriage was in reality a doctrine according
to which Love is the divinizing Eros, everlastingly in
anxious conflict with the fleshly creature and this creature's enslaving instincts.

Accordingly, the appearance of the *passion* of Love
was bound radically to transform the attitude to adultery. Doubtless, unalloyed Catharist doctrine never con-
doned the fault *per se;* on the contrary, it prescribed
chastity. But, as I have pointed out earlier, inextricable
misunderstandings were produced by the courtly symbol
of love for the Lady, obviously a kind of love incompatible with marriage in the flesh. To an uninitiated reader
of the Provençal poems and Arthurian romances, Tristan was no doubt guilty of a fault in committing adultery, but at the same time the fault took on the aspect
of *a splendid experience more magnificent than morality.*
What for Manichaeans was a dramatic expression of the
struggle between faith and the world thereupon became
for such a reader an ambiguous and searing "poesy."
And this poesy was seemingly altogether secular. Its
seductive power was intensified by the reader's own ignorance of the mystical significance of its symbols, for
he supposed these to point merely to some *vague* and
pleasing riddle.

---

[1] According to Father B. M. Lavaud, the Roman Catholic sacrament is open to being justified by the account of the miracle at
Cana ("a mere hypothesis," he says, however), by the passage in
which Jesus states that what God has joined man must not put
asunder, or, finally, by the conversations between the risen Jesus
and his disciples regarding the Kingdom of God, "which the Evan-
gelists and the Acts mention, but do not describe in detail." Father Lavaud points to nothing more substantial than these three
"hypotheses" as ground for attributing to the traditional dogma
a *biblical* authority. Vide his article in *Ètudes carmélitaines,* April
1938, p.186.

[2] The Gnostics (e.g. Carpocrates) often asserted that "crimes
are a tribute paid to life." Cf. Schultz, *Dokumente der Gnosis,*
op. cit.

Only thus can we account for the fact that in the twelfth century an adulterer or adulteress suddenly became somebody "interesting." King David, in lying with Bath-sheba, was held to have committed a crime and to have made himself into an object of contempt. But when Tristan carries off Iseult, his deed turns into romance, and he makes himself into an object of admiration. What had hitherto been a "fault" and what could only give rise to edifying remarks on the perils of sin and on remorse now became—in symbol—something mystically virtuous, and later on was degraded (in literature) into a disturbing and alluring entanglement.

I do not want directly to suggest that the present breakdown of marriage is simply the latest aspect of the discord between a medieval heresy and orthodoxy. The heresy, as such, exists no longer; and if orthodoxy does still exist, it must nevertheless be admitted no longer to play a direct part in the lives of our contemporary societies, to the formation of which it contributed so much. In my opinion, the present general demoralization reflects a confused strife in our lives as a result of the co-existence of two *moral* systems, one inherited from religious orthodoxy, but no longer sustained by a living faith; the other derived from a heresy of which the "in-essence-lyrical" expression has come down to us in a form altogether profaned and therefore distorted. On the one hand, we have today a morality concerned for the species and the general well-being of society, though none the less bearing some impress of religion—what are called middle-class morals. On the other hand, there is a morality spread among us through our literary and artistic atmosphere and general culture—and this produces passionate or romantic morals. The whole of middle-class youth in Europe was brought up to regard marriage with respect; and yet at the same time all young people breathe in from books and periodicals, from stage and screen, and from a thousand daily allusions, a romantic atmosphere in the haze of which passion seems to be the supreme test that one day or other awaits every true man or woman, and it is accepted that nobody has really lived till he or she "has been through it." Now, passion and marriage are essentially irreconcilable. Their origins and their ends make them mutually exclusive. Their co-existence in our midst constantly raises insoluble problems, and the strife thereby engendered constitutes a persistent danger for every one of our social safeguards.

In bygone times it fell to the myth to restrain this latent lawlessness, and to fit it symbolically into moral categories. The myth provided an outlet, and operated to the benefit of civilization. But it came about that the myth was abased and profaned together with the formal modes which had furnished its physical embodiment. If it were now to strive to rise into existence again, we know that no powers of *resistance* would be strong enough to serve as its mask and excuse. Every month sees a flood of articles and books about the breakdown of marriage. They are not in the least likely to settle the problem; for only the myth—that is to say, our unawareness—could bring about in behalf of passion a kind of *modus vivendi*. In making us more keenly alive to the problem, these articles and books contribute, on the contrary, to hampering the elaboration of a settlement. They are themselves evidence of the breakdown, and signs also of our inability to repair it with things as they are. For the institution of marriage was founded on three sets of values which subjected it to *compulsions*, and it was precisely in the effect and interaction of these that the myth achieved expression.[1] But today the compulsions have been either relaxed or abandoned.

There were, in the first place, sacred compulsions. Pagan races have invariably made marriage the subject of a ritual, vestiges of which long survived in our own customs. The ritual covered the purchase, abduction, and exorcism of the bride. Nowadays, owing to economic uncertainties, dowries (even on the Continent) have lost importance. The customs derived from nuptial abduction now only live on as rustic practical jokes. In France no longer does a mother call on the parents of the girl whom her son wishes to marry and formally ask for her hand. Nowhere now is a betrothal very often the occasion for a lawyer's presence at a full-dress reception. And few couples feel any "superstitious" need of having their union "blessed" by a priest.

There were, in the second place, social compulsions. But today considerations of rank, blood, family interests,

[1] Cf. Book I, above.

and even money, are receding into the background so far as democratic countries are concerned, and hence the mutual choice of a marriage partner tends more and more to depend on individual circumstances. That is why divorce is steadily on the increase. Likewise epithalamial ceremonies have either been greatly simplified or else are dispensed with altogether. Customs of remote and sacred origin such as that of "the semi-publicity of the nuptial bed"[1] were kept up in the French provinces right into the seventeenth century. The original mystery had been forgotten, but the ritual continued to give weddings their social character and to fit them into the life of the community. But in the eighteenth century the ceremony of "bedding the bride" had already become nothing more than an occasion for mild and picturesque gallantries. Nowadays the honeymoon, to the extent that it survives and retains any significance, must be held to indicate a wish for escape from habitual social surroundings and an insistence on the private nature of what is called wedded bliss.

There were, finally, religious compulsions. But the modern mind, in so far as it is still able to distinguish between Christianity and sacred and social compulsions, recoils from it with horror. For a religious vow is taken for "time and eternity," which means that it makes no allowance for temperamental vagaries, alterations of character, and changes in taste and external circumstances, such as every couple must expect to experience. And it is on there being no such ups and downs that modern couples make what they call their "happiness" depend. I shall return to this presently.

From such a general decay of institutional obstructions a slackening of tension was bound to ensue, so that it is no wonder that there is now a vast confusion. Adultery has become a topic either for delicate psychological analysis or else for facetious jokes. Fidelity in marriage has become slightly ridiculous: it is so conventional. Strictly speaking, the two hostile moral systems are no longer in *conflict* (and hence no myth is any longer possible), but are approaching a state of mutual neutralization, which will be reached when the old values—not transcended, but abased—have finally dissolved.

---

[1] *The Waning of the Middle Ages,* op. cit.

2

The Modern Notion of Happiness

Now that marriage has ceased to enjoy the safeguards of a system of social compulsions, the only possible basis on which it can rest is individual choice. This means, actually, that the success of any given marriage depends upon an individual notion of the nature of happiness, which at best may be assumed to be identical in the minds of both parties. And yet if in any event it is perplexing enough to define happiness in general, definition becomes impossible when account has to be taken of the contemporary wish to control one's own happiness, or—what doubtless amounts to the same thing—to be able *to experience* the ingredients of one's happiness and to be able to analyse them and roll them over the tongue, so as to give here and there a neat pat of improvement. Your happiness, it is being asserted from the pulpits of magazines, depends on this or on that; and this or that is invariably something that must be *acquired*, usually for cash. The consequence of this propaganda is that we are obsessed by the notion of a facile happiness and at the same time are rendered incapable of being happy. For everything thus suggested introduces us to a world of comparisons in which, until there are men like gods, no happiness can be established. Happiness is indeed a Eurydice, vanishing as soon as gazed upon. It can exist only in *acceptance*, and succumbs as soon as it is laid claim to. For it appertains to being, not to having, as the moralists in all ages have insisted; and our own age brings no new factor to disprove them. Every wish to experience happiness, to have it at one's beck and call—instead of *being* in a *state* of happiness, as though by grace—must instantly produce an intolerable sense of want.

To wish marriage to be based on such "happiness" implies in men and women today a capacity for boredom which is almost morbid, or else a secret intention not to

294

play fair. Perhaps it is only this intention or hope that can account for the readiness of couples to get married "without believing in it." The dream of potential passion acts as a perpetual distraction to paralyse the revulsions of boredom. People are not unaware that passion is a woe, but they imagine that such a woe will be splendid and "vital" in a way ordinary life cannot be, and more exciting than the "happy-go-lucky" present. Either a resigned boredom or else passion—this is the dilemma our lives come up against as a result of the contemporary notion of happiness. In any case this notion threatens the ruin of marriage as a social institution that is defined by its stability.

3

"It's Wonderful to be in Love!"

In the twelfth century in Provence love was regarded as a dignity. It not only imparted a titular nobility, but actually ennobled. Troubadours were raised socially to the level of the aristocracy, which treated them as equals. That is perhaps how there has been imposed on us today through the medium of literature the altogether modern and romantic notion that passion is something morally noble, and need know no law and no custom. Whoever loves passionately is supposed to be thereby made one of an exalted section of mankind among whom social barriers cease to exist. A Tzigane may carry off a princess; a mechanic, marry an heiress. Likewise, a beauty queen has some hopes of becoming the wife of an earl or millionaire. This is a modern "adaptation"—to use a cinematographic term, such as is alone appropriate here[1] —of the theory that love is above the established social order.

The profane passion is something absurd, a kind of

[1] German films in the days of Hitlerism freely used the Hollywood plot in which a workman or chauffeur comes "to deserve" his employer's daughter.

drug, a "sickness of the soul," as the Ancients supposed, everybody is ready to grant, and moralists have said so *ad nauseam*; but in this age of novels and films, when all of us are more or less drugged, nobody will *believe* it, and the distinction is capital. The moderns, men and women of passion, expect irresistible love to produce some revelation either regarding themselves or about life at large. This is a last vestige of the primitive mysticism. From poetry to the piquant anecdote, passion is everywhere treated as an *experience*, something that will alter my life and enrich it with the unexpected, with thrilling chances, and with enjoyment ever more violent and gratifying. The whole of possibility opens before me, a future that assents to desire! I am to enter into it, I shall rise to it, I shall reach it in "transports." The reader will say that this is but the everlasting illusion of mankind, the most guileless and—notwithstanding all I have said—the most "natural"; for it is the illusion of freedom and of living to the full. But really a man becomes free only when he has attained self-mastery, whereas a man of passion seeks instead to be defeated, to lose all self-control, to be beside himself and in ecstasy. And indeed he is being urged on by his nostalgia, the origin and end of which are unknown to him. His illusion of freedom springs from this double ignorance. A man of passion wants to discover his "type of woman" and to love no other. Gérard de Nerval, in one of his poems, tells of a dream in which a noble Lady appears to him in a landscape of childhood memories.

She's fair, dark-eyed, and in old-fashioned clothes
That in another life I may withal
Have seen before, and now but do recall.

Without question this is a mother-image, and psychoanalysis has shown what tragic impediments that may imply. But to quote a poet is either of no value or of too much. I want to confine myself to the illusion which most people in the present century have been *taught*: what obsesses them far more than a mother-image is "standardized beauty." Nowadays—and we are only at the beginning—a man who falls passionately in love with a woman whom he *alone* finds beautiful is supposed to be a prey to nerves. So many years hence he will have to undergo treatment. Admittedly, every generation forms a standardized notion of beauty as a matter of course, even as fashion concentrates at various times on heads, bosoms, hips, or the slim lines of the open-air girl. But nowadays our sheep-like aesthetic tastes exert a greater influence than ever before, and they are being fostered by every possible technical and sometimes political means. A feminine type thus recedes more and more from personal imponderables and is selected in Hollywood or by the State. This influence of standardized beauty is a double one. On the one hand, it preordains who shall be an appropriate object of passion (and to this extent the object is drained of personality); on the other hand, it disqualifies a marriage in which the bride is not like the obsessing star of the moment. In short, the present so-called "freedom" of passion is a question of advertising power. A man who imagines he is yearning for "his" type, or a woman for "hers," is having his or her private wishes determined by fashionable and commercial influences; i.e. by novelty.

4

Marrying Iseult?

Now suppose that, in spite of everything, a man succeeds in plumping for a particular type as his type—a type which will be a cross between what naturally appeals to him and what the cinema has taught him to like. He meets a woman of this type, and identifies her. There she is, the woman of his heart's desire and of his most intimate nostalgia, the Iseult of his dreams! [1] And of course she is already married. But let her get a divorce, and she shall be his! Together they will experience "real

[1] The title of a novel by Max Brod, *Die Frau nach der man sich sehnt*—the women we yearn after, of our nostalgia—supplies the best definition of Iseult. Passionate love wants "the *faraway* princess," whereas Christian love wants "our *neighbour*."

life," and the Tristan he nurses like his hidden daemon
in his bosom will wax and bloom. As regards the revelation of the myth, that is all that matters. There we have
the real "marriage for love" of our time—with passion
as the bride! But thereupon the onlookers (or the public) display a certain uneasiness. Will the lover with all
his desires gratified continue to be in love with his Iseult
once she has been *wed*? Is a cherished nostalgia still desirable once it has recovered its object? For Iseult is ever
a stranger, the very essence of what is strange in woman
and of all that is eternally fugitive, vanishing, and almost
hostile in a fellow-being, that which indeed incites to pursuit, and rouses in the heart of a man who has fallen a
prey to the myth an avidity for possession so much more
delightful than possession itself. She is the woman-from-
whom-one-is-parted: to possess her is to lose her.

And thereupon begins a new "passion." There is a
deliberate effort to renew both obstacle and struggle. The
woman in my arms I must imagine as other than she is.
I give her another guise, I cause her to recede in my
dreams, I strive to disturb the emotional tie that is gradually being formed thanks to the smoothness and serenity of our lives. For I must devise fresh obstructions if I
am to go on desiring, and if I am to magnify my desire to
the dimensions of a conscious and intense passion that
shall be infinitely thrilling. And only suffering can make
me aware of passion; and that is why I like to suffer and
to cause to suffer. When Tristan carries off Iseult to the
forest, where there is nothing any longer to obstruct
their union, the daemon of passion sets down a drawn
sword between their two bodies. Let us descend a few
centuries, stepping down at the same time the whole gam-
ut that stretches from the age of religious heroism to
the drab confusion in which men and women of our own
profane era are struggling: instead of the knight's sword,
it is the sly dream of the husband that comes between
him and the wife he can only continue to desire by imagining she is his mistress.[1] In countless nauseating novels
there is now depicted the kind of husband who fears the
flatness and same old jog-trot of married life in which his
wife loses her "allure" because no obstructions come

---

[1] The recipe was made available as early as Balzac's *Physiolo-
gie du mariage* (1828).

between them. Such husbands are the pathetic victims of a myth the mystical promise of which long ago faded out. In the eyes of Tristan, Iseult was nothing but the symbol of luminous Desire: his other world was the divinizing death that was to release him from terrestrial ties. So Iseult had to be the Impossible, for every possible love recalls us to its bonds, reduces us to those limits of time and space without which there are no "creatures"—whereas the one goal of infinite love is compelled to be the divine: God, our idea of God, or the deified Self. For a man whom the myth now haunts without disclosing its secret, there is no other world beyond passion except another passion, which he must pursue in another turmoil of appearances each time more fleeting. Originally it was of the essence of mystic passion to be *without end*, and that is how this passion became distinct from the throb of carnal desire. But whereas infinity in the eyes of Tristan was an eternity from which there could be no return and in which his lacerated spirit would at last dissolve, men and women today can look to nothing but the everlasting return of an ardour constantly being thwarted.

Formerly victims of the myth could not throw off its spell except by escaping out of the finite world. Today a passion calling itself "irresistible" (as an alibi for the discharge of responsibility) cannot even discover how to be *faithful,* since its end is no longer transcendence. One after the other, it exhausts illusions it has found all too easy to grasp. Instead of leading to death, it is broken off by her unfaithfulness. How patent the degradation of a Tristan who has *several* Iseults! But it is not he who should be blamed; for he is the victim of a social organization in which the obstructions have been cheapened. They break down too soon, before the undertaking has been completed. A soul that sets out to rise in opposition to, and above, the world, has incessantly to begin its ascent afresh. And thereupon a modern Tristan lets himself turn into the antithetical Don Juan type—the man of successive love affairs. The categories break down, and the experience itself ceases to be outstanding. Alone the mythical Don Juan could evade this consummation. But he knew no Iseult, no unattainable passion, neither past nor future, nor sensual anguish. He lived always in the present, having no time to love, to wait, or to remember; and nothing that he desired could resist him, because he *loved* not what did resist.

To love in the sense of passion-love is the contrary of to live. It is an impoverishment of one's being, an *askesis* without sequel, an inability to enjoy the present without imagining it as absent, a never-ending flight from possession. To love with passion-love meant "to live" for Tristan; as the true life which he summoned was transfiguring death. But we have lost transcendence. Death is but a slow consumption.

It is evident in the light of a knowledge of the original myth that the popular novels and films of the present day are the sign of a decay of the individual person; the sign of a sort of sickness of being. Nearly all the complications to which plots resort do not amount to more than a monotonous arrangement of the contrivances of an enfeebled passion in quest of *secret* obstructions. Passion now only wants somehow to keep going. For instance, there is the psychology of jealousy, a jealousy that has been wished for and that is provoked and surreptitiously encouraged—and not only in "the other"! A man or woman wants the beloved to be unfaithful in order that he or she may once again go forth in pursuit and once again "experience" love for its own sake. Rapture is now no more than a sensation, and it leads nowhere. Married people are constantly being thrown back into a realm of comparison, which is the realm of jealousy. Extruding from his or her own self and also from the present as it is given, unable to take the other as he or she is, because that would mean being first of all content with oneself, a man or woman now sees on every side nothing but things to be coveted, qualities that he or she feels the want of, and grounds for comparison that invariably turn against the comparer. It hurts a husband to find that other women seem beautiful in a way his wife is not, even when everybody else insists that hers is the greater beauty. For he does not understand either how to possess or how to enjoy what reality has given him. He has lost the one essential—a sense of constancy. For to be faithful is to have decided to accept another being for his or her own sake, in his or her own limitations and reality, choosing this being not as an excuse for excited elevation or as an "object of contemplation," but as having a matchless and independent life which requires *active* love.

I am not trying to attack passion here. I confine myself to describing it, well aware that I shall convince not a single victim of the profaned myth. But it was necessary to show briefly by means of a few features *how* this passion leads to a number of psychological fates the effects of which are beyond dispute. It has got to be admitted that *passion wrecks the very notion of marriage at a time when there is being attempted the feat of trying to ground marriage in values elaborated by the morals of passion.* Of course it would be going too far to suggest that a majority of people today are a prey to Tristan's frenzy. Few are capable of the thirst that would cause them to drink the love-potion, and still fewer are being elected to succumb to the archetypal anguish. But they are all, or nearly all, dreaming about it, or else have mused upon it. And however worn and faded the mark of the original myth, it still hugs the secret of the anxiety that is nowadays disturbing married couples. The contemporary mind recoils from nothing so much as from the notion of a limitation deliberately accepted; and nothing pleases this mind more than the mirage of infinite transcendence which the reminiscent impress of the myth keeps up. To try to *grow conscious* of the nature of the situation—that sums up the ambition that inspired the preceding analyses; but I realize that they have taken me to the limits of the displeasing. We are too fond of our illusions to suffer gladly any attempt even to name them.

5

From Lawlessness to Eugenics

Nevertheless, modern marriage, which may be said by antiphrasis to be founded upon the remnants of the myth, amounts to a permanent state of lawlessness, and this must obviously involve perils such as no *social* order can tolerate. I say nothing of the spiritual peril to which the morals of escape engendered by the myth must expose a moral being. The social peril is enough to account for the number of attempts made since the first world war "to re-establish" marriage.

There were the respectable efforts of the Churches to define the institution afresh, together with the moral duties which it implies.[1] Humanists restated the arguments of Goethe and Engels in favour of marriage. According to the former, marriage is the greatest achievement of European culture and the solid foundation of any private life; according to the latter, monogamic unions provide the most sensible relation between the sexes in a society that has been emancipated from the restraints of money and class. Others sought to found a science of conjugal relations. Jung analysed the "psychological conflict" and the "neuroses" that lie, in his opinion, at the root of the evil; he hinted that medical psychology could put everything straight. Van de Velde and Hirschfeld suggested that the best course would be to spread a more accurate knowledge of sex.

So many inquiries and so many panaceas indicate how serious the question is, but they have not produced any adequate means of settling it. Curiously enough, too, every one of these learned authors devotes a few lines to extolling passion, or at least to seeming to countenance it. There are obvious reasons for hesitating to offend readers in their most intimate and assured convictions. To do so would seem "puritanical." Some of these writers, however, go further, indulging in the paradox that loving passion may crown a union that has been perfectly achieved (according to their recipe). Nobody, so far as I know, has dared to say that love, *as understood nowadays,* is the flat negation of the marriage to which it is claimed that love can serve as support. The reason is that nobody seems to know exactly what passionate love may be, and neither where it comes from nor whither it may lead. There is indeed a feeling that something is wrong, but writers also fear (quite correctly) that if they attacked

---

[1] The encyclical *Casti connubii* replied to the decisions of the Anglican Lambeth Conference. The oecumenical meetings at Stockholm and Oxford of representatives of all the non-Roman Churches also touched on the problem.

passion they would pass for Philistines. So the fundamental problem is passed over with a simulated lightness. "We must get ourselves read, and win confidence. There is no going against the tide of a whole epoch. Passion has always existed, it therefore always will exist; and we are no Don Quixotes." No doubt! And yet something *must* be done. Hence the one question confronting the historian and sociologist is: What *mechanism* will be released in order to put matters right—what mechanism or what collective reflex?

Two large-scale experiments furnish one kind of answer, and perhaps point to the solution to which we shall all be brought.

Revolutionary Russia was the scene of a youthful "outburst" of sex which it is tempting to regard as unprecedented in European annals.[1] As for marriage, theoretically it was swept away during the early stages of the Soviets. Nihilist or romantic intellectuals had inspired the young Bolshevist leaders with a doctrine that found expression in unmarried cohabitation, abortion, and the desertion of babies—in short, in whatever was imagined to defy reactionary prejudices mistakenly thought to have been fostered by bourgeois capitalism. Lenin, in a famous letter to a woman Bolshevist named Zetkin, describes this collapse of morals, and protests with all the vigour of a "professional" revolutionary—and hence of a Puritan—against the sexual lawlessness which—using the words in their contemptuous Marxian sense—he termed "petit bourgeois." Twenty years later, a "restoration of morals" had been achieved, not owing to any sudden revival of virtue nor thanks to the efforts of some philanthropic society, but as a result of the deliberate action of a dictatorship fully alive to the conditions requisite for its survival. Stalin's immediate aim was to rebuild the framework of his nation. For in the absence of a framework economic life was in danger of collapse, and "national defence" could not be organized without constant appeal to the passion of the early revolutionaries, and it was precisely this passion that Stalin had determined to get

[1] Actually, similar happenings occurred among the youth in so-called bourgeois countries. But in Russia principles of "emancipation" were advertised; elsewhere the young were content to put these principles into practice.

rid of. To lay down new social foundations, and especially
that most stable and most stabilizing of units: the family,
became therefore a vital necessity. The nature of the
mechanism of productivist dictatorship compelled the so-
called Socialist State to decree a series of laws against
divorce—which was made more burdensome—and against
abortion and the deserting of babies born out of wedlock.
The sudden severity of these laws, the psychological
shock which they inflicted, propaganda, and measures
enabling the police to keep a watch on private life, transformed the moral atmosphere of Russia round about the
year 1936.[1] Marriage was instituted again on strictly
utilitarian, collectivist, and eugenic principles; and there
was promoted a spirit in which individual problems tended
to lose all their dignity, legitimacy, and lawless virulence.[2]

In pre-Hitlerite Germany the level of lawlessness to
which sex sank was possibly quite as low as that reached
in Russia before Stalin. The gradual decay of social restraints was not accompanied by any outward violence,
but on that very account the marriage morals of the
young were all the more seriously undermined. At the
same time the decline of the passion myth in the father-
land of romanticism involved far more complicated consequences than in France, and they seemed of the greatest variety. The morbid shamelessness of the German
post-war years, the *neue Sachlichkeit* promoted by ad-
vanced writers and artists, the homosexuality so common
in the secret societies that were a prelude to Hitlerism,
the sadistic outbursts in the Baltic *Freikorps,* the so-
called "political" crimes committed by leagues of youth,
certain forms of nudism, the "trial betrothals" that became customary among students, the serious manner in
which passionate quarrels involving "threes" or "fours"
were treated—on the model of Friedrich Schlegel's *Lu-
cinde*—all these were so many signs of the sex stampede
that followed the weakening of matrimonial restraints and

---

[1] Cf. Hélène Iswolsky, *Femmes soviétiques* (Paris, 1937).

[2] When dealing with the U.S.S.R. the words "family," "eugenics," and "abolition of passion" should all be put in quotation
marks. The headlong drop in population compelled Stalin to
encourage births. But who can be sure that his plans were carried
out? And his motives, I repeat, were not in the least "moral";
rather were they military.

the decline of the myth of fatal love. Already the elements of despair and of private surrender to impulse, which are implicit in any pseudo-legitimization of a strictly individual "happiness," were rising to the surface.

But Hitler's dictatorship, for the very reason that it claimed to operate for racial and military ends, was bound to address itself at the very outset to repairing this breakdown in the nation's morals. To begin with, the anti-social ideal of "happiness" and that of "living dangerously" were countered by the promotion of a collective ideal. *"Gemeinnütz geht vor Eigennütz!"* The general interest comes before that of individuals! Next, by means of every spectacular, didactic, and even religious instrument that it could devise, Hitlerism effected the extraordinary *transference* [1] which resulted in making the one legitimate and possible object of passion the concept of a Nation symbolized in its Führer. First, woman was bereft of her romantic halo and relegated to the position of wife, her only function being to bear and to bring up children till at the age of four or five they could be handed over to the Party. Next, certain steps in eugenics were taken. A "school of future brides" was opened in order to supply wives to the S.S. (*Schutz-Staffeln*), Nazi protective squads, troops selected as supposedly incarnating the racial ideal. Entrance to this school was confined to girls of fair complexion, of Aryan blood, and at least five feet eight inches in height. Hence, in Germany, a man's "type of woman" was fixed for him, not by the recollections of his unconscious nor by exotic fashions, but by the scientific section of the Ministry of Propaganda. In 1938 similar schools were set up for all German women, and attendance at these schools may well have become compulsory. It was decreed that marriages would henceforth be celebrated "in the name of the State." The ultimate aim is obvious. It was to reach a point at which only eugenic marriages would be legal, and would be allowed to take place entirely according to social, racial, and physiological data; they would not be affected in any way by individual "taste." Then scientific marriage would have fulfilled the dream of Lycurgus: it would have become a stage in military training.

Stalin's experiment failed, if we can trust the accounts

---

[1] Referred to in Book V, above.

of the present state of the manners of youth in the U.S.S.R.
Nazi-ism belongs to the past. Yet the totalitarian temptation is still there. We are not forbidden to imagine that
our democracies will one day yield to it in the name
of some "science" or sociological hygiene. The enforced
practice of eugenics *may* succeed there where all moral
doctrines had failed, resulting in the effective disappear-
ance of any "spiritual"—and hence artificial—need of passion. The cycle of courtly love would be complete. The
Europe of passion would be no more. A new and unforeseeable Europe would be taking its rise in the laboratory.

6

The Significance of the Breakdown

The better to see our situation, let us look at America
—that other Europe which has been released from
both the routine practices and traditional restraints of the
old. No other known civilization, in the 7,000 years that
one civilization has been succeeding another, has bestowed on the love known as *romance* anything like the
same amount of daily publicity by means of the screen,
the hoarding, the letter-press and advertisements in magazines, by means of songs and pictures, and of current
morals and of whatever defies them. No other civilization has embarked with anything like the same ingenuous assurance upon the perilous enterprise of making
marriage coincide with love thus understood, and of making the first depend upon the second.

During a telephone strike in 1947, the women operators in the county town of White Plains, near New York,
received the following call: "My girl and I want to get
married. We're trying to locate a justice of the peace.
Is it an emergency?" The women telephone operators
decided forthwith that it was. And the newspaper which
reported the item headed it: "Love is Classified as an
Emergency." This commonplace newspaper cutting provides an example of the perfectly natural beliefs of Amer-
icans, and that is how it is of interest. It shows that in
America the terms "love" and "marriage" are practically
equivalent; that when one "loves" one must get married

instantly; and, further, that "love" should normally overcome all obstacles, as is shown every day in films, novels,
and comic-strips. In reality, however, let romantic love
overcome no matter how many obstacles and it almost
always fails at one. That is the obstacle constituted by
time. Now, either marriage is an institution set up to be
lasting—or it is meaningless. That is the first secret of
the present breakdown, a breakdown of which the extent
can be measured simply by reference to divorce statistics,
where the United States heads the list of countries. To
try to base marriage on a form of love which is unstable
by definition is really to benefit the State of Nevada.
To insist that no matter what film, even one about the
atomic bomb, shall contain a certain amount of the romantic drug—and romantic more than erotic—known as
"love interest," is to give publicity to the germs that
are making marriage ill, not to a cure.

Romance feeds on obstacles, short excitations, and
partings; marriage, on the contrary, is made up of wont,
daily propinquity, growing accustomed to one another.
Romance calls for "the far-away love" of the troubadours; marriage, for love of "one's neighbour." Where,
then, a couple have married in obedience to a romance,
it is natural that the first time a conflict of temperament
or of taste becomes manifest the parties should each ask
themselves: "Why did I marry?" And it is no less natural
that, obsessed by the universal propaganda in favour of
romance, each should seize the first occasion to fall in
love with somebody else. And thereupon it is perfectly
logical to decide to divorce, so as to obtain from the
new love, which demands a fresh marriage, a new promise of happiness—all three words, "marriage," "love,"
"happiness," being synonyms. Thus, remedying boredom
with a passing fever, "he for the second time, she for
the fourth," American men and women go in quest of
"adjustment." They do not seek it, however, in the old
situation, the one guaranteed—"for better, for worse"—
by a vow. They seek it, on the contrary, in a fresh "experience" regarded as such, and affected from the start
by the same potentialities of failure as those which preceded it. That is how divorce assumes in the United
States a less "disastrous" character, and is even more
"normal," than in Europe. There where a European regards the rupture of a marriage as producing social disorder and the loss of a capital of joint recollections and

experiences, an American has rather the impression that "he is putting his life straight," and opening up for himself a fresh future. The economy of saving is once again opposed to that of squandering, as the concern to preserve the past is opposed to the concern to make a clean sweep in order to build something tidy, without compromise. But any man opposed to compromise is inconsistent in marrying. And he who would draw a draft on his future is very unwise to mention beforehand that he wishes to be allowed not to honour it; as did the young millionairess who told the newspaper men on the eve of her marriage: "It's marvellous to be getting married *for the first time!*" A year later, she got divorced.

Whereupon a number of people propose to forbid divorce, or at least to render it very difficult. But it is marriage which, in my opinion, has been made too easy, through the supposition that let there be "love" and marriage should follow, regardless of outmoded conventions of social and religious station, of upbringing and substance. It is certainly possible to imagine new conditions which candidates for marriage—that true "co-existence" which should be enduring, peaceable, and mutually educative—should fulfil. It is possible to exact tests or ordeals bearing on whatever gives any human union its best chances of lasting: aims in life, rhythms of life, comparative vocations, characters, and temperaments. If marriage—that is to say, lastingness—is what is wanted, it is natural to ensure its conditions. But such reforms would have little effect in a world which retained, if not true passion, at least the nostalgia of passion that has grown congenital in western man.

When marriage was established on social conventions, and hence, from the individual standpoint, on chance, it had at least as much likelihood of success as marriage based on "love" alone. But the whole of western evolution goes from tribal wisdom to individual risk; it is irreversible, and it must be approved to the extent it tends to make collective and native destiny depend on personal decision.

It is also clear that the present breakdown of marriage, in Europe as in America, results from a plurality of profound or proximate causes, of which the cult of romance is but an instance. (But it was my due to myself to insist on it here.) For the quest for individual happiness to have precedence on social stability, and for respect of psychological evolution to have precedence on the meaning of a vow, is something which can be connected with the romantic complex. But there is more to it, and in other domains, or at other levels of reality, at times social and at other times psychical.

Woman's emancipation—her entrance into the professions and her claim to equality of treatment—is a perceptible factor in the breakdown. The popularization of psychological knowledge is another. Men and women of the twentieth century, even with only a smattering of the existence of Freudian complexes, of the play of repressions and inhibitions, and of the origin of neuroses, are inclined to require more than their ancestors did from marriage and from conjugal life. Those demands will go on growing with the diffusion of the "human sciences," the early stammerings of which have already in perceptible measure modified the self-awareness of western man. Finally, there are signs of a more profound event—one possibly comparable to that which invaded the collective psyche in the twelfth century, and which I called in Book II the "Reascent of the Shakti." The strong revival of Mariology in the Roman Catholic Church with its popular millions; the most recent work of C. G. Jung and his school,[1] on the eternal Sophia, Wisdom, and Mother-Virgin; and also (and really otherwise) the revival of interest in Catharism shown by the *avant-garde* of European literature, and in the elevation of the "Child-Woman," saviour of rational man, or the repeated announcement that the feminine principle is about to get even with patriarchal pretensions [2]—all that allows the premonition of a vast evolution of the modern psyche in prospect, and even though the first principle and the implications of such an evolution are withheld from us, nevertheless an evolution that will possibly provide the

[1] Cf. C. G. Jung, *Antwort auf Hiob* (1952), where the author does not hesitate to write that the proclamation in 1950 of the Dogma of the Assumption of the Virgin marks the most important religious event since the Reformation. See also Henry Corbin's study of the Eternal Sophia in *Revue de Culture européenne*, No. 5, 1953.

[2] Cf. notably, and in addition to the works cited above on Catharism and Courtly Love, such books as *Arcane 17* by André Breton, the lyrical novels of Julien Gracq, the studies by Robert Graves concerning the Great Goddess, and by Adrian Turel on matriarchates.

future historians of our western society with the key to a breakdown of which we so far see but the superficial, sporadic, and incoherent symptoms.

We can feel how vain any attempt would be at present "to resolve" the contradictions which so many men and women put up with in marriage. Harmonization or a new equipoise is being worked out, perhaps—invisibly. Its nature keeps it for the present out of range of individual awareness. Any solution that I might be tempted to offer, even if deemed "it" in the next century, would be stamped today as ineffectual, or, if it could effect anything, would do more harm than good. If I had hit upon it, and had the power to make my contemporaries adopt it, I should carefully refrain from doing so. For a breakdown of this sort is no accident. To try to arrest it as a fever is stopped would be not so much to cure it as to deprive ourselves of any prospect of one day understanding its secret. And it would be at the same time a kind of cheating, either because a solution would mean really no more than an attempt to get back to the former equipoise, and how precarious that was the breakdown itself shows, or else because any solution must cast over the future of the community a theory or precepts reasonable enough in themselves, but the remote effects of which cannot be estimated so long as the general *significance* of the breakdown escapes us.

We shall be better employed in deciphering the message and in patiently decoding the ambiguous tidings which the breakdown brings us concerning ourselves—concerning our secret wishes, the genuine tendency—possibly creative—sometimes betrayed in our rebellions, our ingenuous illusions, and our sins. To seek to repair the breakdown of marriage by means of moral, social, or scientific measures inspired by the sole desire to stop further damage, might very well be to deny arbitrarily to this breakdown what seems to be its actual character —namely, that of a quest as yet carried on blindfold for *a fresh equipoise* of the married couple—a harmony that will reconcile the invariably simultaneous, contrary and legitimate demands of the stability and evolution of both the species and the individual, and indeed the needs both of the fulfilment of the person and of the Absolute that alone judges and raises up that person.

Book VII

ACTIVE LOVE, OR KEEPING FAITH

1

We Must Take Our Stand

How futile the intellectual attitude that would describe itself as being against passion! There is no arguing with passion, no reasoning with it; for it does not wish to have reason on its side. To succumb to passion is precisely to rest content with being in the wrong according to the world—in the great, irrevocable wrong of preferring death over life. To attack passionate love successfully would require a spiritual violence more lethal than this love itself. For first and last, at the beginning and the end of passion, there is no "delusion" about man or about God—and *a fortiori* no moral delusion—but a crucial decision: a man wishes to be his own god. [1] Passion brands the heart the moment the cold-blooded serpent—the complete cynic—has whispered his eternally unfulfilled promise: *Eritis sicut dei*! How artless and innocent the moralist who thought to turn a man from taking this fatal, divinizing road by "demonstrating" to him that it leads to ruin! By pleading every earthly reason, offering him the support of all the arts of *living*, when earth is what this man contemns, and life is the fault he regards as needing to be redeemed! Such a man's passion can be overcome only by killing him before he can kill himself, and in some other way than he wishes to die.

As for rendering innocuous the area of culture into which passion has dug its roots, that is a task that the State will probably see to as part of its hygienic policy. But for me, here and now, the problem offers no loop-

---

[1] I confine myself to the limiting case of Tristan. There are cases of passion in Christian marriage, and in passion cases of the married status.

nole through relying upon the time to come. If indeed we must assume that nobody can be aware of the nature of his own desires nor plumb the depths of his own most secret inclinations, at least each may survey what he has done and face the consequences of the decisions he has ventured. All I now intend to offer, then, is a statement of the stand I personally have taken—of the choice that I am conscious of having made in my own life. It is no cut-and-dried solution. Probably there is no solution, as I have said above. Even were such a solution possible, it could avail only for me alone: nobody ever decides except for himself. But having written a whole book about passion, I must not shirk *completing* the description with an account of this feature of the subject, thanks to which the book will be lifted, not into some abstract sphere where passion cannot subsist, so that discussing it must be triviality, but into the concrete world where choice determines our lives.

2

A Critique of Marriage

If no argument that I can see is valid against true passion, so likewise it seems to me that reason is equally powerless to justify marriage; I feel indeed that every one of the extremely varied objections that the finest minds have ever urged against it is still *fully* valid. At all times the Philistine's reasons have betrayed a bad conscience beside the romantic's ironies; but in the face of plain veracity these reasons are utterly put to rout. The notorious peaceful fireside only exists at the level of a certain political speechifying, either middle-class or aiming to edify. Tolstoy describes it as "hell." And I think he deserves the greater credence. Inasmuch as when taken one by one most human beings of both sexes are either rogues or neurotics, why should they turn into angels the moment they are paired? Push open the first door that offers. The quiet which a wife is supposed to ensure the noble breadwinner, on his returning home at night exhausted and anxious to relax in domestic peace, ranges nine times out of ten from a restless running to and fro of little attentions to an uncontrolled bawling. Were some of the "peaceful" conversation that enlivens "the domestic hearth" of a business man or mechanic selected at haphazard and made into a gramophone record, censorship would for once have established a *raison d'être*!

Yes, the romantics are right; and so are the realists; and so are the scholars who declare in the name of their vocation that one must choose between writing books and producing children. *Aut liberi aut libri*, as Nietzsche put it. And Kierkegaard is right over them all, because, first, he extolled passion as being the highest value in the "aesthetic stage" of life; then rose above passion by extolling marriage as being the highest value in the "ethical stage" (the "fullness of time"); and finally condemned marriage as the highest obstruction in the "religious stage," since marriage fetters us to time where faith requires eternity. What objections can be brought against this man that he himself has not already more accurately stated? Kierkegaard is able to praise both the Philistine and the romantic, and to put them both so thoroughly in the right as to make them ashamed of ever having doubted themselves; but in the end he not only crushes the Philistine who is content to marry a brewer's widow or the young lunatic who is in love with a king's daughter, but also the pious man who has imagined that religion ought to be a happy union—a marriage with his own virtue. For the sinner's love of God is "essentially unhappy," and this Christian passion is the only truth, a truth from which every one of our human "duties" (including that of being happy) does but turn us aside. Kierkegaard first denounces the Protestant ministers who objected to celibacy; then Luther and Calvin who were both married; then the Fathers who praised marriage; and finally Saint Paul who suffered marriage. Christ alone lived like a Christian! How refute this extremist? Unbelievers are referred to the arguments of the romantics, which are valid against their secular moralizing; and believers to the arguments of Saint Paul, which are valid against their humanism. What does the Apostle say?

"It is good for a man not to touch a woman. Never-

theless, to avoid fornication, let every man have his own
wife, and let every woman have her own husband. The
wife hath not power of her own body, but the husband;
and likewise also the husband hath not power of his own
body, but the wife. Defraud ye not one the other,
except it be with consent for a time, that ye may give
yourselves to prayer; and come together again, that Satan tempt you not for incontinency. But I speak this by
permission, and not of commandment. For it is better to
marry than to burn. But as God hath distributed to every
man, as the Lord hath called every one, so let him walk.
Let every man abide in the same calling wherein he was
called. They that use the world be as not abusing it;
for the fashion of this world passeth away."

And here comes the finishing stroke:

"He that is unmarried careth for the things that belong
to the Lord, how he may please the Lord: But he that
is married careth for the things that are of the world,
how he may please his wife."

Everything to be urged against marriage is true, and
therefore should be urged against it, either from the romantic standpoint—if we believe in Iseult—or from the
standpoint of the whole-hearted scholar—if we believe in
our work—or from the purely spiritual standpoint—if we
believe. Hence it is impossible to uphold marriage till we
have passed beyond the first two criticisms, and are on the
way to the third—that is, till we are keeping steadily
before us the inhuman requirement of perfection as a
perpetual question, as a goad that can prevent us from
again exposing ourselves to human objections.

If I fail to consider the state which is not only beyond
marriage but also beyond every human order, the state
called the Kingdom of God ("There shall be neither men
nor women"), my wisdom and hope are *restricted* to a
relative perfection—the poise in imperfection that is marriage. Thereupon, if I cannot reach this poise, all I may
do is to rebel against my creature state; yet if I reach
this poise too readily, I become the Philistine pilloried by
the romantics, or the moral being caught in the toils of
society, and I am thereupon denied any understanding of
those "cruel" truths of the spirit spoken of by Nietzsche.

But if I am convinced that the Apostle is right and
agree with him, I adopt an open mind towards the imperfect poise of marriage and—happily or unhappily—

live in wait of perfection. I realize that it is a *wild* attempt I am making (although at the same time an altogether natural one) to live perfectly in imperfection. But I also realize that this attempt must possess an unshakable truth if it incessantly bears witness to what transcends every kind of consequence, however excellent.

3

Marriage as a Decision

Once we ask ourselves what is involved in choosing a man or a woman *for the rest of one's life,* we see that to choose is to wager. Both in the lower and the middle classes the wiseacres urge young men "to think it over" before taking the decisive step. They thus foster the delusion that the choice of a wife or husband may be governed by a certain number of accurately weighable pros and cons. This is a crude delusion on the part of common sense. You may try as hard as you like to put all the probabilities at the outset in your own favour—and I am assuming that life allows you the spare time for such nice calculations—but you will never be able to foresee how you are going to develop, still less how the wife or husband you choose is going to, and still less again how the two of you together are going to. The factors involved are too diverse. Suppose you could weigh them as they are now (assuming them to be finite in number) and you were so deeply versed in the conduct of human affairs as to know the values of every one of them and their order, you would still be unable to foresee how a union entered upon with all the *facts* duly weighed was going to shape. Nature is said to have required several hundreds of thousands of years for the selection of those species which now seem to us adapted to their surroundings. And yet we have the presumption to suppose that all of a sudden in the course of a single life we may solve the problem of the adaptation to one another of two highly organized physical and moral beings! For this is what all unsatisfactorily married persons suppose whenever they grow convinced that a second or third trial is going to yield a closer approximation to "happiness," notwithstanding that everything goes to show that even a hundred thousand trials would not provide the first inchoate and altogether empirical data upon which to build a science of "happy marriage." It needs to be recognized frankly that the problem with which we are confronted by the practical necessity of marriage becomes the more hopelessly insoluble the more we strive "to solve" it in a rational way.

True, I have not stated the case quite fairly; for as a rule everything happens as if the happiness of a married pair actually did depend on a finite number of factors—character, beauty, fortune, social position, and so on. But as soon as individual demands are put forward, these external data lose importance, and it is imponderables that determine our decision. [1] Thereupon it is common sense that turns out to have argued unfairly in recommending that our choice should result from a mature and reasonable submission of the data to impersonal criteria.

But after all the logical fallacy is negligible; what matters is the moral fallacy which the logical implies. When a young engaged couple are encouraged to calculate the probabilities in favour of their happiness, they are being distracted from the truly moral problem. The attempt to minimize or to conceal the fact that, when considered objectively, a choice of this kind is a wager fosters the belief that everything depends on wisdom or on a set of rules, when actually everything depends on a *decision*. And yet, inasmuch as no set of rules can be anything but imperfect and provisional, if we are to be guided by rules we also need some kind of guarantee. But the only possible guarantee would be one supplied by the strength of the decision whereby we commit ourselves during the rest of our lives "for better, for worse." And it is precisely to the extent that we persuade ourselves that the matter is above all one of calculation and of weighing up that the decision in itself is made to seem secondary or

---

[1] The further we get away from the *species* and the nearer we come to the *person,* the more choice becomes particular. And to this endowment of the beloved with a particular personality there may correspond an increasingly specific quality of instinctive behaviour. Such is Dr. Marañon's argument in favour of monogamy.

superfluous. I therefore feel that it would be more appropriate, both to the essential nature of marriage and to the facts for young people to be taught that their choice must always have an arbitrary element, of which they are undertaking to bear the consequences, whether the consequences turn out happy or unhappy. I do not seek to defend acting on "rash impulse"; to the extent that probabilities can be weighed, it would be stupid not to weigh them. But I insist that the guarantee of a union in appearance sensible never lies in this appearance. It must lie in that irrational event, a decision that we venture upon in spite of everything and that lays the foundation of a new life in being a consent to take new chances.

Let me forestall any misunderstanding. "Irrational" in no way means "sentimental." To choose a woman for wife is not to say to Miss So-and-So: "You are the ideal of my dreams, you more than gratify all my desires, you are the Iseult altogether lovely and desirable—and endowed with a suitable dowry—of whom I want to be the Tristan." For this would be deceit, and nothing enduring can be founded on deceit. Nobody in the world can gratify me; no sooner were I gratified than I would change! To choose a woman for a wife is to say to Miss So-and-So "I want to live with you just as you are." For this really means: "It is you I choose *to share* my life with me, and that is the only *evidence* there can be that I love you." If anybody says, "Is that all?"—and this is no doubt what many young people will say, having been led by virtue of the myth to expect goodness knows what divine transports—he must have had little experience of solitariness and dread, little experience indeed of solitary dread.

Alone a decision of this kind, irrational but not sentimental, sober but in no way cynical, can serve as the basis for a real fidelity; and I do not say: "A fidelity that will prove a recipe for 'happiness'"; I only say: "A feasible fidelity, because it is not being wrecked at birth by some necessarily inaccurate calculation."

4

On Keeping Troth

The morals of marriage are distorted by the way the plighting of a troth is made into a problem when no problem ought to arise till *after* a troth has been plighted and is considered to be absolute. The problematical element in marriage belongs not to *cur* but to *quomodo*, to the "how" and not to the "why." Kierkegaard says: "Morality does not set out from an ignorance which needs to be changed into knowledge, but from a knowledge that requires to be put into practice." It is not the nature of the pledge exchanged in marriage that is problematical, but the consequences involved by the pledge. (Likewise, theology is distorted by setting out from the "problem of God"—exactly as though in unbelief—when the *real* problem is to know how to obey Him.) For a troth does not have to give its reasons, or then it is not a troth, any more than anything else potentially noble and great would be; any more than passion!

The moralists, and also some of the sociologists, have tried to maintain that monogamy is natural, and, moreover, beneficial. The theme is one open to interminable discussion. And it will become highly pertinent the day men behave rationally and in obedience to their own best interests, the day they no longer have passions and cease to prefer error as such, and no longer deserve the disturbing epithet of "human" in the active sense. Meanwhile, I fancy that men and women as they are now must look upon fidelity as the least natural of virtues, the one most inimical to "Happiness." In their eyes and as they put it, faithful marriage can only exist as the result of an "inhuman" effort. Their fundamental claim, their religion of Life, is diametrically opposed to it. They think fidelity is a discipline dictated (to our spontaneous impulses and desires) by an absurd and cruel prejudice, or else is a prudent abstinence. Or else again they regard it as the

320

consequence of an inability to live to the full; of a spirit-less liking for what is comfortable and conventional; of a lack of imagination; of a contemptible timidity; or of a sordid calculation. The habit of people today, their acquired nature, is to make the most of every situation for its own sake, without any longer referring their conduct to what "judges" and "measures" the enjoyment which they thereby obtain. Actually, an acquired respect for the social order is the only thing that still upholds the notion of fidelity. But this is not treated as a serious obstruction, and is circumvented in a hundred ways. Listen to the excuses of a husband who deceives his wife. He may say: "It's of no importance, it doesn't alter our relations, it's merely a passing affair, a lapse without a sequel," or else: "It's absolutely vital for me, and tremendously more important than all your petty morals and assurances of bourgeois happiness!" Between a cynical attitude and tragic romanticism there is no real contradiction, as I showed earlier.[1] In each case it is a matter of *escaping* from some actual pledge, because a pledge is thought to be a hateful limitation.

Forgoing any rationalist or hedonist form of apology, I propose to speak only of a troth that is observed *by virtue of the absurd*—that is to say, simply because it has been pledged—and by virtue of being an absolute which will uphold husband and wife as persons. Fidelity, it must be admitted, stands emphatically athwart the stream of values nowadays admired by nearly every one. Fidelity is extremely *unconventional*. It contradicts the general belief in the revelatory value of both spontaneity and manifold experiences. It denies that in order to remain lovable a beloved must display the greatest possible *number* of qualities. It denies that its own goal is happiness. It offensively asserts first, that its aim is obedience to a Truth that is believed in, and secondly, that it is the expression of a wish to be constructive. For fidelity is not in the least a sort of conservatism, but rather a construction. An "absurdity" quite as much as passion, it is to be distinguished from passion by its persistent refusal to submit to its own dream, by its persistent need of acting in behalf of the beloved, by its being persistently

[1] *Gauloiserie* as much as passion having been an escape from reality, a way of idealizing it. Cf. p. 197, above.

in contact with a reality which it seeks to control, not to flee.

I maintain that fidelity thus understood sets up the person. For the person is manifested like something made, in the widest sense of making. It is built up as a thing is made, thanks to a making, and in the same conditions as we make things, its first condition being a fidelity to something that before was not, but now is in process of being created. Person, made thing, fidelity—the three terms are neither separable nor separately intelligible. All three presuppose that a stand has been taken, and that we have adopted what is fundamentally the attitude of creators. Hence in the humblest lives the plighting of a troth introduces the opportunity of making and of rising to the plane of the person—on condition, of course, that the pledge has not been for "reasons" in the giving of which there is a reservation which will allow those reasons to be repudiated some day when they have ceased to appear "reasonable!" The pledge exchanged in marriage is the very type of a *serious* act, because it is a pledge given once and for all. The irrevocable alone is serious. Every life, even the most disinherited one, has some immediate potentiality of dignity, and it is in an "absurd" fidelity that this dignity may be attained—in a readiness to say "No" to dazzling passion, when there is every earthly reason for saying "Yes"—to say "No" by virtue of the absurd, by virtue of an old promise, of human unreason, of a reason of faith, of a pledge given to God and underwritten by God. And perhaps later on, afterwards, a man or woman may find that the folly of the accepted sacrifice was the greatest wisdom; and that the happiness he or she has forgone is being restored, even as Isaac was restored to Abraham. But this can only happen if he or she has not expected it. And it may also be that nothing rewards our loss: we are among dimensions where ordinary worldly measures no longer avail. But are we still capable of imagining a dignity and greatness in no way romantic and the opposite of excited ardour? The fidelity of which I am speaking is foolish, and yet our folly is then of the most sober and everyday kind. *A sober folly that rather closely simulates behaving sensibly;* that is neither heroic nor challenging, but a patient and fond application.

However, everything has still not been made plain.

Tristan also was faithful. And so is every true passion.
(Not to mention the successive fidelities which we display in one after another of our "affairs" nor the fidelity
of all those Tristans who are really Don Juans in slow
time.) It remains accordingly to show where the difference lies, and to ascertain why a faithful husband should
not simply be the man who has identified his wife with
Iseult.

When the lover in the Manichaean legend has undergone the great ordeals of initiation, he is met, you remember, by a "dazzling maiden" who welcomes him with the
words: "I am thyself!" So with fidelity in the myth, and
Tristan's. Fidelity is then a mystic narcissism—usually
unconscious of course, and imagining itself to be true
love for *the other*. In analysing the courtly legends, however, we saw that Tristan is not in love with Iseult, but
with love itself, and beyond love he is really in love with
death—that is, with the only possible release there can
be for a self guilty and enslaved. Tristan is true neither
to a pledge nor to a symbolical being named Iseult. She
is but a lovely pretext, and all the time he is being true
to his most profound and secret passion. The myth seizes
on "the death instinct" inseparable from any form of
created life, and transfigures it by bestowing upon it an
essentially spiritual goal. To destroy oneself, to despise
happiness is thereupon a way of salvation and of ac-
ceding to a higher life, to "the highest bliss of being"
sung of by the expiring Isolde. It is a fidelity destructive
of life, but that also destroys the fault in divinizing the
now "innocent" *self*!

Of this original mystical form, "passionate troth" has
by now preserved no more than the illusion of giving
access to a more ardent life. But the power of the illusion betrays that the original religion still obscurely survives—a religion that was prior to our modern "instinct"
and that secretes the intimate riddle of passion at depths
which our psychologists are unable to plumb.

"Our vows were not exchanged for this world," Novalis
wrote, having in mind his lost love. The words are at
once a moving expression of courtly fealty and an *irrevocable* negation of life. But the troth of marriage is,
on the contrary, a pledge given for *this* world. Inspired
by an unreason "mystical" (if you like) and, if not hostile,
at least indifferent to happiness and the vital instinct,

fidelity in marriage requires a re-entry into the real world, whereas courtesy meant only an escape from it. In marriage the loving husband or wife vows fidelity first of all to *the other* at the same time as to his or her true self. And whereas Tristan showed himself constant in a steadfast refusal, in a desire to exclude and deny creation in its diversity and to prevent the world from encroaching upon spirit, the fidelity of the married couple is acceptance of one's fellow-creature, a willingness to take the other as he or she is in his or her intimate particularity. Let me insist that fidelity in marriage cannot be merely that negative attitude so frequently imagined; it must be active. To be content not to deceive one's wife or husband would be an indication of indigence, not one of love. Fidelity demands far more: it wants the good of the beloved, and when it acts in behalf of that good it is creating in its own presence the neighbour. And it is by this roundabout way through the other that the self rises into being a person—beyond its own happiness. Thus as persons a married couple are a mutual creation, and to become persons is the double achievement of "active love." What denies both the individual and his natural egotism is what constructs a person. At this point faithfulness in marriage is discovered to be the law of a new life, though not of natural life (that would be polygamy) and not of life for the sake of death (that was Tristan's passion).

The love of Tristan and Iseult was the anguish of being *two*; and its culmination was a headlong fall into the limitless bosom of Night, there where individual shapes, faces, and destinies all vanish: "Iseult is no more, Tristan no more, and no name can any longer part us!" The other has to cease to be the other, and therefore, to cease to be altogether, in order that he or she shall cease to make me suffer and that there may be only "I myself am the world!" But married love is the end of anguish, the acceptance of a limited being whom I love because he or she is a summons to be created, and that in order to witness to our alliance this being turns with me towards day.

A life *allied* with mine, for the rest of our lives—that is the miracle of marriage. Another life that wills my good as much as its own, because it is united with mine: and were this not for the rest of our lives, it would be a

menace, such as is ever present in the exchanged pleasures of an "affair!" But few people now seem to be
able to distinguish between an obsession which is undergone and a destiny that we shoulder.

Hence it must be shown with the help of a plain example.

To be in love is not necessarily *to love*. To be in
love is a state; to love, an act. A state is suffered or
undergone; but an act has to be decided upon. Now, the
promise which marriage means cannot fairly be made to
apply to the future of a state in which I am at the moment, but it can and should mortgage the future of conscious acts which I take on—to love, to remain faithful,
to bring up my children. That shows how different are the
meanings of the word "to love" in the world of Eros and
in the world of Agape. It is seen even better when it is
noticed that the God of Scripture *orders* us to love. The
first commandment of the Decalogue is: "Thou shalt
love the Lord thy God with all thy heart, with all thy
soul, and with all thy mind;" it can only be concerned
with acts. It would be altogether absurd to demand of
a man a state of sentiment. The imperative, "Love God
and thy neighbour as thyself," creates structures of active
relations. The imperative, "Be in love!" would be devoid
of meaning; or, if it could be obeyed, would deprive a
man of his freedom.

5

Eros Rescued by Agape

Thereupon charitable love, Christian love—which is
Agape—appears at last and risen to its full height. It
is the expression of being in action. And it is Eros, passionate love, pagan love, that spread through the European world the poison of an idealistic *askesis*—all that
Nietzsche unjustly lays at the door of Christianity. And
it is Eros, not Agape, that glorified our death instinct and
sought "to idealize" it. But Agape has got its own back

by rescuing Eros. For Agape is incapable of destruction, and does not even wish to destroy what destroys.

"I desire not the death of a sinner, but that he may live."

The god Eros is the slave of death because he wishes to elevate life above our finite and limited creature state. Hence the same impulse that leads us *to adore* life thrusts us into its negation. There lies the profound woe and despair characterizing Eros, his inexpressible bondage; and in making this bondage evident Agape has delivered Eros from it. Agape is aware that our terrestrial and temporal life is unworthy of adoration and even of being killed, but that it can be accepted in obedience to the Eternal. For, after all, it is here below that our fate is being decided. It is on earth that we must love. In the next world, we shall meet, not divinizing Night, but the forgiveness of our Creator and Judge.

This prospect is one that natural man was unable to imagine. He was condemned to put his faith in Eros—to trust in his most powerful desire and to expect release through this desire. Yet Eros could lead him but to death. But a man who believes the revelation of Agape suddenly beholds the circle broken: faith delivers him from natural religion. Now he *may* hope for something; he is aware that there is some other release from sin. And thereupon Eros in turn has been relieved of his fatal office and delivered from his fate. *In ceasing to be a god, he ceases to be a demon.*[1] And he finds his proper place in the provisional economy of Creation and of what is human.

The Pagans could not do otherwise than make Eros into a god; Eros was the most powerful force within them, the most dangerous and the most mysterious, the most deeply bound up with the event of living. All pagan religions deify Desire. All seek to be upheld and saved by Desire, which is thus instantly transformed into the greatest enemy of life, the seduction of Nothingness. But once the Word was made flesh and had spoken to us in human language, we learned the tidings that it is not we who have to deliver ourselves but God Who will deliver us, *God Who loved man first* and came down to

---

[1] Sin, it has been remarked by R. de Pury, is not Eros, but the sublimation of Eros.

him. Salvation is no longer something beyond, and ever a little more out of reach during the interminable ascent of Desire, the consumer of life; it is here below and is attainable through obedience to the Word.

And hence what have we to fear from desire. It loses its absolute hold over us the moment we cease to deify it. This is attested by the display of fidelity in marriage. For the foundation of this fidelity is an initial refusal *on oath* "to cultivate" the illusions of passion, to render them a secret worship, or to expect from them any mysterious intensification of life. I may also indicate how it is so by consideration of something well known. Christianity has asserted the complete equality of the sexes, and this as plainly as possible. Saint Paul says:

"The wife hath not power of her own body, but the husband; and likewise also the husband hath not power of his own body, but the wife."

Once she is man's equal, woman cannot be "man's goal."[1] Yet at the same time she is spared the bestial abasement that sooner or later must be the price of divinizing a creature. But her equality is not to be understood in the contemporary sense of giving rise to rights. It belongs to the mystery of love. It is but the sign and evidence of the victory of Agape over Eros. For a truly mutual love exacts and creates the equality of those loving one another. God showed His love for man by exacting that man should be holy even as God is holy. And a man gives evidence of his love for a woman by treating her as a completely human person, not as if she were the spirit of the legend—half-goddess, half bacchante, a compound of dreams and sex.

But from these premises let us proceed to the concrete psychology of married equality. When a man is faithful to one woman, he looks on other women in quite another way, a way unknown to the world of Eros: other women turn into persons instead of being reflections or means. This "spiritual exercise" develops new powers of judgement, self-possession, and respect.[2] The opposite in

---

[1] As Novalis supposed, thereby effecting a revival of courtly mysticism and of the old Celtic tradition.

[2] "Respect," as I use the word here, means that we recognize in a being the fullness of a person. A person, according to Kant's famous definition ["A person is the subject whose actions are imputable."—Translator], is what cannot be used by man as an instrument or thing.

this of an erotic man, a steadfast man no longer strives to see a woman as merely an attractive or desirable body, as merely an unintended movement or a fascinating expression; he feels, as soon as tempted, the difficult and serious mystery of an independent, alien existence; he realizes that he has been desiring only an illusory or fleeting aspect of what is actually a complete life, and that perhaps this aspect has been but a projection of his own reverie. Thus temptation recedes disconcerted instead of *making* itself into an obsession; and fidelity is made secure by the clear-sightedness it induces. The sway of the myth is by so much weakened, and although this sway is unlikely ever to be entirely abolished without leaving traces in hearts drugged by images, hearts such as men harbour today, at least it loses its efficacy. The myth no longer determines a person.

In other words, it may be said that fidelity secures itself against unfaithfulness by becoming accustomed not to separate desire from love. For if desire travels swiftly and anywhere, love is slow and difficult; love actually does pledge one for the rest of one's life, and it exacts nothing less than this pledge in order to disclose its real nature. That is why a man who believes in marriage can no longer believe seriously in "love at first sight," still less in the "irresistible" nature of passion. "Love at first sight" is no doubt a legend that was accredited by Don Juan, as the "irresistible" nature of passion was earlier accredited by Tristan. Neither the excuse nor the alibi can deceive any one who does not wish to be deceived because he thinks deception will be to his advantage; they are tropes of a romantic rhetoric, and allowable in that form, but only becoming ridiculous if confused with psychological truth.

My analysis of the myth has made it plain why people *like to believe in* irresistibility, which is an alibi invoked by the guilty. "I didn't do it, I wasn't there; it was an irresistible power that acted in the stead of my person." That is the pious lie [1] of a minister of Eros. But what a lot of self-encouragement resides in the word "irresistible!" As for "love at first sight," it is supposed to excuse Don Juan's lapses. All literature invites us to accept it as the sign of a very strongly sensual nature. Don Juan,

[1] On the unmistakable connexion between passion and lying, I have insisted, pp. 48–51, and p. 176, above.

the man of loves at first sight who led a "tempestuous" life, passes for a kind of superman or supermale. This is a myth with an indeterminate power, hovering over moral contingencies; but we may be confident that it is a product of *compensatory dreams*—compensating either for an imposed and detested fidelity, or for a masochistic jealousy, or for the beginnings of impotence. Indeed, Don Juan's behaviour is typical enough of one kind of sexual weakness. It is in a state of general weariness, sexually localized, that the body is led to commit these sudden lapses, not unakin to the puns that obsess a weary mind. But when body and mind are normally vigorous the chances of love at first sight must be very slender. It would thus seem that monogamy, in making sexual relations normal, becomes the best assurance of pleasure— that is, of the entirely carnal eros, which is not in the least to be deified.[1]

It may be objected that marriage must then be simply "the grave of love." But it is of course the myth once again that suggests this, thanks to its obsession of obstructed love. It would be more accurate to echo Croce and to say that "marriage is the grave of savage love," [2] and more often the grave of sentimentality. Savage and natural love is manifested in *rape*—the evidence of love among all savage tribes. But rape, like polygamy, is also an indication that men are not yet in a stage to apprehend the presence of an actual person in a woman. This is as much as to say that they do not know how to love. Rape and polygamy deprive a woman of her equality by reducing her to sex. Savage love empties human relations of personality. On the other hand, a man does not control himself owing to lack of "passion" (meaning "power of the libido"), but precisely because he loves and, in virtue of his love, will not inflict himself. He refuses to commit an act of violence which would be the denial and destruction of the person. He thus indicates that his dearest wish is for the other's good. His egotism

[1] I must repeat, however, that arguments of this kind cannot serve as a foundation for the institution of marriage. It is simply a matter of observation that refutes the current fancies which we owe to the Tristan myth and its Donjuanesque negative. But such "reasons" are altogether ineffective as regards anyone who prefers the myth and wishes to believe in the revelations of passion.

[2] Benedetto Croce, *Etica e Politica*.

goes round via the other. This, it will be granted, is a notable revolution.

And we may now pass beyond that altogether negative and private statement of Croce's, and at last define marriage as *the institution in which passion is "contained," not by morals, but by love.*

6

Paradoxes of the Western Attitude

These few remarks on passion and marriage will have set forth the fundamental antagonism of Eros and Agape—that is to say, the antagonism of the two religions that are struggling for the upper hand in the West. It seems to me that once we are aware of this antagonism, of its historical and psychological origins, and of the spiritual issues involved, we must feel the need of revising a number of our current opinions—in the sphere of morality first and foremost, but in the spheres of culture and philosophy as well. As a conclusion to this work, I need doubtless only state the *corrective principle* which my inquiry into passion may be said to establish.

In the eyes of Orientals, the outstanding characteristic of the European attitude is the importance it attaches to passionate forces. They regard this as a heritage of Christianity and as the explanation of our strenuousness. And it is true that the three terms, "Christianity," "passion," and "strenuousness," correspond to the three predominant features of the European psyche, so that such opinions seem self-evident. Yet if the conclusions which I have drawn from my investigation of the courtly myth are accurate, this view of Christian Europe calls for considerable correction.

In the first place, it was not Christianity that caused passion to be cultivated; it was a heresy of Eastern origin. This heresy began by spreading in precisely those regions which Christianity had not yet fully evangelized and where pagan cults still flourished in secret. Passionate love is not Christian love, nor even what has been called "a Christian by-product," nor "the change of address of a force which Christianity aroused and directed towards God." [1] It is rather a by-product of Manichaeism. More accurately, it became a cult through the collaboration of the Manichaean religion with our most ancient religious beliefs and through the struggle that ensued between heresy and Christian orthodoxy. That is a first important correction. Next, it is imperative to point out that our well-known "Western strenuousness" has two distinct sources. If the term is intended to refer to our war frenzy I have shown that historically this frenzy is connected in the clearest possible manner with passion. Like passion, the taste for war follows on a notion that life should be ardent, a notion which is the mask of a wish for death. It is an inverted strenuousness, and self-destructive. But our strenuousness has another aspect, and one not to be connected with passion for a moment. I mean, our mechanical genius, which is the reflection of a human attitude the exact opposite of passionate: a faith in the value of created things, of matter, and of the action of the mind upon the visible world. Neither passion nor the heretical faith out of which it sprang could have inspired a belief that the control of Nature should be the aim of our lives, inasmuch as originally this control was held to be a function of the Demiurge, and salvation was held to lie precisely in an escape away from his devilish rule. [2]

We may ask ourselves whether this most striking expression of the restlessness of the European mind has not resulted from a disposition peculiar to our Continent, or whether it is not due to some indirect influence of the Christian ambition defined by the Apostle as the deliverance of the creature from the bondage of corruption—an ambition that may be taken as tending to re-establish the Cosmos under the original rule from which sin has caused it to break away. In Europe the Christian ambition to change the souls and conduct of sinners has given rise to an ambition to transform the human environment

[1] Leo Ferrero, *Désespoirs*. The problem of passion is admirably defined by this little book in its psychological data.

[2] "The theory of the Ancients that work is unworthy of a free man recurs in chivalry," Henri Pirenne remarks in his *Histoire de l'Europe*, p. 113.

(whence came the attention bestowed on technics). But supposing Christianity had been established in India or China two thousand years ago, would the results there be by now the same? The answer to this question is irrelevant here. It is enough to note that the Christiano-occidental (or creative) components of European strenuousness have been inspired by a will exactly the opposite of that of passion.

What is misleading, and what indeed has produced an inevitable misunderstanding about our contemporary restlessness, is that war and our mechanical genius have been in collusion. When at the French Revolution war became "national," it at once needed the assistance of every creative force, and that of mechanical force in particular. Thus did the passion of war become the principal motive power of mechanical research. This has been very obvious since 1915. The truly monstrous combination of the death-dealing and creative forces changed the nature both of war and of our technical genius. Mechanized war got rid of passion, and technics, in becoming lethal, were unfaithful to the ambitions with which they had originated. Europe is possibly going to succumb to the fate it has thus prepared for itself. But obviously it is not Christianity—as so many writers allege—that will be responsible for the disaster. The catastrophic spirit in Europe is not Christian.[1] On the contrary, it is Manichaean. That is what those who identify Christianity with Europe commonly overlook. Everything European is not Christian. If therefore Europe were to succumb to its evil genius, it would be through having for too long cultivated the para-Christian or anti-Christian religion of passion.

Should we infer that passion has been *the Eastern temptation held before Europe?* Inasmuch as passion did not spread in our history and culture earlier than the twelfth and thirteenth centuries—and then only thanks to a peremptory impulsion from heresy in Southern France—it turns out that our "fatal" beliefs reached us out of the Near East and Persia, the regions in which

[1] It will be said: What about the Apocalypse? But the disasters heralded in the Book of Revelation represent our *punishment* and not our *deliverance*. It is not death or disincarnation that offers salvation; but the act of grace performed by God.

unmistakably the Heresy first sprang up. Yet the same beliefs did not have the same effects in the East? No doubt, but in the East they were not obstructed and attacked as they were among us. *Hence it has been our dramatic luck to have opposed passion with weapons foredoomed to foster it.* Such is the persistent temptation to which we owe our finest creations. But what gives rise to life gives rise also to death. Let merely an accent be displaced, and strenuousness changes its sign. We may at least declare that the religious attitude of Europeans and the institution most typical of their morals—marriage—are now at a point where it is possible to behold this displacement of accent upon which everything depends.

Unquestionably a Christianized European differs from an Oriental in that he has the capacity to delve into the particularity of created beings. There lies the real clue to our faithfulness. The wisdom of the East pursues understanding in the progressive abolition of diversity. We, on the other hand, seek the density of being in the distinct person, and have constantly explored it more deeply as thus manifested. "The more we understand individual things, the more we understand God," Spinoza says. This attitude amounts to defining my West, and likewise the ultimate conditions of fidelity, the person, and marriage—and of the rejection of passion. It assumes the acceptance of diversity, and that our way of taking hold of the concrete is first to accept its limitations. A Christian takes the world as it is, and not as he may dream that it is. His "creative" activity thereupon consists in recapturing in the depth of individual things all the diversity of the created universe, and that is how it happened that man at the Renaissance was called a microcosm.

Whatever destroys this essential will, or distracts from it, must compromise fidelity and furnish passion with new opportunities. It is *our* life and *our* death. Hence the present breakdown of marriage is the least misleading indication of a western decadence. There are of course other indications, and in the most various spheres—the cult of multiplicity, the poetry of escape, the way nationalist passions encroach upon culture—whatever tends to wreck the person. But they are complex and collective happenings which often elude personal apprehension. The indication given by the breakdown of marriage can be brought home to us, and it warns us quite unmistakably. No other sign is more obvious or more everyday, no other is so fully confirmed within our secret selves.

7

Beyond Tragedy

In many respects this book appears to be the account of a gradual decay. It has insisted on the degradation of the myth, on the breakdown of marriage, on the disparagement of convention and of formal modes, on the extrusion of the passionate frenzy into spheres where it may be in course of encompassing the collapse of civilization. All that is fact, and all that holds out a threat to us. Indeed, it is the more perilous in proportion as we ignore or dispute it. Yet my gradual diagnosis of it has repeatedly yielded glimpses of how it might be overcome. For instance, it may be that Europe, after a *crisis* of totalitarianism (and assuming that this is not fatal), will recover the significance of a fidelity that is secured by substantial institutions—to the person's measure. Perhaps, the very excesses of passion will excite a reaction in the guise of new *formal modes*, and there will thus be set up a new classical age. After all, however, is not this anxious concern over the morrow now lining so many brows another of the temptations of passion? Our lives are not staked in the temporal beyond, but in the decisions establishing our faithfulness that must always be taken in the present. Whatever may befall, hap or mishap, the fate of the world matters much less to us than does an understanding of our immediate duties. "For the fashion of this world passeth away," but our vocation is always *hic et nunc,* in that act performed by the Eternal, thanks to which we grasp our hope.

Two themes for reflection, adumbrated already here and there in these pages, can provide an *open* conclusion. I have striven to unravel certain problems propounded in terms of history and psychology; but the entirely objective observations to which I have been led are not self-sufficient. They call for certain decisions. They introduce a fresh uncertainty which is not altogether as simplified as the passion-fidelity dilemma may suggest. Actually, no problem is ever *understood* till we have foreseen how to solve it and pass beyond it. And it is no good trying to pass beyond the passion-fidelity dilemma by simply denying one of its horns. I have already said, and I insist again, that to doom passion in theory can only be to try to suppress one pole of our creative tension. Actually, such a thing is not feasible. The Philistine who is ready "to condemn" all passion *a priori* confesses thereby never to have experienced passion of any kind. He is not one who has passed beyond the point of conflict, but one who has not yet reached it. The only advance it can be hoped that he might make would be achieved through the breakdown of his confidence—that is, through his being engulfed in some dramatically passionate experience.[1] But beyond a passion that has been experienced all the way to its fatal dead-end, what can we henceforth have an inkling of? The two themes for reflection I am about to sketch indicate two ways of going beyond, consistent with this book, but outside the schematic limits of all exposition.

The first theme is given its bearings by reference to a personal drama the biographical details of which are

[1] Must we go still further than Kierkegaard went beyond the "ethical stage?" I sometimes feel, indeed, I sometimes realize, that from the standpoint of the Christian faith there is doubtless nothing to be gained by a "regulation of morals" for non-Christians. On the contrary, that would be a way of protecting them from the authentic human despair which might bring them to believe. The cure of a soul, not in the sense of middle-class moral hygienics, but in the Christian sense that makes the desired end that an unbeliever should come to believe, ought to make us wish that non-Christians might go right through to the far side of the "happiness" of passion. But all efforts are directed to keeping them on *this side* of it. So that the only concrete *far side* that they are able to wish for or imagine is the "disorder of the passions." But it needs to be added that a man abandoned to his disorderliness experiences a despair for which the remedy may well seem to him to be what St. Paul calls the Law. And it is only by renunciation of the Law *as thus understood* that we can be led to faith.

common property. The event which proved for Kierkegaard to be the starting-point of all his reflection was his
breaking off his engagement to Regine. The private causes
of the break are still partially mysterious. It was an un-
sharable and unutterable "secret" that in Kierkegaard's
view obstructed his entering into marriage, because this
marriage was to have been happy according to the
world. The indispensable *obstruction* to the advance of
passion was on this occasion so thoroughly subjective,
peculiar, and unamenable to comparison, that its gravity
will not be suspected unless with the help of a reference
to Kierkegaard's faith. According to him, the relations
which man—finite and sinful—can have with his God—
who is Eternal and Holy—are exclusively those of a
love *fatally* unhappy. "God creates everything *ex nihilo*,"
he says, and whomsoever God elects by His love, "He
begins by reducing to nothing." From the standpoint of
the world and of natural life, God thus appears as
"my mortal enemy." Here we are being brought up
against the extreme limit, the pure springs of passion;
and in the same moment we are thrust into the heart of
the Christian faith! For, behold! the man now dead to the
world, killed by infinite love, has to go forward and to
live in the world, as if he had no more urgent and higher
task. "The knight of faith," when met with in the street,
has nothing superhuman about him: "he looks like a tax-
collector," and behaves like any decent middle-class citizen. And yet "he has renounced all things with an infinite resignation, and if he has recovered all things in the
sequel, it is *by virtue of the absurd* [that is, by virtue of
faith]. He is constantly leaping into the infinite, but
faultlessly and with complete confidence, so that he drops
back into the finite, and nothing is noticeable about him
but the finite." [1]

Thus the extremity of passion—death in love—introduces a new life, where passion never ceases to be present, but is under the most jealous incognito; for it is now
far more than regal, it is divine. On the analogy of faith,
it may thereupon be understood how *passion*—whatever
the plane in which it is manifested—attains its true future state and salvation thanks only to that *act* of obedience which is a life steadfast and true. To live "like ev-

---

[1] Soren Kierkegaard, *Frygt og Baevan* (Fear and Trembling).

erybody else" and yet "by virtue of the absurd" becomes
an offensive piece of deceit in the eyes of any one who
does not *believe* in the absurd; but it is far more than a
synthesis, and something infinitely more and other than
a "solution," for any one who does believe that God
keeps faith, and that love never deceives the beloved.

No doubt Kierkegaard did not succeed in "recovering"
the finite world except in his *awareness* of its loss, a loss
that was tremendously fruitful for his genius. He never
recovered Regine, but he never stopped loving her or dedicating his books to her. And perhaps it is in the life-work
put into those books that he was most truly faithful. We
need not seek anywhere but in his unquestionably unique
vocation for being a Solitary the explanation of his failure as a man. Others are endowed with some other vocation; they marry Regine, and passion lives again in their
marriage, but then "by virtue of the absurd." And they
are day by day astounded to find that they are happy.
Such things are too elementary and too complete for
words to interpose their dilatoriness between the question which they raise and the answer returned in our living
experience.

The other theme for reflection is perhaps not entirely
unconnected with this. It may even be regarded as a particular aspect of the transition back to passion that
Kierkegaard describes. At the summit of the spiritual
ascent which Saint John of the Cross narrates in the most
ardently passionate language, he knows that the soul attains to a state in which it is perfectly in the presence of
the loving object of love. He calls this mystic marriage.
The soul then treats its love with a kind of semi-divine
indifference. It has got beyond doubt and beyond the
point at which separateness seems to be like a rending; it
wishes for nothing that its love does not wish for; it is at
one with this love in duality, and the duality is now simply
a dialogue of grace and obedience. And the desire for the
highest passion is thereupon being gratified in the very
act of obeying, so that the soul is no longer being cauter-
ized and branded; there is not even any awareness of
love, only the happy moderation of acting.

Thus, on the analogy of faith, passion, born of a fatal
desire for mystical union, may be regarded as open to
being surpassed and fulfilled only thanks to the *meeting*
with some *other*, and the admission of this other's alien

life and ever distinct person, which, although distinct, holds the promise of unending alliance and begins a real dialogue. Then dread having been banished by response and nostalgia by presence, they both cease to summon the happiness it is expected to feel and savour, cease to suffer, and accept our daylight. It is then that marriage is possible. We are two in contentment.

A last time, however, I shall side with moderation. Married couples are not saints, and sin is not some error which we may renounce one of these days in order to adopt a more accurate truth. We are unendingly and incessantly in the thick of the struggle between nature and grace; unendingly and incessantly unhappy and then happy. But the horizon has not remained the same. A fidelity maintained in the Name of what does not change as we change will gradually disclose some of its mystery: *beyond tragedy another happiness waits*. A happiness resembling the old, but no longer belonging to the form of the world, for this new happiness transforms the world.

21 February–21 June 1938 (Revised 1954).

Index